Cultural Boundaries and the Cohesion of Canada

Raymond Breton
Jeffrey G. Reitz
Victor F. Valentine

with the collaboration of

Daiva Stasiulis
Réjean Lachapelle
Ilze Petersons Taylor

The Institute for Research on Public Policy
L'Institut de recherches politiques

Montreal

ISBN 0 920380 37 9
(Version française ISBN 0 920380 39 5)

Legal Deposit Second Quarter
Bibliothèque nationale du Québec

Cette publication existe également en version française.

The Institute for Research on Public Policy/L'Institut de recherches politiques
2149 Mackay Street
Montreal, Quebec H3G 2J2

Founded in 1972, THE INSTITUTE FOR RESEARCH ON PUBLIC POLICY is a national organization whose independence and autonomy are ensured by the revenues of an endowment fund, which is supported by the federal and provincial governments and by the private sector. In addition, The Institute receives grants and contracts from governments, corporations, and foundations to carry out specific research projects.

The *raison d'être* of The Institute is threefold:

— To act as a catalyst within the national community by helping to facilitate informed public debate on issues of major public interest

— To stimulate participation by all segments of the national community in the process that leads to public policy making

— To find practical solutions to important public policy problems, thus aiding in the development of sound public policies

The Institute is governed by a Board of Directors, which is the decision-making body, and a Council of Trustees, which advises the board on matters related to the research direction of The Institute. Day to day administration of The Institute's policies, programmes, and staff is the responsibility of the president.

The Institute operates in a decentralized way, employing researchers located across Canada. This ensures that research undertaken will include contributions from all regions of the country.

Wherever possible, The Institute will try to promote public understanding of, and discussion on, issues of national importance, whether they be controversial or not. It will publish its research findings with clarity and impartiality. Conclusions or recommendations in The Institute's publications are solely those of the author, and should not be attributed to the Board of Directors, Council of Trustees, or contributors to The Institute.

The president bears final responsibility for the decision to publish a manuscript under The Institute's imprint. In reaching this decision, he is advised on the accuracy and objectivity of a manuscript by both Institute staff and outside reviewers. Publication of a manuscript signifies that it is deemed to be a competent treatment of a subject worthy of public consideration.

Publications of The Institute are published in the language of the author, along with an executive summary in both of Canada's official languages.

iv

Dr. Mark Eliesen
Director, Federal NDP Caucus Research
Bureau, Ottawa
W.A. Friley
President, Skyland Oil, Calgary
Judge Nathan Green
The Law Courts, Halifax
Donald S. Harvie
Chairman, Devonian Foundation, Calgary
Dr. Leon Katz
Department of Physics, University of
Saskatchewan, Saskatoon
Tom Kierans
Vice-Chairman, McLeod, Young, Weir,
Toronto
Dr. Leo Kristjanson
Vice-President, Planning
University of Saskatchewan, Saskatoon
Andrée Lajoie
Director, Centre for Research on Public
Law, University of Montreal
Allen T. Lambert
Chairman, Toronto-Dominion Bank,
Toronto
Terry Mactaggart
Executive Director, Niagara Institute,
Niagara-on-the-Lake
Professor William A.W. Neilson
Faculty of Law, University of Victoria
Marilyn L. Pilkington
Tory, Tory, DesLauriers, Binnington,
Toronto
Adélard Savoie, Q.C.
Yeoman, Savoie, LeBlanc & DeWitt,
Moncton
Philip Vineberg, Q.C.
Phillips, Vineberg, Goodman, Phillips &
Rothman, Montreal
Dr. Norman Wagner
President, University of Calgary
Ida Wasacase
Director, Saskatchewan Indian Federated
College, University of Regina
Professor Paul Weiler
Mackenzie King Professor,
Harvard University
Dr. John Tuzo Wilson
Director General, Ontario Science Centre,
Toronto
Rev. Lois Wilson
Rector, Chalmers United Church, Kingston
Ray Wolfe
President, The Oshawa Group, Toronto

Ex Officio Members
Dr. Owen Carrigan
Representing the Canada Council
Denis Cole
President, Institute of Public
Administration of Canada
A.J. Earp
President, Association of Universities &
Colleges of Canada
Dr. Claude Fortier
President, Science Council of Canada
Larkin Kerwin
President, Royal Society of Canada
Dr. William G. Schneider
President, National Research Council
Dr. René Simard
President, Medical Research Council
Dr. David Slater
Acting Chairman, Economic Council of
Canada
Professor André Vachet
Representing the Social Science Federation
of Canada

Foreword

Canadian society is composed of many groups of individuals connected by formal and informal associations, and divided by differences in language, ethnic origin, wealth, education, and a variety of other social and economic characteristics. How these groups interrelate largely determines the degree of cohesion in Canadian society. This study addresses the question: "Are ethnicity and language always divisive elements in social life, or can certain forms of ethnic diversity become factors in the development of a national identity?"

This report is the Canadian contribution to a UNESCO project entitled "Cultural Development in Countries Containing Different National and/or Ethnic Groups." It was initiated by the UNESCO National Commission for Yugoslavia, and included participants from Belgium and Finland, as well as Yugoslavia and Canada.

The Multiculturalism Directorate of the Department of the Secretary of State agreed to participate in the project and asked The Institute for Research on Public Policy to undertake the study on its behalf. The Institute's task was to describe the impact of ethnic and linguistic diversity on the cohesion of Canadian society, and to suggest policy alternatives and their implications for the future.

The report bases its analysis on three intergroup relationships: English/French; "founding peoples"/immigrant communities; and native peoples/national community. The Institute is pleased to have contributed this synthesis of theoretical and empirical research to the understanding of Canada's national identity.

Gordon Robertson
President
May 1980

Preface

This study is the Canadian contribution to a project entitled "Cultural Development in Countries Containing Different National and/or Ethnic Groups," which in turn is part of a series called the "European Joint Studies." The latter is an outcome of the "Intergovernmental Conference on Cultural Policies in Europe," which was held under the auspices of UNESCO in June 1972, in Helsinki, Finland, and in which Canada participated. Within UNESCO, Canada is a member of the European Regional Group of Member States. One of the important recommendations of the conference suggested that European member states of UNESCO carry out joint studies involving persons or institutions from a group of countries on subjects of cultural policy of interest to them. Although UNESCO was asked to act as the general liaison agency, the co-ordination of particular studies was entrusted to the national commissions for UNESCO in interested member states.

The project with which this study is concerned was initiated by the National Commission for Yugoslavia. Other participating commissions are those of Belgium, Canada, and Finland. The objective is to provide a comparative analysis of the implications of ethnic and linguistic diversity for national unity.

Following an invitation of the Canadian Commission for UNESCO, the Multiculturalism Directorate of the Secretary of State Department accepted to ensure Canadian participation in the project, and asked The Institute for Research on Public Policy to undertake the study.

The Institute was assigned the task of describing how various dimensions of ethnic and linguistic diversity are related to the cohesion, or lack of cohesion, of Canadian society, and of providing sufficient background information—demographic, legal, or other—for the reader to understand the issues and their underlying components. Moreover, the analysis was to be carried out in such a way as to indicate the broad policy alternatives that Canadians face with regard to the issues of national cohesion and their main implications. The analysis presented in the report was carried out separately for the three main types of interethnic relationships in Canada: relationships between the anglophone and francophone communities; between the so-called "founding peoples" and ethnic groups composed of immigrants and their descendants; and between the native peoples and the rest of Canadian society.

The study does not represent original research in the sense that no new data have been collected and analysed; rather, its objective is to synthesize the main lines of theoretical and empirical research carried out in the last two decades or so and having greatest relevance to the cohesion of Canadian society. Furthermore, the synthesis is selective: because of the time-frame

ix

and the amount of literature, more attention had to be given to some works than to others. Moreover, many works were useful even though they are not quoted or referred to in the text. So although the bibliography is not exhaustive, it does extend beyond the references.

The overall objective of this study is to present a review of the Canadian situation with regard to national cohesion by decomposing the issues in terms of the three main types of interethnic relationships that exist in the country and by examining some of their interconnections.

We wish to thank Janet Lum and Gail Grant for their assistance in the review of the literature. We also wish to express our gratitude to those who read an earlier draft of this book and offered criticisms and suggestions that were very helpful in preparing the final version: Jacques Brazeau, Jean Brunet, Douglas Campbell, Charles Castonguay, James Frideres, Jacques Henripin, Michèle Gervais-Meunier, Michael Ornstein, Howard Palmer, Maurice Pinard, Norbert Robitaille, Mildred Schwartz, Diane Vanasse, Sally Weaver, Yvan Bordeleau, Arthur Davis, Danielle Lee, and Pierre Laporte. Needless to say, they are not responsible for the use we have made of their comments. We are also grateful for the support of the Multiculturalism Directorate of the Department of the Secretary of State and the guidance provided by members of its Canadian Ethnic Studies Advisory Committee. In particular, we wish to acknowledge the valuable assistance of Helen Eriks in handling various administrative matters throughout the study. Finally, we wish to thank Nouella Challenger, Grace Muldoon, and Ruth Wright for their efficient secretarial assistance.

R.B.
J.G.R.
V.F.V.

Table of Contents

List of Tables and Figures

TABLES

FIGURES

General Introduction

Over the years, Canada has been beset with many problems of "national unity" or societal cohesion. Recently, attention has been focused on the French-English conflict and the prospect of Quebec national sovereignty. However, English-French relations are embedded in a whole matrix of other matters such as regional disparities, political tensions, economic problems, external domination, constitutional disputes, integration of people of different cultures and racial backgrounds—all of which present problems for the cohesion of Canadian society.

Divisions among Canada's various provinces and regions have produced a highly decentralized political system with powerful provincial governments. Federal political institutions have proven inadequate to regulate regional conflicts, which often must be dealt with by conferences of provincial premiers rather than through the federal parliamentary apparatus. Economic problems have generated intense conflicts in labour-management relations, and Canada has experienced a high degree of industrial disruption in recent years. The controversy over inflation, and wage and price controls is only one aspect of this problem. External domination by British, and then American, interests contributes to the lack of a strong Canadian identity or a powerful, unifying national ideology. The satellite status of Canada is important for political, economic, and cultural reasons. At the political level, for instance, the British tradition in Canadian institutions and Quebec's links with France aggravate the English-French conflict. In terms of economics, the various parts of Canada become oriented toward foreign economic interests rather than toward their interests in relation to each other. In the Maritime provinces, the U.S. link is so important that a recent poll showed nearly a third of the population in favour of outright annexation to the United States. In terms of culture, the printed and electronic media of mass communication, and the educational institutions have been heavily influenced by materials foreign (mainly American) in origin. The Canadian Constitution itself still is an act of the British Parliament, and efforts to "patriate" it have so far foundered on failure to agree on an amending formula.

All of these problems, and others as well, are interrelated and intertwined in the effects on the cohesion of Canadian society. None can be understood in isolation from the others. For example, regional and ethnic lines of conflict tend to overlap. One consequence is that the alienation of western Canada, arising partly from economic disadvantage, but perhaps mostly from an inadequate political integration at the federal level, is intensified by the bilingualism issue.

In this context, the present study examines the effects of ethnic and linguistic diversity in Canada on societal cohesion. This topic of course includes the French-English conflict in several of its aspects. During the past two decades, this issue has become an important concern throughout Canada—a concern that has been triggered by, and reflected in, events such as the emergence of an independentist movement in Quebec; political violence in Quebec culminating in the October 1970 events; the formation of an independentist political party, the Parti Québécois, and its election in 1976; the assertive stance adopted by francophones in Quebec, as reflected in such gestures as the language legislation; the decision to set up a Royal Commission on Bilingualism and Biculturalism, and the debates and research it occasioned; the bilingualism policy and programmes of the federal government. Because of that concern, writers on the topic may be expected to formulate some kind of prognosis for the near future. The present study does not have this objective. Rather, we want to identify the basic social forces at work in French-English relations that affect the strength or weakness of national cohesion. Such a study may prove to be an aid in understanding current events, but will certainly not predict the future.

The French-English conflict is not an isolated event, and a second objective of the study is to broaden our scope by considering other aspects of interethnic relations in Canada. The native peoples, though small in number, are an important presence in vast areas of Canadian territory. There have been various expressions of protest on the part of native peoples; they have articulated land claims and aboriginal rights, and nationalistic movements have emerged among them. The so-called "other" ethnic groups together comprise over 26% of the population. The presence of these groups has led to a "multicultural" movement and debates over appropriate public policies, a heated controversy over the revision of the Immigration Act, and the occurrence of racial violence in some cities.

By including these issues, the study explores whether general understanding is increased by posing the issue of ethnicity and societal cohesion more broadly. In what ways do various types of interethnic relationships differ in their impact on societal cohesion? Are ethnicity and language always divisive elements in social life, or can certain forms of ethnic diversity become factors in the development of a national identity? In Canada, some have hoped that ethnic diversity, by creating a general atmosphere of tolerance and pride in one's cultural heritage, might itself become a symbol promoting national unity. The study attempts to explore in a broad context both the negative and positive effects of ethnic and linguistic diversity on national cohesion.

By focusing on language and ethnicity in relation to societal cohesion, we are not stating that cohesion is only affected by linguistic and ethnic factors. Nor are we saying that these factors are necessarily the most important determinants of the degree of cohesion. Other factors could have been adopted as a primary focus. Recent events and past history clearly show, however, that the ethnolinguistic configuration of Canada has a bearing on the degree of its cohesion. Our task is to identify some of the specific features of this configuration and show how they affect the degree of cohesion. In pursuing this task, it will be necessary to examine how language and ethnicity interact with other features of our society, such as regional disparities, American economic dominance, and socio-economic inequalities.

CONCEPT OF NATIONAL OR SOCIETAL COHESION

National unity is an expression that evokes a variety of issues, ideas, and feelings: the absence of conflict; loyalty to the national government; the possible secession of one part of the country from Confederation; harmony or positive feelings among people in different parts of the country; pride and other good feelings about being Canadian; co-operation, rather than tension, between levels of government; giving precedence to one's Canadian identity over one's regional identity; the feeling of getting a good or bad deal from being part of the country; and so on. In international events, feelings of pride in the accomplishments of one's fellow countrymen have salience; the language question conjures up images of possible conflicts; certain policies or ways of operation of the central government bring up the question of its legitimacy among some citizens.

In recent years, it has been frequently used in relation to the possible secession of Quebec from the rest of Canada. Promoting the "national unity" cause has become, in the minds of many people, synonymous with fighting the Quebec independentists and counteracting the propensities of Quebecers in that direction. This study is not restricted to that aspect of the phenomena, but includes some of the other meanings that the expression evokes. The concept of cohesion has, we feel, a broader meaning.

As mentioned, the concept of societal cohesion has many facets. Two general dimensions underline these: one pertains to the relationships between people and institutions of society as a whole, particularly political institutions; the other, to relationships that people have with each other, either as individuals or as groups. Members of a society can be in conflict with the institutions of that society and they can be in conflict with each other. Mutually satisfactory accommodations for both kinds of conflict can be worked out, at least for certain periods of time. The degree of cohesion has to do with the extent of such mutually satisfactory accommodations and resolution of the conflicts that emerge from time to time.

People live within, or in relation to, institutions such as governments, businesses, factories, schools, churches. Because their lives are tied to institutions, people form expectations about what institutions should do and be. In other words, institutions are not only instruments to accomplish things or solve problems; they also embody political, economic, and social values. These appear in ideologies and symbols, and are built into the structures, rules, and procedures of the institutions. "The British parliamentary system," "the free market economy," "federalism"—these and many other symbolic expressions evoke a whole range of values and expectations concerning institutions. As a result of what they are and accomplish, institutions may gain varying degrees of legitimacy and they may be more or less successful in mobilizing the emotional attachment of the population. These effects are indications of the degree of societal cohesion.

The relationships that people have with each other are also important for the cohesion of a society. These can take place between individuals or groups: friendship ties, intermarriage, interpersonal contacts at work, in recreation, at church, or in the neighbourhood; or between organizations, such as business firms, churches, labour unions, professional associations, or governments. These relationships may be valued because they are useful: commercial transactions, mutual assistance, pooling of programme costs, and so on; or because they are based on feelings of a common identity as a people.

Clearly, societal cohesion is a matter of degree, whether we are looking at the legitimacy given to institutions, at the public attachment to those institutions, at the value people attach to their social relationships with other groups, or at the images and feelings that members of different groups have for each other. Moreover, the different components of cohesion are not independent of each other; they can reinforce each other in their positive or negative effects. For example, a favourable attitude toward the institutions of society may foster a feeling of a common identity and solidarity; the feeling that the central government is favouring another group or region will not only affect the degree of legitimacy that it receives, it will also be a source of ill-feelings and conflicts among groups or regions.

To a certain degree, the members of the various ethnic, linguistic, and regional communities in Canada relate to each other directly at work, at church, in voluntary associations, and so on. To a considerable extent, they relate to each other only indirectly through such institutions as government and the media. For this reason, the prevailing intergroup attitudes and feelings may affect what goes on in the government bureaucracy or political parties; it may affect the content of what is communicated through the media or decided in the boardrooms of business corporations. Reciprocally, what goes on in an institution and its social results may affect the degree of legitimacy the institutions will receive, at least in certain parts of the society.

Even though it may appear awkward, the expression *societal* cohesion is used, rather than *social* cohesion. We are dealing with the cohesion of the society, which inevitably involves institutions and groups in relation with each other. Social cohesion is an expression that has the disadvantage of being either too general or too specific. In one sense, it includes the societal cohesion as one among several types of social cohesion (the family, neighbourhood, profession, and political party are some other levels at which social cohesion can occur). In another sense, it concerns relationships that are social in the restricted sense of the term, thus excluding the economic and political relationships. *Societal* indicates that our ultimate preoccupation is at the level of the society, and that it includes relationships with institutions as well as between groups in different spheres of activity.

THREE AXES OF ETHNIC DIFFERENTIATION

As already indicated, the concern of this study is with the impact of ethnic and linguistic diversity, and of the factors that interact with it on the degree of societal cohesion. A first question is the appropriate way of approaching this diversity. This is not an easy matter. The configuration of ethnic and linguistic diversity in Canada is complex: (1) the native peoples in relation to the rest of Canadian society; (2) the English-speaking people in relation to the French-speaking people; (3) a number of ethnic groups, composed of immigrants and their descendants, in relation to the rest of society.

Within these lines of differentiation, further distinctions need to be taken into account. The native peoples comprise several different groups, including the Métis population. The anglophone-francophone distinction cuts across the other lines of diversity. The anglophone community is highly differentiated ethnically; so is the francophone community, although much less so. The "other" ethnic groups are numerous. They exhibit a considerable range of variation in factors such as size, acculturation, complexity of social organizations, and geographic concentration.

Despite such internal variations, at a general level there are a number of issues that pertain to all three axes of diversity. Among these is the question of the patterns of inequality across ethnic and linguistic groups, and their impact on the cohesion of society. There is also the matter of the modes of incorporation of members of different ethnic or linguistic communities into the political, economic, educational, and other institutions of the country. Not all communities are integrated into Canadian society in the same way; their relationships to institutions are not the same. This is a matter that has considerable bearing on the cohesion of society. Another issue is the degree of contact and cross-cultural communication across communities. The development of a common culture that each collectivity shares and of common symbols with which each identifies is an issue that is related to that of cross-cultural communication. The survival of ethnic and linguistic groups as distinct socio-cultural entities is another matter of relevance for societal cohesion. It is important to consider the extent of such survival, the conditions under which it occurs and under which it becomes a political issue, and the nature of its impact on societal integration. Finally, there are questions pertaining to the mechanisms and procedures for the resolution of conflicts between communities and their relevance for societal cohesion.

Each analysis of a particular axis of differentiation considers the processes through which societal cohesion is more or less severely threatened. For instance, each study is concerned with the economic circumstances, the political tensions, and the status issues that are sources of tension between ethnic and linguistic collectivities. These of course relate to the matters mentioned earlier, namely, patterns of cultural survival, selection of symbols and values for the society, choice of language and other conditions for cross-cultural communication, and of mechanisms and procedures for the management of conflicts between collectivities. Attention is also given to the factors that contribute to an increase in the level of such strains and to their possible impact on societal cohesion, given the structural and demographic factors mentioned above.

In addition, at one point or another, each study examines the role of nationalistic, ethnic, and social ideologies in shaping a community's perception of its economic and political situation, and of its status in the society as a whole. Changes in the level and character of group consciousness may occur in each type of ethnic differentiation. Socio-political mobilization of ethnic and linguistic groups is another critical element in the conflict-generating process. Groups mobilize for institutional changes that will lead to an improvement in their situation. Ideologies and group consciousness are important in this process, but so is organization. The conditions necessary for the emergence of leadership, the accumulation of resources, and the development of an organization for concerted action are discussed in each study. In each case, the reactions of the other collectivities and of the societal institutions are considered. Such reactions are critical for the evolution and outcome of the conflict, and for its impact on the degree of societal cohesion.

The three axes cannot be considered as roughly equivalent instances of ethnic diversity or interethnic relationships. This may be the case at a certain level, but to be useful, the analysis must consider the specificity of each axis. Indeed, each axis of ethnic differentiation is characterized by a variety of demographic, economic, political, and socio-cultural features, which have historical, as well as contemporary, dimensions. As a result, the occasions of conflict, the forces affecting the evolution of conflicts, and the problems of accommodation differ from one line of diversity to the other. The general question to which we are addressing ourselves is the same—how does diversity impinge on the degree of societal cohesion? However, the search for factors and processes with an explanatory value follows a somewhat different route for each axis of differentiation.

The different approaches needed to grasp the complexity of the Canadian ethnic and linguistic reality led to the present organization of the project. Each of the three major axes of ethnic differentiation become the object of separate analysis by groups of researchers who worked from a common set of objectives, but who to a considerable degree carried out their analysis independently of one another. Each of the three studies then deals with the relation between ethnicity and societal cohesion from the perspective of the issues and concepts most pertinent to the respective axis of ethnic differentiation.

Thus, somewhat different conceptual frameworks were formulated in order to identify the factors and processes specific to each axis of differentiation, whether these pertain to demographic, social, political, or economic dimensions of social structure. The differences between the studies reflect differences in reality. They also reflect the state of the art—the concepts and research results—with respect to the study of ethnicity and language in a social organization.

To provide a context for the analysis of each axis of ethnic differentiation, it was felt that a demographic analysis showing the evolution of the ethnic and linguistic diversity in Canada over time was essential. Part one presents such an analysis. It deals with three basic questions: the evolution of the ethnic composition of the population since 1871; the linguistic and territorial duality of Canada; and the linguistic mobility of individuals and persistence of linguistic groups.

The analysis of the native communities in part two is distinctive for several reasons. Firstly, the native communities are in fact not yet incorporated in our society. Instead, they exist as a cluster of satellites at the margin of the wider society. Secondly, native groups have a long historical background as on-going societies on this continent. Because of this, they are "nations" rather than ethnic minorities in the usual sense of the term. This historical background also carries with it an internal diversity. This is a third element of their situation; it is appropriate to talk of native peoples because there are several of them. The diversity is also increased by the presence of non-status Métis and other categories of people of Indian ancestry. A fourth element is territory; it constitutes an important basis of native communities in their economic, political, and socio-cultural dimensions. Fifthly, both in absolute and relative terms, the population of people of Indian ancestry is quite small.

There are two other elements, perhaps the most important. Native communities have a very low level of economic development, and they exist in a situation of sociological and administrative dependence *vis-à-vis* the larger society and its institutions. To a considerable extent, control over the administration and development of native communities is external. Their socio-economic condition, the definition of what they are, and their continued existence as distinct subsocieties are largely determined by remote centres of power, the federal government in particular.

The linguistic cleavage is examined in part three, and it also presents a number of distinctive characteristics. Foremost among these is the existence of a social and institutional segmentation between the two communities, each functioning to a significant extent in its own social circles and organizations. Some members think of their collectivity as a nation, a people. Even though they are a numerical minority, francophones reject the conception of themselves as an ethnic minority. As far as the societal institutional system is concerned, both collectivities have been, and still are, in competition, if not in conflict, with each other over the determination of the system's forms and cultural character, and over the rules of language use in it. Because language is an instrument of communication, it poses particular requirements with regard to the incorporation of the two linguistic communities in a common set of institutions as well as for cross-cultural communication.

The two language collectivities differ in size, but both are large. Moreover, even though anglophones are in a position of advantage with regard to wealth, power, and status, francophones nevertheless wield considerable economic and political power. One of the bases of this power is the francophones' concentration in a region of the country, namely, Quebec and the adjacent areas.

Finally, the growth of an independentist movement and the presence in power of an independentist political party add a critical element to the configuration of linguistic factors.

The "other" ethnic groups and their relationship with what are sometimes referred to as the "founding" groups offer still another configuration of characteristics. Their situation is discussed in part four. Generally, these groups have a rather limited set of institutions of their own. Their communities tend to be based on a system of informal relations and a set of associations, rather than on a well developed institutional system. By and large, members of these groups function within anglophone institutions, and to a limited extent, within francophone institutions.

Another characteristic of the "other" ethnic groups is their large number: there are people from over forty different ethnic origins in Canada. The groups vary in size, culture, race, and period of immigration to Canada; they also differ in level of socio-economic achievement and in numerical importance of the second and third generations relative to the immigrant generation. This latter element reflects the fact that for some groups the country of origin supplies virtually no more new immigrants, while for others the flow of newcomers is substantial. Given the fairly high degree of acculturation of members of ethnic groups, at least over generations, the situation with regard to cultural survival, and community life generally, is significantly different for groups with a regular supply of newcomers as compared to those without it. Finally, even though some groups are much larger than others, none approaches the size of either the British- or the French-origin groups. Moreover, most groups are spread over the various regions of the country, with concentrations in various urban centres.

Thus, for these and other reasons related to their history and culture, the "other" ethnic groups show important variations in the degree and form of community organization.

Societal cohesion depends not only on the links that various social groups, such as occupational, ethnic, and religious groups, have with the institutions of the society, but also on the links that they have with each other. But again there are important differences. Foremost among these, at least in the present context, is that in certain instances some types of groupings, such as ethnic, religious, and regional, may have the potential for creating a separate nation-state, while other groupings, such as those based on occupation, age, business interests, or sex, do not have such potential. An occupational group, one of the sexes, an age category, or social categories of that nature cannot maintain a society over generations, either because they are complementary to each other or disappear with time. On the other hand, if the circumstances are favourable, an ethnic, religious, or regional grouping may establish or maintain a national society, essentially because these factors can cut across the other bases of group formation. Thus the interaction of ethnicity and language with conditions of societal cohesion such as those indicated would seem to be particularly critical. The actual effects of ethnic and linguistic diversity on national cohesion are clearly highly variable, and depend on the characteristics of a specific group in relation to those of other groups in the society, and in relation to the structure of political and other institutions.

Given these substantial variations between the three axes of ethnolinguistic diversity, the issues pertaining to inequality, modes of institutional incorporation, cross-cultural contact and communication, group survival, diffusion of common values and symbols, and processes of conflict resolution can be expected to vary from one axis to the other. For instance, it seems clear that the nature and intensity of the strains will be different in the case of the relationships involving native peoples and other Canadians, francophones and anglophones, other ethnic groups and the ''majority'' groups. The content of the ideologies will be different in each instance, as well as the basic ideas underlying the solutions proposed. The degree of mobilization will also vary as the groups do not have the same possibilities for social and political organization, and given differences in factors such as size, wealth, and organization, the reactions of other groups and the societal institutions will not be the same when one or another axis of differentiation is involved. Finally, the processes of conflict resolution, and the particular accommodations that are likely to result, will differ also in each instance of differentiation. It has been necessary, therefore, to formulate frameworks that incorporate the various demographic, ecological, historical, structural (both economic and political), and other characteristics of the collectivities involved in each axis of diversity, and to make it possible to address the issues of inequality, conflict resolution, and so on, in a meaningful way in each case.

These points can be made another way. Language and ethnicity do not *by themselves* have any relevance for societal cohesion. The mere fact of ethnic and linguistic diversity is not a source of disunity. These phenomena are relevant for societal cohesion only to the extent that they are associated with various conditions such as those discussed above. The institutions may function in such a way as to restrict a group to a marginal position in the economy, endanger its cultural security, and assign it a dependent and inferior status in the society as a whole. Negative attitudes and stereotypes may be transmitted from generation to generation, or a group may attempt—directly or indirectly—to impose its culture on other groups. The cultural distinctiveness of ethnic or linguistic groups may make the emergence of a national culture more difficult or may undermine attempts to diffuse a national ideology. Ethnic, and especially linguistic, differences may act as barriers to exchange and communication. An ethnic group may, or may not, possess the resources necessary for engaging in conflict with other groups. Finally, an ethnic group may, or may not, possess its own structure and mechanism for regulating conflict with other groups in the society.

GENERAL OBSERVATIONS ON THE STUDY OF SOCIETAL COHESION

The information for assessing societal cohesion as affected by each axis of ethnic differentiation is highly variable.[1] With respect to the legitimacy of institutions, in each case we have considered information on one group or subgroup in relation to different levels of government or other parts of the society. In the case of French-English relations, for example, the attitudes of the French are more important; in the case of the relation between natives and the rest of the society, the attitudes of the natives are crucial; in the case of the "other" groups, each has its own distribution of attitudes.

But government legitimacy often is not studied directly. No standard methodology exists. In the case of native peoples, the apparent degree of resistance to government policy is the only available measure. By this measure, legitimacy is not high and is decreasing. In the case of the French, there are numerous polls showing attitudes toward independentist proposals. This is far more direct, and again the implications seem to be that legitimacy is not high and tending to decrease. For the groups composed of immigrants and their descendants, a variety of potentially relevant measures are available: interethnic attitudes, Canadian identification, political participation, and even crime rates. But the overall assessment of increasing cohesion between the established "other" groups and the rest of the society is based not only on information from these current indicators but on the fact that

---

[1] Each study is based on materials available in existing theoretical and research literature, rather than on original data collection. They draw upon Canadian and other literature relevant to understanding the Canadian situation. The studies have been prepared with a view toward a non-Canadian audience, or to put it differently, readers requiring a general introduction to the Canadian situation. Basic background information is provided and additional sources listed.

interethnic conflict, particularly in the economic sector, is not as visible today as it was once.

Cross-cultural contact and communication are less readily assessed, and there is a tendency in each study to rely on measures of conflict. The native peoples remain fairly isolated and little information is available, but in what there is, conflict is the main theme. The greatest amount of systematic information on intergroup contact exists for French-English relations, though some of a very general nature is available on the ''other'' ethnic groups. The main conclusion is that a great degree of isolation exists between francophones and the various anglophone ethnic groups, coupled with somewhat negative attitudes across this axis. But in a sense, also, there is a stronger bond between British and French groups than between either group and the ''other'' ethnic groups.

It may seem ironic that intergroup conflict is taken as a main indicator of lack of cohesion, after taking pains to point out that conflict may be a positive force for unity and cohesion. The reason is that the outcomes of current conflicts are difficult to assess, and when the question of cohesion is raised, attention naturally focuses on these conflicts. This does not mean that the ultimate outcome of these conflicts will not contribute to the cohesion of the society. Theory and methodology in this whole area are clearly in need of improvement and refinement.

The objective degree of socio-economic inequality among ethnic groups appears to have a limited impact on societal cohesion. At least a consideration of our three studies shows that the most extreme inequality does not lead to the most serious conflicts. Native peoples experience very serious inequality and are in fact engaging in increasingly intense conflict. But inequalities between anglophones and francophones are less extreme than inequalities along either of the other two axes of ethnic differentiation, and yet by far the greatest problems for societal cohesion exist between these linguistic groups.

It is worth stressing that each of the studies devotes substantial space to a description of inequality, particularly economic, but also political, social, and organizational. This reflects the importance of this particular aspect of intergroup relations. It will be noted that although objective socio-economic conditions may be the source of many problems for societal cohesion, the problems they raise frequently become actualized in the distribution of the means to do something about these conditions. There is thus a potential for conflict over the control of the relevant institutional mechanisms. Moreover, it is clearly the case that a group's perception and evaluation of inequality, its capacity for socio-political mobilization, and the available means of conflict resolution are crucial for societal cohesion. Indeed, it is not sufficient that there be dissatisfaction with the society and its institutions for the cohesion of that society to be seriously threatened; it is not sufficient that there be antagonisms among segments of the society. Cohesion is seriously threatened when the dissatisfaction and antagonism are mobilized into social and collective action. A process disruptive of national cohesion cannot get under way unless individuals and groups have the resources to organize and undertake action. The condition of organization for collective action and the capacity to present viable alternative institutional structures are important aspects of the social mobilization process.

Problematic situations can exist for a long time without the cohesion of the society being seriously threatened (but no doubt without increasing either). What will produce change is the emergence of conditions permitting the socio-political organization of discontent into collective action. These conditions include leadership, the recruitment and training of the required technical expertise, the promotion of structures and communication networks, the development of an ideology, the accumulation of resources, and so on. Such organized mobilization usually brings about conflict between those in the society who have an interest in maintaining the existing institutional arrangements and those who see their interest in establishing a different one. Again, it is worth stressing that the occurrence of conflict between segments of a society is not necessarily disruptive of cohesion. It may in fact be part of the process by which unity is constructed. Much depends on whether there exist agencies and procedures by which conflicts can be regulated in a way that leads potentially to an accommodation of opposing sides. These topics require far more scrutiny than they have so far received.

Each of the studies makes several observations on the capacity of government to manage conflict, if not resolve it (in fact, the distinction between regulating and resolving a conflict can become very critical in examining concrete cases). Each study considers first of all political representation. But interestingly, there is also a focus on the structure of government, and in particular on the degree of its centralization or decentralization. The issues vary greatly. In the case of native peoples, decentralization is seen as a means of conflict avoidance and assimilation. In the case of French-English relations, decentralization is examined from the point of view of its impact on solidarity. In the case of the ethnic groups composed of immigrants and their descendants, decentralization is discussed as a way of dealing with different types of ethnicity and a variety of ethnic groups. In each case, decentralization is controversial; there is no clear agreement on its effects. Each study identifies the dimension as an aspect of conflict resolution, though with various interpretations of its relevance.

The theoretical literature stresses that societal cohesion is also potentially affected by the extent to which the population shares a set of values and beliefs, and an ideology justifying the authority of the institutions, particularly of the State. It is generally thought that to some extent a country may be unified by sharing a common culture that marks its adherents as destined to live together. The importance of ideologies that legitimize institutions is also generally recognized. For example, the speeches of government officials, and the advertising and public relations activities of business corporations frequently make references to the values and beliefs that legitimate "our system of government" and "our economic system." But under certain conditions, those ideologies may be challenged, and new ones may be formulated and diffused. And it is possible that an ideology is acceptable to one group but not to another. These circumstances are occasions of possible tension and disunity. But to what extent a common culture and ideology are necessary is still very much an open question. The importance of shared culture may vary from one society to another.

The virtual absence of a common culture and the weakness of common ideologies have been seen as a particular problem in Canada. Yet there is little systematic study of this dimension or of its consequences. Thus, most studies repeat speculation. With respect to native peoples, it is assumed that cultural distinctiveness is a source of tension; in the case of French-English relations, there can be speculation on the direction of cultural change—for example, that Americanization increases cultural homogeneity (though if it affects primarily the anglophones, it may actually drive the two linguistic groups further apart). The impact on cohesion cannot really be assessed. The same is true for the "other" groups. In those groups, it seems clear that cultural homogeneity increases, but the consequences are unknown.

In the studies that follow, attention is given to the importance of contact and communication among members of the various groups and regions of the country. Group isolation does not promote intergroup cohesion. Frequent contact may provide the opportunity for mutual reward, the development of common ideas, and the regulation of possible conflict. It will be seen, however, that it is not only the amount of contact and exchanges that is important. They must be mutually profitable. Unequal exchanges on a continuing basis are the source of negative attitudes and may lead to conflict.

Each of the studies raises the question of the modes of incorporation of ethnic and linguistic groups in the social and institutional framework of society. Frequently the occasions for the most intense conflicts concern precisely the ways in which the institutions will be shaped in order to accommodate ethnic and linguistic diversity. The shaping of institutions involves issues of power, social recognition, and status, as well as the distribution of scarce resources. It will be seen that for all three axes of differentiation, the situation has evolved over time. For instance, the overall orientation of the majority segment of Canadian society *vis-à-vis* the native peoples has basically shifted from accommodation to domination. In recent years, a new transformation has begun to take place, and much of the debate and conflict, both within the native groups, and between them and the rest of society, concerns the direction of this transformation: should it be integration or assimilation? The study of native peoples inquires whether government may favour assimilation as a strategy for resolving difficulties, and the implications of such an option.

In the case of the "other" ethnic groups, circumstances have also changed: the historical stance of assimilation has been successfully challenged in the sense that by and large it is now socially unacceptable to discuss their incorporation in Canadian society in terms of assimilation. "Multiculturalism" as an orientation has gained some social and political momentum, although the specific institutional forms it will eventually take are not clear. Some of these issues are explored in the study of the "other" ethnic groups, while considering the impact of intergroup contacts on the survival of group distinctiveness. The demographic study is also relevant in this context. In any case, assimilation in itself is seen as a problem for intergroup relations, rather than a solution, at least in the short term. Thus, the reduction of cultural differences may, or may not, contribute to societal cohesion over the long run, but strategies to maximize this outcome may undermine societal cohesion in the short run.

Finally, the question of the modes of societal incorporation is particularly critical for societal cohesion in the case of the two main linguistic groups. As will be seen, throughout the history of the country, the linguistic dualism, which manifests itself in demographic, geographic, economic, political, and socio-cultural dimensions of our society, has been a constant source of conflict over the institutional arrangements that each would find acceptable. These conflicts, and the role of "other" groups in them, are explored.

Part One

Evolution of Ethnic and Linguistic Composition

by

Réjean Lachapelle

Evolution of Ethnic and Linguistic Composition

There is a standard procedure for describing and analysing the demographic evolution of a country. It consists of first presenting the variations in population growth; isolating the natural from the migratory growth; describing the movements of mortality, fertility, emigration, and immigration; and finally, defining the effects of these phenomena on composition by sex and age. Certainly this strategy facilitates comparisons, but it carries the risk of failing to shed light on the specific characteristics of each country.

While this strategy is often used as a basis for analyses of the demographic situation in Canada, attempts are also made to bring out the country's federal nature by describing the evolution of population distribution by provinces and by presenting interprovincial migratory movements (Stone and Siggner 1974). There is no doubt that this is a useful and highly pertinent addition, as it makes it possible to grasp and clarify one of Canada's two major socio-political dimensions, the regional one. As for the ethnolinguistic dimension, it is often dealt with in a vague and sketchy manner. Researchers often content themselves with describing the evolution of composition according to ethnic origin, sometimes confusing the concept of ethnic origin with that of ethnic group.

Censuses ordinarily stress the presentation of *objective* statistics related to the concerns of socio-political agents. However, by force of circumstances and the very limitations of census-taking operations, statistics always reflect reality imperfectly and incompletely, and thereby contribute to an equivocal and sometimes misleading picture of the situation. On this subject, the introduction of the concept of ethnicity offers a very interesting example. Although Canadian censuses provide only totals according to ethnic origin, these are most often described as if they were statistics relating to ethnic groups. We shall examine this question in the first section, while describing the major movements of ethnic composition over the last one hundred years.

Two major linguistic groups alone comprise more than 90% of the Canadian population: the anglophone group and francophone one. The anglophones are the majority in Canada as a whole, but form the minority in Quebec. The francophones are a minority in every province except Quebec, where they are in majority. The second section will be devoted to the description and analysis of the evolution of the linguistic composition during the past twenty-five years, both in Quebec and the rest of Canada.

Finally, the third section will deal with linguistic mobility and the modes of renewal among minority linguistic groups. Particular attention will be paid to francophones living outside Quebec and to groups whose language is other than French and English.

Although on occasion we will isolate Amerindian ethnic origin or languages, we will not attempt to make a detailed analysis of the demographic situation of the native peoples.[1] As traditional sources, especially censuses, are not always reliable, we would have had to have recourse to special sources and methods. This would have forced us to break the continuity of the analysis.

EVOLUTION OF ETHNIC COMPOSITION IN PAST ONE HUNDRED YEARS

We may distinguish four major periods in the settlement of Canada. The first period extends over several thousand years and leads to a very scattered occupation of the territory by the native peoples. The second coincides with French colonization; settlement is confined to the lowlands along the St. Lawrence River and to Acadia (now the Maritime provinces). French colonization, which developed over approximately one hundred and fifty years, came to an end with the conquest of New France in 1759−1760. Canada, surrendered to Great Britain by the Treaty of Paris (1763), was henceforth opened to British immigration. Although the British population grew slowly as a result of the attraction exercised by the United States, the British outnumbered the French before the middle of the nineteenth century. In the second half of the nineteenth century, the population stagnated: during the last four decades, from 1861 to 1901, net migration was, moreover, negative (Stone and Siggner 1974). The fourth period coincides to a large extent with the settlement of the Prairies. It began vigorously at the beginning of the twentieth century. Between 1901 and 1914, Canada profited from the strongest wave of immigration in its history; in 1913 alone, Canada received 400,000 immigrants. This influx was brought to an abrupt halt by the war. Although the British were still well represented, this wave of immigration nonetheless was much more diversified ethnically than those of the nineteenth century.

These major periods of settlement had a profound impact on the ethnic composition of the population. To the native peoples were added, successively, French, British, and finally a very mixed group, the ''other ethnic groups.'' The population of these four groups can be known and compared from 1871 onwards by means of the ten-year census.

In the 1871 census, the population of the first four provinces federated in 1867 is almost 3.5 million (table 1.1). The composition by ethnic origin shows that the British are decidedly in the majority (60.5%). The French are

---

[1] An analysis of the demographic situation of the native peoples appears in part two of this book.

TABLE 1.1
NUMBER AND COMPOSITION OF CANADIAN POPULATION
ACCORDING TO ETHNIC ORIGIN, 1871 TO 1971

YEAR	ALL ORIGINS		BRITISH		FRENCH		NATIVE[a]		OTHER[b]	
	Number (×1,000)	%	Number (×1,000)	%	Number (×1,000)	%	Number (×1,000)	%	Number (×1,000)	%
1871[c]	3,486	100.0	2,111	60.5	1,083	31.1	23	0.7	269	7.7
1901[c]	4,623	100.0	2,619	56.7	1,606	34.7	38	0.8	360	7.8
1901[d]	5,371	100.0	3,063	57.0	1,649	30.7	128	2.4	531	9.9
1911[d]	7,207	100.0	3,999	55.5	2,062	28.6	106	1.5	1,040	14.4
1921[d]	8,788	100.0	4,869	55.4	2,453	27.9	113	1.3	1,353	15.4
1931[d]	10,377	100.0	5,381	51.9	2,928	28.2	129	1.2	1,939	18.7
1941[d]	11,507	100.0	5,716	49.7	3,483	30.3	126	1.1	2,182	18.9
1951[d]	13,648	100.0	6,372	46.7	4,309	31.6	165	1.2	2,802	20.5
1951[e]	14,009	100.0	6,710	47.9	4,319	30.8	165	1.2	2,815	20.1
1961[e]	18,238	100.0	7,997	43.8	5,540	30.4	220	1.2	4,481	24.6
1971[e]	21,568	100.0	9,624	44.6	6,180	28.7	313	1.4	5,451	25.3

SOURCE: Royal Commission on Bilingualism and Biculturalism (1970), p. 257; Dominion Bureau of Statistics (1953), table 34; and Statistics Canada (1973b), cat. no. 92−723, table 2.

NOTES: a. Erratic movements of population of Indian and Inuit origin are explained largely by changes in census practices, in particular with respect to assignation of Métis. As for rest of Canadian population, origin of natives is determined through paternal line since 1951, while in previous censuses, special criteria were used to enumerate them: from 1911 to 1931, they were defined by maternal line; in 1941, all Métis were counted separately; prior to 1911, they seem to have been included, as a rule, in the native population.

b. This residual category also includes those who did not declare their origin in cases where these were not distributed. However, numbers seem to be negligible and probably have no effect on the *general* picture of evolution of numbers and relative size of this category.

c. Comprises only Nova Scotia, New Brunswick, Quebec, and Ontario.

d. Does not include Newfoundland.

e. Includes Newfoundland.

in second place with 31.1% of the population; they are concentrated in the province of Quebec, where moreover they form the majority of the population (78%). The population of other than British, French, or native origin is composed primarily of Germans (203,000) and Dutch (30,000): these two groups alone constitute more than 85% of the population of ''other ethnic origins.''

Despite the high birth rate (Henripin 1968), the population of the first four federated provinces grew at an average annual rate slightly below 1% between 1871 and 1901. Immigration was not sufficient to compensate for those who left for the United States (Lavoie 1972). For many immigrants, Canada was nothing more than a way station on the southward route.

Between 1871 and 1901, the fraction of the population that was of French origin increased from 31.1% to 34.7% in the first four federated provinces, while the British strength diminished from 60.5% to 56.7%. But other provinces had joined the Canadian federation since 1867: Manitoba in 1870, British Columbia in 1871, and Prince Edward Island in 1873. In addition, the federal government administered the Prairie territories, which were to become Saskatchewan and Alberta in 1905, as well as the vast northern territories. In this expanded Canada, Canadians of British origin comprised 57.0% of the population in 1901, while those of French origin accounted for 30.7%.

Following the great wave of immigration at the beginning of the century, the Canadian population increased from 5,371,000 to 7,207,000 between 1901 and 1911, which corresponds to an annual average growth rate of 3%. Interrupted by the World War I, immigration stagnated until 1919. Nevertheless, the Canadian population continued to grow at an annual rate of 2% between 1911 and 1921.

Between 1901 and 1921, the proportion of the population of British origin shrank from 57.0% to 55.4%; similarly, the population of French origin decreased from 30.7% to 27.9%. In contrast, the "other ethnic origins" rose from 9.9% to 15.4%. In 1901, only the Germans numbered more than 100,000 persons: the Scandinavians passed this mark in 1911, the Jews, Dutch, Russians, and Ukrainians in 1921. Several of these groups made a significant contribution to the settlement of the Prairies. Moreover, in this region, the "other ethnic origins" represented between 30% and 40% of the provincial populations in 1921.

Immigration resumed in the 1920s. However, its character had changed. It was no longer a question of populating new territories, but of contributing to industrial development. This explains the tendency for immigrants to establish themselves in the centre of the country, in Quebec and Ontario, and more particularly, in the large cities, Montreal and Toronto. The economic crisis and World War II once more cut immigration to a thin trickle between 1930 and 1945.

From 1921 onwards, and especially between 1931 and 1951, there was a relatively rapid increase in the proportion of the population that was of French origin. It rose from 28.2% in 1931 to 31.6% in 1951, while the fraction of the population of British origin shrank from 55.4% in 1921 to 46.7% in 1951. The entry of Newfoundland into the Canadian federation in 1949, however, increased the share of the British-origin population to 47.9% in 1951.

Two facts profoundly affected the evolution of the ethnic composition following World War II: first, the vigorous revival of immigration from 1951 onwards (Kalbach 1970 and 1974), and second, the progressive reduction in the very high French-Canadian birth rate (Henripin 1974). While scarcely differing from that of other Canadian women in the period around 1870 (Henripin 1968), the fertility among French-Canadian women subsequently decreased much more slowly, to the point where it was 70% higher than among other Canadian women in 1931, and 60% higher in 1941 (Lieberson 1970). The post-war "baby boom," however, had much less impact on French-Canadian women: their lead was thus down to 30% in 1951. Toward the end of the 1960s, it seems that French-Canadian fertility was once more, after the lapse of a century, roughly equal to that of other Canadians (Henripin 1974).

The proportion of the population of British origin continued to fall between 1951 and 1961. However, contrary to all expectations, the British strength rose from 43.8% in 1961 to 44.6% in 1971. However, this is a purely artificial increase resulting from modifications in the data-collecting procedures used in the 1971 census (Castonguay 1976*a*, 1977; Henripin 1974; Statistics Canada 1976; Lachapelle 1977; Rochon-Lesage and Maheu n.d.). J. Henripin (1974) attempted a correction that would make the 1971 ethnic composition *approximately* comparable to that of 1961. According to him, in 1971, the proportions of British, French, and origins other than British and French would have been, respectively, 42.1% (instead of 44.6%), 29.2% (instead of 28.7%), and 28.7% (instead to 26.7%). It would therefore seem that the proportion of persons of British origin continued to diminish between 1961 and 1971. The proportion of persons of French origin also diminished between 1951 and 1971, as was to have been expected. In contrast, the "other ethnic origins" (excluding native peoples) saw their fraction rise from 20% in 1951 to over 25% in 1971,[2] due to the high rate of immigration during this period.

In one century, Canada's ethnic composition underwent profound changes. Between 1871 and 1971, the proportion of the population of British origin shrank from about 60% to slightly over 40%. This reduction in the relative strength of the British took place essentially to the advantage of the "other ethnic origins," whose fraction more than tripled in the course of a century. The strength of the population of French origin hovered in the neighbourhood of 30%, increasing in periods of net emigration and diminishing during periods of net immigration.

Should we conclude that Canada has progressively become, in terms of its demographic base, a country of minorities? That depends, of course, on what we mean by "a country of minorities." Do we wish to express the idea that in Canada there is no longer one ethnic origin that alone comprises the majority of the population? That is hardly an original idea, since it can easily be postulated that in a sense Canada has been a "country of minorities" for over a century.[3] Or do we wish to claim that henceforth no ethnic group corresponds to the majority of the population? In the latter case, we must consider the conditions that make it possible to assimilate the concept of

---

[2] The approximately 5,451,000 people that in 1971 declared their origin as other than British, French, or native form a highly heterogeneous group. Only those declaring German as origin numbered more than one million (1,317,000); those declaring Italian came next with 731,000; followed Ukrainian with 581,000; Dutch with 426,000; Polish with 316,000; Jewish with 297,000; Norwegian with 179,000; Hungarian with 132,000; Greek with 124,000; Chinese with 119,000; Yugoslav with 105,000; and Swedish with 102,000; listing only groups that number over 100,000.

[3] In fact, if we divide British origin into its English, Scottish, and Irish components, as the censuses invite us to do, French origin would be at the top in most censuses, except in 1921 and 1971, when the English origin took first place by a slight margin (Kalbach 1978). In this sense, for over a century, no ethnic origin has represented the majority of the Canadian population.

ethnic group into the concept of ethnic origin as defined in the Canadian censuses.

The concept of an ethnic group is certainly not easy to define with precision. It has to do with the feelings of affiliation presently experienced by individuals, based on characteristics capable of being transmitted from one generation to the next, such as language, religion, or physical attributes. The terms *ethnic identity* or *ethnicity* are readily used in this context. But ethnicity is not an immutable characteristic of an individual; it alters and sometimes undergoes profound changes in the course of a lifetime. The respective strengths of the various ethnic groups may be modified within generations and from one generation to the next. In an ethnically heterogeneous population, it is consequently difficult to accept that ethnic affiliations of the past faithfully reflect those of the present. However, this is the supposition we implicitly entertain when we discuss compositions based on ethnic origins as though they corresponded to compositions based on ethnic groups.

Canadian censuses have never attempted to determine the ethnic affiliations of individuals. Obviously censuses do not lend themselves well to so-called subjective questions. The difficulty has been side-stepped by attempting to establish the ethnic or cultural group of the paternal ancestor who immigrated to North America. This variable—ethnic origin—assigns the population on the basis of characteristics related to the moment—sometimes very distant and verging on the legendary—of the family's arrival in North America. With the possible exception of individuals born outside Canada, nothing ensures that this ethnic origin constitutes a satisfactory approximation of the population's real ethnic affiliations, unless we assume that ethnic mobility has always been negligible in Canada, which seems hardly plausible.

But can we propose a better approximation of the concept of the ethnic group than the measures related to ethnic origin? Although ethnic groups can be distinguished on the basis of many characteristics—physical, religious, linguistic, and so on—there is no doubt that in Canada linguistic characteristics are the most salient differentiating criteria. Of course, the concept of an ethnolinguistic group does not always coincide with the broader concept of the ethnic group, especially in the case of affiliations based on religion or physical characteristics. In any case, we do not have access to information that would make it possible to assign the population according to ethnolinguistic affiliations. However, we can try to make use of two related concepts: home language and mother tongue. Requested for the first time in the 1971 census, the home language designates the language used most often by an individual within his family at the time of the census. The mother tongue corresponds roughly to the home language during early childhood (Lachapelle 1977, n.d.). More precisely, in censuses carried out since 1941, mother tongue means the first language spoken and still understood by the individual.

To grasp clearly the meaning of the concepts of mother tongue and home language, it is enlightening to compare them to two concepts to which they are *formally* related: the region of birth and that of residence. Strictly speaking, an individual does not choose his region of birth any more than he chooses his mother tongue: these are characteristics that his parents have passed on to him. But just as he may live during his lifetime in regions other than his region of birth, he may adopt a home language that is different from his mother tongue. This formal relationship between the region of birth/ region of residence and the mother tongue/home language is undoubtedly worth developing further. We will limit ourselves here to a single observation. In describing regional population distribution, no one hesitates between the variable ''region of birth'' and the variable ''region of residence''; the second is invariably selected. In so doing, we are guided by a simple yet decisive consideration: to describe the situation existing in the present, it is better to adopt a variable that reflects a recent situation rather than one reflecting a past situation. In the matter of linguistic composition, this consideration leads us to prefer the home language to the mother tongue. This does not signify, obviously, that the mother tongue variable is without interest. Coupled with the home language, the mother tongue in fact makes it possible to define a very interesting phenomenon: linguistic mobility. We will return to this subject later.

Having said this, let us return to the examination of the statistics from the 1971 census. Table 1.2 allows us to compare the numbers of the population by ethnic origin, mother tongue, and language of use. As noted earlier, 9,624,000 people declared themselves to be of British origin: 44.6% of the population. However, English as a mother tongue corresponds to a much larger number: 12,974,000 people (60.1%); and English as a home language to many more again: 14,446,000 people or 67.0% of Canada's total population. This means that a substantial fraction of those of other than British origin have English as their mother tongue. In some cases, no doubt, the moves toward English preceded arrival in Canada. But the extent of the moves suggests that the English group constitutes an important centre of attraction. Whatever the case, we must bear in mind that these moves occurred prior to the birth of the census subjects. They involved primarily their parents and grandparents. On the other hand, a comparison of the mother tongue with the home language makes it possible to appreciate the linguistic mobility that the census subjects were willing to accept during their lives. Here again, English exerts an unparalleled force of attraction. Its effect is most felt on the ''other'' languages, but it also affects the French and native languages.

In the last century, Canada was a country whose majority was anglophone *and* British. Immigration subsequently transformed its demographic basis. The newcomers, however, gave up their own languages and massively adopted English. If Canada is not henceforth a country with a

TABLE 1.2
POPULATION ACCORDING TO ETHNIC ORIGIN, MOTHER TONGUE
AND HOME LANGUAGE, CANADA, 1971

ORIGIN OR LANGUAGE	NUMBER (×1,000)			INDEX OF ETHNOLINGUISTIC CONTINUITY $(2) \div (1)$	INDEX OF LINGUISTIC CONTINUITY $(3) \div (2)$
	Ethnic Origin (1)	Mother Tongue (2)	Home Language (3)	(4)	(5)
British or English	9,624	12,974	14,446	1.35	1.11
French	6,180	5,794	5,546	0.94	0.96
Native	313	180	137	0.58	0.76
Other, of which:	5,451	2,620	1,439	0.48	0.55
German	1,317	561	213	0.43	0.38
Italian	731	538	425	0.74	0.79
Ukrainian	581	310	145	0.53	0.47
Dutch	426	145	36	0.34	0.25
Scandinavian[a]	385	84	10	0.22	0.12
Polish	316	135	71	0.43	0.53
Hungarian	132	87	51	0.66	0.59
Greek	124	104	87	0.84	0.84
Chinese	119	95	78	0.80	0.82
Yugoslav[b]	105	74	29	0.70	0.39
Total	21,568	21,568	21,568	——	——

SOURCE: Statistics Canada (1973*b*), cat. no. 92−723; *idem* (1973*c*), cat. no. 92−725; and *idem* (1973*d*), cat. no. 92−726.
NOTES: a. Includes Danes, Icelanders, Norwegians, and Swedes.
    b. Includes Croatians, Serbs, and Slovaks.

British majority, it nevertheless has remained a country with an anglophone majority. Thus, except in a very limited sense and one which, moreover, is far removed from reality, Canada does not seem to have become a "country of minorities." It still possesses a majority, even though one whose character has altered. The concepts of a mother tongue and especially of a home language reflect this situation in a much more satisfactory manner than the traditional concepts of ethnic origin.

LINGUISTIC AND TERRITORIAL DUALITY

The Canadian population is made up of two major linguistic groups, the anglophones and the francophones. Certainly other linguistic groups also form part of the Canadian reality, but on a much smaller scale, as the statistics of the 1971 census relating to the home language indicate. In fact, the English comprise 14,446,000 persons, and the French, 5,546,000 persons; Italian was declared by only 425,000 persons; German, by 213,000; Ukrainian, by 145,000; native languages, by 137,000; Greek, by 87,000;

Chinese, by 78,000; Portuguese, by 75,000; Polish, by 71,000; and Hungarian, by 51,000; to list only those languages frequently spoken within the family by more than 50,000 persons. Thus, the French and English languages together represent nearly 93% of the Canadian population. The expression *linguistic duality* characterizes very well this demographic situation, and in any case expresses it far better than the expression *linguistic diversity*, which is too vague and general.

Anglophones form the majority in all the provinces except Quebec. In 1971, persons whose home language was English represented 15% of the population of Quebec and 87% of the rest of Canada. In contrast, francophones are in the minority everywhere, except in Quebec, where they constitute the majority. In Quebec, nearly 81% of the population had French as its home language in 1971; elsewhere in Canada, also in 1971, French was frequently spoken within the family by only slightly more than 4% of the population. Thus, territorial duality coincides almost exactly with linguistic duality: on the one hand, we have Quebec, where francophones are strongly in the majority; on the other, the rest of Canada, where anglophones form a massive majority.

In the course of the last twenty-five years, the territorial duality of anglophones and francophones has become more distinct (table 1.3). In fact, the fraction of the population that is of French mother tongue and resides in Quebec has gone from 82.3% in 1951 to 84.0% in 1971 and 84.8% in 1976, while the proportion of anglophones living outside Quebec increased from 93.3% in 1951 to 94.4% in 1976. Moreover, the English minority (in Quebec) and the French minority (in the rest of Canada) together only represented 7% of the Canadian population in 1976, as compared with 9% in 1951. Linguistic duality thus seems to have an increasing tendency to become "territorialized." Hence the importance of distinguishing Quebec from the rest of Canada in any study of the demolinguistic situation.

From the end of the eighteenth to the beginning of the twentieth century, the territories located to the west of Quebec were settled one after another. There is, therefore, nothing surprising in the fact that Quebec's demographic importance progressively diminished. In 1921, it seems to have reached its low: the population of Quebec was at that time 26.9% of the population of Canada. In the following decades, Quebec's demographic importance increased rapidly as a result of strong natural growth due to a very high relative birth rate of (francophone) Quebecers. In 1951, Quebec contained 29.7% of the Canadian population (28.9% if the residents of Newfoundland are added to the population of Canada). Between 1951 and 1966, the situation remained stationary: Quebec's higher natural growth rates compensated for its lower rates of migratory growth (Lachapelle n.d.). Since then the balance has been disturbed. Quebec's relative demographic strength went from 28.9% in 1966 to 27.9% in 1971 and 27.1% in 1976. Not only are Quebec's natural growth rates now lower than those of the rest of Canada, but in

TABLE 1.3
DISTRIBUTION OF POPULATION BY MOTHER TONGUE, 1951–1976

YEAR & MOTHER TONGUE	CANADA		QUEBEC		CANADA WITHOUT QUEBEC	
	Number (×1,000)	%	Number (×1,000)	%	Number (×1,000)	%
1951						
English	8,281	100.0	558	6.7	7,723	93.3
French	4,069	100.0	3,347	82.3	722	17.7
Other	1,660	100.0	150	9.0	1,509	91.0
Total	14,009	100.0	4,056	28.9	9,954	71.1
1961						
English	10,661	100.0	697	6.5	9,963	93.5
French	5,123	100.0	4,270	83.3	853	16.7
Other	2,455	100.0	292	11.9	2,162	88.1
Total	18,238	100.0	5,259	28.8	12,979	71.2
1971						
English	12,974	100.0	789	6.1	12,185	93.9
French	5,794	100.0	4,867	84.0	926	16.0
Other	2,801	100.0	371	13.2	2,430	86.8
Total	21,568	100.0	6,028	27.9	15,541	72.1
1976[a]						
English	14,150	100.0	797	5.6	13,353	94.4
French	5,967	100.0	5,058	84.8	908	15.2
Other	2,876	100.0	379	13.2	2,497	86.8
Total	22,993	100.0	6,234	27.1	16,758	72.9

SOURCE: Lachapelle (n.d.); Dominion Bureau of Statistics (1953), table 56; *idem* (1963), table 66; Statistics Canada (1973*a*), cat. no. 92–715, table 18; and *idem, 1976 Census of Canada*, unpublished tables.
NOTES: Due to rounding of figures, totals do not always correspond to sum of parts.
a. Results of 1976 census have been adjusted to make them *approximately* comparable to results of 1971 census; method of adjustment is described in appendix.

addition, her migratory balances have become negative. Certainly Quebec still gains in her migratory exchanges with foreign countries, but she shows significant deficits under the heading of interprovincial migratory movements (Statistics Canada 1977).

It is often considered—implicitly or explicitly—that the study of demographic facts and phenomena in Quebec and the rest of Canada provides an initial approximation of the respective demographic situations of francophones and anglophones in Canada as a whole. No doubt this is so, but it gives us very little information on the development of the linguistic composition within the two major regions, as the various linguistic groups may be affected differently by demographic movements of the whole. In order to satisfactorily describe and analyse the evolution of the linguistic composition within each of the major regions, it would obviously be necessary to have access to a breakdown of the population according to home language. Unfortunately these data were not collected until the 1971 census. However, the composition of the population by mother tongue is available from a number of censuses (table 1.4). This is a poor substitute, since the evolution of the composition by mother tongue is hardly sensitive at all to variations in linguistic mobility, except in an indirect manner by way of births. Whatever the case, we may undoubtedly assume as a first approximation that the *movements* of composition according to mother tongue reflect the *movements* of composition according to the language of use.[4] Even so, the composition according to mother tongue must be comparable from one census to another. If, as seems to be the case, we may assume that the results of the censuses of 1941, 1951, and 1961 are at least approximately comparable, we may still have doubts concerning the comparability of composition according to mother tongue between the censuses of 1961 and 1971 (Lachapelle 1977). Moreover, it does not seem improbable that the methods of data collection and analysis used in the 1971 census resulted, in contrast to those used in the 1961 census, in at least a slight inflation of the importance of the English language. As for the last two censuses, their comparability is equally problematical; we have tried to adjust the results of the 1976 census in order to make them approximately comparable to the results of the 1971 census (method of adjustment used is described in appendix). It is advisable, therefore, to be prudent in interpreting the movements "observed" between 1961 and 1971, and between 1971 and 1976.

Two trends seem to persist throughout the past twenty-five years, both concerning the minorities. In Quebec, the proportion of the population of English mother tongue diminished slowly but steadily between 1951 and 1976; symetrically, in the rest of Canada, the fraction of the population of French mother tongue went from 7.2% in 1951 to 5.4% in 1976.[5] It seems, then, that the relative strength of the minorities has a tendency to decline progressively in Quebec as in the rest of Canada. The process, however, is more advanced and much more rapid in the rest of Canada than in Quebec.

As for the evolution of the French group in Quebec and the English group elsewhere in Canada, it seems to be inversely linked to the movements

---

[4] This hypothesis is possibly less cumbersome than would appear at first glance, due to the compensations established between natural growth and linguistic transfers. This would be worth closer examination with the help of models.

[5] The rapid reduction in the percentage of francophones outside of Quebec results from the combination of several factors. First, they have profited very little from the strong immigration since the war. In addition, their traditionally high birth rate has become progressively lower over the past twenty-five years. Last, a notable decline in their ethnolinguistic continuity has been observed (Arès 1975; Henripin 1974; Joy 1967; Lieberson 1970; Vallée and Dufour 1974).

TABLE 1.4
COMPOSITION OF POPULATION ACCORDING TO MOTHER TONGUE
AND HOME LANGUAGE, 1951—1976

REGION AND LANGUAGE	MOTHER TONGUE				HOME LANGUAGE
	1951 (%)	1961 (%)	1971 (%)	1976[a] (%)	1971 (%)
Quebec					
English	13.8	13.3	13.1	12.8	14.7
French	82.5	81.2	80.7	81.1	80.8
Other	3.7	5.5	6.2	6.1	4.5
Total	100.0	100.0	100.0	100.0	100.0
Rest of Canada					
English	77.6	76.8	78.4	79.7	87.2
French	7.2	6.6	6.0	5.4	4.4
Others	15.2	16.6	15.6	14.9	8.4
Total	100.0	100.0	100.0	100.0	100.0

SOURCE: Table 1.3; and Statistics Canada (1973*d*), cat. no. 92—726, table 26.
NOTE: a. Results of 1976 census have been adjusted to make them *approximately* comparable to results of 1971 census; method of adjustment is described in appendix.

of the population whose mother tongue is neither English nor French. In Quebec, the proportion of the population that is of French mother tongue shrank from 82.5% in 1951 to 80.7% in 1971 and increased to 81.1% in 1976, while the fraction of the population whose mother tongue is neither English nor French increased from 3.7% in 1951 to 6.2% in 1971 and diminished to 6.1% in 1976. Similar movements can be observed in the rest of Canada, although the pivotal year was 1961 instead of 1971.

All this suggests that the respective positions of the two majorities, francophone in Quebec and anglophone elsewhere in Canada, are solidly established. Actually the situation of francophones is more precarious than it seems at first glance. Researchers who have studied Quebec's demolinguistic situation (Charbonneau and Maheu 1973; Henripin 1974; Lachapelle 1977; Rochon-Lesage and Maheu n.d.) are in general agreement on the following points:

1. Differences in mortality rates, though unfavourable to francophones, are now too slight to be a significant factor in the evolution of numbers within linguistic groups.

2. Francophones profited for a long time from a very high relative birth rate; this advantage diminished during the 1950s and disappeared almost completely during the 1960s.

3. Linguistic mobility of persons whose mother tongue is other than English or French occurs more toward English than toward French; also,

francophones display a slight negative balance in their linguistic "exchanges" with anglophones. In total, "other" languages incur important losses, anglophones profit from substantial gains, and francophones remain more or less stationary.

4. When the migratory balance is positive, as it was from 1951 to 1961, the effect of migration is a notable increase in the relative size of the population whose mother tongue is neither English nor French, at the same time that it slightly increases the fraction of anglophones and consequently diminishes the fraction of francophones.

Some researchers (Charbonneau and Maheu 1973; Rochon-Lesage and Maheu n.d.) go further: they postulate, on the basis of a *residual estimate* of net migration by mother tongue between 1961 and 1971, that the migratory phenomenon would be unfavourable to francophones even during periods of net emigration. This hypothesis, however, seems to be contradicted by the evolution of the composition by mother tongue between 1971 and 1976. It also seems difficult to reconcile this hypothesis with the latest data available by mother tongue on migratory movements between Quebec and the rest of Canada (table 1.5).

During the five-year period between 1966 and 1971, in fact, Quebec shows net losses of 75,400 persons in its migratory exchanges with the rest of Canada. These losses are distributed as shown below, according to mother tongue:

English	52,200	(69.2%)
French	13,500	(17.9%)
Other languages	9,700	(12.9%)

Although all linguistic groups show losses, the migratory movements nonetheless seem less unfavourable to francophones than to anglophones.

The evolution of the composition according to mother tongue of Quebec's population thus seems difficult to interpret, especially since 1961. The problem, however, is easy to isolate: it concerns the migratory phenomenon. If we rely on the residual measures of net migration according to mother tongue for the period 1961–1971, we are led to the conclusion that even when the migratory balance is negative, migration reduces the relative size of the francophone population and increases that of the anglophone group; if, on the other hand, we study the census statistics on migration according to mother tongue for the five-year period from 1966 to 1971, we are inclined to support the conclusion directly opposed to the preceding one.

Let us attempt to clarify, and if possible, remove, this contradiction. To analyse the evolution of the composition according to mother tongue, we break down the movements of numbers according to mother tongue into two elements: natural growth (births minus deaths) and migratory growth. In fact, this breakdown is most often used to estimate migratory growth, but the estimates obtained in this way are to be identified with the real net migrators only on condition that we assume that the same individuals always declare the

TABLE 1.5
POPULATION OVER FIVE IN 1971, BY REGION OF RESIDENCE IN 1966
AND BY MOTHER TONGUE

REGION OF RESIDENCE IN 1966 AND MOTHER TONGUE	REGION OF RESIDENCE IN 1971		
	Quebec	Canada without Quebec	Canada
Quebec			
English	643,745	99,075	742,815
French	4,400,400	46,860	4,447,260
Other	274,945	14,365	289,310
Total	5,319,085	160,300	5,479,385
Canada without Quebec			
English	46,905	10,551,160	10,598,070
French	33,360	797,780	831,140
Other	4,635	1,980,410	1,985,045
Total	84,905	13,329,350	13,414,255
Outside Canada			
English	36,940	376,655	314,595
French	38,465	12,750	51,215
Other	62,215	296,540	358,755
Total	137,620	685,945	823,565
All Regions			
English	727,590	11,026,890	11,754,480
French	4,472,225	857,390	5,329,615
Other	341,795	2,291,315	2,633,110
Total	5,541,610	14,175,595	19,717,205

SOURCE: Statistics Canada, special 1971 census tables commissioned by Institute for Research on Public Policy.
NOTE: Migrants who did not declare their place of residence in Canada in 1966 were distributed on a *pro rata* basis among intraprovincial and interprovincial migrants.

same mother tongue from one census to the next, or at least that any substitutions of mother tongue cancel each other out. If we do not make this assumption, the residual estimates of migratory growth correspond to the sum of the real net migrations *plus* the net substitutions of mother tongue. It is not impossible that the English group was increased by substitutions of mother tongue between 1961 and 1971, and also between 1971 and 1976, to the detriment of French and other languages. This might account for part of the discrepancies between direct and indirect measurements of migratory growth.

Thus we can advance another explanation of the anomalies that we have observed. During the past twenty-five years, the situation in Quebec with regard to migration has presented sharp contrasts: between 1951 and 1966, migratory growth was generally positive, while between 1966 and 1976 it was generally negative. We expect that periods of net immigration will be less profitable to the francophone group than to the anglophone and other groups, but that periods of net emigration will be more disadvantageous to the anglophones than to the francophones.[6] While the available data concerning migratory movements in the five-year period from 1966 to 1971 (table 1.5) support the preceding proposal, it can easily be conceived that the residual measurements of net migration between 1961 and 1971 are still difficult to interpret, as they deal with a period that is composed of a mixture of two migratory situations.

Speaking only of composition by mother tongue, it would seem that between 1966 and 1976, the fraction of francophones has increased, at least slightly, in Quebec. This may be imputed to migration, which has been more to the advantage of francophones than of other Quebecers, or more precisely, has been less disadvantageous to francophones than to non-francophones, since the migratory balance has been negative during the last two five-year periods. But the situation of francophones nonetheless shows signs of fragility, as shown by the linguistic transfers, which largely benefit the English group.

LINGUISTIC MOBILITY AND RENEWAL OF LINGUISTIC GROUPS

In isolating and defining the evolution of the linguistic situation, we had to be content with describing and analysing the movements of the composition according to mother tongue. We have seen that it definitely would have been preferable to study composition trends based on the home language, but this variable was not introduced until the 1971 census. Having ascertained both the mother tongue and the home language of those enumerated in 1971, it then becomes possible not only to determine the differences between the compositions according to mother tongue and home language, but also to measure linguistic mobility fairly satisfactorily.[7] Despite its obvious importance, this phenomenon has only been very superficially studied up until now (Castonguay 1974 and 1976b; Statistics Canada 1976; Vallée and Dufour 1974). It would therefore be premature to attempt a synthesis. We will subsequently confine ourselves to a brief

---

[6] This proposition would require lengthy developments that are impossible to present within the framework of this study. We should just mention that due to the linguistic isolation of Quebec francophones, it is permissible to suppose that they are, all things being equal, underrepresented among people that leave Quebec, as well as among those that enter.

[7] We should emphasize, however, that the available data at best allow us to measure the linguistic transfers consented to by the census subjects since their birth. Therefore, as far as linguistic mobility is concerned, we are appreciably in the same situation as a researcher who, wishing to describe internal migration, only has access to totals from one census according to region of birth and residence.

description of linguistic mobility and a few general considerations concerning the renewal of linguistic groups.

We will try first to clarify the idea of linguistic mobility. In the 1971 census, the home language designates the language most often spoken by an individual within his family. As for the mother tongue, it signifies the first language spoken, on the condition that it is still understood. This restrictive clause, strictly speaking, does not allow the mother tongue to be identified with the home language from early childhood. However, we will subsequently allow the mother tongue to constitute an approximation of the home language from early childhood. This introduces a bias[8] whose impact is not known, but whose direction is clear: linguistic persistence is overestimated while, on the contrary, linguistic mobility is underestimated. This must be kept in mind.

In order to determine the degree of linguistic mobility or the degree of linguistic persistence, we will use two indicators: the index of linguistic continuity and the rate of persistence. The index of linguistic continuity of language A is equal to the ratio of the number of people whose home language is A to the number of people whose mother tongue is A. As for the rate of persistence of A, it corresponds to the percentage of people whose mother tongue and home language are both A in relation to those whose mother tongue is A. Let us use an example to clarify these definitions. In Quebec in 1971, 788,830 people declared English their mother tongue; among these, 729,920 also declared English their home language. In total, 887,875 people were counted whose home language was English. The index of English continuity is therefore equal to 887,875/788,830 (or 112.6%), and the rate of persistence of English at 729,920/788,830 (or 92.5%).

By definition, the rate of persistence is between 0 and 1. The complement of the rate of persistence corresponds to the overall rate of linguistic mobility. The index of continuity sometimes exceeds the unit: moreover, it is almost always the case for English, even in Quebec (table 1.6). On the other hand, it should be mentioned that the continuity index is always equal to, or higher than, the rate of persistence.

While the rate of persistence allows us to determine a language's capacity for preservation or conservation, the index of continuity expresses a language's capacity to endure and develop. In most cases, this distinction between preservation and perpetuation capacity is superfluous. Languages generally have strong or weak capacities for preservation and perpetuation: those that maintain themselves well are very attractive, those that retain poorly are not.

---

[8] Naturally there are also other biases, particularly those that result from methods used by Statistics Canada to resolve cases of multiple declarations of mother tongue and/or home language. We should mention, without entering into details, that these methods undoubtedly result in a slight inflation of the linguistic transfers of people whose mother tongue is English.

TABLE 1.6
LINGUISTIC CONTINUITY, PERSISTENCE, AND TRANSFERS, 1971

REGION AND MOTHER TONGUE	CONTINUITY INDEX (%)	RATE OF PERSISTENCE (%)	% OF LINGUISTIC TRANSFERS	
			Toward English	Toward French
Quebec				
English	112.6	92.5	—	83.5
French	100.1	98.4	92.0	—
Native	89.1	85.1	89.4	10.6
Other,	71.4	67.0	70.5	29.5
of which:				
German	45.4	40.9	80.8	19.2
Italian	79.9	76.8	46.1	53.9
Ukrainian	70.2	63.6	87.4	12.6
Canada without Quebec				
English	111.3	99.2	—	21.1
French	73.0	70.2	99.1	—
Native	75.3	69.8	99.6	0.4
Other,	52.1	49.1	99.5	0.5
of which:				
German	37.7	35.8	99.7	0.3
Italian	78.6	73.8	98.1	1.9
Ukrainian	45.8	41.9	99.9	0.1

SOURCE: Statistics Canada (1975), cat. no. 92–776, tables 1 and 2.

However, the Quebec situation is more complex. Judging by the rates of persistence (table 1.6), French has a stronger capacity for preservation than English, but the latter exhibits greater capacity for perpetuation than the former: the continuity index for English is actually 112.6%, as opposed to 100.1% for French. Despite its demographic minority situation, the English group not only manages to attract around 70% of the transfers from ''other'' languages, but it also wins over nearly 25,000 people in its linguistic exchanges with the French group. As for French, its rate of retention is high (its rate of persistence is 98.4%), but its attraction is low: it just manages to maintain its position, as indicates its continuity index (100.1%).

Outside Quebec, the situation is very clear. English remains intact, or very nearly, and attracts all. French, as well as the ''other'' languages, has a low preservation rate and attracts nothing. The same situation exists with the ''other'' languages in Quebec.

With the exception of English in Quebec, all the minority languages seem to have preservation difficulties. The intensity of linguistic mobility nevertheless varies according to whether autochthonal (native) or ''other'' languages are involved, and in the case of French, according to the regions outside of Quebec. In order to compare the situations for these different subpopulations, table 1.7 contains the rates of linguistic persistence observed among young adults, with a distinction being made between those born in Canada and those born outside the country.

More than 80% of the young adults born in Canada who declared an "other" language as their mother tongue no longer speak it in their family. This very strong linguistic mobility is probably found in the majority of immigrant languages, certainly in the most important ones (O'Bryan, Reitz, and Kuplowska 1976; Reitz 1974). These languages do not seem to persist beyond the generation that introduced them to Canada. Moreover, around 90% of the adults who declared them as home language in 1971 were born outside Canada. These linguistic groups can therefore not renew themselves except with the help of regular influxes from outside. They do not seem to have a true Canadian existence.

The linguistic persistence of native languages and French outside of Quebec is much stronger than that of other languages. In fact, among young adults born in Canada, the rate of persistence of other groups does not reach 20%, while it is slightly over 60% for French and native languages outside of Quebec. Undoubtedly it could be said that one part of the difference between the mobility of French in a minority situation and the mobility of other languages results from the weak linguistic mobility of people of French mother tongue who come from Quebec. But this hypothesis is far from being confirmed, judging from the rates of persistence given in table 1.8. With the

TABLE 1.7
RATE OF LINGUISTIC PERSISTENCE FOR POPULATION AGED 20 TO 39, 1971

PLACE OF RESIDENCE AND BIRTH	MOTHER TONGUE			
	English (%)	French (%)	Native (%)	Other (%)
Canada				
Born in Canada	99.1	92.4	64.7	17.6
Born outside Canada	96.4	79.4	47.6	59.9
Total	98.7	92.1	64.3	49.4
Quebec				
Born in Canada	90.0	98.1	84.7	23.3
Born outside Canada	91.4	89.1	51.3	72.0
Total	90.3	97.9	83.3	65.5
Canada without Quebec				
Born in Canada	99.6	62.4	62.2	17.1
Born outside Canada	96.9	46.4	47.7	57.5
Total	99.3	61.9	61.8	46.8

SOURCE: Statistics Canada, special 1971 census tables commissioned by Institute for Research on Public Policy.

exception of the northern territories and the provinces west of Manitoba, there is little difference between the linguistic mobility of people born in Quebec and that of people born in the area. This probably accounts for the strong selectivity of migration from Quebec toward the rest of Canada.

As concerns the demolinguistic situation of French outside of Quebec, three groups of provinces can be distinguished:

— In the northern territories and the provinces west of Manitoba, linguistic mobility always exceeds 60%: the French group cannot reproduce itself in the area; in order to maintain its numbers, it will have to count on influxes from outside.

— On the contrary, in New Brunswick, linguistic mobility is lower than 15%: in the absence of migrations and under the condition that the linguistic situation does not deteriorate, francophones can hope to maintain their numbers there on the condition that their fertility be at least slightly higher than the generation replacement threshold (around 2.1 children per woman).

— In the other provinces, linguistic mobility is intermediate (40%); in order to preserve their numbers, francophones must either count on a high fertility (at least 3.5 children per woman), or else receive relatively large contingents of immigrants.

With the possible exception of Ontario and the New Brunswick regions that border on Quebec, it definitely seems that renewal of the French group is

TABLE 1.8

LINGUISTIC PERSISTENCE OF PEOPLE OF FRENCH MOTHER TONGUE, BORN IN CANADA AND AGED 20 TO 59, ACCORDING TO PROVINCE OF BIRTH, 1971

PROVINCE OF RESIDENCE IN 1971	PROVINCE OF BIRTH			
	Total (%)	Same Province(s) (%)	Quebec (%)	Other Parts of Canada (%)
New Brunswick	87.4	88.3	87.1	53.2
Other Atlantic provinces	56.8	60.6	52.7	30.8
Quebec	98.0	—	98.3	89.2
Ontario	62.1	62.0	69.6	39.2
Manitoba	53.9	56.2	58.7	35.2
Saskatchewan	38.9	38.2	56.3	33.9
Alberta	35.2	37.1	59.0	17.9
British Columbia	20.3	10.9	38.4	14.8
Northern territories and Yukon	36.3	30.8	55.2	25.9
Canada	92.1	—	—	—

SOURCE: Statistics Canada, special 1971 census tables commissioned by Institute for Research on Public Policy.

difficult to ensure without sizeable migratory influxes from territories that have a large francophone concentration (Joy 1967, 1978).

CONCLUSION

Canada comprises two major linguistic groups, the anglophones and the francophones. In 1971, English was the home language of 67% of the population, French, of 26%. Excluding native peoples, other groups do not have a true Canadian linguistic existence. In fact, their members are very quickly losing the use of their language of origin, most often in favour of English. A clear territorial duality superimposes itself on the linguistic duality. Francophones are the majority in Quebec (81%), while anglophones heavily dominate the demographic scene in the rest of Canada (87%). Over the last twenty-five years, the process of "territorialization" has become accentuated: the francophones are concentrated more and more in Quebec, and the anglophones, in the rest of Canada.

Francophones profited from a very high birth rate for a long time. This diminished in the years following World War II and practically disappeared during the 1960s. Some feared that this would lead to a rapid reduction in francophone strength not only throughout Canada but also in Quebec. If the percentage of francophones in the Canadian population diminished rapidly between 1951 and 1976, the state of affairs is nevertheless more complex in Quebec. Due to the mediocre migratory situation, the proportion of francophones seems to have increased slightly over the last ten years. As francophones are much less inclined to emigrate than non-francophones, it is not surprising that their strength increases during periods of net emigration.

Due to the orientation toward English of third-group linguistic transfers, the French majority in Quebec, no longer benefiting from an appreciably higher fertility, faces a disturbing alternative: either the economic situation is satisfactory and immigration exceeds emigration, in which case Quebec maintains or drops slightly in demographic strength in the Canadian picture, but the proportion of francophones risks a strong drop in Quebec; or the economic situation is mediocre and emigration exceeds immigration, in which case the percentage of francophones is likely to rise in Quebec, but the strength of Quebec will decrease in the Canadian population. This undoubtedly partially explains why the Quebec government called for increased power over immigration, and in 1974 and 1977, adopted two very important laws designed to protect and improve the position of the French language.

Adjustment of 1976 Census Results by Mother Tongue

Although the data of the 1971 and 1976 censuses were collected by the same method, auto-enumeration, and appreciably the same question was asked concerning mother tongue, the compositions according to mother tongue are not comparable. Two main reasons account for this. First, the cases of multiple declarations of mother tongue were not resolved in the same manner: in comparison to the methods adopted in the 1971 census, those used in 1976 resulted in inflating the English and French languages at the expense of other languages. Second, Statistics Canada did not use the same methods in attributing a mother tongue to people who did not declare one: in fact, in 1976, those who did not declare one were simply not distributed by mother tongue.

In another study (Lachapelle 1977), we tried to adjust the data from the 1976 census in such a way as to make them approximately comparable to the data published from the 1971 census. We will present the main results and complete them.

In order to make the compositions by mother tongue comparable for the last two censuses, we first applied to the 1976 census the procedures for resolving multiple declarations of mother tongue that were used in the 1971 census. This adjustment was significant, as can be seen in table 1.A.1. In fact, on a Canada-wide scale, the use of the 1971 procedures instead of those of 1976 reduced the English-mother-tongue population by more than 250,000, and the French-mother-tongue population by approximately 18,000; as for the population whose mother tongue is neither English nor French, it augmented it by almost 275,000, which is equivalent to an increase of 11% over the figures published from the 1976 census.

Those who did not declare a mother tongue in the 1976 census must now be distributed. We tried to be guided by the method used in the 1971 census, more exactly by the results it gave. It would seem that it led to a distribution by mother tongue of those who did not declare any, which is close to the distribution of people who declared one or more (Lachapelle 1977), at least on a Canada-wide scale. In a first approximation, it therefore does not seem excessive to assume that those who did not declare a mother tongue would be

TABLE 1.A.1
NUMBER OF PEOPLE DECLARING AT LEAST ONE MOTHER TONGUE, 1976

MOTHER TONGUE	1976 PROCEDURES			1971 PROCEDURES		
	Canada	Quebec	Canada Without Quebec	Canada	Quebec	Canada Without Quebec
English	14,123,000	801,000	13,322,000	13,867,000	778,000	13,089,000
French	5,887,000	4,989,000	898,000	5,869,000	4,977,000	893,000
Other	2,538,000	334,000	2,204,000	2,811,000	369,000	2,442,000
All languages	22,548,000	6,124,000	16,424,000	22,548,000	6,124,000	16,424,000

SOURCE: Lachapelle (1977).
NOTE: Due to rounding of figures, totals do not always correspond to sum of parts.

distributed in the 1976 census along the same lines as the estimated distribution by mother tongue among those who did declare at least one. We put this hypothesis into effect province by province (Lachapelle 1977). The estimates obtained appear in table 1.A.2. These results were criticized (Castonguay 1978) on the basis that it would have been preferable to distribute those who did not declare a mother tongue among all the census divisions, or even among census subdivisions or enumeration areas. Thus we redid our calculations, census division by census division. These new estimates are also given in table 1.A.2. They differ very little from the preceding ones. However, we have used them in the text.

TABLE 1.A.2
POPULATION BY MOTHER TONGUE, 1976

MOTHER TONGUE	DISTRIBUTION OF THOSE WHO DID NOT DECLARE AT PROVINCIAL LEVEL[a]			DISTRIBUTION OF THOSE WHO DID NOT DECLARE AT CENSUS-DIVISION LEVEL[b]		
	Canada	Quebec	Canada Without Quebec	Canada	Quebec	Canada Without Quebec
English	14,147,000	792,000	13,355,000	14,150,000	797,000	13,353,000
French	5,976,000	5,066,000	910,000	5,967,000	5,058,000	908,000
Other	2,870,000	376,000	2,494,000	2,876,000	379,000	2,497,000
All languages	22,993,000	6,234,000	16,758,000	22,993,000	6,234,000	16,758,000

SOURCE: Statistics Canada (1978), cat. no. 92–821; Lachapelle (1977).
NOTES: Due to rounding of figures, totals do not always correspond to sum of parts.

    a. We assume that people who did not declare a mother tongue were distributed in same manner as those who declared at least one. This hypothesis obviously was put into effect province by province (Lachapelle 1977).

    b. Hypothesis stated in note (a) was put into effect province by province, except for three provinces that contain appreciable numbers of francophones. For New Brunswick and Ontario, we proceeded census division by census division; likewise for Quebec, with exception of Island of Montreal, where we proceeded by federal electoral district.

Although we feel that we have improved the comparability of the compositions according to mother tongue from the 1971 and 1976 censuses, the many uncertainties that persist cannot be ignored. We have therefore not counted the variations in underenumeration according to mother tongue from the 1971 and 1976 censuses. In addition, in most of the analyses, we are forced to assume implicitly that the same people always declare the same mother tongue from one census to the other, or at the very least that the movements compensate for this. This hypothesis has obviously not been demonstrated, but would definitely be worth investigation.

References and Bibliography

Arès, Richard
1975 *Les positions ethniques, linguistiques et religieuses des Canadiens français à la suite du recensement de 1971*. Montreal: Les éditions Bellarmin.
Canada, Dominion Bureau of Statistics
1953 *1951 Census of Canada*. Vol. 1, *Population: General Characteristics*. Ottawa: Queen's Printer and Controller of Stationery.
1963 *1961 Census of Canada*. Vol. 1 (Part 2), *Population: Official Language and Mother Tongue*. Cat. no. 92–549. Ottawa: Queen's Printer.
Canada, Royal Commission on Bilingualism and Biculturalism
1970 *Report*. Book 4, *The Cultural Contribution of the Other Ethnic Groups*. Ottawa: Queen's Printer.
Canada, Statistics Canada
1973*a* *1971 Census of Canada*. Vol. 1 (Part 2), *Population: General Characteristics—Age Groups*. Cat. no. 92–715. Ottawa: Information Canada.
1973*b* *1971 Census of Canada*. Vol. 1 (Part 3), *Population: General Characteristics—Ethnic Groups*. Cat. no. 92–723. Ottawa: Information Canada.
1973*c* *1971 Census of Canada*. Vol. 1 (Part 3), *Population: General Characteristics—Mother Tongue*. Cat. no. 92–725. Ottawa: Information Canada.
1973*d* *1971 Census of Canada*. Vol. 1 (Part 3), *Population: General Characteristics— Official Language and Language Most Often Spoken at Home*. Cat. no. 92–726. Ottawa: Information Canada.
1975 *1971 Census of Canada*. SP–6, *Special Bulletin: Population Statistics on Language Retention and Transfer*. Cat. no. 92–776. Ottawa: Information Canada.
1976 *1971 Census of Canada*. Vol. 5 (Part 1), *Profile Studies: Demographic Characteristics—Language in Canada*. Cat. no. 99–707. Ottawa: Supply and Services Canada.
1977 *International and Interprovincial Migration in Canada, 1961–62 to 1975–76*. Cat. no. 91–208. Ottawa: Supply and Services Canada.
1978 *1976 Census of Canada*. Vol. 2, *Population: Demographic Characteristics—Mother Tongue*. Cat. no. 92–821. Ottawa: Supply and Services Canada.

Castonguay, Charles

1974 "Dimensions des transferts linguistiques entre groupes anglophone, francophone et autres d'après le recensement canadien de 1971." *Bulletin de l'Association des démographes du Québec* 3, sp. no. 1: 110–24.

1976a "Quelques remarques sur les données du recensement de 1971 concernant la langue et l'origine ethnique." *Cahiers québécois de démographie* 5, sp. no. 3: 211–41.

1976b "Les transferts linguistiques au foyer." *Recherches sociographiques* 17: 341–51.

1977 "La mobilité ethnique au Canada." *Recherches sociographiques* 18: 431–50.

1978 "La répartition des non-répondants à la question sur la langue maternelle aux recensements de 1971 et de 1976." Paper read at Association canadienne française pour l'avancement des sciences Congress, demography section.

Charbonneau, Hubert, and Maheu, Robert

1973 *Les aspects démographiques de la question linguistique.* Commission d'enquête sur la situation de la langue française et sur les droits linguistiques au Québec, synthèse S3. Quebec: Éditeur officiel du Québec.

Henripin, Jacques

1968 *Tendances et facteurs de la fécondité au Canada.* Ottawa: Queen's Printer.

1974 *Immigration and Language Imbalance.* Canadian Immigration and Population Studies. Ottawa: Information Canada.

Joy, Richard J.

1967 *Languages in Conflict: The Canadian Experience.* Ottawa: The author.

1978 *Canada's Official Language Minorities.* Montreal: C.D. Howe Research Institute.

Kalbach, Warren E.

1970 *The Impact of Immigration on Canada's Population.* Ottawa: Queen's Printer.

1974 *Effect of Immigration on Population.* Canadian Immigration and Population Studies. Ottawa: Information Canada.

1978 "Growth and Distribution of Canada's Ethnic Populations, 1871–1971." In *The Canadian Ethnic Mosaic: A Quest for Identity,* edited by Leo Driedger. Toronto: McClelland and Stewart.

Lachapelle, Réjean

1977 "Quelques notes à propos de la comparabilité de la composition par langue maternelle aux recensements de 1971 et de 1976." *Cahiers québécois de démographie* 6, sp. no. 3: 93–137.

n.d. "Regards sur la population québécoise." In *Annuaire du Québec 1977/1978*, pp. 228−38. Quebec: Éditeur officiel du Québec.

Lavoie, Yolande

1972 *L'émigration des Canadiens aux États-Unis avant 1930; mesure du phénomène*. Montreal: Les Presses de l'Université de Montréal.

Lieberson, Stanley

1970 *Language and Ethnic Relations in Canada*. Toronto: John Wiley & Sons (Canada).

O'Bryan, K.G.; Reitz, J.G.; and Kuplowska, O.M.

1976 *Non-Official Languages: A Study in Canadian Multiculturalism*. Ottawa: Supply and Services Canada.

Reitz, Jeffrey G.

1974 "Language and Ethnic Community Survival." *Canadian Review of Sociology and Anthropology*, sp. no., *Aspects of Canadian Society*: 104−22.

Rochon-Lesage, Madeleine, and Maheu, Robert

n.d. "Composition ethnique et linguistique de la population du Québec." In *Annuaire du Québec 1974*, pp. 206−12. Quebec: Éditeur officiel du Québec.

Stone, Leroy O., and Siggner, Andrew J., eds.

1974 *The Population of Canada: A Review of the Recent Patterns and Trends*. Monograph commissioned by the United Nations Committee for International Coordination of National Research in Demography for World Population Year, 1974. Ottawa: Statistics Canada.

Vallée, Frank G., and Dufour, Albert

1974 "The Bilingual Belt: A Garrotte for the French?" *Laurentian University Review* 6, no. 2: 19−44.

Part Two

Native Peoples and Canadian Society: A Profile of Issues and Trends

by

Victor F. Valentine

with the research assistance of

Ilze Petersons Taylor

Introduction

A common view of Canada's native peoples is that they constitute a social class or subclass within Canadian society. Since they are the most impoverished group in Canada, the class position assigned to them is the lowest, lumped in with unskilled, immigrant workers recently arrived in Canada. A major difficulty with this view is that it obscures the extraordinary relationship that native people bear to the federal government. This relationship was established through treaties signed by them and successive governments over the years, was later spelled out in legislation (the Indian Act), and though vaguely worded, was included as one of the articles in Canada's Constitution (British North America Act). More recently, recognition of their special-status position was reaffirmed in the contractual agreement dealing with the disposition of aboriginal land in the James Bay area.

Native societies, rather than forming an integral part of Canadian society, exist as a cluster of satellites. Control over their direction is determined through the instrumentalities of government. Indeed, since Confederation in 1867, the link between native societies and the rest of Canada has been through the federal government. The definition of who they are is influenced by government legislation as is their continued existence as distinct societies with special rights. One of the consequences of this relationship has been that native people have become isolated from the main stream of Canadian social and economic life. Another has been almost total dependence on government to satisfy their essential needs.

Native people have the lowest incomes, the poorest health, and the highest rates of unemployment of any single group in the country. As satellite societies, the major item for negotiation is the entry point—at what level and under what guarantees will that special status not be jeopardized should they enter Canadian society. Officialdom and other bodies have assumed that they should enter in a manner similar to that of immigrants who came to Canada and worked their way up the ''class ladder.'' Native spokesmen, on the other hand, do not accept this as a suitable entry point, and argue for special assistance or more equitable sharing of the profits derived from their lands; so that they, too, might enjoy the benefits associated with middle-class life. Native people have categorically rejected the view that they are an ''ethnic group'' to be treated uniformly along with those groups in Canada whose ancestors came from a foreign country.

Among other things, special status carries with it the rights to certain tracts of lands that have been set aside in perpetuity for those recognized as being an ''Indian'' according to the Indian Act. The Métis and non-status Indians who constitute three-quarters of the native population are not recognized at the present time as having special status, and with the exception of five or so small ''colonies,'' control no lands equivalent to those controlled by status Indians. Many live in sparsely populated, remote areas, and have always regarded the land on which they live and that they have used for generations as belonging to them, but this has been disputed by provincial governments who claim that the Indians have no legal title and are merely ''squatters'' on Crown-owned lands. Concern over the possibility of displacement has increased with the expansion of the search for new energy sources. The Métis and non-status Indians are pressuring the government to accord them special status in order to clarify land entitlements in the provinces (Daniels 1979*a*, *b*).

The possibility of land alienation and of being economically displaced by large-scale developments has become a major concern for all native groups, including the Inuit. Native leaders are raising questions about control over the pace of development on lands that they have traditionally used, and are demanding a more equitable distribution of the profits accruing from such development. They argue that in past periods of internal economic expansion, native people were excluded from the new economy that emerged, suffered underdevelopment of their own economy, and were driven deeper into poverty. Recent proclamations by some native groups to be recognized as ''nations'' with clearly delineated territories and sufficient political powers to control development reflect this concern.

Government response has been to offer reassurance that the policy of special status for status Indians and Inuit will not be abandoned, and negotiations have been initiated to settle long-standing specific land claims. However, on the question of according special status to Métis and non-status Indians, it has remained mute, leaving their affairs to be administered by provincial governments as those of ordinary citizens.

Fragmented, ambiguous, and uncertain native policy is being pushed into new directions by the conflict generated over these issues. This is taking place under pressure for large-scale development. Both provincial and federal governments are anxious to see development proceed, not only to replenish diminished energy stocks but to create new jobs in order to relieve high unemployment rates. The direction this policy seems to be taking, and the implications for native people and societal cohesion, are the focus of this paper.

In reviewing the published literature, government reports, and statements by native spokesmen dealing with the current situation, a fundamental difference of opinion was found to exist between authors over questions related to the cause of native poverty and remedies required to improve their lot. The difference was found to boil down to the ideological position held by each author over which should take precedence—the right of all individuals within the State, regardless of race, and so on, to equality of access to opportunities, or the right of historical national minorities within the state to self-determination. Those who give precedence to equality of opportunity use a "liberal" social-class model for explanation, while those who give precedence to nationalist aspirations employ a variant of the internal colonial or centre-periphery model, such as the one developed by Johan Galtung (1971). Since each leads to different definitions and recommends different solutions to native problems, a brief summary of the more salient arguments advanced by each is in order.

For those who employ a social-class model, native people are viewed as constituting a disadvantaged subclass at the lowest level of the class system. The native problem is perceived essentially as one of removing socio-psychological and cultural impediments to advancement within the system. These impediments are believed to have been caused by past paternalistic practices, segregation of native communities, racial discrimination, and mental disorders associated with *laissez-faire* acculturation. Special status and the reservation system are regarded as being part of the problem since they are thought to perpetuate the isolation of natives from other Canadians and lead to increased dependence on government. Recommended ameliora-tive measures place emphasis on quasi-psychotherapeutic techniques, such as group dynamics and community development, as well as on media campaigns aimed at improving the self-image of the native and reducing incidences of anti-native racial discrimination. Though emphasis is also placed on encouraging natives to become involved in small, self-help economic development projects, increased government expenditures through welfare assistance, and better educational and employment measures are recom-mended to alleviate the immediate effects of poverty. In other words, the alleviation of poverty is to be accomplished through catch-up programmes aimed at encouraging greater participation in Canadian society. This participation is believed to be inevitable and a more realistic alternative to the possibility of native collectivities being recognized as politically autonomous entities within Confederation.

By contrast, those who employ an internal colonial, or centre-periphery, model view the native problem in terms of economics and power, that is, in terms of domination and exploitation of one socio-cultural system by another. Native poverty is seen to be the result of domination by central authorities, who have permitted the exploitation of native lands and labour for the benefit of the dominant society. In the process, native economies have not developed, and the basis of cultural survival has been imperilled. Special status and the rights to land are believed to be necessary if native societies are to survive in the manner guaranteed by land-cession treaties made over the years and by government promises since Confederation. The alleviation of poverty is to be achieved through a new political and economic formula that would transfer greater authority to native collectivities for the control over the lands claimed by them, with the profits derived from any development on those lands retained locally for the long-term benefit of native communities. The current practice of creating dual economies in development areas—one based on pre-capitalist modes of production for natives, the other on financial capitalism for whites—is questioned, as is the view that natives benefit from centrally controlled developments through an increase in job opportunities at the community level. Political and economic equality, as well as cultural coexistence, is seen as essential if the State is to meet its obligations as the guarantor of native rights.

The debate—if it can be called that—engendered by these two approaches is not a new one.[1] In one form or another, it has emerged in every modern polynational state. In Canada, it is taking place against the background of Parti Québécois demands for a new form of political and economic association, and the rejection by the federal government of these demands or any form of special status for cultural or linguistic groups. Public pronouncements to this effect have raised questions among native spokesmen as to the actual status of native groups in Confederation, and anxiety over whether continued recognition of their rights will be forthcoming. It is the contention of this analysis that ambivalence on the part of federal and provincial governments over which of the two approaches should, or does, take precedence is increasingly becoming the source of conflict between them and native groups. It is also contended that rather than attempting to resolve the question decisively one way or the other, governments have chosen to manage and contain the conflicts generated. To this end, various strategies for incorporating and controlling native collectivities have emerged, as have techniques for conflict management emphasizing bargaining and negotiations rather than hostile confrontations. The discussion that follows attempts to examine the more salient characteristics of these strategies and techniques, in the hope that some understanding of the way in which Canada goes about the business of maintaining cohesion in a culturally diverse polity might be forthcoming. Clearly, because of the difficulty of interpreting government actions, and the motives behind these, the attempts made are suggestive rather than rigidly conclusive.

---

[1] In Lenin's time, it was called the nationalities' question, and took the form of whether the universal class struggle advocated by Marx should take precedence over the right of historical national minorities within the Tzarist state to self-determination. Though the debate split the socialist party at the time, it resulted in a declaration of the rights of nationalities and the transformation of Russia, after the events of 1917, into several territorially based, autonomous republics. However, according to a number of writers, the issue is still unresolved, and the actual status of autonomous groups is a matter of considerable friction within the U.S.S.R. (Pipes 1975).

As indicated earlier, this paper was prepared to form part of a series sponsored by UNESCO on the theme of diversity and unity in several modern states. Consequently, some of the sections contain detailed background information already familiar to some Canadian readers, but which may be new to those not as knowledgeable about Canada. Because of this, some sections are descriptive expositions and others are more analytical. In the latter, theories of conflict management and dependence control are utilized.

Discussion is divided into seven main sections. The first provides the historical background. A brief overview of native cultures in pre-contact times is presented in which emphasis is placed on illustrating the similarities and differences in cultural forms, as well as the variety of languages spoken.

The second is a brief summary of who is, and is not, considered to be an ''Indian'' for purposes of the Indian Act, to illustrate the different categories of people that have emerged inadvertently as a result of legislation. Some of the implications, both legal and in terms of personal identity, are touched on, but have not been taken up at length.

The third is a discussion of the principal methods used to incorporate and control native societies from the time of first contact to the recent past. The size and distribution of the native population is outlined in the fourth section, along with some socio-economic indicators of levels of health, education, unemployment rates, and so on. The fifth examines the rise of modern native organizations in terms of organizational form, leadership effectiveness, and the conflicts now taking place between native groups, governments, and other sectors of Canadian society.

The sixth examines contemporary conflicts in which native peoples have been involved: those over economic development projects, native land claims, language, urban migration, and native status. This section employs theories of conflict management and dependency control. An assessment is made of whether government strategy and policy have either integration or assimilation as objectives.

Lastly, a summary conclusion is offered in which policy directions, and some of the implications of these, are discussed in terms of the diversity-unity theme.

At this point, a few words must be said to explain the use of certain terms and concepts. These are offered not as exhaustive definitions, but as a guide to the reader.

The term *conflict* is used to refer to the competition that arises when two or more actors or parties are in simultaneous pursuit of scarce resources. The parties to the conflict may make use of violent, aggressive acts or more passive means, such as bargaining and negotiations, for resolution. In the latter case, emphasis is placed on compromise and some form of sharing of the resources under dispute, rather than on the complete elimination of one or both parties (Schelling 1960). The conflict is not resolved in a decisive sense, but managed and kept from escalating into violent confrontations that could be mutually destructive to both parties. It is this form of conflict that characterizes the relations between natives and governments today.[2]

The words *assimilation* and *integration* are often used interchangeably in everyday speech. Here, they are used to refer to different outcomes resulting from the culture contact process between two socio-cultural systems, in which one system is dominant and the other subordinate. Assimilation is said to be the outcome when individuals of the subordinate system are incorporated into the dominant one, such that they look to it for the satisfaction of needs, goals, and aspirations. They may either become members of the dominant social class structure, or depending on factors such as conditions of entry, rules of inclusion, attitudes held toward them by dominant group members, and so forth, may form a subclass within the class structure. Total assimilation of such individuals is said to occur when identification with the dominant system is complete, that is, when the individuals no longer make reference to the subordinate system as a viable life-style alternative. Integration, on the other hand, is used to refer to the outcome when the members of both systems participate in one or more common socio-cultural dimension, but not in others. For example, there may be participation of members from both groups in common economic and political arrangements, but not in social or cultural ones. This condition could be described as one in which the two systems have achieved economic and political integration, while permitting cultural and social coexistence, that is, recognizing the continued existence of both forms of cultural and social institutions. Complete coexistence is the outcome when each system continues to exist independently of the other and without commonality of participatory institutional arrangements. In reality, however, a combination of the three outcomes may take place simultaneously.[3]

Because of the functional interrelation of elements in a socio-cultural system, it is problematic whether integration is a permanent condition or a transitional stage in the assimilation process. The view taken in this discussion is that it is a transitional stage, and as applied to native societies, forms part of the strategy by which the dominant society controls and incorporates collectivities into the polity.

A bibliography is provided, but as will be noted, it contains many references to primary documents in the form of government reports, memoranda, and so on. Though there is growing literature dealing with native affairs, there are still many gaps to be filled dealing with specific

---

[2] For a more complete discussion of these two forms of conflict, the reader is referred to the game theoretical analysis of conflict made by Thomas Schelling (1960) and Anatol Rapoport (Von Clausewitz 1968), especially the distinction they make between zero-sum and non-zero-sum games.

[3] A useful way of thinking about the concepts of coexistence, integration, and assimilation is in terms of elementary set theory. By analogy, coexistence corresponds to the condition of separate sets; integration, to the condition of overlapping sets; and assimilation, depending on the degree, to the conditions of the subset and "fuzzy" subset.

aspects of native life. Statistical data were found to be difficult to obtain, especially for the Métis. Consequently, greater reliance was placed on data dealing with status Indians, since they are enumerated in the census as a category, while the Métis are not. Time, space, and availability of data made it impossible to deal with each group separately, as initially intended; thus some of the generalizations made, as a result of lumping groups together, may have to be modified by the findings of future, detailed studies.

Chapter 2.2

Native Peoples in Aboriginal Canada

As European explorers and fur traders began to move into what is now Canada in the sixteenth century, they encountered a number of native cultures that because of their technological simplicity were thought to be uncivilized and backward. There was no system of writing, no metallurgy beyond the pounding of copper in one or two regions, no practical use of the wheel, and no domestication of animals except the dog.

Only recently has the ingenious nature of native cultures been recognized, particularly their value as adaptive strategies to deal with regional or local environmental conditions. Native languages were thought to be rudimentary, primitive, not really worth learning; religions, pagan and pantheistic; and social and political structures, almost non-existent, based on custom rather than a coded system of laws.

Misnamed "Indians" by Columbus and commonly referred to as "savages" by both French and English explorers, Europeans generally believed that all Indians were alike—without refinement of manners and occupying a stage of barbarism not unlike the one that Europeans believed themselves to have passed through centuries before. In fact, there were a variety of native cultures with quite sophisticated languages capable of expressing profound philosophical and religious ideas. Rather than being simple, some aspects of social organization were extremely complex, as Lewis Henry Morgan (Morgan 1966) found in his studies of Iroquois kinship systems.

A full and detailed account of just how remarkable and varied these cultures were is beyond the scope of this paper. All that can be done here is to outline their more salient features, and illustrate some of the similarities and differences in social life that existed in aboriginal Canada.

LINGUISTIC VARIATIONS

The actual number of people in Canada in pre-Columbian times is not known. Estimates range from two to three hundred thousand persons spread from east to west across the continent and as far north as the arctic archipelago. Diamond Jenness (1963) has identified twelve distinct linguistic families, each with fifty-four or more dialects often so different from one another that persons of the same linguistic stock, but who were geographically distant, could barely understand one another. Figure 2.2.1 gives the name of each family and its geographical location.

This linguistic diversity apparently presented no barrier to inter-nation contact in pre-contact times. Trade, intermarriage, and sometimes war brought groups into frequent interaction requiring a degree of multilingualism. On the northwest coast in the post-contact period, a synthetic version of the Chinook language became the *lingua franca* for many of the coastal nations (Jenness 1963, p. 19).

CULTURAL VARIATIONS

The linguistic divisions correspond only imperfectly to the various types of native cultures that existed. There were examples of peoples who spoke dialects of the same linguistic family, yet were geographically and culturally remote from each other. On the other hand, the culturally similar nations of the northwest coast spoke radically different languages. Variations in cultural forms appear to have been more related to Canada's ecological regions than to anything else.

Various methods of classifying aboriginal cultures have been devised by anthropologists. Jenness's (1963) system, although a rudimentary version of the modern culture-ecology approach, still has considerable utility and is the one adopted for the limited purposes of this discussion. He identified six cultural regions that roughly correspond to geographic areas (see fig. 2.2.2). In modified form, these are:

1. The Eastern Woodlands
2. The Plains
3. The Pacific Coast
4. The Cordillera
5. The Mackenzie and Yukon river basins
6. The arctic barren grounds

Indians of the Eastern Woodlands. The Eastern Woodlands encompasses two distinct regions—the Laurentian Shield of northern Ontario and Quebec, and the geographically related Maritime provinces, and the fertile lowland of the Great Lakes, including the eastern extension into the St. Lawrence River Valley. The Laurentian Shield region was occupied by migratory hunting and gathering peoples of the Eastern Woodlands, while the lowland region was occupied by the agricultural Iroquoian-speaking peoples.

The migratory nations included the Beothuk, of Newfoundland (now extinct); the Micmac, of Nova Scotia, New Brunswick, Prince Edward Island, and the Gaspé region of Quebec; the Malecite, of the St. John River region of New Brunswick; the Montagnais-Naskapi of Labrador and northern Quebec; the Cree, of the marshy lowlands of James Bay; the Algonkians, of the Ottawa Valley; and the Ojibwa, of Lake Superior and Lake Huron. All

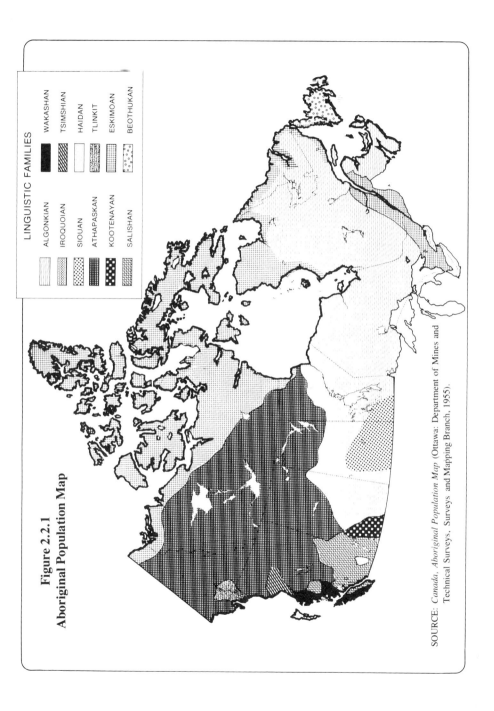

Figure 2.2.1
Aboriginal Population Map

LINGUISTIC FAMILIES

ALGONKIAN
IROQUOIAN
SIOUAN
ATHAPASKAN
KOOTENAYAN
SALISHAN

WAKASHAN
TSIMSHIAN
HAIDAN
TLINKIT
ESKIMOAN
BEOTHUKAN

SOURCE: *Canada, Aboriginal Population Map* (Ottawa: Department of Mines and Technical Surveys, Surveys and Mapping Branch, 1955).

Figure 2.2.2
Aboriginal Cultural Regions

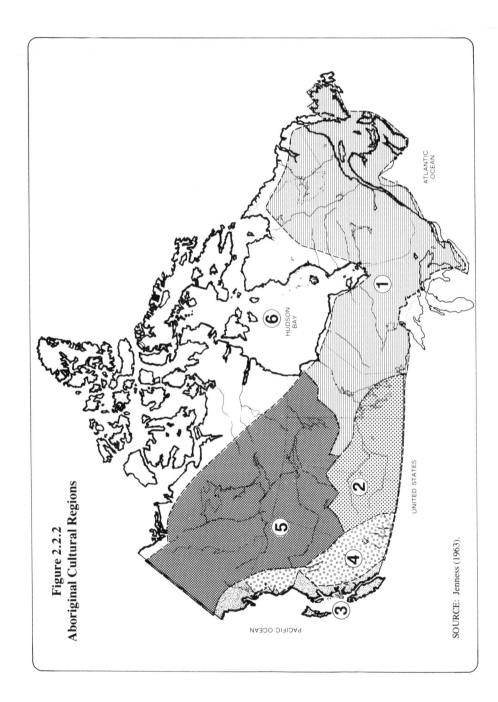

SOURCE: Jenness (1963).

these groups spoke dialects of the Algonkian language, and although regional variations existed, they shared a distinctive overall pattern of life. Migrations within delineated hunting territories occurring seasonally, the groups relied on a combination of hunting, fishing, and gathering for subsistence. Hunting and gathering were done by individual families, and collections of families or bands of up to one hundred persons, depending on the season or the wildlife to be exploited. The division of labour was on the basis of sex and age, in which each family produced its own food, clothing, shelter, and tools. When game was scarce, a band would disperse into smaller hunting units of two or three nuclear families often related by ties of kin.

Social organization was flexible and adaptive to environmental conditions. Formal political structures did not exist. Leadership, when it was forthcoming, was informal, based on the spiritual or hunting abilities of an individual, rather than social class or other systems of ranking. Individuals were under no compulsion to follow a leader, or for that matter, to share food and other amenities with others beyond the kin group. Since constant mobility made the accumulation of large quantities of material goods rather difficult, these societies tended to stress egalitarian values in which prestige accrued to an individual skilled in the daily task of making a living. Individuals who exhibited wisdom, generosity, or supernatural powers were also highly regarded, and frequently could attract a following over which they were able to assert a measure of authority. They remained, however, first among equals.

The Iroquoian-speaking agriculturalists of the fertile lowland area, by contrast, practised a considerably different life-style from that of the migratory hunters surrounding them. They were basically an agricultural people who supplemented a diet of corn, beans, and squash with game animals and fish. Unlike the migratory hunting societies, they lived in semi-permanent villages, often with palisaded walls.

A village consisted of a cluster of relatively large buildings called *longhouses*, each accommodating from a few to a dozen or so families. As with migratory hunting groups, no elaborate system of rank or class existed, and the division of labour was on the basis of sex and age. To the women fell the full responsibility for planting, weeding, and harvesting crops; storing food; gathering wood for fuel; making pots and baskets, and running the household. Men were involved in the activities associated with war, hunting, and trading; and were responsible for the building of houses, canoes, tools, and weapons.

The political organization of the Iroquoians was also quite different from that of the migratory hunting bands. Distinct and cohesive nations were united under an overriding political structure that welded them into confederacies. The Iroquois Confederacy, or League of Five (later Six) Nations, consisted of the Mohawk, Seneca, Cayuga, Oneida, Onandaga, and following the American Revolutionary War, the Tuscarora. (Most of these

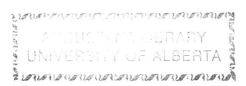

tribes were located in what is now Upper New York State, between the Hudson River and the southern shore of Lake Ontario; but as they were allies of the British in the wars with the French and later the Americans, they came to southern Ontario and Quebec following the defeat of the British by the Americans in order to remain under British protection.)

Although Lewis Henry Morgan (1966) has described the functioning of the Iroquois Confederacy in some detail, much less is known about the political structure of the other confederacies. The Council of the Iroquois Confederacy was composed of fifty hereditary chiefs known as *sachems*. All were of equal rank, but the larger tribes were entitled to send more representatives to council than the smaller tribes. The council was the legislative and governing body of the league, all matters of concern to the league as a whole—principally interaction with tribes outside of the league—being within its jurisdiction. The sachems of the council, in turn, formed the councils of their respective tribes and controlled its domestic affairs. Although their influence was considerable, and their decisions respected, the sachems possessed no coercive power and could not compel obedience.

Indians of the Plains. The aboriginal peoples of the prairie grasslands lived in the southern region of the present-day Prairie provinces and spoke dialects of either the Algonkian or Siouan linguistic families. They were organized into scattered, migratory bands that aggregated during the spring and summer months for communal buffalo hunts. The large herds of buffalo on the prairies ensured a steady source of food, and hides for clothing and shelter. Though considerable co-ordination of action was required for large-scale communal hunts, formal political structures with emphasis on managerial and leadership roles were not prevalent. Like the Woodlands peoples, leaders were supported or followed because of the personal influence they exercised or because of their ability as hunters and warriors. In other respects, too, their social organization was similar to that of neighbouring Woodlands peoples, especially in the organization of family life and the production by each family of all of the requirements for daily life. Here also the division of labour was based on age and sex: the men hunted, and made weapons and tools, while the women managed the household, gathered edible plants, and made the family clothing (Cox 1975, pp. 179−80).

The main languages spoken were offshoots of Algonkian and Siouan families. The Algonkian-speaking nations of the Blackfoot Confederacy, the Blood and the Piegan, occupied huge territories up to the middle of the eighteenth century extending from the Rocky Mountains into Saskatchewan, and as far south as the upper Missouri River (Jenness 1963).

After the eighteenth century, Woodlands Indian groups moved on to the plains, and in the process displaced the original inhabitants by driving them southward. The Cree and Ojibwa-Saulteaux from the Hudson Bay region, both Algonkian-speaking peoples, were the principal groups to invade the plains. Since they were the first in central Canada to receive goods from the European traders located on the shores of Hudson Bay, these groups were armed with steel axes, knives, and firearms, making it possible to drive back other groups, such as the Blackfoot, less well armed with traditional stone implements.

The Siouan-speaking Assiniboine Indians also arrived on the Canadian plains in the post-contact period. Originally, they inhabited a region farther to the south and moved northward as a result of pressure from the westward movement of white settlers in the United States.

The exact date of the introduction of the horse onto the plains is unknown, but it is generally believed to have been introduced by the Spanish far to the south and traded northward from nation to nation, reaching the Canadian prairies in the middle of the eighteenth century. It revolutionized the life of the Plains people and increased their mobility as well as hunting range. The increased mobility and exploitative efficiency brought the various nations into fierce competition with each other for hunting territory. Horses became a new source of wealth, raiding and horse-stealing forming the basis of the prestige system.

Indians of the Pacific Coast. The cultures developed by the Indians living along the Pacific coastal region were unique in aboriginal Canada. An elaborate system of social stratification existed based on inherited rank. Assured of an abundant supply of food in the form of fish, whales, and other sea mammals, people lived in relatively permanent villages, in ingeniously constructed large wooden dwellings.

The Tlingkit of southeastern Alaska; the Haida of the Queen Charlotte Islands; the Tsimshian of the Nass and Skeena Rivers; the Wakashan-speakers of Vancouver Island; the Nootka and the Kwakiutl; the Salish-speaking Bella Coola and Coast Salish, all possessed a social structure that distinguished between aristocracy, commoners, and slaves.

The basic economic unit was the autonomous local group, consisting either of a lineage or an extended family group based on bilateral descent. Such local groups owned various resource areas, and absolute ownership rights to the territory were vested in an hereditary chief. The local group consisted of a resident noble family, a chief and his slaves, and a fluctuating number of commoners. Such a group shared one large dwelling, and a number of such dwellings might group together at a winter village site to form a political and ceremonial unit. Slaves were the only group that formed a distinctive class. The distinction between ''nobles'' and ''commoners'' was less clear cut since status was based on relative degrees of kin relationship to the current chief.

As the holder of his family's rights, a chief had access to a diverse set of resources. Marriage provided an important means of gaining access to rights held by other groups. A chief who wished to ratify his claim to a particular name and its attendant right to exploit a resource did so at a gift-giving ceremonial known as the "potlatch." The quantity and quality of goods distributed at such a ceremonial enhanced the prestige of a chief and guaranteed him the support of the commoners for his claim. Such feasts also acted as a mechanism to ensure the distribution of resources throughout the community.

Indians of the Cordillera. Peoples of the Cordillera region of the interior of British Columbia were divided into three distinct groups:

  i. The Lillooet and Thompson people, the Shuswap, the Lake and Okanagan, and a few Nicolet bands

  ii. The Kootenay of the southeastern corner of the province

  iii. The Dené of the northern region, which included the Tahltan, Tstelsaut, Carrier, and Chilcotin peoples

Of these groups, all but the Kootenay subsisted on some combination of salmon and game, such as elk, bear, and beaver. The Kootenay originally dwelt on the eastern side of the Rockies, but were driven west by the Blackfoot. They retained a basically Plains Indian life-style, and although driven from their territory, made frequent trips across the Rocky Mountains to hunt buffalo on the plains.

All the Interior tribes other than the Kootenay spoke an Athapaskan dialect. Many engaged in trade with the coastal peoples, and in the process seem to have acquired some of the cultural traits of these peoples, particularly their system of social stratification, slavery, and the potlatch. The Interior Salish, despite extensive trade contacts with the coast and with the exception of two groups, retained a social structure similar to that of the Athapaskan-speaking people of the Yukon and Mackenzie basins in which the local unit was the small band. Their affairs were sometimes directed by an informal council of elders.

Indians of the Mackenzie and Yukon river basins. Although few in number—like the Inuit—the Athapaskan- or Dené-speaking peoples roamed over a vast northern territory. The combined size of the territories of both groups comprised half the land mass of Canada.

Dependent on hunting and collecting from forest lands for subsistence, the Dené lived in tiny bands made up of a few families that migrated seasonally in search of wildlife within a recognized hunting territory. In social organization and elements of material culture, they closely resembled the cultures of the Eastern Woodlands. There were no paramount chiefs or headmen; division of labour was based on age and sex; and authority was derived from the personal qualities exhibited by an individual. The family was the basic unit of production, and provided or manufactured all that was required to sustain life.

The principal groups included: the Chipewyan of the Churchill River; the Yellowknife of the Great Slave and Great Bear lakes; the Dogrib, the Slave, and the Beaver, of the Mackenzie, Athabaska, and Peace rivers; and the Kutchin, Nahani, and Sekani of the Yukon and upper Peace rivers.

Inuit of the arctic barren grounds. In a number of respects, the Inuit[1] were culturally quite distinct from all of the other peoples of aboriginal Canada. Archaeologists suggest that while the ancestors of all the Indian groups came from Asia in migratory waves at least fifteen thousand years ago, the Inuit came in the last wave some thirty-five hundred years ago. These dates are not firm since recent archaelogical investigations indicate a longer time span, but how long is still a matter of conjecture. The Inuit, interestingly, are the only aboriginal group in the Americas with culturally and linguistically related people still living on the Asian side of Bering Strait, the two thousand or so Inuit-speaking people of Siberia.

Their traditional territory in Canada extended along the whole arctic coastline from Alaska to Labrador and some of the Arctic islands. This territory extended southward to about the limits of the treeline. Jenness (1963) classified them, primarily on the basis of subsistence patterns, into coastal and inland peoples, with further subdivisions based on locale. By and large, the bulk of the population was concentrated along the coastline, living in tiny, isolated settlements of a few families. These people hunted and depended primarily on sea mammals for food, clothing, fuel, and shelter, while those living inland depended on fresh water fish and the migratory caribou herds of the subarctic barren grounds west of Hudson Bay.

Although sea mammals were fairly abundant, their availability varied considerably with the seasons and sea ice conditions. The harshness of the arctic climate and the scarcity of edible plants or even wood made survival precarious. The Inuit nonetheless developed a remarkable technology based on bone, stone, drift-wood, and animal hides, which made adaptation to the environment possible. All available natural resources were utilized, even snow for the construction of winter dwellings.

In contrast to their ingenious technology, Inuit social organization was simple in the extreme. Like other hunting and gathering groups, the nuclear family was the basic unit of production. No formal political structure existed and there were no chiefs or headmen. The division of labour was based on age and sex, where the men did the hunting, manufactured tools and implements, and constructed the snow house or summer skin tent, while the women managed the household, made the family's clothing from animal skins, and gathered edible berries and fish in the vicinity of the camp. Also, like other hunting societies, the Inuit were semi-nomadic, moving back and forth across large hunting territories in search of food. Again, as in other hunting societies, egalitarian values pervaded the culture.

The picture that emerges from this all-too-abbreviated review of aboriginal Canada is one in which there is considerable similarity in material

---

[1] Formerly called Eskimo, a term rejected by the people in recent years in favour of their own word for themselves.

culture, but with variation in social organization and linguistic expression. With the possible exception of the Iroquois, the Blackfoot Confederacy, and the Indians who lived along the Pacific Coast, no formal political structures existed with clearly recognized, authoritative leaders. The majority of societies were egalitarian with a rudimentary division of labour based on age and sex. Custom and oral tradition, rather than coded laws, were the basis of social control. Status and prestige were based on achievement rather than on ascription, as almost everywhere except the Pacific Coast.

All of the various cultural groups identified with a specific hunting territory, as well as with a particular language or cultural unit. Very frequently, the word they used to refer to their own kind simply meant "man" or "the people." This sense of cultural uniqueness is being recreated by native leaders today and is expressed in the desire to be recognized as distinct "nations" within Canada.

Who Is a Native?

Though there were diverse societies speaking a variety of languages spread across Canada in aboriginal times, culture and language played almost no part in the official definition of an Indian developed by the federal government.

This definition grew out of the first Indian Act of 1876 (Smith 1975, p. 87), in which the principle of patrilineal descent was used to determine who was eligible for registration. This principle is still in force and has been interpreted to mean that only those persons of native ancestry who can trace descent through the male line to a person originally entitled to be registered are Indians for purposes and benefits of the Indian Act. For example, a registered Indian man who marries a white woman or a person of Indian ancestry *not* entitled to be registered remains an Indian, and his wife and children are entitled to be registered as such. A registered Indian woman, on the other hand, who marries a white man or a person of Indian ancestry *not* entitled to be registered loses her registration status, and her children and husband are not entitled to be registered (Cumming and Mickenberg 1972, pp. 6−7).

Intermarriage between whites and Indians over the years has produced a situation in which there are individuals who have white physical characteristics and are registered as Indians, and those who have Indian physical characteristics, speak an Indian language, or follow an Indian life-style, but are not entitled to be registered.

Four categories of native persons,[1] each with its own set of social and economic problems, have emerged from the consequences attendant upon the

---

[1] In fact, there are at least thirteen terms for native persons in official usage, but only the four principal ones are dealt with here. These are listed to give some idea of the terminological confusion that has resulted from the legal definition of Indian and to warn the reader to be cautious when reading official reports, statistical compilations, or census material dealing with native people since these often lump categories together for one purpose, but not for another, and use different definitions at different time periods:

— Native Indian   — Treaty half-breed
— Status Indian   — Enfranchised Indian
— Non-status Indian   — Métis (this term has five different regional pronunciations)
— Treaty Indian   — Half-breed
— Non-treaty Indian   — Inuit
— Registered Indian   — Eskimo
— Reservation Indian

The list excludes slang terms as well as those invented by anthropologists, such as Amerindian and the recently discovered ''urban Indian'' of the sociologists.

In the absence of systematic research, we can only speculate on what effect this terminological confusion is having on the search for identity among today's young natives.

legal definition of an Indian, and Indian-white intermarriage. The names commonly applied to them are:

— Status Indians (may also be called registered or treaty Indians)
— Non-status Indians (also frequently referred to as non-treaty Indians)
— Métis
— Inuit

STATUS INDIANS

Status Indians are those entitled to be registered under the Indian Act. The majority are members of a band, have access to land in the form of reservations, and depending on the treaty of surrender each band signed with the Crown, may also have rights to large tracts of land or resources adjacent to a reserve for specific purposes. Their educational, health, and welfare needs are the responsibility of the federal government, which provides these services free of charge in the context of the reservation. Those who leave the reservation or become enfranchised (i.e., lose their Indian status) are expected to apply to the provincial governments in the provinces in which they live for these services, like other citizens of a province. In addition, some bands, particularly those that have leased their lands for resource or other developments, have accumulated funds that are held in trust by the federal government for use by the band.

Income earned on reserves is exempt from federal taxes, and in recent years the federal government has introduced special employment, housing, and economic development projects to improve living conditions on reserves.

Status Indians are organized into 554 bands of varying sizes. The total number of reserves is 2,274, but only about 70% of the status-Indian population actually live on reserves; young adults, particularly in recent years, have been migrating to adjacent cities and towns in search of wage employment. Reserves vary in size from less than 1 acre to 349,000 acres.

MÉTIS AND NON-STATUS INDIANS

The non-status Indians are those of native ancestry who, because of the patrilineal rule, or voluntary or involuntary enfranchisement, have been denied registration status. Consequently, they are excluded from the provisions of the Indian Act and the treaties that their ancestors may have signed. They of course may refer to themselves as Indians, but they are excluded from band membership, reserves, and any special federally run status-Indian programmes in the fields of health, education, and welfare. Having no special rights to lands, they are considered to be the responsibility of provincial or local governments, similar to the non-Indian citizens in the areas in which they live. The fact that they may look like Indians, speak an Indian language, have close relatives living on reserves, and even follow so-called traditional Indian occupations of hunting, fishing, and trapping is entirely overlooked by officialdom.

The public, on the other hand, does not understand the legal distinctions between status and non-status Indians. Thus, they are subjected to the same treatment, discriminatory or otherwise, prevalent in the white community in which they happen to live.

The same situation holds true for the Métis, who are in some ways a special case of non-status Indians. They also are the descendants of interracial marriages, but have chosen to identify themselves as a distinct people—a ''new nation''—with special rights inherent in that status, at least equivalent to those accorded status Indians. This view is especially prevalent in the three Prairie provinces, but is by no means shared or accepted by all those of mixed white-Indian ancestry. The idea that they were a new nation was largely developed by Louis Riel, a Manitoba Métis of mixed French-Indian ancestry, in the late 1800s. At that time, western Canada was mainly populated by Métis of predominantly French and Scottish ancestry. The more successful of them had given up fur trapping and buffalo hunting (the occupations of the majority) to become private fur traders, merchants, and transportation contractors.

When the Métis discovered that the federal government had ignored their political, linguistic, and land rights in arranging the transfer of the West to Canadian sovereignty, they formed a provisional government and attempted to negotiate a new arrangement for Métis and western Canada. While Riel's government was responsible for bringing the province of Manitoba into Confederation in 1870, a similar attempt to get special concessions for the Métis in Saskatchewan in 1885 met with failure. An insurrection ensued in which the Métis were defeated. Riel was arrested, found guilty, and hanged for treason (Stanley 1978).

Some Métis families in Manitoba and other parts of western Canada were given land grants in roughly the same proportion of government land grants given to white settlers who came to western Canada in large numbers, especially after the construction of the railway in 1885. The vast majority of Métis land grants were alienated to speculators, and the Métis land grant system came to an end early in this century.

Displaced from the land in the fertile south and excluded from the new economy that the developments of the time brought, many Métis families moved to the more remote northern frontiers of the Prairie provinces and eked out a marginal living as trappers, traders, fishermen, or migrant labourers. Many Métis communities today still follow this mode of existence.

Unlike status Indians, Métis and non-status Indians are not included as a special category in the official census. Being a Métis or non-status Indian is a matter of personal identity choice, influenced, of course, by the reaction of the dominant white community to one's physical appearance and life-style (especially the type of occupation and educational achievement level). The psychological problems posed for Métis and non-status Indians over the choice of identity have not been sufficiently studied, but there is evidence to suggest considerable strain and identity shifting on the part of individuals during the course of his or her lifetime. Depending on physical appearance, an individual may try to identify with, and be accepted as, a white, an Indian, or Métis. Circumstances may dictate, as Barth (1969) has pointed out for ethnic groups, a shift from one identity to another, if it is advantageous to do so.

Today, with increased tolerance of native peoples by the population as a whole, individuals who formerly attempted to identify as whites have rediscovered aboriginal ancestry and in increasing numbers are coming forward proudly, proclaiming that they are Indian or Métis.

While this trend may have positive, psychological therapeutic value, it complicates the task of accurate enumeration. The size of the Métis and non-status Indian population grows not only through natural increase, the enfranchisement of status Indians, the loss of status by Indian women and their children through marriage to non-status persons, but also through personal choices made by those with native ancestry who suddenly discover or rediscover their native heritage and no longer wish to be identified as a white. This phenomena has enormous ramifications for the whole business of native land claims, payment of compensation monies, or the provision of special government assistance programmes.

INUIT

In Canada's Constitution, the British North America Act, no mention is made at all of the Inuit. It simply states that the federal government is responsible for the administration of Indians and the lands reserved for their use. Though excluded from the Indian Act, Inuit do come under the jurisdiction of the federal government. Their aboriginal status was confirmed by a Supreme Court decision in 1939 (Cumming and Mickenberg 1972, p. 7). Although they never made treaties with the government, and no special lands, funds, or monies were set aside for their use, the federal government provides for all of their health, welfare, housing, and educational needs. In recent years, the government has recognized that they have a claim to land, and negotiations are going forward to determine the size and extent of their claim.

There is almost no interaction between the Inuit and other native groups. The thirty-seven hundred or more living in northern Quebec did come together with the Cree Indians of the James Bay region to negotiate a land claims settlement, but the terms of the settlement gave them almost complete freedom of action from the decision of other groups. In the main, the Inuit appear to identify more with other Inuit groups in the circumpolar basin (Greenland and Alaska) than they do with southern Canadians (Rowley 1972).

The Inuit population, comprising about seventeen thousand people, lives in tiny isolated settlements above the tree line across the vast Arctic region stretching from Labrador in the east to Alaska in the west. Communication between settlements is difficult, but improvements in telecommunications and air travel in recent years have made possible the formation of Inuit organizations capable of dealing with issues that transcend merely local or regional interests.

Throughout the ensuing discussion, the word *native* is used to refer to all people of Indian or Inuit ancestry, regardless of legal status.

Evolution of Early Government Policy: Strategies of Incorporation and Control

Both before and after Confederation, governments employed different strategies to incorporate and control native peoples. At least three can be identified, and for purposes of this discussion, may be termed as strategies of accommodation, domination, and integration. Each refers to the mode of relating to a vital dimension of native society, for example, cultural accommodation, economic domination, and corporate political integration.

Reference to a strategy implies only an emphasis corresponding roughly to a different set of circumstances in the expansion and development of Canadian society without implying the absence of other strategies, nor in the case of accommodation, that its use took the same form at all times, if in fact it was employed at all at certain times.

Because contact between white and native societies varied over time in terms of geography, intensity, and many other factors, the applicability of each mode of incorporation is not necessarily related to precisely dated periods of history. Due to varying rates of economic development, the Dené peoples of the sparsely populated Northwest Territories, and the Algonkian peoples living in relatively isolated communities in the great Canadian forest belt (which stretches across the continent), are in many respects only now experiencing intervention by governments and entrepreneurs on a scale comparable to that experienced two hundred years ago by other native groups living in the more densely populated southern and eastern regions.

In this historical section, the pre- and post-Confederation strategies of accommodation and domination will be discussed. The integration strategy, which characterizes the contemporary period, will be discussed in a subsequent section on contemporary issues and conflicts.

PRE-CONFEDERATION POLICY: ACCOMMODATION

Accommodation as a strategy for dealing with native groups was first utilized by the French and English at the time of initial contact in what are now the Maritime provinces. The intruders, being few in number, needed the assistance of the Indians they met for survival, and later as allies in the French-English wars.

The Indians were never conquered. During the contact period, treaties and friendships were made, but they were not asked to surrender land. Some groups, such as the Iroquois, were allies of the English against the Americans and came to Canada after the defeat of the English in the American War of Independence.

The accommodation strategy was employed by the English-owned Hudson Bay Company, established in the 1600s, and later by the Montreal-based Northwest Company. By the time European whaling vessels visited the shores of arctic Canada, the strategy was extended to deal with the Inuit as well. They, too, were never conquered, but unlike other native groups, they signed no treaties and never surrendered rights to land.

The trading companies wanted fur and encouraged natives to abandon hunting, as their primary form of subsistence, for trapping and barter. This shift set in motion a whole series of events that led to far-reaching social changes as well as changes in the relative power positions of the various tribal or linguistic groups. The Cree Indians, for example, a Woodlands people originally from the vicinity of the James Bay-Hudson Bay area, were one of the first northern groups to receive steel axes and knives, guns and ammunition, flour and other concentrated foods from the Company's post at Hudson Bay. Thus armed, they marauded westward along the waterways to the Rocky Mountains, driving the conventionally armed Plains Indian tribes to the south and into pockets in southern Alberta (Jenness 1963, p. 284). It was not until the Company branched out from the shores of Hudson Bay and established trading posts in the interior that some balance in intertribal power relations was restored, though at great territorial loss to those indigenous tribes who were displaced.

Both companies followed more or less the same policies in dealing with native peoples. They were less interested in systematically changing the cultures of the groups encountered than they were in maximizing profits from trade; the former interest was left to missionaries and later to government officials, who followed in the wake of the companies.

The western Métis were born during this period. White traders were encouraged to cohabit with native women. Indeed, the Hudson Bay Company even paid pensions to these women when they were left behind (and they nearly always were) by their male partners on retirement to Scotland or England after a number of years of service. The role of the two companies in the population mix that resulted is still evident today. The Northwest Company employed mainly Canadians from Quebec, while the Hudson Bay Company imported men from the Scottish Isles. Thus, in the areas dominated by each company, the Métis were either English-speaking with Scottish surnames, and Protestant in religion, or French-speaking with French surnames, and Roman Catholic in religion.

Native people were excluded from the senior managerial positions in the companies. They were relegated to the role of trappers or to working for the companies in such fields as transportation, construction, and maintenance of trading posts. The Métis more frequently than other workers filled these jobs and acted as middle men between the whites and native groups whose language they spoke.

Having established themselves as free traders, transportation and building contractors, lumber and flour mill owners, and in some cases, dry goods and other small manufacturing entrepreneurs, by the 1850s, when free trading was permitted, a few Métis families emerged as a bourgeois class. This class, and its role in the economy of the West, was displaced in 1867 by the new economic order emanating from eastern Canadian financial centres and London, England, in co-operation with the first federal government of Canada. After the defeat by federal forces of the Métis insurrection of 1885, the massive settling of the West by European immigrants, and the decline of the fur trade, the Métis were displaced territorially and excluded by and large from the new order.

The context in which accommodation was used as a strategy in dealing with native people may be summarized at this point. Native peoples were incorporated into a commercial system as primary producers on a family basis, not unlike the cottage industries of old Scotland. They became increasingly dependent on trade goods and the foreign-owned companies for tools, clothing, food, and so on. Land-use patterns were changed along with life-goal aspirations and expectations. Families were induced to seek work in the new ''growth centres'' or trading-post settlements. Cultural coexistence was tolerated, but only insofar as it did not interfere with commercial interests. Although race mixing was tolerated, those with native ancestry were excluded from white society, its class system, and high status occupations, including positions of political power. Overt conflict, at least initially, was managed without armed, organized policemen or soldiers, through a system of interpersonal relationships between white traders and natives, emphasizing particularist rather than universalistic selection criteria. Mechanisms of social control included the use of positive and negative sanctions, through the credit and debt system. Selected native families or leaders were favoured over others and given higher amounts of credit to purchase goods at the trading post in times of need. This was particularly the case for the relatives of a native woman cohabiting with a white trader. The manipulation of economic rewards was also used to co-opt the support of dominant personalities with a potential for troublesome behaviour.

As indicated above, the strategy of accommodation, as pursued by the companies in the northwest, the whalers in the Arctic (and the military on the eastern seaboard earlier), was indifferent to questions related to the survival of native cultures and languages. Maximization of profits from trade took precedence over all else, including clarification of native land rights. The traders and whalers wanted productive trappers and hunters, not North American versions of themselves.

It is notably its indifference to the survival of native culture and language that characterizes the strategy of accommodation, but insofar as its effects were the subordination of native society, it may be indistinguishable from other strategies also aimed at control and incorporation. Accommodation was an attribute of prudence at a stage of white reliance on native co-operation and native labour for gaining a material and economic foothold in the new world. In the process, however, exploitative forces were released that diminished native social, economic, political, and cultural strength, allowing the relegation of native society to an inferior status and the use by white society of what may be regarded as the more deliberate and comprehensive strategy of domination.

POST-CONFEDERATION POLICY: DOMINATION

The development of domination as a strategy coincided with western expansion and settlement, which followed Canada's change in status from a British colony to an independent state in 1867. The new federal government, after consolidating territorial boundaries through negotiations with the Americans, made treaties with the principal Indian bands living in central and prairie western Canada. In these treaties, the bands surrendered large tracts of land in exchange for reserve lands, usually one square mile per family of five, for their exclusive use. In some cases, they were also given the use of unoccupied lands adjacent to the reserve for hunting, fishing, and trapping, as well as monetary compensation in the form of a payment of five dollars per year to each member of the band in perpetuity, a suit of clothing every three years for the chief or headman, and promises of social assistance by way of literacy instructions, rudimentary medical supplies, materials for house building, simple hand tools, and the like.

The reserve lands, and monies derived from them, were placed in a Crown trust. Lands could not be sold, and the trust monies that a particular band had accumulated could not be spent without the consent of the minister of the federal department responsible for administering the Indian Act. These and similar protective provisions have been in all Indian acts since 1874. Possibly the federal government was concerned that native peoples would be alienated from their land holdings by unscrupulous white settlers, who after completion of the railway across the Prairies to the Pacific Coast in the 1800s, began to populate central and western Canada in large numbers. It has also been suggested that the patrilineal principal was introduced into the act, not only to limit the size of the native population, thereby reducing claims to land and special treatment, but to stop enterprising white men from marrying Indian women and eventually taking control of Indian lands. More research is required to validate these suggestions.

A casual reading of successive Indian acts soon reveals that all are basically concerned with land, with spelling out who is entitled to its use, how it may be used, and how it and its products may be disposed of. The net effect of the various provisions of the Indian Act, as implemented over the years, has been the control by government over every aspect of native life. The bureaucracy that emerged to administer the act developed a paternalistic approach in which the status of the reserve Indian became that of ward of the Crown. In memoranda, letters, and other writings of government officials of the 1920s, 1930s, and 1940s are to be found such phrases as "the reserve is a cradle whereby Indians are to be rocked to full citizenship," and "Christianization and education are to go hand in hand." The ensuing relationship of unilateral dependency is well illustrated by some of the more protective sections of the 1951 Indian Act. Questions of the paternity of illegitimate children born to status-Indian women are to be determined by officialdom to safeguard the patrilineal principle; status Indians are declared not to be responsible for debts incurred off the reserve; the reserve land is to be held collectively and cannot be sold without ministerial consent; the consumption of alcoholic beverages is prohibited; produce from the land, such as grain, cannot be sold without a permit from the local government official responsible for administering band affairs; voting in federal elections is prohibited unless individuals become enfranchised; and a number of other exemptions related to taxation and compulsory military service. It was not until the late 1950s and 1960s that some of the prohibitions—voting and consumption of alcohol—were removed from the act. The others were revised to permit more individual freedom or control over band affairs.

Generally, freedom of movement was unrestricted. At times, individuals were encouraged to leave the reserve to seek wage employment in towns or cities. Once off the reserve, however, the question arose of whether the federal or provincial government was responsible for an individual's health, welfare, and educational needs. Today this has become a thorny issue in federal-provincial relations.

The unit of bureaucratic control became the reserve and band councils. Many bands did not have chiefs or headmen, nor a system of councils. The authorities overcame this by introducing a rudimentary form of democratic elections. Often those who signed treaties on behalf of a band were elected or appointed to do so by the treaty negotiation party. Local chiefs and councils were given very limited jurisdiction and in the main became advisory bodies to the government official responsible for administering their affairs.

Band councils interacted with officialdom independently and in isolation from one another. Furthermore, funds held in trust for a particular band could not be used by another, a similar situation existing with respect to land. Large-scale developments of oil or gas resources on some reserve lands were, and still are, undertaken by foreign corporations under terms established by the government. Annual royalty payments based on production were made to the band, part of which were paid to members in cash and the remainder to the band's trust fund. Even today, reserves with oil- and gas-bearing lands in Alberta may yield families an annual cash payment of several thousand dollars. The majority of bands, however, are not so well off. Until recently, band funds could not be used for land-claims litigation. This partially explains why the number of cases of litigation over land and resources has increased so dramatically in the 1970s. The formation of effective provincial and national organizations that attempt to cut across tribal as well as band ties has occurred only in the last decade.

Social interaction with white society was minimal. Indians were being displaced from their traditional lands and at the same time excluded from the new economy. Separate federal health facilities, welfare services, and schools placed status Indians outside normal or regular provincial arrangements.

Relegated in most parts of the country to labour-intensive, seasonal occupations, such as hunting and trapping, with low monetary returns, dependency on the federal government for assistance and administrative services increased to the point where the federal budget is now close to one billion dollars, exclusive of categorical assistance programmes applicable to all Canadians, such as unemployment insurance, family allowance, and Canada's pension plan.

The relations between officials and native groups during this phase of domination may be characterized as impersonal and legalistic. A bureaucratic hierarchical structure was created in which those at the top were responsible for all important decision making. The mode of incorporation and control was through bureaucratic extension, whereby band organizations were absorbed, in effect, into the administrative bureaucratic structure itself. Through preferential treatment, the administration permitted a small, select group of Indians to flourish and become affluent (Dosman 1972, p. 56). These persons usually became native spokesmen and were listened to because of their moderate, supportive views and white-man-like behavioural characteristics. Such individuals were unkindly called "professional Indians" by the more cynical. Nevertheless, little or no real opportunity existed for the majority of native peoples to work in the bureaucracy itself or to participate in the decision-making process through extra bureaucratic means. In the main, all communication in the hierarchical system was governed by the "chain-of-command" principle, offering native peoples few opportunities to make their grievances known to senior officials or the government in distant headquarters at Ottawa.

The public and government image of Indians, Métis, and Inuit seemed to classify them as adjuncts of wildlife resources to be managed and gradually improved in quality. Government reports abound with references to natives as "human resources"—a mobile labour force that may be shifted here or there to meet a development need. Until recently, officials frequently rationalized the policy of gradual assimilation using a variant of the cultural evolutionary theory of change of Lewis Henry Morgan (1907). It was naively assumed that hunting societies must pass through the stages of pastoralism and agriculture before entering industrial society. The establishment by government of a reindeer station in the Mackenzie delta in 1936 to shift the Inuit from hunting to reindeer herding is an example of the application of this approach. This attempt was not successful. With the movement of Inuit and other natives into wage-labour occupations, this theory was gradually, but not entirely, abandoned. Native workers showed how quickly they could shift from hunting to operating complicated construction machinery when it was to their advantage.

The domination strategy, though having the effect of isolating natives from the white society, was nevertheless aimed at gradual assimilation into either the English or French languages and cultural modes. In the federally financed, but missionary-run, reserve and residential schools, the speaking of native languages by native children was prohibited. The curriculum emphasized the white point of view, making little or no mention of native history or accomplishments. Even in Quebec, in many schools sponsored by the federal government for native children, the language of instruction was English.

Domination and paternalism produced a peculiarly ambivalent situation whereby native people, relegated to a pre-capitalist mode of production, were isolated from the mainstream of Canadian life; yet at the same time, they were expected to become assimilated into the dominant white culture.

Presented elsewhere, the synopsis dealing with native peoples' present-day quality of life illustrates the extent of underdevelopment that inevitably follows a domination strategy. The dominance/dependency relationship created by the imposition of a separate legal and administrative status upon native peoples resulted in unequal access to the rewards of Canadian society—a situation that Galtung refers to as "structural violence" (1969).

Aside from this form of violence imbedded in the socio-political structure, Canada's native-white relations historically have been free (with the exception of the Riel insurrection of 1885) from violent conflicts, such as wars and massacres experienced by natives in the United States and Latin America.

Population Characteristics and Socio-Economic Conditions

There is no lack of general observations on the impoverishment of native communities. Contact with native society readily attests to the state of poverty and deprivation characterizing the native collectivity. The statistics available confirm the observations that native people are less adequately housed, poorer in health and education, and more frequently jobless, drunk, and imprisoned for infractions of the law than any other group in the general population. This section will attempt to provide a statistically based synopsis of the extent to which marginality is experienced in terms of poorer conditions of life relative to those prevailing among other Canadians.

While there is little doubt that current statistical interpretation concerning native life is generally correct, it must be acknowledged that the state of statistics collection pertaining to native people is far from desirable. Federal departments, for example, use varying definitions of the terms *native* and *Indian*. The Department of Indian Affairs and Northern Development reports only on "registered" Indians, thus excluding some 798,000 Métis and non-status Indians. On the other hand, census figures compiled by Statistics Canada in recent years apply to anyone claiming a native language as "mother tongue," even though not legally registered. Also, data collected by provincial and territorial governments are not always indicated by ethnic categories; in the case of the territories, however, the data would apply largely to native society, which forms the highest percentage of the population, although any attempt to interpret data from the Northwest Territories relating primarily to the Inuit, as distinguished from other native groups, would be frustrated.

Native organizations are attempting, with government funding, to remedy deficiencies in the collection of native statistical information, but are far from achieving desirable results in all sectors. A combination of more funding and better co-ordination of data collection, including agreement on terminology to be used, is required before reliable, comparative information is available for all vital dimensions of native life.

POPULATION

Recent estimates place the size of the combined native population in 1977 at about 1.1 million people, composed of: 291,171 status Indians; 798,250 Métis and non-status Indians; and 22,760 Inuit. The number for status Indians was derived from official registration records maintained by the Department of Indian Affairs and Northern Development, while those for the other two groups are estimates supplied by their national association headquarters in Ottawa.[1]

Native people constitute a small percentage of the country's total population, about 4.8% (table 2.5.1). The percentage relative to each provincial or territorial population varies from a low of .6% in Newfoundland to a high of 80% in the sparsely populated Northwest Territories. It is in those areas where the ratio of natives to whites is relatively high that the most vociferous demands are heard for land rights, self-determination, and improvements in general living conditions. Also, it is in the relatively small cities of these regions that social problems and antagonism between natives and whites are most noticeable.

The exact number of native people now living in urban centres is not known. For status Indians in 1974, Statistics Canada (1977*c*) estimated that 27% were living off reservations, but actual location was not given. There is some evidence to suggest that in the three Prairie provinces, up to one-third of the combined native population is living in urban centres, and that the migration of natives from reservations, and rural and remote areas to these centres is increasing each year at a rate roughly equal to their annual rate of natural increase (Rudnicki 1976). The majority of status Indians, however, still live on reserves or Crown lands, and in small settlements or communities in the forest belt, which stretches across the continent, or in the Arctic; that is, in the sparsely populated, less industrialized regions of the country. Nearly all Inuit now live permanently in small settlements along the Arctic coastline and depend on government almost entirely for subsistence.

As indicated in table 2.5.2, the rates of natural increase for both status Indians and Inuit have been declining, but are still considerably higher than the national rate. Comparable data are not available for the Métis and non-status Indians.

---

[1] The Inuit estimate was arrived at by taking the 1971 census figure of 17,550 and projecting the average annual natural rate of increase over a six-year period. Since Métis and non-status Indians are not enumerated separately from the rest of the population, the estimate for them is difficult to confirm. It is based on a survey of 346 communities across Canada (Schwartz 1977), conducted by the Native Council of Canada in 1976, and extrapolations made from the survey results. The estimate is probably low, especially for Ontario and Quebec where contacts between whites and Indians have been going on for hundreds of years. Also, because of the exclusionary patrilineal rule of the Indian Act, the population is expanding by inclusion of new members each year as well as by natural increase.

Since native associations receive funding grants from government based on population estimates, the possible influence this might have on native or government calculations must be borne in mind.

Based on a survey, conducted in 1976, of 24,365 Métis and non-status Indian households across Canada, Schwartz (1977) calculated the age distribution of Métis and non-status Indians. The distribution closely resembles that for status Indians. Both populations have the highest percentages in the under-fourteen-years-of-age group: 41.3% for status Indians and 43% for Métis and non-status Indians, as compared with 26.4% for the Canadian population as a whole. In the over-sixty-five category, both have similar percentages, but these are about half the percentage for the rest of the country (table 2.5.3).

TABLE 2.5.1
DISTRIBUTION OF NATIVE POPULATION, 1977

Province	Population	Status Indian Population	Estimated Métis and Non-Status Indian Population	Estimated Inuit Population	Estimated Total Native Population	% Native
Newfoundland	557,700	—	1,200	2,200	3,400	0.6
Prince Edward Island	118,200	466	1,400	—	1,866	1.6
Nova Scotia	828,600	5,417	8,100	—	13,517	1.6
New Brunswick	677,300	5,096	7,600	—	12,696	1.9
Quebec	6,234,500	31,333	78,200	4,410	113,943	1.8
Ontario	8,264,500	63,685	159,200	—	222,885	2.7
Manitoba	1,021,500	42,630	127,800	—	170,430	16.7
Saskatchewan	921,300	43,651	130,950	—	174,601	19.0
Alberta	1,838,000	34,537	103,600	—	138,137	7.5
British Columbia	2,466,600	54,192	162,500	—	216,692	8.8
Yukon Territory	21,800	2,766	7,200	—	9,966	45.7
Northwest Territories	42,600	7,397	10,500	16,150	34,047	80.0
Canada	22,992,600	291,170	798,250	22,760	1,112,180	4.8

SOURCE: Statistics Canada (1978*b*), cat. no. 91–201; Siggner, Locatelli, and Stewart (1978); and unpublished data supplied by Native Council of Canada and Inuit Tapirisat of Canada.

TABLE 2.5.2
RATE OF NATURAL INCREASE

Year	Status Indian	Inuit	Canada
1964	3.5	5.0	1.6
1974	1.9	2.3	0.8

SOURCE: Statistics Canada (1977*c*), p. 282.

TABLE 2.5.3
AGE AND SEX COMPOSITION

AGE GROUPS	MÉTIS AND NON-STATUS INDIANS		POPULATION OF CANADA		STATUS INDIANS[a]	
	% of total males	% of total females	% of total males	% of total females	% of total males	% of total females
14 and under	43.6	42.4	27.1	25.8	41.2	41.4
15–19	13.5	13.1	10.3	9.9	12.4	12.8
20–24	8.7	9.1	9.4	9.2	9.3	10.0
25–44	20.5	22.8	27.1	26.4	22.4	21.8
45–64	10.3	9.6	18.7	19.2	10.3	9.7
65 and over	3.4	3.0	7.4	9.5	4.4	4.3
Total	100.0	100.0	100.0	100.0	100.0	100.0

SOURCE: Schwartz (1977), p. 5; Statistics Canada (1976*a*), cat. no. 91–202; and unpublished data supplied by Department of Indian Affairs and Northern Development.
NOTE: a. Treaty and Registered Indians only.

HEALTH

Generally speaking, health standards among native people have improved considerably over the past two decades, due in large measure to massive government spending for housing, welfare, and medical services. For those living in northern, remote regions and urban slums, health conditions still remain below national standard.

Tuberculosis, once rampant among native peoples and a principal cause of death, has been brought under control, but not entirely suppressed. The rate of new cases is nine times that for the general population, and the reactivation rate, seventeen times greater (Statistics Canada 1977*c*, p. 285).

Nutrition, once a serious problem in isolated northern regions, is gradually improving, but not uniformly for all age groups. Nutrient intake, now judged to be adequate by medical surveys for status Indian and Inuit children, is less so for adolescents and adults, and dangerously inadequate for the elderly and for pregnant women. Elderly men were judged to be seriously deficient in calorie intake, much below the standards for the general population, and the intake of pregnant Inuit women was so low that fetal growth could be adversely affected (Health and Welfare Canada 1975*b*, pp. 139, 148*c*). The infant mortality rate for status Indians and Inuit has declined dramatically since 1960, but still remains high relative to that for the general population. In 1974, the status Indian rate was three times the national average, and the Inuit rate, five times (table 2.5.4).

Approximately 50% of native infant deaths are caused by upper respiratory diseases and accidents (Siggner, Locatelli, and Stewart 1978). Native infants face greater risks of death than do Canadians infants:

Major Causes of Infant Deaths	Risk Factor Compound To Other Canadian Infants
Perinatal causes	1.4 times
Respiratory diseases	6.4 times
Infective parasitic diseases	8.2 times
Accidents, violence	3.0 times
Congenital anamolies	0.3 times

Life expectancy is lower for status Indians than for the general population by twenty-two years (68 versus 46) for males, and twenty-eight (75 versus 47) for females (Canada 1978*a*).

The general standard of housing for all categories of native people is below that for the rest of Canada, but is improving as a result of special government subsidized housing programmes. Progress has been slow in rectifying deficiencies uniformly across the country, and many are still without basic utilities such as sewer and water (table 2.5.5). In 1973, a survey of housing conditions on Indian reserves judged 22.4% good, 21% fair, and 56.6% poor. The standards used were those developed by the Department of Indian Affairs and Northern Development (Statistics Canada 1977*c*, p. 288) and are below those for the country as a whole.

TABLE 2.5.4
INFANT MORTALITY RATES, 1960 AND 1974

	1960	1974
Status Indian	7.9	3.9
Inuit	18.8	6.4
Canada	2.7	1.5

SOURCE: Health and Welfare Canada (1975*a*).

EDUCATION

The extent to which native languages are being retained and used as the principal means of communications is not known. There is some evidence to suggest, however, that a higher percentage of native peoples are shifting to English as the principal means of expression, even in Quebec (Statistics Canada 1976*e*, p. 53). DeVries and Vallée (1975, p. 46), in their analysis of 1971 census data on native language usage, report that of those who claimed Indian or Inuit ancestry, the proportions using native languages in the home varied according to whether the respondents lived in urban or rural environments. Of those living in urban centres, only 16% spoke a native language at home most often, compared to 56% for those living in rural or remote areas. They also report a percentage decline from 87% in 1951 to 57% in 1971 for those claiming Indian or Eskimo as mother tongue. While their

TABLE 2.5.5
HOUSING UTILITIES—REGISTERED INDIANS AND
TOTAL POPULATION—CANADA, 1971 AND 1973

GEOGRAPHIC AREA	AVERAGE NUMBER OF PERSONS PER HOUSEHOLD		AVERAGE NUMBER OF PERSONS PER ROOM	
	Registered Indians	Total Canada	Registered Indians	Total Canada
Canada	5.1	3.5	1.49	0.64
Total rural	—	3.9	1.71	0.68
rural non-farm	—	3.8	1.73	0.67
rural farm	—	4.3	1.45	0.67
Urban	—	3.4	0.96	0.63

GEOGRAPHIC AREA	% HOUSEHOLDS WITH NO RUNNING WATER		% HOUSEHOLDS WITH SEWAGE SYSTEM		% HOUSEHOLDS WITH BATH & TOILET	
	Registered Indians	Total Canada	Registered Indians	Total Canada	Registered Indians	Total Canada
Canada	50.27	3.97	64.90	90.44	41.38	93.52
Total rural	67.77	15.85	—	63.63	22.09	76.02
rural non-farm	67.94	14.94	—	66.25	21.74	77.08
rural farm	63.93	18.54	—	55.96	30.33	72.83
Urban	8.57	0.72	—	97.75	87.34	98.31

SOURCE: Siggner, Locatelli, and Stewart (1978).

data give no indication of prospects for survival of native languages, they do indicate a trend toward decreased usage.

Though not conclusive, the data from Schwartz (1977) on Métis and non-status Indians, and that from the Department of Indian Affairs and Northern Development's school records for status Indian students (1978*h*) support the view that a shift to English usage is taking place. The data are not comparable since they deal with different segments of the respective populations and since different collection techniques were used. Also, neither source gives information indicating how fluency was measured, nor is there indication of how frequently a language was spoken nor in what context.

The school records for 1977 (table 2.5.6) indicate that 23.1% of the status-Indian student population reported a native language as the one most frequently spoken, and 33% reported English. Less than 1% claimed to be bilingual in English and French, while 34.8% said they were bilingual in English and a native language (ibid.).

TABLE 2.5.6
STATUS-INDIAN
STUDENT POPULATION BY LANGUAGE SPOKEN, 1976

Language Spoken	Number of Students	%
Any native Indian language	18,017	23.3
English	24,198	32.9
French	621	less than 1
Native language and English	27,203	34.8
Native language and French	604	less than 1
Native language, English, and French	59	less than 1
English and French	268	less than 1
No information	7,118	9.0
Total	78,088	100.0

SOURCE: Department of Indian Affairs and Northern Development (1978*d*).

Of those who responded to the language question in the 1976 Métis and non-status Indian survey, 68.4% reported English as the language most frequently spoken; 12.3%, a native language; and 7.1% said they were bilingual in English and French (Schwartz 1977, p. 13). Compared to status Indians, the higher percentage of bilingual speakers in both official languages is not surprising since a high proportion of Métis in western Canada as well as in Quebec have French ancestry and were educated by French-speaking missionaries in French schools (table 2.5.7).

The apparent shift from native languages to English is due primarily to the fact that English was the language of instruction in federal schools for status Indians and Inuit, even in Quebec. Until about 1960, the speaking of native languages by students in school was actively discouraged, and in some schools operated by missionaries, a punishable offence. This situation has changed in federal schools, and native languages may be spoken and even taught as a special subject; however, English still remains the main language of instruction.

Modern elementary school facilities exist in virtually all native communities, even in tiny arctic settlements. For status Indians and Inuit, the federal government pays the full cost of education for elementary and secondary schooling, and provides grants for those qualified to attend post-secondary institutions. It makes no special provisions for the education of the Métis and non-status Indians, nor do the provinces. They are entitled to the same educational services offered other provincial residents.

Proportionately, native people have considerably lower educational attainment levels than do their counterparts in the general population. In 1971, 64% of status Indians over fifteen years old had grade eight or less, compared to 33.5% for the same age segment in the general population; and only 2.7% had some post-secondary education, compared to 18.6% for the rest of Canada (table 2.5.8).

TABLE 2.5.7
MÉTIS AND NON-STATUS INDIANS BY LANGUAGE SPOKEN, 1976
%

Languages	Spoken Most Fluently
English	68.4
French	12.2
Bilingual (English and French)	7.1
Native languages	12.3
Total	100.0

Source: Schwartz (1977), p. 13.

TABLE 2.5.8
DISTRIBUTION BY AGE ACCORDING TO EDUCATIONAL ATTAINMENT, CANADA, 1971

HIGHEST EDUCATIONAL ATTAINMENT	15–24		25–34		35–44		45–54		55–64		65+		Total	
	Indians	Canada	Indians	Canada	Indians	Canada	Indians	Canada	Indians	Canada	Indians	Canada	Indians	Canada
Up to grade 8	45.6	12.9	54.7	23.1	78.5	36.3	85.9	42.3	88.8	51.6	88.6	63.7	64.0	33.5
Up to grade 13	52.4	65.9	40.3	48.0	19.1	43.8	13.5	41.0	8.6	35.4	8.3	28.1	33.3	47.9
Some post-secondary	2.0	21.3	5.1	28.6	2.4	19.7	0.6	16.8	2.6	13.0	3.0	8.2	2.7	18.6
Total percentage	100.0	100.1	100.1	99.7	100.0	99.8	100.0	100.1	100.0	100.0	99.9	100.0	100.0	100.0
Public use sample total	555		355		251		170		116		132		1,579	

SOURCE: For total Canadian population, Statistics Canada (1977b), cat. no. 99-708, pp. 30–31; for native Indians, Statistics Canada, 1971 Census of Canada Public Use Sample Tapes, individual data.

NOTE: "Native Indians" are all those coded as so on the census ethnicity question, and born in Canada or the United States.

TABLE 2.5.9
DISTRIBUTION ACCORDING TO EDUCATIONAL ATTAINMENT, CANADA, 1976
%

Highest Educational Attainment	Métis and Non-Status Indians		Population of Canada
No schooling	4.2		
Grade 6 or under	19.2	49.8	24.6[a]
Grades 7 and 8	26.4		
Grades 9 to 12	47.7		49.5[b]
Grade 13 or higher	2.5		25.9[c]
Total	100.0		100.0
Average	8.1		n/a

SOURCE: Schwartz (1977).
NOTES: a. 0–8 years of schooling.
b. High school; includes persons who have either completed secondary education or at least some secondary education, but with no post-secondary education.
c. Some post-secondary, or post-secondary and university degree.

TABLE 2.5.10
ENROLMENT BY GRADE, CANADA, 1967, 1976, AND 1977

LEVEL	STATUS INDIANS				POPULATION OF CANADA
	1967		1977		1976
	Number	%	Number	%	%
Preschool–Grade 8	53,328	82.0	59,260	74.0	60.8
Grade 8–12/13	5,967	9.2	12,457	15.0	26.9
University	142	0.2	1,632	2.0	5.4
Other post-secondary	5,581	8.6	7,077	9.0	6.2
					(0.7 graduates)
Total	65,018	100.0	80,426	100.0	100.0

SOURCE: Stewart (1977); and Statistics Canada (1977*a*), p. 320.

Schwartz (1977) found a similar disproportionate distribution for the Métis and non-status Indians in 1976. Forty-nine per cent had grade eight or less, compared to 24.6% for the general population. Only 2.5% had some post-secondary education, compared to 25.9% for Canada as a whole (table 2.5.9).

While status-Indian school enrolment has increased over the past ten years (table 2.5.10), the retention rate, as calculated in 1977, of those from grade two who continue school to complete grade twelve is very low (17.9 for status Indians and 75.4 for Canada in 1976) and has been consistently low in about the same proportions since 1966 (Siggner, Locatelli, and Stewart 1978). Of those who managed to enter secondary school and were enrolled in

1977, 54.5% dropped out. The drop-out rate has been consistently high, averaging about four times that for the general population (table 2.5.11).

Over the past ten years, status-Indian enrolment in universities has increased from 142 in 1967 to 1,632 in 1977. The increase started in the early 1970s and is coincidental with the start made by a number of universities to offer undergraduate-degree programmes in native studies. Vocational training and short-term special course work still retain the highest percentage (73.1% in 1977) of those enrolled in post-secondary institutions (table 2.5.12). By comparison and in proportion to each total population, the representation of the status-Indian segment in universities in 1977 was only 2%, compared to 5.4% for the general population. Given the low retention rate and the high drop-out rate in secondary schools, it is unlikely that these proportions will change over the next few years.

TABLE 2.5.11
ACHIEVEMENT LEVEL OF
STATUS-INDIAN SECONDARY-SCHOOL STUDENTS, 1974–1977

ACHIEVEMENT	1974		1975		1976		1977	
	Number	%	Number	%	Number	%	Number	%
Graduated	352	5.5	664	6.2	796	7.7	745	8.3
Promoted	2,741	42.5	543	5.1	606	5.9	1,480	16.5
Failed	386	6.0	267	2.5	221	2.2	462	5.2
Dropped out	1,924	29.8	4,996	46.4	5,853	56.6	4,897	54.5
Partially promoted	529	8.2	259	2.4	208	2.0	120	1.4
Transferred	531	8.3	4,054	37.6	2,667	25.8	1,288	14.4
Total	6,463	100.3	10,783	100.2	10,351	100.2	8,992	100.3

SOURCE: Department of Indian Affairs and Northern Development (1975*a*, 1976*a*, 1977*a*, and 1978*a*).

TABLE 2.5.12
ENROLMENT OF STATUS INDIANS IN POST-SECONDARY COURSES, 1967–1977

YEAR	UNIVERSITY		TEACHING		NURSING		VOCATIONAL		SPECIAL COURSES		TOTAL	%
	Number	%	Number	%	Number	%	Number	%	Number	%		
1967–1968	142	2.5	23	0.4	21	0.4	1,901	33.3	3,636	63.6	5,723	100.0
1968–1969	189	3.7	38	0.8	20	0.4	1,779	34.2	3,178	61.1	5,204	100.0
1969–1970	321	3.2	49	0.5	24	0.3	2,528	25.3	7,102	70.9	10,024	100.0
1970–1971	432	4.0	48	0.5	24	0.3	2,307	21.1	8,135	74.4	10,946	100.0
1971–1972	559	4.6	63	0.6	15	0.2	2,680	22.0	8,879	72.8	12,196	100.0
1972–1973	911	7.0	104	0.8	25	0.2	3,465	26.6	8,558	65.6	13,063	100.0
1973–1974	1,055	10.2	115	1.1	13	0.2	2,256	21.7	6,989	67.1	10,428	100.0
1974–1975	2,047	20.2	195	2.0	64	0.7	2,230	22.0	5,627	55.4	10,163	100.0
1975–1976	2,071	18.7	421	3.8	36	0.4	2,609	23.5	5,966	53.8	11,103	100.0
1976–1977	1,632	18.8	570	6.6	87	1.0	1,795	20.7	4,625	53.1	8,709	100.0

SOURCE: Department of Indian Affairs and Northern Development (1978*e*).

DEVIANCE

Underrepresented in universities, native people are overrepresented in penal institutions. Though they make up less than 5% of the population, in 1976 they constituted 8.4% of the total number of inmates in federal penitentiaries (Department of Indian Affairs and Nothern Development 1977*f*). The ratio has been much more disproportionate in provincial jails. Earlier studies (Canadian Corrections Association 1967) found that 80% of the female and 66% of the male populations of the Prince Albert prison were persons of native ancestry; in larger cities, such as Regina, they constituted 48% of the prison population; and in remote areas where they form the largest segment of the population, such as the Pas and Inuvik, percentages for local prisons were much higher, 100% and 95% respectively.

Mann (1975, p. 54) estimated the Inuit crime rate to be ten times that for the general population. Finkler (1975), in comparing the crime rates for Inuit and non-Inuit living in Frobisher Bay, found the Inuit rate four times higher. The majority of offences (80%) were drug and alcohol related.

While there are no doubt reasons for serious concern, statistical indicators of native crime rates must be interpreted with caution. Very little is known about the circumstances surrounding arrest and conviction, or how relations between whites and natives in a given community influence the commission of a crime or the enforcement of law.

EMPLOYMENT

Limited by education and opportunity, native people are rarely found in the professions, managerial class, or corporate élite. A notable exception is a recently retired vice-president of the Union Carbide Corporation, a Mohawk Indian from Brantford, Ontario. He worked as an engineer on the Manhattan project during World War II, and is currently president of a branch of the U.S. Academy of Sciences for native people. Other exceptions include old, established Métis families of Manitoba, some of whom are very wealthy and form part of the business élite of that province. They rarely identify themselves publicly as persons of native ancestry and seldom become involved in those native associations aimed at gaining recognition of native rights. Though still few in number, talented native persons are achieving international recognition as artists and actors. Others have received acclaim in professional sports, particularly hockey and rodeo.

Apart from the exceptional few, the majority of natives who enter the labour force are engaged in the semi-skilled, unskilled, clerical, or service sectors of the economy; that is, in occupations low in socio-economic status and subject to high seasonal unemployment rates. This is particularly the case for those living in rural and remote parts of the country, and for those migrating from these regions to urban centres (Frideres 1974, p. 97). Conducted in the Northwest Territories in 1969, a survey of male status-Indian occupations found that 36.4% had no occupation, 22% were unskilled labourers, and 16.8% were engaged in hunting, fishing, and trapping. Less than 1% worked in one of the established professions; the remainder were either unemployed, or held clerical or semi-skilled service positions (Owen 1976, exhibit 3–17).

A more recent survey, conducted in 1976, of Métis and non-status Indian occupations across Canada revealed a similar clustering at the lower end of the occupational-status scale. Only 2.4% fell into the managerial or professional categories and 50.2% into those for clerical, semi-skilled, and unskilled manual workers (Schwartz 1977, pp. 11, 12, 44).

Native people have a continuous history of having the highest unemployment rates of any group in the country, even in times of economic growth. One estimate for 1969 placed the status-Indian unemployment rate in western Canada as high as 65.4% (Owen 1976, exhibit 3–24), and another by Frideres (1974, p. 97) for 1971 placed it at 68% for those in the twenty-to-thirty age group living in urban centres. The rate for the Inuit has not been calculated, but is probably much lower since the majority in the work force is employed almost exclusively by the governments of Canada and of the Northwest Territories in a variety of service occupations. It has been estimated that approximately 60% of Inuit-earned income is derived from those sources, 37% from hunting and trapping, and only 3% from employment in the private sector.

In 1976, the unemployment rate for Métis and non-status Indians was slightly more than four times the national rate (Schwartz 1977, p. 18). The rates were highest for the fourteen-to-nineteen age group—54.5%—compared to the national rate of 13.3% for the equivalent age group (table 2.5.13).

Because of high rates of unemployment and irregular participation in the labour force, native workers earn consistently less per year than their counterparts in the general population. In 1976, for example, it was estimated that while 49.7% of Manitobans earned more than $4,000 per year,

TABLE 2.5.13

UNEMPLOYMENT RATES FOR MÉTIS AND NON-STATUS INDIANS, AND CANADA, 1976

Age Group	Male	Female	Both Sexes	Population of Canada
14–19	52.4	57.2	54.5	13.3[a]
20–24	32.7	30.4	31.9	11.3
25–44	25.1	25.5	25.2	6.1
45–64	32.5	29.3	31.7	4.9
Total[b]	32.3	34.7	33.0	7.6

SOURCE: Statistics Canada (1976b), cat. no. 71–001; and Schwartz (1977), p. 23.
NOTES: a. 15–19 age group.
    b. Population 65 years of age and over included in calculation of total unemployment rate.

only 10.8% of status-Indian workers had equivalent earnings. Approximately 48% had annual incomes of less than $1,000, as compared to 12% of those in the general provincial work force (Owen 1976, exhibit 3—33). The average weekly earnings for employed Métis and non-status Indian workers in 1976 was 16% lower than the comparable national average for industrial workers (Schwartz 1977, pp. 22, 23).

A substantial portion of native family income is derived from a variety of provincial and federal welfare assistance programmes (see table 2.5.14). In 1974, 40.7% of status Indians living on reserves and Crown lands received welfare assistance for health, social, and economic reasons in the amount of $53.3 million. As indicated in table 2.5.14, of the total number of recipients, 16.8% cited health reasons; 24.3%, social reasons; and 58.9%, inadequate personal or family income, brought about by a lack of employment opportunities (Statistics Canada 1977c, p. 291). In 1978, expenditures for welfare increased to $85.7 million (Department of Indian Affairs and Northern Development 1979b). Welfare costs for the Métis and non-status Indians are not known since they receive welfare assistance from the provinces in which they live and are lumped in with the general population. Provincial authorities in the western provinces claim that they are as high, if not higher, than those for the status Indians (Rudnicki 1976).

Financial institutions in the private sector of the economy have always shown a conspicuous reluctance to extend credit in the form of loans and

TABLE 2.5.14
STATUS INDIANS LIVING ON RESERVES AND CROWN LANDS, AND
RECEIVING FEDERAL WELFARE ASSISTANCE, 1973—1974

PROVINCE	REASON FOR WELFARE ASSISTANCE[a]			NUMBER OF RECIPIENTS	% RECEIVING ASSISTANCE
	Health %	Social %	Economic[b] %		
Maritimes	11.2	27.5	61.3	6,453	83.4
Quebec	10.7	19.7	69.6	6,348	27.3
Ontario	29.5	—	70.5	7,611	18.7
Manitoba	21.1	20.9	58.0	14,763	47.6
Saskatchewan	11.7	29.7	58.6	16,743	56.7
Alberta	17.2	28.1	54.7	15,400	57.9
British Columbia	17.1	41.7	41.2	11,102	32.3
Yukon Territory	16.3	26.1	57.6	1,018	44.6
Canada	16.8	24.3	58.9	79,438	40.7

SOURCE: Statistics Canada (1977c), p. 291.
NOTES: a. Includes direct relief payments to needy individuals and families, but not other forms of assistance, such as health and educational services, housing subsidies, funds for community improvements, or categorical assistance programmes available to all Canadians.
b. Recipients lacking employment opportunities or having inadequate incomes.

mortgages to native people unless backed by substantial collateral or unless promised ironclad government guarantees. Those living on reserves have been unable to use the land as collateral for loans since it is held in trust and cannot be alienated without complicated legal procedures, including approval by the federal minister responsible for administering the Indian Act. An intricate government system of financing status Indian and Inuit development enterprises has evolved, of which the Department of Indian Affairs and Northern Development's Economic Development Fund is a prime example.

From 1974 to 1978, a total of 5,452 business enterprises were financed by the fund, in the amount of $124.8 million (Department of Indian Affairs and Northern Development 1979b). Table 2.5.15 indicates the number and type of enterprises funded. While some enterprises, such as co-operative agricultural projects and real estate investment in British Columbia, have had notable success, others have incurred substantial losses. In 1977, losses of up to $23.9 million were reported, due largely to insufficient financing of projects on a continuing basis, poor management, and investment in too many projects with doubtful economic potential (*Toronto Globe and Mail*, 15 September 1977). Frideres (1974, p. 177) noted in 1971 that the 900 businesses found on reserves employed only 1,000 people. In 1974, a survey of status-Indian economic development activity (Department of Indian Affairs and Northern Development 1976d) revealed that of the 5,873 development projects in the sample, the average man-month per status Indian employed was 6.6 and the average total income per person employed was $1,780.

TABLE 2.5.15
STATUS-INDIAN ECONOMIC DEVELOPMENT FUND, 1974–1978

DEVELOPMENT ACTIVITY	PROJECTS		FUNDING	
	Number	%	$	%
Agriculture	1,740	32.0	25,513,548	20.4
Forestry	261	4.8	11,039,953	9.0
Fishing and trapping	340	6.2	3,016,479	2.4
Manufacturing (handicrafts)	320	5.8	16,287,121	13.0
Construction	252	5.0	6,020,772	4.8
Transportation	700	12.8	6,852,713	5.4
Wholesale and retail trade	533	9.7	9,882,143	8.0
Real estate	39	0.7	23,357,175	18.7
Services	1,101	20.0	19,965,043	16.0
Indian fishermen's assistance programme	166	3.0	2,879,810	2.3
Total	5,452	100.0	124,814,757	100.0

SOURCE: Department of Indian Affairs and Northern Development (1979a).

Both exclusion from the labour force and the perpetuation of a dual economic system—one for all whites and a less affluent one for natives— carry with them social, as well as financial, consequences. Very few native people are members of trade unions, or business or professional associations of the kind that transcend regional or cultural boundaries. Diminution of normal relations with other Canadians in the daily social and economic life of the country serves to weaken the already tenuous links between native and Canadian societies, and to increase dependence on government to provide a substitute version of those services accessible to other Canadians, but not to them.

Modern Native Associations

Over the years, efforts to ameliorate the effects of unilateral dependence and impoverishment have led native peoples to form mutual benefit associations that transcend band or local community organizations. Until the last decade, these associations were weak and relatively ineffective, suffering from lack of funds and membership confidence. Relying solely on contributions from members and benevolent voluntary organizations such as church groups, dedicated leaders often went unpaid, using personal funds to cover the cost of travel and other organizational expenses. In the main, they advanced no ideological or political point of view beyond an appeal to natural justice for recognition of special rights to communal land, some form of self-government, and the right to preserve their languages and cultures. By pointing to the impoverishment and displacement in their own land, their leaders hoped to appeal to the conscience of the country as a whole for a new deal (Whiteside 1973*b*).

Though governments ignored by and large their existence and continued to deal with band or local groups individually, it was the leaders of these associations who mobilized opposition to the "white paper" in 1969. In concert with prominent Métis spokesmen and band chiefs, they were able to convince the federal government in 1970 to fund native organizations and establish a policy consultative process. Reflecting the existing divisions within the native population, three national associations were recognized along with thirty provincial or regional affiliates. Each is funded separately by the federal Department of the Secretary of State—the same department responsible for funding multicultural programmes for ethnic groups. At the national level, status Indians have formed the National Indian Brotherhood (NIB), the Métis have joined with the non-status Indians to form the Native Council of Canada (NCC), and the Inuit have formed the Inuit Tapirisat of Canada (ITC). In 1977, for example, about nine million dollars were distributed to qualifying associations to cover salaries, office operations, and travel costs for the year.

Each national association has a president and two other officers who are elected by delegates at an annual national assembly. Until recently, the term of office was one year, but this varies and has been changed to up to three years in some associations. Salaries also vary in amounts; presidents may receive between thirty and forty thousand dollars per year, while the vice-president and secretary-treasurer may be paid amounts ranging from twenty to thirty thousand dollars.

Provincial or regional affiliates repeat more or less the national organizational pattern, with the difference that in the NIB, band chiefs represent a local constituency rather than a president. Bands have status under the Indian Act, and their participation is tempered by legal constraints and responsibilities.

A council normally made up of the three elected officers and the president and vice-president of each provincial or regional affiliate determines the business of the national office. In the NCC, for example, members of the board of directors are not elected at the annual meeting, but are automatically directors by virtue of their election at their own provincial meetings. Built into the organizational structure is an attempt to countervail the powers of the national office in the interest of provincial or local freedom of action. Affiliation is on a consensus basis, and each provincial or regional association may withdraw membership at any time. The method of funding reinforces this option, since each association receives funds directly from the government, whether or not it remains affiliated with the national organization. Thus, as is the case with the NCC at the present time, three provincial associations, British Columbia, Saskatchewan, and Manitoba, have withdrawn membership over disputes with the national office yet continue to be funded as independent organizations. The powers of the purse rest with the federal government, and it alone decides which organizations to recognize for funding, in what amounts, and for how long.

Though circumscribed in powers and operating under the enormous difficulties inherent in the consensual method of decision making, the associations have achieved significant gains in the space of less than ten years, most notably in the fields of native housing, employment, and education. Even government bureaucracies, provincial, as well as federal, and traditionally resistant to the employment of natives, have responded to their appeals to recruit more natives into government service. Also, there has been considerable success in presenting the native point of view to the Canadian public, and in the process, enhancing native peoples' self-image, as well as the image held by the population at large. On the other hand, progress in resolving the fundamental issues concerning the definition of an Indian, of special status, and of aboriginal rights has not been so spectacular, and for some leaders, even discouraging (Manuel 1974).

Part of the reason for this is that common ideology and a unified approach to the resolution of problems have not yet evolved, nor is there what might be called a unified native movement. The three national associations operate completely independently of each other. There is very little interaction between the leaders. They neither convene joint assemblies, nor often attend one another's meetings. Communication between respective leaders, when it does occur, is informal, based on shared social or regional ties. The issues that originally divided native peoples continue to do so, especially the question of recognition under the Indian Act. Status Indians, as already mentioned, actively oppose inclusion of Métis and non-status individuals into the existing band and reservation system. The Inuit remain aloof from both groups, preferring to join with the Inuit of Alaska and Greenland.

The issues that separate the associations at the national level are reflected at local levels, and here, too, there is little or no action on common problems. A notable, current example is the Northwest Territories, where the federal government has recognized all native groups as having a valid land claim and has offered to negotiate the terms of a settlement. However, the status-Indian association refuses to meet with the Métis organization, and the Inuit have put forward a claim independently of the other two. During the negotiations over the James Bay Agreement, Métis and non-status Indians were not invited to participate in the actual negotiations by the status-Indian and Inuit associations, though both the federal and Quebec governments recognized they had a claim. In this case, the issue was settled unilaterally by the status Indians with the governments, leaving it up to the status-Indian communities to decide which local non-status persons were to be eligible for inclusion.

The leadership of each national association is constantly required to maintain a delicate balance in responding to the demands of internal factions or special interest groups. Native politics in the process have become a fine art in which considerable diplomatic and administrative skills are required to deal with competing tribal, regional, and ideological view-points. Recently, native women have challenged the male-dominated leadership. Women are active in all the associations, but those who are members of the NIB, for example, at the provincial and national levels seldom get elected to offices other than the ''housekeeping'' one of secretary-treasurer. Part of the reason lies in traditional attitudes toward women, and more importantly, in the NIB's case, in the reluctance of the male-dominated band organizations and chiefs to have the patrilineal rule changed.[1] By comparison, the NCC has been much more active in supporting native women's rights. In the past seven years, out of five national presidents, one was a woman, and currently two women are presidents of provincial affiliates in the eastern provinces. Resentment over the loss of status because of the patrilineal rule is no doubt an important consideration for non-status women and is one of the major reasons why they joined the NCC in the first place. Noteworthy here is the

---

[1] The problem is compounded by the fact that the government is reluctant to increase the size of existing reserves and the amount of funding to bands to accommodate the increase in population that would result if the rule were changed.

NCC's membership composition: in the eastern provinces, women predominate, while in the rest of the country, the sex ratio is more balanced.

In the main, tribal and linguistic affiliations are diminishing in relative importance as the process of participating in provincial, regional, and national organizations goes forward and English becomes the language of everyday use. These affiliations cannot be discounted entirely, however, especially in the more remote regions, where native languages are commonly spoken. The Dené Indians of the Northwest Territories, as has been mentioned previously, wish to form a separate Dené Nation and have issued a declaration to this effect (Dené of the Northwest Territories 1975). They are willing to include Métis in this nation, if the latter agree to sign a statement accepting Dené political and cultural objectives. In both the NIB and NCC, all of the presidents have been from western Canada, and generally speaking, the most vocal, high profile leaders tend to be of Cree ancestry, followed by British Columbian natives who have had a more active history than most other groups in organizing native associations.

Conflicting regional interests and demands are as characteristic of native politics as they are of politics in the country as a whole. Indeed, the provincial elected affiliates tend to identify as "provinces," and the leaders jealously guard what they regard as provincial powers and functions from encroachment by the national association. Unlike the federal system of Canadian politics, the membership at large does not elect the national council directly, as the voters of Canada do the federal government. In an organization such as the NCC, the appointed presidents and vice-presidents of provincial affiliates on the national council tend to give low priority to objectives that are national in scope, in favour of short-term objectives of a kind immediately beneficial to the provincial constituents and likely to assist in their re-election. Continual wrangling over the division of responsibility has led to the conception of the national office as being little more than an information co-ordinating body or lobbying group with the federal government for the provincial affiliates. Thus, national presidents find themselves relatively powerless to speak out on issues of national importance because of the difficulty of obtaining a consensus acceptable to each region. If they do speak out, they frequently find themselves reprimanded by a council for having expressed as national policy a course of action that contradicts that of a provincial affiliate. This occurred recently with the NCC when the president publicly announced NCC support for the recommendations made by Justice Thomas Berger on the Mackenzie Valley pipeline, without having knowledge that the president of the Northwest Territories affiliate had the same day condemned the recommendations (Native Council of Canada 1977*b*). The problem of balancing regional interests with national, long-term goals has led national presidents to become cautious and often indecisive. Only those with great diplomatic skills have been able to keep their associations intact, and at the same time give direction aimed at national policy formulation.

The power struggle between national and affiliate association leaders is not simply over loss or gain of status or prestige. Dedicated though many may be, there is a pecuniary interest as well. Election to executive offices, paying relatively high salaries, is one of the few career opportunities open to native peoples. In nearly all cases, native leaders have less than a high school education, and some have come from impoverished family backgrounds (Manuel 1974). Like executives in other enterprises, fear of loss of job and steady income has become an important factor affecting leadership behaviour. Those who perform in accordance with membership expectations and within the constraints imposed by the consensus process may seek re-election, but increasingly after completing a term, many seek employment in the federal or provincial government bureaucracies. The shift from administering the affairs of native associations to government bureaucracy is facilitated by the fact that national and provincial association offices have themselves become somewhat bureaucratic, employing relatively large support staffs, consultants, and highly qualified specialists. National and provincial associations, which receive funds in addition to the basic organizational core funding for programme development purposes or land claims research, may have annual budgets running into the millions of dollars. Thus, the experience gained by the younger native leaders, especially those with high public profiles, in association work at the executive level, improves career opportunity prospects in government service. An ambitious, career-oriented leader cannot ignore the impression formed of him by officialdom. Because career opportunities for native leaders are few, an increasing number are leaving association work for government middle-management positions.

When the funding programme for native associations was first implemented, it was linked to a consultative process in which native leaders were to have access to federal ministers at the Cabinet level. With this in mind, a Cabinet committee was established, reporting to the prime minister to receive representations. Initially, contact between native leaders and ministers took place at regular intervals. Today, meetings between native leaders and ministers take place less frequently. These have gradually been replaced by meetings of ''joint committees'' made up of senior bureaucrats and representatives of native associations. The committees cover all of the programmes of concern to native peoples—housing, land claims, employment, and so on. The routinization of interaction between native leaders and officialdom via the joint committee structure is resulting in the role of the native leader being transformed from that of equal partner in a consultation process to that of an equivalent functionary, that is, unofficial member of the bureaucratic structure itself. The incorporation of the leadership in this fashion increases the risk that the associations will be turned into career opportunity structures that operate as extensions of the bureaucratic communications network. This possibility is recognized and being actively resisted by some, but how successfully is still in doubt.

The fragility of native associations, as already mentioned, is due to factionalism present among native groups and is aggravated by total dependence on government for funding. Members pay only a token membership fee, and their actual numbers, as well as level of commitment, are not known. As creatures of the government, they are always subject to manipulation and control on the part of career opportunist leaders or government officials wishing to influence the outcome of the consultation process. It would be reasonably accurate to say that native associations are increasingly being used as part of the government's conflict management approach to native affairs.

While both sides use manipulative tactics in dealing with each other, the native leader is a disadvantaged partner in bargaining situations involving the two. Not having the vast resources of government at his disposal, he must rely on appeals to public opinion to bring pressure to bear on politicians in order to influence decisions in his favour. Much time is spent doing just that, with varying degrees of success. Difficult or unsympathetic senior bureau-crats are manipulated by threats of going "over their heads" to the prime minister, and friendly persons in the media are relied upon to publish information embarrassing to the government. These tactics have been employed with skill and considerable success, especially during the late 1960s and early 1970s, when student radical groups could be counted on to ally themselves with native causes. Finally, it is uncertain whether public opinion regarding native groups will be positive or negative in the event of the latter impeding the development of energy resources.

Officialdom, as the advantaged partner in the consultation or bargaining process, relies on more subtle tactics—ones less likely to receive public attention. In handling complex negotiations or difficult native leaders, officials can influence the outcome of negotiations by withholding or curtailing funds. This tactic blames Treasury Board for any cutbacks and has the advantage of leaving the impression that the official is not personally to blame. The consequences for the native leader of a curtailment of funds are considerable, and include inability to meet monthly payrolls of large office staffs in native organizations or a diminution in his political stature if the funds are not forthcoming for local betterment projects. Most leaders campaign for elections with promises to improve local living conditions, and failure to produce projects can result in the loss of an election. Another tactic is for officials to form coalitions with one or another of the many factions present in native associations against a difficult leader. This tactic is played most successfully by officials who are familiar with native politics and is also played by native leaders with officials to remove intractable bureaucrats. The coalition operates through promises of rewards and may take the form of promising additional funds to a provincial president if he does not support the views of a national president on a particular issue. The reward is not always in terms of funds, but may take the form of a future job possibility or simply an appeal to vanity and prestige by creating the impression that the partner is favourably regarded by the powers that be.

Not all dealings between natives and officials, of course, are manipulative. Men of integrity, with a genuine desire to improve conditions, exist on both sides. What is suggested is that the associations as presently structured are not likely to overcome factionalism and become a unified movement aimed at leading native peoples toward mutually beneficial goals, be these within or outside the existing polity. Caught in the dilemma posed by poverty and promises of economic betterment on the one hand, and a desire to preserve identity and culture on the other, native associations have chosen to give priority to economic betterment.

Traditionally, native people have been conservative in the expression of political behaviour and beliefs. For example, socialism in its various forms has never had a large following, and in this, native people reflect the voting behaviour of other Canadians. Ideological differences, if they may be called that, are over questions of identity, culture, and nationhood. At one end of the spectrum are those who welcome assimilation, and at the other, those who reject white society altogether and wish to return to original modes of cultural expression; Canadian natives who are members of the American Indian Movement (AIM) represent this latter extreme. The recent declaration by the Dené concerning nationhood status and a similar declaration by the Inuit are less extreme, since some unspecified ties with the country as a whole for purposes of economic development are envisioned (Watkins 1977). Unlike AIM, the orientation of these quasi-independence movements is to the future rather than to the past. AIM has native religious roots that are anti-materialistic and ambivalent about notions of progress not shared by the majority of native people. The small minority of AIM members in Canada are mainly young people. They receive no funding from the federal government, are subjected to police surveillance, and are rejected by the national and provincial associations and affiliates.

In recent years, the emergence of an élite group of native leaders working either in associations or governments has facilitated the integration of native collectivities. On this point, Galtung's model (1971) dealing with the nature of dependency is instructive. He suggests that these forms of control are only successful when the values and aspirations of the dominant élite group at the power centre are shared by the subordinate élite group that controls those in the periphery.

Current Issues and Decentralization of Conflict

Up to this point, the discussion has referred mainly to relations between the federal government and native peoples. It has been suggested that the government has managed to contain potential conflict over questions of identity, inequality, and aboriginal rights through an elaborate consultation process, the decentralization of certain decision-making powers, and the funding of native associations. It is also suggested in this section that the mode of incorporation is by integration of native collectivities into existing provincial structures, with or without formal agreements. Weak national level organizations facilitate this, with the result that provincial and territorial affiliate organizations increasingly find themselves in disputes with provincial governments over federally unresolved issues. In short, the locus of disputes is gradually being shifted from the federal government to the governments of the provinces and territories. A discussion of these new circumstances will lead to a very brief consideration of the new government strategy with respect to native groups.

SPECIFIC ISSUES

Development Conflicts

Probably the most sensitive area of contention between natives and provincial governments is over the expansion, by multinational corporations in search of energy and other resources, into areas traditionally used by native peoples. This dispute is complicated by the existence in some frontier areas of white merchants, other businessmen, and workers who view development as necessary to their economic well-being. Though white people generally are outnumbered by natives in frontier regions, they control the local economy and community service structures, including local government and law enforcement. Through business networks extending to southern centres and political affiliations, they are able to bring pressure to bear on provincial governments for developments to further their interests, especially when these conflict with those of native peoples. The relations between the two groups are cordial and relatively free of overt discriminatory behaviour, apparently as long as native groups do not challenge existing social arrangements or the supremacy of white developmental priorities.

An example of deterioration in local white-native relations is the controversy over the mercury pollution of the English Wabigoon River system in northern Ontario by a large pulp and paper manufacturing corporation (Rayner 1977*b*). Natives who depend almost entirely on the fish from the river system for subsistence are faced with the possibility of mercury poisoning. Politicians have been reluctant to close the river system to domestic fishing because of pressure from local tourist camp operators and sports fishermen who do not need the fish for food. In the dispute that has erupted over the issue, a provincial Cabinet minister claimed that the symptoms of Minamata disease (irreversible mercury poisoning) found in some natives were due to venereal disease and alcoholism. Another claimed the disease was discovered by Japanese communists and its existence could not be confirmed by Canadian doctors (Rayner 1977*b*, p. 2). The issue, though hotly debated in the provincial legislature as recently as the summer of 1977, is still unresolved. A local native group has been formed, and a law suit against the pulp and paper company believed responsible for the pollution is contemplated.

In northern Quebec, the Cree Indians have launched an $8 million law suit against fourteen companies for mercury contamination of their lands. In the meantime, one of the companies in northern Ontario, whose operations are believed to be the major source of the pollution, has applied for an expansion of timber rights in the area covering some nineteen thousand square miles (Rayner 1977*b*, p. 3). The expansion has been vigorously supported by white businessmen and community leaders in the region, but opposed by native spokesmen. Arguments for expansion are in terms of the number of jobs that will be created, thereby increasing the size of the population and the general level of prosperity in the region. The extent to which native peoples are to share in the prosperity is not clear, although promises of jobs in forestry operations have been made. Environmental effects of the massive timber removal plan are also unclear as are the effects of the cutting on the native, land-based economy.

Land Disputes

In the disputes over both pollution of the watershed and timber removal, the federal government has been conspicuously silent, leaving it to local status Indian associations to deal with the provincial government and corporations. What, if any, "behind the scenes" support is given to status Indians is not known. This has not been the case with the Nelson River diversion project in northern Manitoba. Here a conflict has emerged between the status Indians of five reserves and the provincial government of Manitoba over the flooding of 1,900 acres of land on the reserves. The flooding is required to increase the generating capacity of the hydroelectric stations in the area. The natives demanded compensation for damages; the provincial government objected on the grounds that it was unwilling to accord natives any special status or the rights to hold up public projects. The premier of the province condemned as "pernicious" the doctrine that Indian lands could not be transferred without consent for public purposes. The federal minister of Indian Affairs and Northern Development threatened an injunction against continued work on the project unless compensation was paid. While his threat was reassuring to the native peoples involved, it was in fact almost empty since the federal government was bound by a contract to support the project signed ten years before (Rayner 1977*a*, p. 2). Nonetheless, the relations between the two governments became so strained over the issue that the federal minister recently gave as one of the reasons for his being transferred to another portfolio the pro-native stand he took in the dispute, which at the time of writing, has not yet been completely resolved.

Disputes with provincial governments over land and resource rights are not only confined to status Indians. Recent funding by the federal government of land claims research for Métis and non-status Indians has increased the incidence of disputes similar to those of status Indians over their claims. The federal government has already recognized their rights to land claims in the two territories and, to a more limited extent, in the James Bay Agreement. In addition to this, the federally appointed Indian land claims commissioner has publicly announced that he believes they have a basis for claims, especially in the three Prairie provinces (Indian Claims Commission 1977, p. 23). The situation is further complicated through incidents of tacit recognition by the federal government of special status for Métis and non-status Indians in the special funding it provides for housing, claims research, employment programmes, and core funding for associations. These programmes are regarded with suspicion by the provinces, and some are reluctant to participate in them. There is a growing concern that should Métis and non-status Indian claims prove valid, large tracts of provincial lands will have to be provided to settle the claims. In the sparsely populated western provinces, people of native ancestry represent a higher proportion of the population than they do in Quebec and Ontario, and the provision of large tracts of land to meet the needs of native families might entail losing revenues from potential developments on these lands or might even impede development altogether. Furthermore, almost all provincial lands have been sold, leased, or set aside for parklands and development. It would cost billions of dollars in some provinces such as Manitoba to meet the projected claims already hinted at by the Métis in that province.

Provincial governments have always been uneasy about the existence of reserves in their boundaries and have resisted attempts to expand them. Thus, the possibility of their setting aside additional lands for Métis is highly problematic.

Development Liabilities

Large corporations and governments argue that economic and social benefits automatically accrue to native peoples as a result of large-scale developments undertaken in areas mainly inhabited by them. This argument has been received with skepticism by native peoples, and is central in the disputes occurring with governments at all levels.

Native people claim that they are employed as unskilled workers only during the construction phase of a development project and are laid off when the project becomes operational, while permanent jobs are given to white workers imported from the south by companies and trade unions. Attempts to learn new skills and become members of trade unions are impeded by company labour contracts and union rules, which favour members with experience or skills in a particular trade. The vicious circle implicit in hiring practices has left native peoples with the impression that union membership is for whites only, and few have been successful in breaking the circle.

In fact, this is largely what did happen in every part of northern Canada where mining[1], hydroelectric, and large-scale timber operations have been undertaken—Yellowknife, Northwest Territories; Kitimat, British Columbia; Elliot Lake, Ontario; Thompson, Manitoba, are but a few examples.

In these areas, not only were native peoples displaced by white southern workers, but they were relegated to live in makeshift housing in enclaves on the margins of the new towns that sprung up to accommodate southern workers, businessmen, and company managers.

Working for wages in construction radically alters the life-style of native families. Returns from trapping seldom yield more than $1,500 per year. This sum may be earned in one month in construction wage employment. If the employment only lasts one or two years and the native worker is laid off, he finds it extremely difficult to return to trapping and maintain the standard of living attendant upon steady wage income.

Territorial and Political Claims

Considering the situation described above, it is understandable that native peoples resent and resist major developments undertaken in their vicinity. Today almost half of Canada's land mass is under some form of comprehensive claim by native groups—northern Ontario, Northwest Territories, the Yukon, and most of the Arctic. These land claims must be seen as attempts by native peoples to subvert the process that has created their underdevelopment. Two cases will be discussed: the James Bay Agreement and the Northwest Territories land claims.

---

[1] A recent study by Lazore (1977) reveals that in 1971, there were 129,675 workers in the mining industry in Canada; of these, 1,085 were natives, that is, less than 1 % of the total.

James Bay Agreement. The James Bay Agreement provides the clue to the direction of future government policy, and will probably be the framework for the settlement of the comprehensive land claims outstanding in the two territories and the arctic region. The application of the integration formula to existing reserves is complicated by treaty obligations and past practices, especially the system of band administration, but no doubt the main thrust of integrating native groups into provincial structures will gradually be implemented on reserves as well.

The agreement is closely modelled on the one negotiated by the U.S. government with the natives in Alaska in 1973 (Daniels 1977*b*, p. 22). Both were negotiated under pressure of impending massive energy extraction projects, which threatened to have widespread environmental impact. In the case of Alaska, the construction of a north-south pipeline was the issue, while in northern Quebec, it was the construction of a huge hydroelectric dam and the flooding of thousands of square miles. The land entitlement of natives—Métis, Indian, and Inuit—had never been properly implemented and hardly any reserves had been established. Those that were became incorporated into the new structures provided for in the agreements. Negotiations with governments and corporations were undertaken by native organizations, newly formed and legally incorporated under the law of each region. Lawyers and scientific specialists were employed by each side. In all these respects, the negotiations differed markedly from the one-sided negotiations that characterized the land-surrender, treaty-making period of years ago. The treaties provided tracts of land for use and benefit by native peoples in perpetuity, but were vague on the rights to natural resources. In both the Alaska and James Bay agreements, aboriginal title is forever extinguished in exchange for compensation monies; small community land holdings; environmental protection guarantees; exclusive hunting, fishing, and trapping rights to tracts of land adjacent to the communities; the establishment of economic development corporations; and the organization of native communities into municipalities under government jurisdiction. This latter provision is a radical departure from previous practice and is a basic feature of the integration strategy. In both agreements, the size of the territories surrendered by natives is enormous—325 million acres in Alaska and 262 million acres in northern Quebec.

The compensation monies are considerably more in Alaska ($925 million) than in Quebec ($225 million). The method of payment of this sum is noteworthy. In Alaska, the agreement clearly states a pay-out plan of twenty years, by which time all native communities will be considered like other communities and have no special taxation or other privileges. Assimilation over a twenty-year period is the hope. The Quebec agreement also has a twenty-year, interest-free pay-out plan, but the agreement does not specify the status of native peoples after twenty years. Compensation money is not paid to individuals, but to new corporate structures, and must be used for economic or community betterment purposes. A safe assumption would be that the government hopes all the communities in northern Quebec will be fully integrated into provincial administrative networks by the time the last payment is made. In fact, the James Bay and Northern Quebec Native Claims Settlement Act, passed 4 May 1977 and giving effect to the agreement, repeals the federal trusteeship responsibility for natives and their lands, and paves the way for the Quebec provincial government to assume more responsibility for native affairs in the northern parts of the province. This is the first time the federal parliament, which has constitutional responsibility for native affairs, has shared this responsibility with a provincial government (Daniels 1979*b*, pp. 23–24).

While a detailed plan for the development of native economic ventures is outlined, no provision is made in the agreement for native participation in the hydroelectric corporations as shareholders, members of the boards of directors, or even as workers. Their ability to control the future pace of development in the region is limited to a rather vague consultation role mainly related to environmental questions. The type of economic development envisaged for them is in the provision of community maintenance services, tourist services, handicraft production, and wildlife harvesting—all labour-intensive, low-income, high-risk enterprises.

Northwest Territories Land Claims. Recently, those living in the Northwest Territories have advanced land claims to the whole of the Canadian arctic region. The claim also calls for some form of political autonomy with cultural and linguistic guarantees. A similar claim has been put forward by the Dené Indians to the remaining Mackenzie River corridor portion of the Northwest Territories. In both cases, the federal government has recognized that there is a valid basis to a land claim, but rejects the concept of political autonomy with its implications of separate nation status. Perhaps for the first time it also recognizes—at least in principle—language and cultural retention as a fundamental right.

The Northwest Territories land claims negotiations will likely be modelled on the James Bay formula with modifications in that some language and cultural guarantees will probably be included in the final agreement. The situation here is complicated by the fact that three groups—the Dené Indians, the Métis, and the Inuit—have not arrived yet at a common negotiating position. In fact, the Dené refuse to sit down at the same negotiating table with the Métis. While both desire more control over the land and its development, the Dené have put forward a claim based on their existence as a nation with independent political rights. The Métis reject the Dené nation concept in favour of the continuation of federal control over the area, but with native peoples occupying the senior positions in any new territorial government arrangement. Both groups fear that unless something is done to change the existing political or administrative structures, the decisions of remote corporate or government planners will be imposed upon them without consultation, resulting in adverse consequences for the northern environment and its people.

Such fears are not without foundation. In commenting on the Dené quest for self-determination in the Northwest Territories, the economist Mel Watkins (1977) argues that the real beneficiaries of frontier developments are the industrial and metropolitan centres in southern Canada and the United States, which are largely dependent upon the extraction of resources from frontier areas. Surplus capital in the form of profits are drained off by the corporations that conduct the operations, leaving the frontier region without investment capital to diversify the local economy once operations come to an end due to depressed market conditions or resource depletion factors. A study by the University of Alaska on the possible impact of the Alaska pipeline on the local economy predicts a period of "boom and bust" for related reasons (Tussing 1971, p. 128). The study estimates that of the 21,000 jobs that will be directly created as a result of the construction of the pipeline, the majority will be filled by immigrants to the area from the south. Additional housing, schools, roads, hospitals, and so on, will have to be constructed to meet the needs of the expanded population. In ten years, after the construction is completed, only 600 permanent jobs will remain, and unless the economy is diversified, many will have to migrate from the area, leaving the permanent inhabitants with the cost of maintaining an infrastructure of services expanded far beyond their needs and without sufficient investment capital to diversify the economy.

Language Issues

The current quest for self-determination in frontier areas, expressed in nationalistic terms by the Dené, the Inuit, and a Cree-Ojibwa group in northern Ontario, has as a first objective regional economic independence from southern control centres. This objective is believed to be a necessary concomitant to the development of a social order capable of sustaining native language and culture.

In commenting upon language transfer and retention among native peoples in Canada, John Kralt (Statistics Canada 1976, p. 53) made this observation:

> In Canada, excluding Quebec, only 0.6% have some knowledge of French while 71.1% know only English. In Quebec, 32.7% know only English, 22.3% know only French and 3.2% are bilingual. The native peoples in Quebec are different from all non-official language users in that they are either unilingual English or French, rarely both. For all other language groups in Quebec, bilingualism in the two official languages is a major portion of French knowledge.

In the James Bay Agreement, the status of native languages and cultures was avoided, and a debate has erupted between the province and the Inuit over whether the latter are to be exempt from Quebec's new French language law.

The Inuit of Quebec speak English as a second language because schools were administered by the federal government and English was used as the language of instruction. Also, the missionaries who converted them to Christianity were Church of England members of the Protestant faith, and they reinforced the use of English. The recent legislation (Law 101) by the Parti Québécois government proclaiming French the official language of the province led to protests by the Inuit in the larger settlements that required Quebec provincial police interventions. The Inuit and representatives of the provincial government have agreed to negotiate a compromise, but the details are not yet known. The federal government, though it has a responsibility to protect native rights, has been reluctant to intervene, no doubt to avoid open confrontation with the government of Quebec.

A similar conflict over language rights is occurring on some Indian reserves in Quebec. Here, too, English was used by the federal government as the language of instruction on the reservations, and families are refusing to send their children to schools where French is now the mandatory language of instruction.

Urbanization and Social Problems

With the increase in numbers of native peoples migrating to urban centres, the costs for welfare, health, and other services to off-reserve status Indians have become a matter of contention between the two levels of government (provincial and federal). In the more populous provinces, Quebec and Ontario, with large industrialized urban centres, the plight of the native migrant is less noticeable. Also, the service costs of maintaining him in a city are less of a burden on these provincial treasuries than they are in the less industrialized and less populous provinces in eastern and western Canada.

In Manitoba, for example, a study conducted on the social assistance costs to the province for status Indians not living on reserves (Rudnicki 1976) revealed that about 35% of the status-Indian population lived in the province's urban centres. The total cost in 1975 for welfare, health, education, and other services provided by the province was in excess of $126 million, or $3,000 per native person, an amount double that per non-native resident. The Manitoba status-Indian population is growing at the rate of 3.5% per year; this growth prevails almost entirely in urban areas and not on reserves, where population size is fairly stable. Though the federal government has the responsibility for status Indians, the province increasingly finds itself shouldering a larger portion of service costs. Of the total $216 million spent on status Indians in 1975, the federal government contributed only $80 million. Rudnicki claims that a similar situation exists in the other two Prairie provinces of Saskatchewan and Alberta. Resentment that Indian reserve lands do not produce provincial revenues is an important factor in the dispute over cost-sharing, especially with the oil-producing province of Alberta.

Perhaps more significant than questions of dollar costs are the social problems that have emerged as a result of urbanization in nearly all the Prairie cities affected. Native peoples are relegated to slum dwellings of inner city ghettos. Opportunities to interact socially with residents beyond the boundaries of the core area are minimal; so that the whites with whom they have most contact are often alcoholics or those with histories of petty crime (Brody 1971). The incidence of drunkenness and delinquency is high, to the point where there are frequent clashes between natives and police. Because educational backgrounds are weak, and professional or trade skills lacking, many can only work as seasonal labourers, and families are forced to subsist on welfare. Mobility into the dominant social-class system, of course, is not entirely impeded, and some do succeed in finding work as clerks, stenographers, and so forth. However, very few natives are to be found in the professions or prestige occupations. The social stigma attached to living in the depressed core also impedes interracial marriages with whites, except with those living under the same disadvantaged circumstances.

Federal-Provincial Relations

The increasingly prominent role that provincial governments must now play in resolving important issues affecting native peoples adds a new set of legal, political, and constitutional problems to those regularly burdening federal-provincial relations. The issues are of a nature and complexity that no longer are capable of solution by simple appeal to the federal domain. For this reason, the locus of disputes on native matters has shifted from the federal to the provincial authorities without, however, any clear understanding among all parties as to the respective responsibilities to be exercised at the federal and provincial levels.

The absence of a coherent and comprehensive federal policy on native matters involving the provincial domain—as well as the overall economic one—raises apprehension in the native community over the extent to which the federal government is committed to protect native interests in the interplay of native society with powerful actors, such as provincial governments and multinational corporations. Such apprehensions lead naturally to the suspicion that having publicly withdrawn the ''white paper'' proposing a devolution of responsibilities for native affairs to the provinces, the federal government is nonetheless committed to its implementation unobtrusively, on a selective, piecemeal basis.

OVERALL STRATEGY: INTEGRATION OR ASSIMILATION

The strategy of integration coincides with the recent period characterized by expansion northward of large multinational corporations in search of new energy sources. Other events of significance that accompanied the integration strategy were: the "white paper"; the introduction of the government's multicultural policy; the student protest movement of the late 1960s; and the formation of national native organizations with government funding in 1970.

The government's policies of economic coexistence and cultural assimilation were not openly opposed by native groups until quite recently. Open resistance in the form of a protest crystallized in 1969, when the government put forward a "white paper" or plan in which the concept of "special status" for natives registered under the Indian Act was to be downgraded, if not abandoned entirely. The spiralling cost of administration due to increased dependency by natives on welfare payments was no doubt a major factor in the government's decision to speed up the assimilation process. The plan called for a transfer of responsibility for providing health, welfare, and education services from federal to provincial administration. In addition, the federal Department of Indian Affairs and Northen Development was to be atrophied in an attempt to normalize relations between natives and provincial agencies.

The response of native spokesmen was to reject the government's proposal. In 1970, they issued a plan of their own called the "red paper," which was presented to the prime minister. This called for reaffirmation of "special status," recognition of aboriginal rights, and the establishment of a consultation process whereby native leaders could meet with members of the Cabinet to formulate future policy. The government withdrew the white paper. The consultation process was established, and to a considerable extent, the decision-making authority of the bureaucrats in the Department of Indian Affairs has been curtailed.

As the government's new native policy is still evolving, only its direction, rather than its form, can be charted. The strategy of integration is consistent with the official policy of multiculturalism that applies to the country as a whole. As used by the government, multiculturalism distinguishes between socio-economic integration and cultural coexistence. That is, the various ethnic groups that comprise the population are expected to participate in all aspects of Canadian society as equals without necessarily giving up all distinctive cultural attributes. What exactly the government understands by the word *culture* is a matter of some debate (Porter 1975). Social scientists (Kroeber and Kluckhohn 1963) have identified several hundred usages for the word. The actual meaning is further complicated by the fact that Canada is a bilingual country with two official languages, French and English. None of the many native languages has official status.

In practice, the government's multicultural programme has taken the form of support through special funding to ethnic organizations for the encouragement of folk-art activities in which the quaint or semi-aesthetic aspects of a culture are stressed. Folk-dancing in colourful regional historical costumes, folk-music, and literature are but a few examples. Instruction in languages other than French or English is also supported, but outside the regular school curriculum and in most cases after regular school hours. From the operation of the programme, the impression gained is that the government views ethnic culture as a static, harmless force that belongs in a museum, rather than as a dynamic one that fashions the future. Museums, in this view, become instruments of a policy to remove any vital traces of a past culture from the centre of life—where it is proven to inspire or reinforce nationalist tendencies in marginal groups—and place them where, like cenotaphs to the dead, they may be harmlessly contemplated and even honoured.

The multicultural programme as applied to native peoples has undoubtedly resulted in a revival of interest in selective aspects of native cultures. Indian and Inuit arts and crafts were at first supported partly for aesthetic reasons, partly to improve the public image of native peoples, but mainly as an economic development measure to increase income. More recently, a number of literary works and poetry have been published in the native languages, along with magazines and newspapers. Ancient songs and dramas have been revised and presented on television, radio, and national theatre. In the northern parts of the country, government-run radio and television networks provide news and other broadcasting in native languages. Inuit art has already gained international recognition, and world interest in the art of other native groups is growing.

While the programme has·been of marginal value in improving economic conditions among impoverished native groups, it has contributed considerably to improving the public image of natives, though there still are white communities that openly discriminate against local natives. This is especially the case in northern frontier areas where the interests of the small white communities are at odds with those of the natives. Here, prejudice and discrimination take the form of racial separation in schools and residential areas, discouragement of interracial marriages, as well as type of employment available (Brody 1975). Whether intended or not, the programme has led to cultural revitalization and resistance to assimilation. Interest among native youths in native religious practices, ceremonials, and languages has accelerated, accompanied by a sense of pride, rather than shame, in ancestry. The depth and strength of the revitalization movement has not been sufficiently studied, but given the fact that a majority of young people speak only English or French, and are exposed increasingly to television with predominantly American content, the movement is fragile and possibly transitory. It depends too heavily on government, rather than local, financial support. Also, the desire for improved economic conditions and occupational betterment seems to take precedence in most areas over questions of cultural expression. Native parents want their children to learn English and become educated; so that they can get better jobs.

Integration as a strategy for incorporation recognizes transitional stages in the acculturation process. Its long-term aim is eventual assimilation of native groups into the French or English cultural streams. By encouraging greater participation in the market-place, to use Barth's phraseology (1969), and by allowing the coexistence of selective cultural elements, the potential for racial conflict is reduced in the polity. It is a conflict-management tactic. Questions of social-class inequalities and disproportionate overrepresentation in business and government sectors by one ethnic group are not addressed. Native collectivities are seen as socio-cultural units that are to be integrated into existing social class and political systems. In economic terms, the pre-capitalist economy, based on wildlife harvesting to which native peoples have been relegated, is to be changed to a rudimentary capitalist form. The strategy, for example, does not call for natives to be equal partners in the large-scale economic developments undertaken on their lands by large corporations, but to be paid compensation monies or given grants to start businesses of their own, mainly in tourism or handicraft production. An essential feature of this strategy is the formation of native-run local development corporations. Another is the formation of local native government structures, which are incorporated—like Chinese boxes—into an existing provincial or territorial government's municipal affairs departments. These features are spelled out in detail in the James Bay Agreement (1975) recently negotiated between Hydro-Quebec, the James Bay Development Corporation, the James Bay Energy Corporation, the Government of Canada, the Government of Quebec, the Grand Council of the Crees, and the Northern Quebec Inuit Association.

The integration formula for dealing with native peoples has these characteristics: firstly, the main mode of incorporation is through the integration of native corporate groups into municipal-type structures and economic development corporations. In areas where comprehensive land claims are outstanding, legal agreements replace treaties as the main instrument of land surrender. Compensation monies, communal tracts of land, resource harvesting rights to larger tracts replace reservations as part of the settlement package. Here and elsewhere, band government organizations are strengthened by shifting some decision-making powers to band councils or other leadership bodies. Bureaucracy is decentralized to regional administrative centres whose boundaries correspond to those of provinces or territories. Emphasis is placed on native collectivities becoming integrated as units into existing provincial or territorial governmental arrangements, with an initial period of federal funding for services rendered to those native peoples defined by the Indian Act.

Secondly, as integration proceeds and ties of unilateral dependence are weakened, the role of the federal government becomes less that of protector of, and spokesman for, native rights and more that of mediator or conflict manager in any disputes between native peoples and provincial agencies.

Native organizations at provincial and national levels are established with federal government funding. The elected leaders carry out negotiations and consultation with senior bureaucrats and on occasion Cabinet ministers. Conflict is managed through the techniques of bargaining and negotiations. Though opportunities for face-to-face communications between natives and governments are stressed as being important to the consultative process, both sides rely on lawyers, scientists, or other specialists to negotiate on their behalf. Since the government has overwhelmingly greater resources at its disposal than do native organizations, the latter must rely increasingly on paid white consultants to prepare and present their bargaining positions. Legal, rather than moral or political, solutions are sought to problems, and the threat of court action hangs over difficult negotiations. The reference to law and the courts, it can be said, is one of the principal conflict-management devices that are becoming characteristic of the integration strategy.

Finally, though the strategy tolerates the coexistence of selective cultural behaviour and attempts to incorporate native collectivities into existing governmental structures, it does not deal directly with questions of social segregation between whites and natives, nor with the exclusion of natives from the labour force. Rather, it encourages as a transitional measure the existence of two economic systems—one for whites and one for natives. Impoverished native living conditions are to be improved through funding enterprises controlled exclusively by native collectivities and based on renewable resource and wildlife harvesting, or tourism and handicraft manufacturing. The dual economies are particularly evident in areas in which native lands are required for large-scale energy or mineral developments. The concept of equality, that is, of natives becoming partners with corporations in the development of their lands or even being involved at the senior decision-making levels of the corporate structure, has not been seriously considered by government or corporations.

It is a matter of conjecture whether the integration formula is merely aimed at managing conflicts between natives and governments, or whether its real objective is the eventual assimilation of all native groups into the French or English cultural streams. The response by native spokesmen, mindful of past injustices, is predictably mixed. On the one hand, they welcome the weakening of unilateral dependence ties; on the other, they fear their gain in autonomy may be at the expense of further territorial losses and a diminishing of their ''special status'' position. Native leaders, with the exception of those in northern Quebec, have publicly criticized the James Bay Agreement as being ''assimilationist'' and a violation of aboriginal rights (Daniels 1979*b*).

Chapter 2.8

Summary and Conclusion

This study has attempted to present an overview of current issues and trends affecting native peoples in Canada. This was done to illustrate what, if any, vital role native people play in Canadian society, and how as a group they contribute to its cohesion.

A central contention has been that native societies, rather than forming part of Canadian society, exist as a cluster of satellites. The relationship they bear to other Canadians is through the instrumentalities of government on which they have become heavily dependent not only for financial aid but for guarantees of special status rights and the protection of lands. Government legislation, by defining who is an Indian, has influenced the definition of other native peoples and has resulted in a proliferation of categories or types of native people. Though the legislation was aimed at identifying a sector of the native population for purposes of determining eligibility to live on reserve lands, it has had the divisive effect of separating family members from one another, as well as dividing native communities. Since members of the general public do not know the difference between one category of native person and another, and classify a person as being an Indian on the basis of physical appearance, treatment accorded native persons regardless of category tends to be uniform. In areas where racial discrimination aimed at Indians is prevalent, discriminatory attitudes are extended to all categories of native persons.

This categorization has created difficulties, especially for those who identify as Métis and non-status Indians. Not having the special government protection accorded status Indians nor special tracts of land on which to live, their living conditions are frequently much worse than those prevailing among status Indians. Regarded as ordinary citizens like others in the provinces, they receive no special assistance and are frequently regarded as squatters on lands inhabited by them for generations. Although the Métis and non-status Indians have joined together in one national association, the objectives sought by each group differ. Whereas the Métis are seeking recognition as a distinct people or nation within Confederation, the non-status Indians are seeking recognition as Indians. There is also a difference in the objectives sought by the other categories of native people, and this has led them to form separate associations, which have not yet been able to come together in common cause.

While there were diverse cultures in aboriginal Canada in which members spoke a variety of languages and dialects, neither culture nor language played a significant role in the official definition of an Indian. Identification by individuals with a particular cultural and linguistic group is still a factor in native life today, but is diminishing in significance with each generation.

Few in numbers relative to the population of the country as a whole, native people are dispersed across the country, with many living in small, isolated settlements. With the exception of the Northwest Territories and the Yukon, they constitute a very small percentage of provincial populations. Because of this and the remoteness of communities from each other, they do not constitute a significant political force in either federal or provincial politics. Native people tend to vote as do other Canadians for one or the other of the two large established parties, with preferences for one or the other in some areas that reflect past missionary influences.

Native people as a group are the most impoverished in the country. Compared with the total population, they have the poorest health conditions, shortest life expectancy, and lowest standard of living. Their rate of unemployment is the highest in Canada and very few are represented in the skilled labour force or professions. They are overrepresented in jails and correctional institutions, but underrepresented in secondary and post-secondary schools. Chronic unemployment, low income, and lack of collateral place them at a disadvantage in dealing with private financial institutions, and as a consequence, they have been alienated from the sources of capital open to other Canadians.

Alienated from most of the vital social and economic institutions to which other Canadians belong, including trade unions, they are unable to assert much direct influence on Canadian society. What influence they are able to assert is indirect, through the mediation of government and bureaucracy. With the possible exception of Roman Catholic and Protestant religious organizations, their participation in transnational social institutions is minimal, and in this regard, they are not part of the cohesive network that operates to bind the various sections of Canadian society together. As already mentioned, the link to Canadian society has been primarily through government. This special relationship to the federal government grew out of historical conditions.

Both before and after Confederation, successive governments employed different strategies in efforts to incorporate and control native peoples. Three have been identified and have been termed strategies of accommodation, domination, and integration. The use of each roughly corresponds to periods of internal economic expansion and refers to the principal mode of relating to a vital dimension of native society. Ownership of land and control over resources have been the central issues that have most affected the development of native policy from the time of first contact to the present. In many respects, the Indian Act is a land-administration document describing who is legally entitled to use Indian lands, and how and under what conditions they can be sold, transferred, or assigned.

The accommodation strategy was the principal one employed in the early contact period by trading companies. It is characterized by incorporation of native collectivities into commercial arrangements in which control was effected through barter and the debt system. Though a change was effected in traditional modes of production, no concerted effort was made to change customs or social behaviour. Native people remained by and large separate from European society as represented by the military and commercial agents of the time.

The domination strategy was developed and coincided with western expansion and settlement following Confederation in 1867—that is, during the period when Canada was consolidating its territorial boundaries. Treaties for the surrender of land were entered into with various native groups and the reservation system was established. The first federal Indian Act came into existence in the mid−1870s, and the regulation of the affairs of those living on reserves was introduced. The reservation system best exemplifies the domination strategy, since around it grew a bureaucratic structure that permeated nearly every aspect of reserve life. Native collectivities were incorporated as extensions of the bureaucratic structure. In addition to the application of Canadian law, the principal method of social control was through the manipulation of government services in which certain individuals or groups were favoured over others. The domination strategy was paternalistic and produced a tie of unilateral dependence that still marks the relations between natives and government in some areas. While domination and paternalism had the effect of relegating natives to a pre-capitalist mode of production and led to impoverishment, it was nonetheless aimed at the gradual assimilation of individuals into the dominant society. The spread of Christianity was actively encouraged, and education in English or French was made mandatory.

The development and implementation of the integration strategy coincide with the recent period of northward expansion by large corporations in search of new energy sources. Ownership of land and resources has once again come into dispute, especially in areas where land was not ceded or reserves established. The main features of this strategy include a weakening of unilateral dependence ties, the use of legal agreements rather than treaties for the surrender of land, and reliance on consultation, bargaining, or negotiations to settle disputes. Incorporation and control are to be through the integration of native collectivities into existing provincial or municipal government structures within a dual economic framework, one for natives and the other for whites.

The emergence of national and provincial native associations in present form coincides with the shift to the integration strategy. A principal function of these associations is to participate with high level bureaucrats and politicians in a consultative process in which the native point of view on problems and issues is presented for resolution. While the process has resulted in a weakening of paternalistic bureaucratic control, it has placed native leaders in an ambivalent position. Funded entirely by government, divided in purpose and along other lines, the leadership has become vulnerable to manipulation and control by officialdom. In a number of respects, the associations themselves have become extensions of the bureaucracy, and in this role assist in containing or regulating the disputes between natives and government.

As pressure groups, the associations have had noteworthy success in influencing governments to increase expenditures for programmes aimed at alleviating poverty. Success in influencing policy formulation has not been as noteworthy, however, and basic questions involving native rights to land, extension of special status to all categories of native people, or the status of native societies in Confederation remain unanswered. Land and resource ownership disputes have been dealt with as a local problem, not as a national one requiring policy reformulation. This is resulting in a piecemeal approach to policy evolution, with compromises achieved at the negotiation table determining the direction.

The absence of a comprehensive federal policy covering all categories of native people is creating difficulties for provincial governments. Disputes are increasing concerning jurisdictional responsibilities over ownership of land in areas inhabited mainly by native people, and over cost-sharing arrangements for the provincial services provided for them, especially in urban centres. The shift in the locus of disputes from the federal to provincial domain is placing additional strain on already overburdened federal-provincial relations.

Though the level of discontent is increasing, it is problematic whether native people will be able to resolve their differences and form a united native movement of a kind that might pose a separatist threat to Confederation. These differences emanate not only from imposed status distinctions, differences in cultural backgrounds and regional experiences, and so forth, but also from a lack of consensus among all categories of native people on questions related to the specific nature of the relationship that native societies should have with Canadian society, and whether their collective interests lie in their participation in it.

Finally and by way of conclusion, several of the observations raised during the course of the discussion need to be emphasized.

Firstly, the integration strategy of incorporation, by offering something from both worlds, avoids the question of which right should be given precedence—the right to equality of opportunity within the dominant society or the right of native people, as historical national minorities, to self-determination. Instead, it attempts to promote both at the same time. The multicultural composition of Canada and the official policy of multicul turalism form part of the reason for this. For government to resolve one way or the other the contradiction inherent in the attempt could have repercussions for the rest of the country beyond those for native people. The present official policy of multiculturalism ignores the question of assimilation and is in many respects a variant of the integration strategy. To advocate a policy aimed at assimilating native people would cause concern among other cultural groups about government sincerity. On the other hand, to advocate a policy of self-determination for native people would provide a precedent and might be exploited by separatist elements, such as the Parti Québécois. To resolve the dilemma on the side of self-determination would require a new political formula for Canada going beyond the nineteenth-century Germanic notion of the state as being composed of one nation; this formula has not yet emerged in Canada.

Lastly, it is suggested that integration, as a means of incorporating and exercising control over native societies, is itself a conflict-management strategy. By permitting the coexistence of some dimensions of native socio-cultural systems and maintaining control over vital ones, such as the political and economic systems, the fact of control is made less obvious and resistance to it minimized.

Many policy makers may believe, but do not openly state, that the assimilation of native people into Canadian society is inevitable. For them, integration is viewed as a transitional step to that end. The hope underlying the belief is that through management of local economic enterprises, improved educational opportunities, and the acquisition of occupational skills (all of which are outlined in recent proposals for land-claims settlements), native people will be in a better position to enter Canadian society on a basis at least equal to that of recently arrived immigrants.

References and Bibliography

Armstrong, T.; Rogers, G.; and Rowley, G.
1978 *The Circumpolar North: A Political and Economic Geography.*
London: Methuen & Co.

Arnold, Robert D.
1976 *Alaska Native Land Claims.* Anchorage, Ala.: Alaska Native
Foundation.

Badcock, William T.
1976 "Who Owns Canada? Aboriginal Title and Canadian Courts."
Canadian Association in Support of the Native Peoples Bulletin 17,
July.

Barber, L.I.
1973 "The Implications of Indian Claims for Canada." Paper read at
Banff School of Advanced Management. Mimeographed.
1974 "The Basis for Indian Claims." Paper read at the Saskatoon
Institute of Northern Studies, Saskatchewan. Mimeographed.

Barrados, Maria
1977 "Multilingualism of Natives in the Mackenzie District: An Analysis
of Data from the Northern Manpower Survey Program." Mimeographed. Ottawa: Carleton University.

Barth, Fredrik, ed.
1969 *Ethnic Groups and Boundaries: The Social Organization of Culture
Difference.* London: George Allen & Unwin.

Berger, Thomas R.
1977 *Northern Frontier, Northern Homeland: The Report of the Mackenzie Valley Pipeline Inquiry.* 2 vols. Ottawa: Supply and Services
Canada.

Blishen, Bernard R., and McRoberts, Hugh A.
1976 "A Revised Socioeconomic Index for Occupations in Canada."
Canadian Review of Sociology and Anthropology 13: 71−79.

Bodley, John H.
1975 *Victims of Progress.* Don Mills, Ont.: Cummings Publishing Co.

Booz, Allen, and Hamilton Associates Ltd.
1969 "Study of Health Services for Canadian Indians." Mimeographed.
Ottawa: Health and Welfare Canada.

Bowles, Richard P.; Hanley, James L.; Hodgins, Bruce W.; and Rawlyk,
George A.
1972 *The Indian: Assimilation, Integration or Separation.* Scarborough,
Ont.: Prentice-Hall of Canada.

Brody, Hugh
  1971 "Indians on Skid Row." Mimeographed. Ottawa: Information Canada.
  1975 *The People's Land*. Markham, Ont.: Penguin Books Canada.
Burnford, Sheila
  1969 *Without Reserve*. Toronto: McClelland and Stewart.
Canada, Department of Indian Affairs and Northern Development
  1970 *Linguistic and Cultural Affiliations of Canadian Indian Bands*. Ottawa: Queen's Printer.
  1972 "Registered Indian Social Assistance Expenditures by Region, 1963–1964 to Date." Mimeographed. Ottawa: Department of Indian Affairs and Northern Development.
  1973a "Death Rates by Main Cause and Sex, Registered Indians and Canadian Population, 1968." Mimeographed. Ottawa: Department of Indian Affairs and Northern Development.
  1973b "Indian Inmate Population of Federal Penitentiaries as of January 30, 1973." Mimeographed. Ottawa: Department of Indian Affairs and Northern Development.
  1973c "Percentage of Deaths Due to Violence, Registered Canadian Indians and Canadian Population, 1964–1968." Mimeographed. Ottawa: Department of Indian Affairs and Northern Development.
  1975a "Achievement and Destination of Registered Indian Students by Region, 1974–1975." Mimeographed. Ottawa: Department of Indian Affairs and Northern Development.
  1975b "Enrolment of Indian Students in Federal and Non-Federal Schools by Grade and Region." Mimeographed. Ottawa: Department of Indian Affairs and Northern Development.
  1975c "Registered Indians in Grade 1 and Percentages of Continuing Students in Subsequent Grades, 1949–1950 to 1975–1976." Mimeographed. Ottawa: Department of Indian Affairs and Northern Development.
  1976a "Achievement and Destination of Registered Indian Students by Region, 1975–1976." Mimeographed. Ottawa: Department of Indian Affairs and Northern Development.
  1976b "Crude and Standardized Cause-Specific Death Rates for the Registered Indian Population, 1974." Mimeographed. Ottawa: Department of Indian Affairs and Northern Development.
  1976c "Enrolment of Registered Indian Students in Federal and Non-Federal Schools by Grade and Region, 1975–1976." Mimeographed. Ottawa: Department of Indian Affairs and Northern Development.
  1976d "Indian Economic Activity, 1973–1974–1975, Canada." Mimeographed. Ottawa: Department of Indian Affairs and Northern Development.

1976*e* "Indian Housing Survey, 1975." Mimeographed. Ottawa: Department of Indian Affairs and Northern Development.

1976*f* "Programme Summary: Employment and Related Services Division. Cumulative Totals of Applications Approved to March 31, 1976." Mimeographed. Ottawa: Department of Indian Affairs and Northern Development.

1976*g* "Registered Indian Enrolment in Federal and Non-Federal Secondary Schools by Grade, 1948–1949 to 1975–1976." Mimeographed. Ottawa: Department of Indian Affairs and Northern Development.

1976*h* "Registered Indian Population by Sex and Year for Canada and Provinces, 1970–1974." Mimeographed. Ottawa: Department of Indian Affairs and Northern Development.

1977*a* "Achievement and Destination of Registered Indian Students by Region, 1976–1977." Mimeographed. Ottawa: Department of Indian Affairs and Northern Development.

1977*b* "Average Age of Death for Registered Indians, Selected Years, 1966, 1971, 1975." Mimeographed. Ottawa: Department of Indian Affairs and Northern Development.

1977*c* "Enrolment of Registered Indian Students in Post-Secondary Courses, 1957–1958 to 1975–1976." Mimeographed. Ottawa: Department of Indian Affairs and Northern Development.

1977*d* *Facts and Figures: Northwest Territories*. Ottawa: Supply and Services Canada.

1977*e* "Indian University Students." Mimeographed. Ottawa: Department of Indian Affairs and Northern Development.

1977*f* "Inmate Population of Federal Penitentiaries by Ethnic Origin for All Canada as of December 1, 1976." Mimeographed. Ottawa: Department of Indian Affairs and Northern Development.

1977*g* "Number of Registered Indian Students by School Type and Region, 1975–1976." Mimeographed. Ottawa: Department of Indian Affairs and Northern Development.

1977*h* "Registered Indian Population and Annual Growth Rate for Canada and Regions: For Selected Years, 1949–1975." Mimeographed. Ottawa: Department of Indian Affairs and Northern Development.

1978*a* "Achievement and Destination of Registered Indian Students by Region, 1977–1978." Mimeographed. Ottawa: Department of Indian Affairs and Northern Development.

1978*b* "Annual Percentage Increases in the Registered Indian Population of Canada Since 1924." Mimeographed. Ottawa: Department of Indian Affairs and Northern Development.

1978*c* "Enrolment of Registered Indian Students in Federal and Non-Federal Schools, by Grade and Province, 1976–1977." Mimeographed. Ottawa: Department of Indian Affairs and Northern Development.

1978*d* "Enrolment of Registered Indian Students in Post-Secondary Courses, 1957–1958 to 1976–1977." Mimeographed. Ottawa: Department of Indian Affairs and Northern Development.

1978*e* "Enrolment of Students in Federal and Non-Federal Schools, by Grade and Province, 1977–1978." Mimeographed. Ottawa: Department of Indian Affairs and Northern Development.

1978*f* "Indian University Students." Mimeographed. Ottawa: Department of Indian Affairs and Northern Development.

1978*g* "Registered Indian Enrolment in Federal and Non-Federal Secondary Schools by Grade, 1948–1949 to 1977–1978." Mimeographed. Ottawa: Department of Indian Affairs and Northern Development.

1978*h* "Student Population by Languages Spoken." Mimeographed. Ottawa: Department of Indian Affairs and Northern Development.

1979*a* "Indian Economic Development Fund Approved Offers by Fiscal Year and Business Category." Mimeographed. Ottawa: Department of Indian Affairs and Northern Development.

1979*b* "Registered Indian Social Assistance Expenditures by Region, 1973–1974 to Date." Mimeographed. Ottawa: Department of Indian Affairs and Northern Development.

Canada, Department of Regional Economic Expansion

1970 *Programs of Interest to Indians and Métis*. Ottawa: Queen's Printer.

Canada, Department of the Secretary of State

1973*a* *First Canadian Conference on Multiculturalism*. Ottawa: Supply and Services Canada.

1973*b* *Study of the Problems of Discrimination Against Indigenous Populations*. Ottawa: Secretary of State.

1976 *Multiculturalism as State Policy: Conference Report, Second Canadian Conference on Multiculturalism, Government Conference Centre, Ottawa, February 13–15, 1976*. Ottawa: Supply and Services Canada.

Canada, Government of the Northwest Territories

1977 *Annual Report of the Government of the Northwest Territories: Council in Transition*. Ottawa: Supply and Services Canada.

Canada, Health and Welfare Canada

1975*a* *Annual Report, 1975, Medical Services Branch*. Ottawa: Health and Welfare Canada.

1975*b* *Nutrition Canada. Indian Survey*. Ottawa: Information Canada.

1978 "Health Data Book." Mimeographed. Ottawa: Health and Welfare Canada.

Canada, Indian Claims Commission

1977 *Commissioner on Indian Claims: Statements and Submissions, a Report*. Ottawa: Supply and Services Canada.

Canada, Royal Commission on Bilingualism and Biculturalism
1970 *Report*. Book 4, *The Cultural Contribution of the Other Ethnic Groups*. Ottawa: Queen's Printer.
Canada, Statistics Canada
1973*a* *1971 Census of Canada*. Vol. 1 (Part 1), *Population: Census Subdivisions (Historical)*. Cat. no. 92−702. Ottawa: Information Canada.
1973*b* *1971 Census of Canada*. Vol. 1 (Part 3), *Population: General Characteristics—Ethnic Groups*. Cat. no. 92−723. Ottawa: Information Canada.
1974*a* *1971 Census of Canada*. Vol. 1 (Part 5), *Population: The Out-of-School Population*. Cat. no. 92−743. Ottawa: Information Canada.
1974*b* *Perspective Canada: A Compendium of Social Statistics*. Ottawa: Information Canada.
1976*a* *Estimates of Population by Sex and Age for Canada and the Provinces*. Cat. no. 91−202. Ottawa: Supply and Services Canada.
1976*b* *The Labour Force*. Cat. no. 71−001. Ottawa: Supply and Services Canada, February and March.
1976*c* *1971 Census of Canada*. Vol. 5 (Part 1), *Profile Studies: Demographic Characteristics—Language in Canada*. Cat. no. 99−707. Ottawa: Statistics Canada.
1977*a* *Canada Year Book, 1976−77. Special Edition: Annual Review of Economic, Social and Political Developments in Canada*. Ottawa: Supply and Services Canada.
1977*b* *1971 Census of Canada*. Vol. 5 (Part 1), *Profile Studies: Demographic Characteristics−Educational Attainment in Canada*. Cat. no. 99−708. Ottawa: Supply and Services Canada.
1977*c* *Perspective Canada II: A Compendium of Social Statistics 1977*. Ottawa: Supply and Services Canada.
1978*a* "Birth Rates, Infant Mortality Rates, All Deaths, Indians, Inuit and Canada, 1960−1976." Mimeographed. Ottawa: Statistics Canada.
1978*b* *Estimates of Population for Canada and the Provinces*. Cat. no. 91−201. Ottawa: Supply and Services Canada.
Canada, Statutes of Canada
1857 "An Act to Encourage the Gradual Civilization of the Indian Tribes in this Province, and to Amend the Laws Respecting Indians." 20 Victoria, Cap. 26. Toronto: Stewart Derbishire and George Desbarats.
Canadian Catholic Conference Administrative Board
1975 *Northern Development: At What Cost?* Ottawa: Canadian Catholic Conference.

Canadian Corrections Association
1967 *Indians and the Law*. Ottawa: Canadian Welfare Council.
Caplow, Theodore
1969 *Two Against One, Coalitions in Triads*. Englewood Cliffs, N.J.: Prentice-Hall, Inc.
Cardinal, Harold
1969 *The Unjust Society: The Tragedy of Canada's Indians*. Edmonton, Alta.: Hurtig Publishers.
Chamberlin, J.E.
1975 *The Harrowing of Eden: White Attitudes Toward North American Natives*. Toronto: Fitzhenry and Whiteside.
Cox, Bruce
1973 *Cultural Ecology: Readings on the Canadian Indians and Eskimos*. Carleton Library Series. Toronto: McClelland and Stewart.
1975 "Changing Perceptions of Industrial Development in the North." *Human Organization* 34: 27−33.
Crowe, Keith
1974 *A History of the Original Peoples of Northern Canada*. Montreal: McGill-Queen's University Press for Arctic Institute of North America.
Cumming, Peter A.
1969 "Indian Rights: A Century of Oppression." *Toronto Globe and Mail*, 24 February.
1977 *Canada: Native Land Rights and Northern Development*. Documentation Series, no. 26. Copenhagen: International Work Group for Indigenous Affairs.
Cumming, Peter A., and Mickenberg, Neil H., eds.
1972 *Native Rights in Canada*. 2d ed. Toronto: General Publishing Co. for Indian-Eskimo Association.
Daniels, Harry W.
1979a *The Forgotten People: Métis and Non-Status Indian Land Claims*. Ottawa: Native Council of Canada.
1979b *We Are the New Nation*. Ottawa: Native Council of Canada.
Dené of the Northwest Territories
1975 "The Dené: Land and Unity for the Native People of the Mackenzie Valley: A Statement of Rights." Mimeographed. Yellowknife, NWT: Dené of the Northwest Territories.
Depape, D.W. Phillips, and Cooke, A.
1975 *A Socioeconomic Evaluation of Inuit Livelihood and Natural Resource Utilization in the Tundra of the Northwest Territories*. Inuit Tapirisat of Canada: Renewable Resources Studies, vol. 4. Edmonton, Alta., and Waterloo, Ont.: University of Edmonton and University of Waterloo.

Deprez, Paul, and Bisson, A.
1975 *Demographic Differences Between Indians and Métis in Fort Resolution*. Series 2, research report no. 22. Winnipeg, Man.: Center for Settlement Studies, University of Manitoba.

Deprez, Paul, and Sigurdson, G.
1969 *The Economic Status of the Canadian Indian: A Re-examination*. Series 2, research report no. 1. Winnipeg, Man.: Center for Settlement Studies, University of Manitoba.

DeVries, John, and Vallée, Frank G.
1975 "Data Book on Aspects of Language Demography in Canada." Mimeographed. Ottawa: Carleton University.

Dosman, Edgar J.
1972 *Indians: The Urban Dilemma*. Toronto: McClelland and Stewart.

Driver, Harold E.
1969 *Indians of North America*. 2d rev. ed. Chicago, Ill.: University of Chicago Press.

Drucker, Philip.
1955 *Indians of the Northwest Coast*. New York: Natural History Press.

Dunning, R.W.
1959 "Ethnic Relations and the Marginal Man in Canada." *Human Organization* 18: 117−22.

Elliott, Jean Leonard, ed.
1971 *Minority Canadians*. Vol. 1, *Native Peoples*. Scarborough, Ont.: Prentice-Hall of Canada.

Fidler, Dick
1970 *Red Power in Canada*. Toronto: Vanguard Publications.

Finkler, Harold W.
1975 *Inuit and the Administration of Criminal Justice in the Northwest Territories: The Case of Frobisher Bay*. Montreal: Centre international de criminologie comparée, Université de Montréal.

Forrest, Anne
1976 "An Evaluation of the Alaska Native Claims Settlement Act." Mimeographed. Yellowknife, NWT: Indian Brotherhood of the Northwest Territories.

Fransen, J.J.
1964 "Employment Experiences and Economic Position of a Selected Group of Indians in Metropolitan Toronto." Master's thesis, University of Toronto.

Frideres, James S.
1974 *Canada's Indians: Contemporary Conflicts*. Scarborough, Ont.: Prentice-Hall of Canada.

Galtung, Johan
1969 "Violence, Peace, and Peace Research." *Journal of Peace Research* 6: 167−91.

1971 "A Structural Theory of Imperialism." *Journal of Peace Research* 8: 81–118.

Gibbins, R., and Ponting, J.R.
1977 "Findings and Implications of a National Survey on Attitudes Towards Indians." Mimeographed. Calgary: University of Calgary.

Giraud, Marcel
1945 *Le Métis canadien: son rôle dans l'histoire des provinces de l'ouest.* Paris: Institut d'ethnologie.

Gordon, Milton M.
1964 *Assimilation in American Life: The Role of Race, Religion and National Origins.* New York: Oxford University Press.

Grygier, Tadeusz
1973 "Crime and Social Policy in Churchill: Summary of Findings and Recommendations." Mimeographed. Ottawa: Department of Indian Affairs and Northern Development.

Hawthorn, Harry Bertram, ed.
1966–1967 *A Survey of the Contemporary Indians of Canada: A Report on Economic, Political, Educational Needs and Policies.* 2 vols. Ottawa: Information Canada.

Haycock, Ronald Graham
1971 *The Image of the Indian.* Monograph Series. Waterloo, Ont.: Wilfrid Laurier University Press.

Honigmann, John J., and Honigmann, Irma
1965 *Eskimo Townsmen.* Ottawa: Canadian Research Centre for Anthropology.
1970 *Arctic Townsmen.* Ottawa: Canadian Research Centre for Anthropology.

Hoople, J., and Newbery, J.W.E.
1974 "And What About Canada's Native Peoples?" *Canadian Association in Support of the Native Peoples Bulletin* 15.

James Bay Agreement, The
1975 3 vols. Quebec: Éditeur officiel du Québec.

Jenness, Diamond
1964 *Eskimo Administration: Canada.* Vol. 2. Technical Paper no. 14. Montreal: Arctic Institute of North America.

Jenness, Diamond, and National Museum of Canada
1963 *The Indians of Canada.* Anthropological Series, no. 15. Ottawa: Queen's Printer.

Kenora Social Planning Council, Violent Deaths Committee
1973 "They Were Young People: A Study of the Kenora Area, With Primary Emphasis on Apparent Alcohol Involvement." Mimeographed. Kenora, B.C.: Kenora Social Planning Council.

Kroeber, A.L., and Kluckhohn, Clyde
1963 *Culture: A Critical Review of Concepts and Definitions.* New York: Vintage Books.

Lazore, Glen
 1977 *Native People and Mining: The Opportunity for an Untapped Resource*. Mineral Bulletin MR 171. Ottawa: Supply and Services Canada.
Lotz, James
 1971 *Northern Realities; The Future of Northern Development in Canada*. Chicago, Ill.: Follett Publishing Co.
 1972 "Socioeconomic Development in the Canadian North: Some Perspectives and Problems." In *Education in the North: Selected Papers of the First International Conference on Cross-Cultural Education in the Circumpolar Nations*, edited by Frank Darnell, pp. 229–39. Montreal: Arctic Institute of North America.
Lysyk, K.
 1968 "Resource Paper on Human Rights and Canada's Native People." Paper read at the Ninth Annual Meeting and Conference of the Indian-Eskimo Association of Canada, September, in Toronto. Mimeographed.
Mann, Donald
 1975 *The Socioeconomic Impact of Non-Renewable Resource Development on the Inuit of Northern Canada*. Inuit Tapirisat of Canada: Renewable Resources Studies, vol. 8. London, Ont., and Waterloo, Ont.: University of Western Ontario and University of Waterloo.
Manuel, George, and Posluns, Michael
 1974 *The Fourth World: An Indian Reality*. New York: Free Press.
Marx, Gary T.
 1971 *Racial Conflict: Tension and Change in American Society*. Boston: Little, Brown & Co.
Morgan, Lewis H.
 1907 *Ancient Society: Or Researches in the Lines of Human Progress From Savagery Through Barbarism to Civilization*, edited by E.B. Leacock. Magnolia, Mass.: Peter Smith Publisher Inc.
 1966 *League of the Ho-de-no-sau-nee or Iroquois*. 2 vols. 1904. Reprint, edited and annotations by Henry M. Lloyd. New York: Burt Franklin, Pub.
Nagler, Mark
 1972 *Perspectives on the North American Indians*. Toronto: McClelland and Stewart.
 1973 *Indians in the City: A Study of the Urbanization of Indians in Toronto*. 2d ed. Ottawa: Canadian Research Centre for Anthropology.
 1975 *Natives Without a Home: The Canadian Indian*. Don Mills, Ont.: Longman Canada.

Native Council of Canada
1975a "Economic Development in a Sub-Region." Mimeographed. Ottawa: Native Council of Canada.
1975b "Métis and Non-Status Indian Economic and Social Aims and Priorities." Mimeographed. Ottawa: Native Council of Canada.
1975c "Position Paper of the Native Council of Canada on Aboriginal Rights." Mimeographed. Ottawa: Native Council of Canada.
1977a "Métis and Non-Status Indian Crime and Justice Commission Report." Mimeographed. Ottawa: Native Council of Canada.
1977b "Minutes of the Native Council of Canada National Sixth Annual Assembly Meeting." Mimeographed. Ottawa: Native Council of Canada.
"Native Housing: Overcoming Government Neglect."
1976 *Canadian Association in Support of the Native Peoples Bulletin* 17.
O'Malley, Martin
1976 *The Past and Future Lands: An Account of the Berger Inquiry Into the Mackenzie Valley Pipeline*. Toronto: Peter Martin Associates.
Owen, Thomas, and Associates
1975 "Distribution of Population by Ethnic Group, Age and Sex, 1971." Mimeographed. Ottawa: Department of Regional Economic Expansion.
1976 "Barriers to Native Labour Entry and Employment." Mimeographed. Ottawa: Department of Regional Economic Expansion.
Patterson, E. Palmer
1971 *The Canadian Indian: A History Since 1500*. Don Mills, Ont.: Collier-Macmillan Canada.
Pelletier, W.; Poole, D.G.; Mackenzie, J.A.; Thomas, R.K.; and Toombs, F.C.
1971 *For Every North American Indian Who Begins to Disappear, I Also Begin to Disappear; Being a Collection of Essays Concerned With the Quality of Human Relations Between the Red and White Peoples of This Continent*. Toronto: Neewin Publishing Co.
Pineo, Peter C.; Porter, John; and McRoberts, Hugh A.
1977 "The 1971 Census and the Socioeconomic Classifications of Occupations." *Canadian Review of Sociology and Anthropology* 14: 91–102.
Pipes, Richard
1975 "Reflections on the Nationality Problems in the Soviet Union." In *Ethnicity: Theory and Experience*, edited by Nathan Glazer and Daniel P. Moynihan. Cambridge, Mass.: Harvard University Press.
Porter, John
1975 "Ethnic Pluralism in Canadian Perspective." In *Ethnicity: Theory and Experience*, edited by Nathan Glazer and Daniel P. Moynihan. Cambridge, Mass.: Harvard University Press

Rath, Otto
1975 "Tuberculosis Among the Indian and Inuit." Ottawa: Health and Welfare Canada.
Rayner, L.
1977*a* "Notes on the Nelson River Diversion Project." Mimeographed. Ottawa: Native Council of Canada.
1977*b* "Notes on the Reed Paper Limited Mercury Pollution Case." Ottawa: Native Council of Canada.
Richardson, Boyce
1976 "Lessons From the James Bay Settlement." In *Dené Rights*, vol. 7, pp. 37 – 56. Yellowknife, NWT: Indian Brotherhood of the North-west Territories.
Robertson, Heather
1970 *Reservations Are for Indians*. Toronto: James Lorimer & Co.
Ross, W. Gillies
1975 *Whaling and Eskimos: Hudson Bay 1860 – 1915*. Publications in Ethnology. Ottawa: National Museum of Canada.
Rowley, Graham
1972 "The Canadian Eskimo Today." *Polar Record* 16: 201 – 5.
Rudnicki, W.
1976 "An Assessment of Provincial Costs of Services to Status Indians in Manitoba." Mimeographed. Report to the Government of Manitoba. Ottawa: Policy Development Group Ltd.
Sanders, Douglas E.
1973 *Native People in Areas of Internal National Expansion: Indians and Inuit in Canada*. Documentation Series, no. 14. Copenhagen: International Work Group for Indigenous Affairs.
1976*a* "Aboriginal Title: A Legal Perspective. A Summary of Evidence and Testimony to the Mackenzie Valley Pipeline Inquiry." Vancouver: University of British Columbia.
1976*b* *Land Claims: A Legal History of the Land Claims*. Victoria, B.C.: Vancouver Island Cultural Educational Center.
Schaefer, Otto
1973 "The Changing Health Picture in the Canadian North." *Canadian Journal of Ophthalmology* 8: 196 – 204.
Schaefer, O.; Hildes, J.A.; Medd, L.M.; and Cameron, D.G.
1975 "The Changing Pattern of Neoplastic Disease in Canadian Eskimos." *Canadian Medical Association Journal* 112: 1399 – 1404.
Schelling, Thomas C.
1960 *Strategy of Conflict*. Cambridge, Mass.: Harvard University Press.
Schwartz, G.
1977 "Survey of Métis and Non-Status Indians: National Demographic and Labour Force Report." Mimeographed. Ottawa: Native Council of Canada and Canada Employment and Immigration Commission.

Sealey, P. Bruce, and Lussier, A.S.
  1975 *The Métis: Canada's Forgotten People.* Winnipeg, Man.: Manitoba Métis Federation Press.
Siggner, A.J.
  1977 *Preliminary Results From a Study of 1966−71 Migration Patterns Among Status Indians in Canada.* Working Paper no. 1. Ottawa: Department of Indian Affairs and Northern Development.
Siggner, A.J.; Locatelli, Chantal; and Stewart, Del
  1978 "Socio-Economic and Demographic Trends for the Registered Indian Population: A Working Paper." Mimeographed. Ottawa: Department of Indian Affairs and Northern Development.
Smith, Clagett G., ed.
  1972 *Conflict Resolution: Contributions of the Social Sciences.* Notre-Dame, Ind.: University of Notre-Dame Press.
Smith, Derek G., ed.
  1975 *Canadian Indians and the Law: Selected Documents, 1663−1972.* Toronto: McClelland and Stewart.
Stanbury, W.T.
  1975 *Success and Failure: Indians in Urban Society.* Vancouver: University of British Columbia Press.
Stanley, G.F.G.
  1978 *The Birth of Western Canada: A History of the Riel Rebellions.* Toronto: University of Toronto Press.
Stewart, Delbert D.
  1977 "Socio-Economic Forecasts for Registered Indians in Canada, 1976−77 to 1989−90." Mimeographed. Ottawa: Department of Indian Affairs and Northern Development.
Taylor, John Leonard
  1975 "Historical Introduction to Métis Claims in Canada." Mimeographed. Ottawa: Indian Claims Commission.
Toombs, Farrell C.
  1971 "The Indian in Canada: A Query on Dependence." In *For Every North American Indian Who Begins to Disappear, I Also Begin to Disappear; Being a Collection of Essays Concerned With the Quality of Human Relations Between the Red and White Peoples of This Continent.* Toronto: Neewin Publishing Co.
Tussing, Areon R.
  1971 *Alaska Pipeline Report: Alaska's Economy, Oil and Gas Industry Development, and the Economic Impact of Building and Operating the TransAlaska Pipeline.* Joint Institute of Social and Economic Research Series, no. 31. Seattle, Wash.: University of Washington Press.
Usher, Peter
  1975 "The Class System, Metropolitan Dominance and Northern Development." Paper read at the Annual Meeting of the Canadian Association of Geographers, 29 May, in Vancouver. Mimeographed.

Valentine, Victor F.
1954 "Some Problems of the Métis of Northern Saskatchewan." *Canadian Journal of Economics and Political Science* 20: 89–95.
1966 "The Forgotten People." In *People of Light and Dark*, edited by the Department of Indian Affairs and Northern Development. Ottawa: Queen's Printer.

Valentine, Victor F., and Vallée, Frank G.
1968 *Eskimo of the Canadian Arctic*. Toronto: McClelland and Stewart.

Von Clausewitz, Karl
1968 *On War*. Edited by Anatol Rapoport. London: Penguin Books.

Wah-shee, J.J.
1975 "The Indian and Economic Development." Paper read at the Manitoba Economic Development Conference, 29 January, in Winnipeg, Man. Mimeographed.

Walsh, Gerald
1971 *Indians in Transition*. Toronto: McClelland and Stewart.

Watkins, Mel
1976 "The Meaning of Underdevelopment." In *Dené Rights*, vol. 5, pp. 38–70. Yellowknife, NWT: Indian Brotherhood of the Northwest Territories.
1977 *Dené Nation: The Colony Within*. Toronto: University of Toronto Press.

Waubageshig, comp.
1970 *The Only Good Indian: Essays by Canadian Indians*. Toronto: New Press.

Whiteside, Don
1973a "A Good Blanket Has Four Corners: A Comparison of Aboriginal Administration in Canada and the United States." *The Indian Voice*, (May-June, July).
1973b "Historical Development of Aboriginal Political Associations in Canada." Mimeographed. Ottawa: National Indian Brotherhood.
1974 "Aboriginal Policy in Canada Since World War II." Paper read at the American Civilization Symposium, 7–8 March, at New York State University College.

Wilson, James
1974 *Canada's Indians*. Minority Rights Group, no. 21. New York: Interbook, Inc.

Wuttunee, William I.C.
1971 *Ruffled Feathers: Indians in Canadian Society*. 2d ed. Calgary: Bell Books.

Zentner, Henry
1973 *The Indian Identity Crisis: Inquiries Into the Problems and Prospects of Societal Development Among Native Peoples*. Calgary: Strayer Publications.

Part Three

Linguistic Boundaries and the Cohesion of Canada

by

Raymond Breton

and

Daiva Stasiulis

Introduction

Canada is characterized by the presence of two main linguistic communities: anglophone and francophone. In many ways, Canadians behave, react, think, and feel as members of one or the other of these communities. Of course, language is not the only component of the social identity of Canadians. Their identity is defined by a number of other group memberships, such as occupational, religious, ethnic. However, even though these are important, there are many circumstances in which people behave as members of one or the other of the linguistic communities. In addition, the linguistic cleavage is present within several organizations, such as labour unions, schools, businesses, churches, athletic clubs, and government.

Because of its fundamental character, we can expect the linguistic cleavage to have a significant impact on the degree of cohesion of Canadian society. Not surprisingly, many Canadians perceive problems of national unity as problems pertaining to English-French relations. This cleavage is the concern of this part of the study. Various dimensions of English-French relations and their implications for the cohesion of Canadian society will be explored. Before describing the dimensions considered in the study, we will comment on a few critical features of the linguistic cleavage as a characteristic of Canadian society generally, and as a factor for its cohesion in particular. These features are the existence of parallel social networks and institutions for anglophones and francophones, the size and internal differentiation of each community, and the presence of common institutions.

PARALLEL SOCIAL NETWORKS AND INSTITUTIONS FOR ANGLOPHONES AND FRANCOPHONES

Foremost among the features of the linguistic cleavage is that it results in a far-reaching segmentation of the structure of society and its institutions. Segmentation implies much more than differences between people; it refers to the way in which their social relationships and institutions are organized. To a significant degree, anglophones and francophones live separately in their own social circles and institutions. Segmentation, which is a matter of degree, refers to (1) the enclosure of social networks along ethnic lines; and (2) "a social structure compartmentalized into analogous, parallel, non-complementary but distinguishable sets of institutions" (van den Berghe

1969, p. 67). In Canada, language constitutes the basis of segmentation. The anglophone and francophone segments contain largely self-enclosed social networks and show a high degree of institutional completeness. It is thus possible to refer to the linguistic segments as subsocieties (the expressions *community* and *collectivity* will be used synonymously).

Social enclosure refers to the existence of separate networks of social relations among the members of a society. It refers first to the existence of social boundaries and mechanisms for the maintenance of such boundaries between the linguistic groups. Secondly, it refers to a particular pattern in the contours of such boundaries. Indeed, enclosure involves a certain superimposition of social boundaries, or perhaps more accurately, the containment of the many networks of social affiliations within the more basic and inclusive linguistic boundaries. Group memberships may overlap considerably within the linguistic segments, but the resulting criss-crossing of social affiliations does not extend over the basic linguistic line of social division.

As Barth mentions (1969, pp. 9−10), the existence of a boundary does not mean that there is no interaction between the members of each segment, nor that there is no mobility between them. Rather, the interaction and mobility that take place are regulated in such a way as to preserve the boundaries between the segments.

While enclosure refers to the structure of social relations, compartmentalization refers to the structure of institutions in the society. Each linguistic segment has its own set of institutions. This does not necessarily imply culturally distinct institutions and practices. For example, both English and French in Canada operate within a variant of the British parliamentary system. Compartmentalization is not a statement about cultural pluralism; rather, it is a statement about the locus of the institutional authority and clientele. For example, parallel educational structures refer to the existence of at least two sets of educational organizations serving different clienteles and under the control of different élites, not to their cultural difference. Since both the clientele and the élite are defined along the lines of social segmentation, the processes of institutional compartmentalization and social enclosure reinforce each other.[1]

This is not to say that cultural differences are irrelevant. Indeed, to the extent that they exist, they support and sometimes accentuate the social and institutional segmentation. The task of this study is to try to understand the sources of cohesion and tensions between anglophones and francophones in Canada. It is to identify the factors that bring about strains between the two communities; the conditions leading to the social and political expression of

---

[1] For a further discussion of ethnic segmentation and a comparison with ethnic heterogeneity (a situation of ethnic differentiation involving very limited, if any, social enclosure and institutional compartmentalization—a situation characterizing the ''other ethnic groups''), see Breton (1978, pp. 56−62).

these strains; and the processes through which they are handled. The postulate is that such factors, conditions, and processes are to be found primarily in the existence of parallel social networks and institutions, and in the ways in which they are structured, rather than in the existence of cultural differences.

SIZE AND INTERNAL DIFFERENTIATION OF LINGUISTIC COMMUNITIES

In absolute terms, both linguistic subsocieties are large in population, and even though the francophone community is less numerous in relative terms, it nevertheless constitutes a significant minority. And the two communities are concentrated in different parts of the territory. Thus, to a certain extent, the linguistic and regional cleavages coincide, but not completely. Different regional identities exist within both the anglophone and francophone communities. Being a Newfoundlander, an Ontarian, or a Westerner, for example, are meaningful identities for large numbers of anglophones living in these different parts of the country. Similarly, being an Acadian, a Québécois, a Franco-Manitoban, or an Ontarian are meaningful identities for many francophones in the corresponding parts of the country. Recently, Lee and Lapointe (1979) argued that the francophone community in Canada is becoming progressively more differentiated, in such a way that its members increasingly think of themselves and organize themselves on a regional basis. It should be noted, however, that in the case of the Acadians, this self-differentiation has existed for a long time.

The two linguistic subsocieties are not homogeneous—a fact that is frequently used to argue against the existence of two subsocieties. The anglophone community, for instance, exhibits considerable ethnic heterogeneity. For an important part of that community, language and ethnicity are two distinct components of social identity, the language spoken (and in most cases the only language known) not being the language corresponding to the ethnic origin. The correspondence exists only for those of British origin, although even in their case, the correspondence is not complete, as some people of British origin do not consider English their mother tongue.

The francophone community is also differentiated ethnically, although much less so. Some members of other ethnic groups have become acculturated into the francophone community—a phenomenon that may increase with the greater importance of French in business and industry, and with the application of the legislation requiring immigrants settling in Quebec to send their children to French schools.

Nevertheless, despite internal differentiation of a regional or ethnic character, the anglophone and francophone communities do exist. The linguistic cleavage is significant in terms of identity, social networks, and social organization. This is especially striking in the case of many members of the "other ethnic groups," who at times think of themselves, behave, and react as members of their respective ethnic communities, be it Italian, Ukrainian, Polish, or other; but who frequently think of themselves, behave, and react as English-speaking people, that is, as members of the anglophone subsociety.

COMMON INSTITUTIONS AND SOCIAL NETWORKS

The segmentation of Canadian society along linguistic lines is not complete; if it were, there would be two countries, two societies. There are common institutions that are meant to, and to some degree do, serve the members of each of the two subsocieties. There are also social networks that link together some members of each of the communities.

It is thus possible to think of Canadian society as having two levels of social organization. At one level, there are the anglophone and francophone subsocieties, with their own institutions, social networks, stratification system, and culture. The two subsocieties, however, function within a more inclusive societal framework, which also has its own institutions, social networks, stratification system, and culture. Each member of the society belongs to a societal community and a linguistic subsociety, and functions within each level. There are, of course, some who function in both linguistic communities, but such people constitute a very small proportion of the population. This two-level participation is especially clear at the political level, where citizens relate to, and are affected by, the central government and a provincial government primarily representative of a segment of one or the other of the linguistic communities. But as will be seen, it is also the case in other institutional areas.

DIMENSIONS OF ENGLISH-FRENCH RELATIONS SIGNIFICANT FOR SOCIETAL COHESION

Three basic dimensions constitute the basis of the analysis that follows. Firstly, there are different spheres of activities in which such relations occur: economic, political, and social. Because of the varying character of the activities and the existing institutions in each sphere, the relationships between the linguistic communities are also likely to vary from one to the other. Secondly, both anglophones and francophones have relationships with the common institutions, especially in the political and economic spheres of activity. By relating to a common institution, anglophones and francophones may develop a sense of cohesion, the sense that they belong to the same overarching community. Moreover, through their interaction with the common institutions, such as government, business, and the media, the members of each linguistic community indirectly relate to each other: they learn and develop images, feelings, and attitudes about each other.

However, not only individuals but also institutions from each community interact with the common institutions. Vertical relationships can be either individual-institutional or interinstitutional. One of the characteristics of subsocieties is that they can act to some degree as corporate entities. This involves relationships between institutions, although individuals are the ones who interact with each other as agents of those institutions. Interinstitutional relationships may also be a source of societal cohesion, and for the same reasons, that is, by fostering the sense of belonging to an overarching community and by bringing about mutual knowledge, feelings, and attitudes. Indeed, when the institutions of a language community relate with the central government, it is in effect the members of that community who are relating with the central government through their institutions and their agents. This may sound as though the central government were a foreign government. Of course, it is not; but it may have elements of foreignism from the point of view of a particular subsociety, as when it is perceived as acting in the interest of one part of the country to the detriment or neglect of another.

These "vertical" relationships with common institutions may or may not contribute to cohesion. Through them a sense of separateness may develop, rather than belongingness; negative rather than positive attitudes may crystallize; the weaknesses and problems of each community may become the focus of attention, rather than their strengths and achievements; what each gains may be of greater concern than what each contributes; and so on. The analysis that follows attempts to identify some of the circumstances under which these relationships are likely to contribute to cohesion rather than disunity.

Thirdly, relationships can also occur between individuals and institutions from each community. One can think of these relationships as "horizontal." Personal relationships may occur between members of each language collectivity. Similarly, the governmental agencies, churches, labour unions, professional associations, businesses, and other organizations of each linguistic community may interact with each other. Such horizontal relationships may or may not exist to any significant extent, and if they exist, they may lead to solidarity or conflict. At the interpersonal level, contacts may be the occasion for the formation of networks of social solidarity, but may also encourage the formation of stereotypes and negative attitudes. At the interorganizational level, the interaction may consist of mutually advantageous exchanges and joint projects, or may involve conflicts over resources and areas of jurisdiction. Some of the circumstances leading to these outcomes will be considered in this study.

In short, the degree of societal cohesion is seen as being the result of the character of the relationships that each linguistic community has with the common institutions and with each other in economic, political, and social spheres of activity. An important aspect of these relationships is socio-psychological in nature: on the one hand, loyalty to the common institutions, or the sense, on the part of both linguistic communities, that these institutions are legitimate, and that it is possible to identify with them; and on the other, social solidarity across the two communities or the sense of belonging to the same overarching community.

The analyis will search for the factors and processes affecting the degree of societal cohesion in the character of the vertical and horizontal relationships occurring in economic, political, and social spheres. It will also explore various phenomena that affect the character of these relationships. Among these phenomena are certain features of the existing institutions, the socio-economic circumstances in which they function, such as the patterns of inequality and the economic dominance of the United States, the prevailing values and ideologies, the recent socio-political mobilization for change, the internal ethnic and regional diversity of the two linguistic subsocieties, and ecological and demographic conditions.

The overall framework can be sketched as follows:

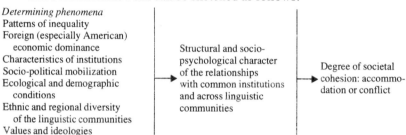

Determining phenomena		
Patterns of inequality		
Foreign (especially American) economic dominance	Structural and socio-psychological character of the relationships with common institutions and across linguistic communities	Degree of societal cohesion: accommo-dation or conflict
Characteristics of institutions		
Socio-political mobilization		
Ecological and demographic conditions		
Ethnic and regional diversity of the linguistic communities		
Values and ideologies		

In short, given the segmentation of Canadian society along linguistic lines, what factors can be said to affect the degree of its cohesion? Under what circumstances do institutions command the loyalty of the members of each linguistic community? What factors affect their legitimacy and their quality as objects of identification? Under what conditions do the members of each subsociety build cohesive ties with each other either individually or through their institutions? In addition to contributing to the identification of relevant factors and processes, it is hoped that as a result of this analysis, it will be possible to formulate at least an opinion, if not a firm judgement, as to the relative importance for the cohesion of Canadian society of horizontal, as opposed to vertical, relationships; of interinstitutional, as opposed to interindividual, relationships; of institutional-individual, as opposed to interinstitutional, relationships; and of the political, economic, and social domains of activity.

ORGANIZATION OF PART THREE

In the next two chapters, relationships in the economic sphere are considered. A critical aspect of these relationships is the degree of inequality both between individuals and between enterprises across linguistic lines, that is to say, inequality in individual condition, possibilities of mobility, and capacity for organizational growth. In other words, the concern is with the participation of members of each linguistic community in the common economic institutions and of the enterprises of each community in the overall economy of the country. A second aspect of these relationships concerns the ways in which common economic organizations relate to each linguistic community as a community. This aspect pertains to the behaviour of enterprises as corporate members of each community.

Chapters 3.4 and 3.5 proceed with a parallel analysis of relationships in the political sphere. The first aspect considered is the representation of each linguistic community in the central government, and the extent to which that government reaches the citizens of each community. The relationships that the provincial governments corresponding to the major segments of each language community have with the central government will also be discussed. In addition, since provincial governments have their own constituencies, they, like the central government, must gain and maintain the allegiance of citizens. Both levels of government must establish their legitimacy *vis-à-vis* the same segment of the population. As a result, there is a possibility of competition between them for the loyalty of that segment. This competition and its possible impact on the degree of societal cohesion will be considered.

Chapter 3.6 deals with horizontal relationships in both the economic and political spheres. Consideration will be given to questions of interprovincial trade and collaboration. The horizontal relationships to be considered include those taking place outside Quebec between anglophone and francophone communities as corporate entities.

Relationships in the social sphere are analysed in chapter 3.7. When going through the proceeding chapters, the reader will notice that the social dimension of economic and political relationships is frequently considered as it is relevant to several aspects of these relationships. Chapter 3.7, however, focuses on social relationships between francophones and anglophones, and more specifically on those at the interpersonal level. Their implications for societal cohesion are explored. Finally, chapter 3.8 presents a summary of the analysis and some conclusions.

Socio-Economic Inequalities Between the Linguistic Communities

A comprehension of the dynamics of French-English relations in Canada requires a prior understanding of the socio-economic inequalities between these two collectivities. Francophones are in a weaker position than anglophones in terms of average income levels, occupational scales, mobility rates, and returns to investment in education. Moreover, they are collectively disadvantaged *vis-à-vis* anglophones as to ownership, control, and management of the economy, and status of their language. These patterns of inequality serve to further differentiate the two communities and help to maintain the boundaries between them in terms of their identity, social networks, and social organization. Also, such socio-economic disparities have ramifications for all classes of relationships that have relevance to societal integration—of both a vertical and horizontal nature and involving both institutions and individuals. Francophone individual and collective weaknesses should not be viewed as isolated factors, but as interactive with other factors, such as the economic predominance of the anglophone nation to the south and the numerical disadvantages of francophones, both within most regions and Canada as a whole.

Socio-economic inequalities impact upon the processes involved in furthering societal cohesion—such as those pertaining to the legitimacy of the national government for various social classes and interests within each collectivity. The stronger anglophone collectivity is likely to have a bias of input in decision-making structures due to the greater resources it can command and the greater responsiveness of such structures to more powerful interests (chapter 3.6). This may lead to greater identification with, and accordance of, legitimacy to "their own" institutions by members of the less favoured group (chapter 3.7). The processes involved in horizontal patterns of collaboration and other forms of interaction are also likely to be affected by the distribution of socio-economic power between collectivities, as evidenced in both interinstitutional and interindividual behaviour (chapters 3.5 and 3.8). At the individual level, for instance, personal contacts of individuals across subsocieties may be discouraged not only by linguistic and cultural barriers but also by differences in social class. Also, the recognition of inequalities may discourage members from the disadvantaged collectivity from participating in joint endeavours with individuals from the dominant group, as greater benefits of participation may be perceived as likely to accrue to the latter.

The pervasive influence of the socio-economic imbalance between the francophone and anglophone subsocieties on all classes of relationships will become evident throughout the analyses contained in the following chapters. Our task here will be to describe the patterns of inequality between English and French Canadians, examining their performance in each of the individual and collective measures specified above.

DISTRIBUTION OF INCOME

In 1961 (the latest year for which data are available), there was a noticeable disparity in average income between Canadians of French and British origins for the country as a whole (table 3.2.1). Males of British origin ranked second highest in average total income and earned approximately $1,000 more than those of French origin, who in turn ranked second lowest among all ethnic groups. Put in other terms of comparison, Canadians of French origin earned about 80% of the average income of those of British origin (Royal Commission on Bilingualism and Biculturalism 1969a).

In all provinces, individuals of British origin have consistently higher incomes than individuals of French origin. The disparity in average income between the two collectivities was particularly pronounced within Quebec, where male employees of French origin earned about 64% as much as similar persons of British origin, and within Montreal, where the corresponding figure was 67% (Morris and Lanphier 1977, p. 13).

TABLE 3.2.1
Average Income of Non-Agricultural and
Total Male Labour Force, Canada, 1961

Ethnic Origin	Non-Agricultural Male Labour Force		Total Male Labour Force
	Income	Index	Index
British	$4,852	109.9	109.8
French	3,872	87.7	85.8
German	4,207	95.3	103.1
Italian	3,621	82.0	81.0
Jewish	7,426	168.2	166.9
Ukrainian	4,128	93.5	86.8
Others	4,153	94.1	98.2
All origins	4,414	100.0	100.0

SOURCE: Royal Commission on Bilingualism and Biculturalism (1969a), p. 16.

TABLE 3.2.2
AVERAGE EMPLOYMENT INCOME FOR MALE WORKERS,
MONTREAL, 1961 AND 1971

ETHNIC ORIGIN	1961		1971	
	Employment Income	Rank	Employment Income	Rank
French	$3,878.97	8	$6,617.32	7
English-Scottish	5,823.79	2	8,575.51	3
Irish	5,373.73	4	8,343.49	5
Scandinavian	5,509.70	3	8,880.14	2
German	4,774.74	5	8,396.79	4
Italian	3,073.95	9	5,676.02	9
Jewish	6,180.01	1	9,686.90	1
Eastern European	4,387.11	6	7,148.29	6
Other ethnic origin	3,975.88	7	6,278.05	8
All workers	4,314.98	—	7,042.28	—

SOURCE: Boulet (1977), p. 5.

In a study based on two large samples from Statistics Canada, Boulet (1977) found that the gap in average income between French and English Canadians within Montreal had closed substantially in the ten-year period since 1961. Whereas in 1961 male employees of French origin earned about 67% as much as individuals of British origin, by 1971 they had increased their proportion to 77% (a figure that approximates their ratio of income *vis-à-vis* British Canadians for all of Canada in 1961; see table 3.2.2). Note, however, that in Montreal the figure for the average income for French Canadians in 1971 was still well below the average income for all workers.

Unfortunately, we have no figures that would indicate whether the trend toward improved francophone income observed in Montreal between 1961 and 1971 occurred in the rest of Quebec and Canada, and whether it has continued to the present time. In any case, one might conclude that there does exist a considerable imbalance in average income between French Canadians and English Canadians in favour of the latter.

OCCUPATIONAL DISTRIBUTION

There are marked differences in terms of occupational distribution between French and English Canadians. In 1961, 21% of the British, as opposed to 14% of the French, were in professional or managerial occupations. Thirty per cent of the British were employed in the two blue-collar categories, craftsmen and unskilled labourers, as opposed to 39% of the French (table 3.2.3).

TABLE 3.2.3

DISTRIBUTION OF MALE LABOUR FORCE BY ETHNIC ORIGIN AND OCCUPATION, CANADA, 1961

OCCUPATIONAL CLASS	PERCENTAGE							
	All origins	British	French	German	Italian	Jewish	Ukrainian	Other
Professional and technical	7.6	9.3	5.9	6.1	2.8	13.7	5.8	6.9
Managerial	10.2	12.1	7.6	8.3	6.6	39.4	7.1	9.5
Clerical	6.9	8.2	6.7	5.0	3.7	6.8	5.7	5.1
Sales	5.6	6.6	5.2	4.4	3.2	14.1	3.5	4.2
Service	8.5	9.2	7.7	6.4	8.5	2.6	7.3	9.6
Transportation and communications	7.5	8.0	8.9	6.2	4.7	2.8	6.4	5.5
Craftsmen and production workers	28.8	25.5	31.4	32.5	43.7	15.6	29.6	29.8
Labourers	6.2	4.6	7.5	5.6	19.2	1.1	6.9	6.8
Farmers	12.2	10.8	10.8	21.0	2.7	0.5	23.0	15.8
Other primary	3.9	3.1	5.3	2.3	2.3	0.0	2.5	4.6
Not stated	2.6	2.6	3.0	3.0	2.6	3.4	2.2	2.2
Total, all occupations								
Number	4,705,518	2,071,417	1,303,280	297,003	137,071	49,820	135,987	710,940
Percentage	100.0	100.0	100.0	100.0	100.0	100.0	100.0	100.0

SOURCE: Royal Commission on Bilingualism and Biculturalism (1969a), p. 38.

Porter's (1965) classic study indicates that the occupational position of French Canadians, in some respects, has worsened over time, while that of British Canadians has improved. Between 1931 and 1961, Canadians of French origin moved further below the national average in the professional and financial categories, while Canadians of British origin advanced. As for income, the disparity between the British and French representation in the professional and managerial categories holds for all provinces in Canada, and is particularly pronounced in the case of Montreal and Quebec generally. In 1970, the Commission d'enquête sur la situation de la langue française et sur les droits linguistiques au Québec (Gendron Commission) found in Quebec this same pattern of anglo overrepresentation (36%) and French underrepresentation (23%) in the high occupational levels (administrative or professional), and the reverse situation for employment as labourers (29% for francophones and only 13% for anglophones; Morris and Lanphier 1977, p. 13).

By 1971, Reitz (1975) found that there was a substantial reduction in occupational inequality between the French and British within Canada as a whole. This improvement for the French appeared to be part of a general trend toward an overall reduction in occupational inequalities among ethnic groups over the ten-year period, 1961 to 1971. Reitz attributed this improvement, which was most pronounced at the middle and upper levels of the occupational structure, to the opening up of educational opportunities and the expansion of industries and organizations controlled by French Canadians. However, as indicated by the Gendron Commission in its study of Quebec, where these factors would have the most effect upon occupational improvement for the French, the gap in occupational inequality is still considerable.

SOCIAL MOBILITY

A study by Jocas and Rocher (1957) comparing the intergenerational mobility of French and English Canadians in urban districts in Quebec showed that the gap in occupational distribution separating those two principal ethnic groups had in fact increased considerably from one generation to the next. For the top occupational categories, it was found that the advantage enjoyed by English Canadians had grown from 8.8% to 22.4% from father to son. Similarly, the gap between English and French Canadians in their representation in the occupations of skilled workers and labourers had grown from 26% to 29.3% from one generation to the next.

A replication carried out in 1964 found that the "distancing" noted in 1954 between the occupational distribution of French and English Canadians from one generation to the next had slowed down considerably (Dofny and Garon-Audy 1969). Whereas in 1954, in three-quarters of the cases, the gap had grown between the two ethnic groups, in 1964 the gap had lessened in five-eights of the cases. The authors concluded that this reduction underlined an acceleration in the speed of mobility of French Canadians. They noted, however, that these findings must be interpreted with caution. First of all, the intergenerational decrease in the disparity of representation in various occupations between French and English must not veil the fact that English Canadians preserve a net overrepresentation in the highest occupational categories. Secondly, the increased mobility of French Canadians is more attributable to changes in the structure of employment, such as the decline in employment in the rural sector and the increase in industrial jobs, than to equalizing factors.

RETURNS TO EDUCATION

One common interpretation of the disparity in occupational income and status between French and English is that this gap exists due to the longer length of schooling undergone by English Canadians. In 1961, Canadians of British origin had spent an average two years more at school than had Canadians of French origin (Royal Commission on Bilingualism and Biculturalism 1969*a*). However, a nation-wide study by Raynauld, Marion, and Béland (1975) showed that the disparity in income existed even when differences in educational achievements were taken into account, and that the higher the occupational level, the greater this disparity was likely to be. Among unskilled workers with primary education, those of French origin earned 95% as much as those of British origin; for clerical and skilled workers with secondary education, the percentage dropped to 90%; for managers, professionals, and sales workers with post-secondary education, it fell further to 86%.

Moreover, that study showed that controlling for occupation, additional years of education did not have the same effect on income for all ethnic origins: additional education is more profitable for individuals of British origin than for those of French origin. Thus, for British-origin individuals, ''the effect of an elementary education compared to no education is $526; for the first two years of secondary education, it is $728−$526=$102; for three to five years of secondary education, it is $1639−$728=$911'' (ibid., p. 223); and for university education, it is $2195. For French-origin individuals, the effect of an elementary education compared to no education is $619; for the first two years of secondary school, it is $230. However, the increment in income gained from three to five years of secondary education is only $308, and for a university education, only $1654 (table 3.2.4).

Thus, it would seem that an investment in an equal amount of education would yield lower returns, in terms of income, for francophones than for anglophones. The results of the study would also lead one to reject the explanation that the socio-economic inferiority of French Canadians is based on their lower levels of education.

TABLE 3.2.4
EDUCATION EFFECTS ON INCOME
(Canadian 1961 Dollars)

ETHNIC ORIGIN	LEVEL OF EDUCATION				
	None	Elementary	Secondary 1−2	Secondary 3−5	University
French	0	619	849	1157	2811
	(0)	(854)	(1255)	(1919)	(4465)
British	0	526	728	1639	3834
	(0)	(938)	(1336)	(2860)	(5836)
Other	0	408	817	1601	2738
	(0)	(476)	(1310)	(2558)	(4345)

SOURCE: Raynauld, Marion, and Béland (1975), p. 224.
NOTE: After three iterations. Income at zero education taken to be zero; effects of education thus increments in income. Increments, in turn, corrected for correlation with "occupation," while figures in brackets are observed differences in income by level of education.

OWNERSHIP OF ECONOMIC ENTERPRISES

Since organizational discrepancies between French and English are most crucial in their effect on societal integration within the province of Quebec, we will deal here with the distribution of ownership of business establishments within Quebec. Placing into perspective the importance of economic activity in Quebec in relation to Canada as a whole, the *Financial Post* (26 July 1975) noted that of the 144 major manufacturing, resource, public service, and financial enterprises in Canada, 33 (23%) had their head offices in Quebec (Sauvé 1976, p. 9).

One measurement used by the Royal Commission on Bilingualism and Biculturalism (1969a) to calculate the size of establishments owned by francophone Canadians, anglophone Canadians, and foreign interests was the percentage of the labour force employed in a number of selected industrial sectors by establishments owned by members from each of these collectivities. Francophone ownership appeared to be strongest in two sectors—agriculture and service—where half of the Quebec labour force working for francophones (and 24% of the total Quebec labour force) was employed. The other half (23% of the total Quebec labour force) was evenly divided among the remaining seven industrial sectors (table 3.2.5).

Within the manufacturing sector, which accounts for 27% of the total labour force, francophone manufacturers employed only 22% of all those working in that sector. Another indication of the weakness of the francophone-owned industries is the fact that they accounted for only 15% of the total value-added in production (that is, the value of produced goods less the cost of energy and raw materials). This is in contrast to the roughly 42% each accounted for by manufacturing establishments owned by anglophone Canadians and foreign interests (table 3.2.6).

TABLE 3.2.5
SIZE OF ESTABLISHMENTS IN PRIVATE SECTOR OWNED BY
FRANCOPHONE AND ANGLOPHONE CANADIANS, AND
FOREIGN INTERESTS, MEASURED BY NUMBERS EMPLOYED, QUEBEC, 1961

INDUSTRIAL SECTORS	NUMBER OF EMPLOYEES (×1,000)	PERCENTAGE OF LABOUR FORCE IN ESTABLISHMENTS OWNED BY			
		Franco-phones	Anglo-phones	Foreign Interests	Total
Agriculture	131.2	91.3	8.7	0.0	100.0
Mining	25.9	6.5	53.1	40.4	100.0
Manufacturing	468.3	21.8	46.9	31.3	100.0
Construction	126.4	50.7	35.2	14.1	100.0
Transportation and communications	102.4	37.5	49.4	13.1	100.0
Wholesale trade	69.3	34.1	47.2	18.7	100.0
Retail trade	178.7	56.7	35.8	7.5	100.0
Finance	62.2	25.8	53.1	21.1	100.0
Services	350.9	71.4	28.6	0.0	100.0
All industries	1,515.1	47.3	37.7	15.0	100.0

SOURCE: Raynauld (1974), pp. 63–64.
NOTE: Excludes forestry, fishing and trapping, the public sector, and unspecified industries.

TABLE 3.2.6
SIZE OF MANUFACTURING ESTABLISHMENTS OWNED BY FRANCOPHONE
AND ANGLOPHONE CANADIANS, AND FOREIGN INTERESTS,
MEASURED BY VALUE-ADDED, QUEBEC, 1961

	PERCENTAGE OF TOTAL VALUE-ADDED IN ESTABLISHMENTS OWNED BY			
	Francophones	Anglophones	Foreign Interests	Total
All industries	15.4	42.8	41.8	100.0

SOURCE: Raynauld (1974), p. 78.

Sales (1977) and Légaré (1977*a*) characterize French-Canadian enterprise as non-monopolist, where ownership and management are often
familial, the number of employees relatively small and poorly paid, and the
assets relatively limited (Sales used the cut-off point of 500 employees and
assets under $10 million). Foreign-owned and English-Canadian establish-
ments, on the other hand, predominate in the monopolist sector, which is
comprised of giant enterprises, some of which are multinational, having the
highest productivity, paying the highest wages, and being the most likely to
expand (Légaré 1977*a*; Morris and Lanphier 1977; Raynauld 1973; Sales

1977). Whereas francophone-owned enterprises are more oriented to local markets, selling a mere 22% of their output outside Quebec, English Canadian establishments sell 49% of their production outside Quebec, and foreign-owned establishments, 60% (Royal Commission on Bilingualism and Biculturalism 1969*a*, p. 57).

The particular sectors of the economy and the type of business enterprises dominated by francophones and anglophones will have repercussions for the occupational status and income of employees from each of these collectivities, for the relative status of the French and English languages, and for the overall status of the two subsocieties. Sales (1977) found that the ethnicity or national origin of the principal stockholders or controllers of the enterprise was the prime determinant of the national or ethnic origin of top managers in business enterprises within Quebec. Very few (only 3.7%) French-Canadian-owned enterprises within Quebec employed managers of other origins, which was not surprising given that in the francophone-owned, non-monopolist enterprises, the managers are often the owners.

Within Anglo-Saxon, Canadian-controlled industry, 28.4% of management were of French Canadian origin, which is a smaller proportion than that accounted for by either the Anglo-Saxon Canadian or ''Neo-Canadian'' categories (the latter of which were half Anglo-Saxon). For Canadian-owned enterprises having their head office outside Quebec (usually in Ontario), the ethnicity of principal stockholders and that of managers was perfectly correlated: both were either Anglo-Saxon or Jewish. In such enterprises, French Canadians were not found within the upper management levels. However, for Canadian-owned businesses that had their head offices within Quebec, the managers were more diversified, with Anglo-Saxons accounting for 53.6% and French Canadians, 26.9%. Sales found that very often a French-Canadian manager at the head of an Anglo-Saxon enterprise could be explained by the ethnicity of the previous owner.

Studies of the economic élite, defined as senior management and directors within dominant corporations (Clement 1975, p. 5), give some indication of the control of the Canadian economy exercised by English and French Canadians. Table 3.2.7 demonstrates the drastic underrepresentation of French Canadians and overrepresentation of British Canadians within the economic élite over time. The index of ethnic representation, which standardizes for population, shows that French Canadians have made slight gains over a period of two decades (from 1951 to 1972), while English Canadians have remained in exactly the same position proportionate to their population. Thus, as for other measures of organizational status, the figures for élite representation reveal a distribution between the two collectivities that clearly favours anglophones.

TABLE 3.2.7
ETHNIC REPRESENTATION IN ECONOMIC ÉLITE, 1951 AND 1972

ETHNIC ORIGIN	PROPORTION OF ETHNIC REPRESENTATION		INDEX OF ETHNIC REPRESENTATION	
	1951	1972	1951	1972
Anglo	92.3	86.2	1.93	1.93
French	6.7	8.4	0.22	0.29
Other	1.0	5.4	0.05	0.20
Total	100.0	100.0		
N	760	775		

SOURCE: Adapted from Clement (1975), pp. 232–34.
NOTE: Index over 1.00 denotes overrepresentation, and one below, underrepresentation. Index arrived at by dividing population into élite representation, thus standardizing over time for changes in ethnic composition of population. It is a ratio of ethnic proportion in the élite divided by corresponding proportion of Canadian population for same time.

STATUS OF LANGUAGE

Although language disputes are usually discussed in terms of culture, the relative status of a language is both a prime indicator and a component of overall group status. The status of a language is determined by factors both internal and external to the particular situation in which the language is used. For example, the dominant language of operations within a business firm will be affected by the linguistic origin of labour at all levels of the firm, an internal factor. It will also be influenced by the relative importance or weight of external transactions (as compared with internal ones) and the language component of goods and services, both external factors (Breton and Mieszkowski 1975).

The dominance of English as the language of the higher levels of business in Quebec is determined by the international status of English (*lingua franca*), which is reinforced by the close ties of the Quebec economy to the rest of English-speaking Canada, the recent presence of American multinational firms in Quebec, and the importance of English-speaking entrepreneurs and financiers in the economic development of Quebec (Breton and Mieszkowski 1975, 1977; Faucher and Lamontagne 1953; Morrison 1970; Simon 1974).[1]

In a bilingual society, the dominance of one language over the other will affect the relative rates of return on bilingualism for members of each linguistic community. The rate of return on investment in a dominant language is greater than the rate of return on investment in a subordinate

---

[1] The bargaining power of francophones in Canada would be larger if the United States were not an English-speaking nation—even if they constituted the same proportion of the population as they now do.

TABLE 3.2.8
ANGLOPHONES AND FRANCOPHONES USING FRENCH AND ENGLISH LANGUAGES AT WORK, QUEBEC, 1971

Occupation	Anglophones %	Francophones %
Administrators	28	47
Office workers	28	48
Salespersons	31	47
Workers in secondary industries	39	25
Workers in primary industries	31	5

SOURCE: Laporte (1974), p. 17.

TABLE 3.2.9
MEDIAN INCOME OF MALES, MONTREAL, 1970

	French	British[a]
Unilinguals	$5,100	$7,250
Bilinguals	6,800	7,200

SOURCE: Veltman (1976), table 32.
NOTE: a. Includes Irish.

language (Breton and Mieszkowski 1977). The asymmetry in rates of return on language training for francophones in English and for anglophones in French can be seen by the fact that francophones in most occupations, especially those that are white-collar, use both languages more frequently than do anglophones (table 3.2.8).

For francophones, bilingualism is the means to occupational mobility and increased social prestige. The return investment in bilingualism in purely financial terms can be seen in table 3.2.9: the median income of unilingual French Canadian males is much smaller (about 30% less) than the income for unilingual British Canadians. This gap narrows considerably for French Canadian bilinguals and British Canadian bilinguals, with the former earning approximately 94% of the median income earned by the latter. The income for bilingual British Canadians is actually slightly less than for unilingual British Canadians. This rather anomalous finding has been explained by the fact that the pressures for bilingualism among anglophones are greater for those lower in organizations than for those in higher positions (table 3.2.8); therefore, anglophones lower in position (and thus income) within a given occupational category are more likely to require a knowledge of French (Lieberson 1970; Morris and Lanphier 1977).

The recent intervention of the Quebec government through language legislation has as its objective the reversal of the trend toward the dominance of English as the language of work. Analyses offering prognosis on the success of "francisation" differ in their predictions of the probable amount and distribution of benefits that could accrue to French Canadians (Breton and Mieszkowski 1975; Vaillancourt 1977).

CONCLUSION

Our overview of the socio-economic status of francophones and anglophones has indicated that anglophone Canadians have maintained a superior economic position even in the province where francophones form the large majority. Although as individuals francophones have made slight gains over the past few decades as to occupational mobility and representation within the economic élite, these gains have indeed been minimal. Moreover, they have remained in an organizationally weak position in terms of ownership and control of major economic enterprises and the status of their language.

The slight improvement in the socio-economic status of francophones *vis-à-vis* anglophones, induced by such factors as the changing labour requirements of the economy and transformation in Quebec's educational system, imply that the patterns of inequality between the two collectivities are dynamic rather than immutable. However, the long-term persistence of these inequalities has proved to be a constant source of grievance for francophones, accentuated by the growth of political nationalism within Quebec. The types of intervention by either federal or provincial governments in altering these inequalities in favour of the disadvantaged francophone collectivity have direct relevance for the form and very survival of the present political arrangements.

In subsequent chapters, we will analyse the effects of inequalities between francophones and anglophones upon the relationships between the two subsocieties and the relationship each has with the federal government, and will examine various interpretations for these inequalities and their repercussions for societal cohesion.

Economic Organizations and Linguistic Communities

Society is held together or disjointed by the forces that give legitimacy to the economic as well as the political institutions. Moreover, its cohesion depends on the nature and intensity of the economic linkages and interactions among its constituting subsocieties as well as on the political interrelationships.

Several characteristics of political and economic structures, such as their accessibility, the way they reach individuals and groups, and their interorganizational relationships, are fundamental in affecting their legitimacy and their potential impact on the cohesion of society. While these factors will be discussed in relation to political institutions in a subsequent chapter, the focus in this chapter is on economic institutions.

It appears useful to concentrate on five types of economic linkages between communities. Some organizations exist in both linguistic communities in that they recruit part of their labour force in each community. In that limited sense, they could be said to be "common" economic organizations. It should be added immediately that the commonality rarely extends to the control of the organizations. Most of the "common" organizations are anglophone controlled, and few are francophone controlled. Presumably, a truly "bridging" organization between communities would be one that is jointly controlled, but this is far from being a widespread phenomenon. Throughout the discussion that follows, the focus is on the dominant, anglophone-controlled organizations recruiting labour in each linguistic community. These are located in the regions of Quebec, New Brunswick, and eastern Ontario, since this is where the francophone population is concentrated.

It can be said that through such organizations, members of the two communities participate in common economic activities. Thus, the cohesion of the society in such situations depends in part on the extent of this participation and especially on the degree to which it is considered equitable. The issues that arise pertain to the conditions of individual mobility and of effective participation at the various organizational levels.

Organizations can be "common" in another way, namely, by selling their products or services in each community. Through advertising, packaging, and distribution channels, the organizations relate to the communities as aggregates of consumers of goods and services. Here the issues related to the sensitivity and responsiveness of organizations to their bicultural market come to mind.

By recruiting labour in a community and by selling products or services to its members and thus drawing profits that allow the accumulation of capital, organizations are "corporate members" benefiting from their activities in the community. The extent and nature of their participation beyond their labour market and commercial activities can therefore be an issue. When the organization is a corporate member of two language communities, its differential involvement in each of them can be a source of tension. This involvement can be in the cultural activities of the community, its health and educational functions, and in the development of its athletic and recreational facilities. More generally, it can be active in relation to the economic health and growth of the community. Some issues raised in this regard are whether corporate members are putting in as much as they are taking from the community; whether their concern is more with one of the communities; and whether they are at all concerned with the development of the community and its institutions.

The above relationships are between organizations on the one hand and individuals or their communities on the other. But there is another level of economic relationship that affects the cohesion of society, namely, relationships among organizations. This parallels the analysis of the subsequent chapters in which a distinction will be made between the relationship of government organizations at the federal and provincial levels. It is pertinent to look at the relationships among anglophone and francophone organizations. These can be described in terms of the patterns of stratification that exist among the organizations, and of the transactions or exchanges that take place among them. As will be seen later, both kinds of relationships affect the degree of societal cohesion.

Thus, there are five types of relationships between economic organizations and the linguistic communities. One is the relationship with consumers which will not be discussed here[1] because it is less directly related to the structure of opportunities. A second, consisting of the transactions between anglophone- and francophone-controlled organizations, will be considered in the next chapter. The three relationships dealt with in this chapter are (1) organizations in relation with the labour force of each linguistic community; (2) the differential involvement of economic organizations as corporate

---

[1] This phenomenon has been studied by Elkin (1969, 1973), whose work is discussed briefly in chapter seven.

members of each community; and (3) the stratification among economic organizations across communities.

RELATIONSHIP WITH LABOUR FORCE OF EACH LINGUISTIC COMMUNITY

In the last chapter, it was seen that the participation of francophones on boards of directors and at management levels of organizations is not proportional to their numbers in Canadian society. Many hypotheses have been formulated to account for this situation. A systematic analysis of these hypotheses will not be attempted, but the most important will be described briefly.

a. The cultural hypothesis places the burden of the existing situation on the value orientations of francophones, values that lead them away from business and industrial ventures. According to this hypothesis, these value orientations are reflected in the educational system and therefore in the kind of training acquired, and aspirations adopted, by the individuals. They are also reflected in a lower desire for geographic mobility because, for example, of the value attached to family and community ties.

b. The language hypothesis argues that since the language of business and industry, especially in the higher organizational levels, is English, francophones are at a disadvantage. An alternate formulation of this hypothesis is that linguistic assimilation is a condition of socio-economic mobility.

c. The discrimination hypothesis states that the relatively lower participation of francophones is the result of outright exclusion from various positions, the degree of exclusion being more pronounced in the higher levels of the organizational hierarchy.

d. The social network hypothesis argues that the level of organizational participation is a function of the structure of the channels through which organizations recruit their labour force. While the discrimination hypothesis argues that recruitment is selective because it is carried out in such a way as to deliberately keep out certain categories of people, the social network hypothesis states that recruitment is selective because the organization is connected only with certain sources of labour and not with others.

Even though all four hypotheses have some validity, the degree to which they account for the differential distribution of francophones and anglophones in the labour force is not well established. The cultural hypothesis, in particular, has been seriously challenged, the argument being essentially that the culture of a community as reflected either in the orientations of its members or in its educational institutions is largely an adaptation to the structure of opportunities available to that community. In other words, if the Quebec school system did not train its people for business and management positions, it is in large part because such positions were not available to francophones for the reason indicated in the three other hypotheses. Once a cultural system is established, however, it may have an effect of its own.

All four sets of factors have also been at the basis of some public policies. For instance, the educational system was transformed; so that people would be better prepared for the requirements of the labour market. Legislation against discriminatory behaviour in the labour market exists and has been reinforced by the passage of the Canadian Bill of Rights in 1960.

Recently, language legislation pertaining directly to the language of work has also been passed by the Quebec government. It is not clear, however, what the specific objectives of this legislation are with regard to the participation of francophones in economic organizations, let alone what its actual effects will be. There appear to be three objectives involved, two of which concern us at this point since they relate to the ''language'' and ''social network'' hypotheses. It seems that one objective is that by making French the language of work, so removing an obstacle to mobility for francophones, greater numbers will be able to move up the organizational hierarchy.[2] In addition, the language obstacle is imposed on anglophones who will now be at a disadvantage in that segment of the labour market, leaving more room for francophones. So it is not only that francophones will be able to work in their own language, but also that more jobs will be available.

Of course, given that the rest of North America is English speaking, anglophones are not likely to react to such obstacles in the same way as francophones. Like the francophones, they will try to avoid the costs of bilingualism, but are likely to do so by moving into anglophone regions of the country. This is occurring, but the anglophone regions may not have enough jobs for all possible migrants, a situation that will lead many to put pressure on those who control the organizations to move the jobs themselves into the anglophone region.[3]

There have been positive responses to the social and political pressure toward the promotion of francophones in business and industry, and toward a greater use of French at work. Some enterprises appear to adjust more readily than others to their social environment. Thus, some had begun to encourage the use of French and to promote francophones before any legislation was passed. Most, however, waited for government intervention before taking any significant measures in that direction. Finally, some have resisted the pressure in one way or another, but especially by moving all or part of their operations outside Quebec.

---

[2] The language of work is not a problem at the lower levels of organizations (Québec 1972).

[3] When the Sun Life Assurance Co. initially announced it was going to move, it was reported that many of their anglophone employees cheered in approval. They would now be able to move *with* their job.

It should be noted that most francophones use French at work most of the time in Quebec. A study carried out in 1971 showed that 64% of francophones work almost only in French; 3% almost only in English; 32% use both languages, and 1% works in another language (Carlos 1973, p. 8). Among anglophones, the percentages are: almost only French, 5%; almost only English, 63%; both, 32%. Among others, they are: almost only French, 14%; almost only English, 36%; both, 40%; another language, 10%. But there are considerable variations depending on the hierarchical level in the enterprise, the kind of activity (i.e., reading, writing), the function (i.e., research, marketing), the industrial sector (i.e., finance, manufacturing), or the geographical area (i.e., Montreal versus the rest of the province). The combination of these factors can result in significant differences: for example, francophone office employees in manufacturing make little use of their own language in reading and writing activities; in contrast, professionals and technicians in personal and social services make an extensive use of French in either reading, writing, or verbal activities. For more information on the question of the language of work in Quebec, see Akian and Breton (forthcoming).

A second objective of the language legislation could be to deal with the phenomenon identified by the social network hypothesis. Migué (1970, 1971) has articulated this hypothesis in terms of the economic theory of information. He formulated this theory in order to explain the underrepresentation of francophones at the higher administrative and technical levels within Canadian firms. He argues that every worker must acquire information about the conditions offered by the firms where he seeks employment. He must do this at some personal cost. However, he will gauge the cost according to the benefits that he expects to gain from one firm or another. On the other hand, the firm must also have information on the labour market. The cost to the firm of getting this information is equal to the resources it must use to gather information on the labour market, to ensure its channelling throughout the organization, to analyse it, and to make a decision. Its benefits will be demonstrated in the firm's increased productivity. The firm tries to reach a balance between the cost of its searches for an employee and the benefits gained from his services. The task of participating in major decisions is only given to individuals who enjoy management's trust.

The role of information networks is to decrease the cost of acquisition of information or to increase its benefits. Many organizations exist in part as centres of communications between individuals and firms for the purpose of filtering information. For example, universities are set up to train students, but they are also important channels for the selection of candidates and for the communication of occupational information. Historically and technologically, educational institutions are in part a by-product of the economic system. The process of employee evaluation therefore begins in the external network through the application of selection mechanisms. Once hired, however, upward mobility depends primarily on the internal network. The interfirm mobility nevertheless depends strictly on the external network.

The cost of information gathering in connection with highly specialized jobs is very high. Historically, the establishment of information networks has been made by "foreign" enterprises and continues to be made outside the French-Canadian community. Information relevant to the French-Canadian labour market is therefore very limited. Consequently, two subgroups exist within the Canadian and Quebec labour markets: the anglophone group having numerous linkages providing information on the needs of potential employers, and the francophone one having fewer such linkages. The segregation of the information industry into two subnetworks increases the marginal costs that an employer must assume in recruiting a francophone employee who is not entirely integrated into his network. Productivity being equal, he will hire the person whose recruitment cost is the least.

It may be, then, that the language legislation was intended as an incitement to firms to connect themselves to the francophone network of labour market organizations in order to recruit the necessary French-speaking personnel. But it may not have this effect, at least in the short run. For instance, many firms are connected with international markets for managers and technicians, and may find it cheaper to use those channels to recruit French-speaking personnel. In addition, anglophones who have become bilingual may also provide some of the required personnel. Finally, francophones outside Quebec who have integrated into anglophone labour market organizations could be recruited. Thus, an exodus of jobs and the existence of these alternatives may slow down the building of links with the francophone system of labour market organizations. It would seem that the establishment of such linkages would require additional, if not alternative, methods to the passing of legislation.

There is a third objective to the legislation: forcing a shift in the control of firms such that the decisions made are more in line with the interests of the francophone community than previously.[4] This objective is explicitly stated in the white paper that was published prior to the introduction of the language legislation by the Quebec government.

Judging from what Newman (1977) says about the Canadian establishment, the effectiveness of the language legislation in achieving a shift of control appears doubtful:

> Canada's Establishment consists of a surprisingly compact, self-perpetuating group of perhaps a thousand men—nearly all of them Wasps—who act as a kind of informal junta, linked much more closely to each other than to their country. Although their power is waning, they still possess the ability to compel obedience, to shape events and trends—political and cultural as well as economic—in their favor. Their exercise

---

[4] This aspect of the legislation is relevant for other economic relationships discussed later in the chapter.

of authority is subtle, not always successful, but constantly aimed at fulfilling Bertrand Russell's definition of power as "the production of intended effects."

Without being a social compact, the confederacy of Canadian Establishments, loosely knit yet interlocking, forms a psychological entity. Whether by accident or design, French-Canadians have been kept out of this magic circle.

On all three counts—putting French at a premium rather than English, forcing a connection with francophone labour market networks, and shifting the control of decision-making centres—the legislation represents a serious attempt to modify the existing system of privileges. Not surprisingly, it was perceived by many anglophones as a first step in an economic war against the anglophone community.[5] And many responded accordingly: by moving out of Quebec, either for self-protection, retaliatory purposes, or both. In Newman's words (ibid.):

> The new government of Quebec is tough and single-minded, determined to have its way whatever the costs, to split up this country, to destroy the great Canadian experiment. In response, the paladins of the Establishment—the men who make the investment decisions that count—have retreated into a kind of protracted sulk. They have withdrawn vital growth funds, cut Quebec right out of their capital investment plans, abandoned the province to its own dark devices.

This statement may be exaggerated, but it describes a relationship akin to an economic war. How far it will go is difficult to say.

The legislation may have gone too far in the sense of having underestimated the costs imposed on anglophones and their organizations—in terms of language requirements, jobs, and organizational control—as well as the power of these organizations and the willingness of those who control them to retaliate. It is also possible, however, that the confrontation was deliberate, that the costs imposed were fairly well known, and the reaction anticipated. On the other hand, the response of the anglophone interests affected constitutes a sort of admission of the criticisms made against them: that these organizations constitute anglophone domains and that there is no intention of sharing them with francophones.

It seems clear that as long as the relationship evolves as a confrontation, the losses are going to be enormous, although a small group of people will no doubt gain. The losses will be inflicted on segments of the population, but segments of the élites will also harm themselves. "If it [the Canadian Establishment] continues in its present course, it will become the main agent of its own destruction, the chief decimator of its own influence" (ibid.).

It has been argued that unless a "third party" emerges to transform the conflict[6] from a confrontation to one where compromises are more or less reluctantly worked out, the resulting social costs are likely to be very high.

---

[5] This was explicitly stated in an editorial of the *New York Times*, 2 May 1977.

[6] On the role of "third parties" in conflict resolution, see, for example, Deutsch (1973), Nordlinger (1972).

These compromises, however, will have to deal with the problems mentioned above, namely, (a) language as an obstacle to mobility; (b) the poor connection of firms with francophone labour market networks; and (c) the highly skewed distribution of organizational control. The compromises will also have to include measures to deal with the timing and process of transition from one state of affairs to another. Unless these matters are effectively dealt with, whatever measures are adopted will be futile in terms of assuring a more equitable participation of francophones in economic organizations.

DIFFERENTIAL INVOLVEMENT AS CORPORATE MEMBERS OF EACH LINGUISTIC COMMUNITY

Community involvement can take a social form, such as the support of artistic, cultural, or recreational endeavours, participation in civic events, or contribution to religious, welfare, educational, and health institutions. It can also take the form of an active concern for the economic development of the community.

No systematic evidence could be found on the social form of community involvement. We would hypothesize, however, on the basis of informal observations that historically the participation and contribution of "common" economic organizations have been primarily oriented toward the English community organizations and associations. We believe that the empirical evidence, if available, would support this hypothesis for Quebec and for Canada in general. In other words, the "common" economic organizations have defined themselves primarily as corporate members of the anglophone community and have been concerned mainly with the development and support of education, the arts, welfare, health research and services, and so on, in that community.

What has been the nature and extent of the involvement of these "common," but mostly anglophone controlled, organizations in the economic development of each of the linguistic communities? Two arguments have been made on this question: on the one hand, some hold that if it had not been for the investments by these organizations and for the establishment of new ones, Quebec's economic development would have been considerably slower than the development of the rest of Canada. The arrogant expression of this view is that Quebec should consider itself lucky: even if its situation is not ideal, it should be thankful to English-speaking Canada, as without its contribution Quebec's situation would be miserable.

The other view, while acknowledging the importance of these investments, argues that there has been little concern for a "balanced" economic growth of the Quebec economy. For instance, it is argued that the investments in natural resource industries have been largely extractive, with little processing done in Quebec. It is pointed out that there is little concern for the development of technological innovation in some areas of activity and that the manufacturing sector, which is considered crucial for the health of an economy, has been declining during the last fifteen years or so. The more severe critics of the involvement of these organizations in the Quebec economy argue that it has been self-serving and exploitative with no interest in building the Quebec economy and strengthening its various institutions. The ease with which some firms have been leaving Quebec in recent years is seen by many as evidence for this second point of view.

The existence of this controversy, and especially the fact that each point of view is articulated by socio-political groups and by people who have decision-making power, represents an important strain on society.

Establishing the relative merit of these two views would be a monumental task since there are a large number of factors to be considered in assessing the impact on an economy of various organizations and of their decisions. Moreover, not only are economic factors at stake but also social and political ones. For instance, one argument used to explain the aloofness of "common," anglo-controlled economic organizations *vis-à-vis* the francophone community is that the élites of the latter were, and still are, opposed to anything more than a peripheral involvement on the part of anglophone organizations or are lukewarm about it. The argument is that at an earlier time, the clerical, and more recently the social and political, élites and the rising economic bourgeoisie prefer to have the anglophone-controlled organizations as a scapegoat, rather than active participants in the affairs of the francophone community. This attitude on the part of the élite would be based on their perception of the corporate economic power as a threat to their own power and to the cultural survival of the community. It is argued that these economic organizations are seen both as a source of power and as agencies of assimilation.

A basic question is whether the basic interests of a group of organizations and of those who control them are compatible with, or complementary to, those of the particular community in which these organizations operate. If the compatibility or complementarity is low, there will be a tendency for members of the community to perceive a dissociation between power and responsibility in the functioning of the economy. That is to say, certain classes of people will be perceived as having power over the economic condition in the community without having a corresponding sense of responsibility for what happens to that community. Whenever such a situation is felt to exist, the legitimacy of the economic institutions as corporate members of a community may be questioned.

Two structural conditions may lead to the perception of a dissociation between economic power and social responsibility in the behaviour of economic actors. One is a difference in linguistic affiliation between those who control economic organizations and those who work and pursue careers in them. When there is such a difference, the controllers can easily be perceived as acting primarily in the interests of people in their own linguistic group and only secondarily in the interests of the other community. Of course, such a perception will be heightened if they actually behave this way. The second structural condition pertains to the fact that contemporary economies are organized, to a considerable extent, on a national, continental, and world basis. A characteristic of such financial, industrial, and commercial enterprises is that their prosperity, and therefore the power and economic rewards that accrue to their élites, has a relatively weak relationship with what happens in any particular region. The mobility of capital, except perhaps in certain sectors such as the resource industries, has the effect of dissociating to a degree the interests of economic élites from those of any given regional community. In other words, the predominant patterns of economic organization in modern western societies seem to be such as to encourage the dissociation of economic power from social responsibility with regard to any particular region.

There is a further phenomenon of significance in this connection. It is the dissociation between economic and political power:

> ...a society becomes ripe for social transformation when the stratification order is in disequilibrium; that is, when the class which is...economically dominant through its control of the productive process is not the class which is politically dominant. The tensions which this imbalance generates can only be resolved by one and the same class winning mastery over all the elements of power—social, economic and political (Parkin 1976, p. 129).

This is definitely the case in the francophone subsociety: the class that is economically dominant is different from the one that is politically and socially dominant; the two are also poorly connected with each other, either in terms of interorganizational or interpersonal linkages.[7] Moreover, as indicated above, the interests of the economically dominant class are based on a nationally and internationally organized system, and therefore depend relatively little on the condition of a particular region. In contrast, the interests of the politically and socially dominant élite are very much tied to the socio-economic conditions of their region.

As a result of this situation, the political and social élites of a region, which in this case are francophone, from time to time face a double disadvantage: on the one hand, their own organizational and career interests

---

[7] Guindon (1968a) describes the interélite relationships established with the advent of industrialization as a mutually satisfactory accommodation. Quebec society provided political stability, an abundant supply of unskilled labour seeking employment, and an "ideologically co-operative" élite, "sensitive only about its continued control over its demographic substructures. This fitted in quite well with the aims of the incoming groups, which could develop their economic pursuits and enterprises with minimum involvement in the local society. The local élite of politicians and clergy welcomed the transaction of business and the development of business institutions. Industry was relieving the economic burden of the demographic surplus of French-Canadian rural society. The local élites' leadership was not being challenged" (p. 161). Guindon also points out that this pattern of mutually satisfying accommodation has been challenged since World War II, and that making room in the managerial levels of industry and government for the middle class that has emerged in Quebec "is the crucial test of Canadian unity."

are affected by the decisions of an economic élite that belongs to another community, with which they are poorly connected, and over which they have little influence; on the other hand, the interests of that economic élite, because it operates at a different level of economic organization, may be in opposition to those of the regionally based political and social élites. This double disadvantage, whenever it is experienced, constitutes a double source of tension that is likely to be detrimental to the cohesion of society.

Further, since their interests are partly tied to the state of the economy, the political and social élites will attempt to exercise as much control over economic decisions as possible. This will be attempted through the provincial State apparatus. However, the State apparatus that can best serve the interests of the economically dominant élites is that of the central government. Thus, tension rooted in the economic and social organization of society has ramifications at the political level in tensions between central and regional governments.

STRATIFICATION OF ORGANIZATIONS ACROSS LINGUISTIC COMMUNITIES

Closely related to the character of the relationship between anglophone-controlled organizations and the francophone community is the matter of their relationship with francophone-controlled economic organizations. Economic organizations, like any other type, vary in their relative importance, which is determined by their size and the impact of their decisions on other organizations and the community. There exists, in other words, a stratification of organizations on which the socio-economic ranking of individuals partly depends, but which is clearly distinct from it.

There are different ways of classifying economic organizations. One, for instance, is in terms of the function it performs: extractive, processing of new materials, manufacturing, technological development, financing, and so on. These board categories may also be differentiated in terms of product or service (for example, textiles as opposed to electronic equipment; oil as opposed to coal). Organizations in these different categories vary in terms of the economic resources they command, their possibilities for growth, and their impact on the rest of the economy. It is frequently said, for instance, that manufacturing has a ''motor role'' in the economy in contrast to the extraction and export of raw materials.

A related classification of organizations is in terms of their size and influence. Averitt's description of two broad types of organizations in the North American economy illustrates this dimension.[8] He argues that part of the economy

---

[8] Averitt (1968) makes it clear that the two types of organizations are interconnected and interdependent. He is not referring to separate economies of the sort that the expression *dual* sometimes refers to.

...is composed of firms large in size and influence. Its organizations are corporate and bureaucratic; its production processes are vertically integrated through ownership and control of critical raw material suppliers and product distributors; its activities are diversified into many industries, regions, and nations. Financial support is readily available from both internal and external sources. Firms in the large economy serve national and international markets, using technologically progressive systems of production and distribution. . . .

The other economy is populated by relatively small firms. These enterprises are the ones usually dominated by a single individual or family. The firm's sales are realized in restricted markets. Profits and retained earnings are commonly below those in the center; long-term borrowing is difficult. Economic crises often result in bankruptcy or severe financial retrenchment. Techniques of production and marketing are rarely as up to date as those in the center. These firms are often, though not always, technological followers, sometimes trailing at some distance behind the industry leaders (1968, p. 7).

In the present context, we are concerned with the location and control of these different types of organizations by region, but particularly by linguistic subsociety. Organizations differ in terms of their possibilities for growth, their impact on the rest of the economy, their dominance *vis-à-vis* other organizations. One approach to regions and linguistic subsocieties is to look at the kinds of organizations in each of them and at the location of the control of these organizations.[9] An examination of the location of organizations and of their control reveals that nation-states are stratified with respect to each other as are regions within nation-states. It has been frequently observed that the Canadian economy is dominated by the American economy and that central Canada dominates the other regions.

As noted in the previous chapter, francophone economic organizations tend to be lower in the hierarchy than anglophone organizations. First, francophone-controlled organizations tend to be smaller. Second, a number of observers have pointed out that the firms controlled by francophones are located in the most static and slow-developing industries and are tied to a limited market. Heavy industry, producer goods, and complex and expensive consumer goods industries through which "one can reasonably expect economic growth through industrial expansion and technological development" are controlled by non-francophones (Milner and Milner 1973, p. 35).[10] Some changes have occurred in recent years, such as the increased francophone control in the financial sector within Quebec, but the overall pattern has not been altered (Niosi 1977).

This point has also been argued by different authors in terms of the distinction between manufacturing and the supply of raw materials dichotomy. Clement, for example, states that:

---

[9] Control is partly a question of ownership, financial manipulations, ability to set prices, to determine what will be produced, or to connect with markets, domestic or foreign.

[10] See also Dinsmore (1975) and Tremblay (1977).

Canada is not unequivocally an industrial society. *Part* is industrialized—but the rest is more aptly characterized as a resource hinterland. Most of Canada's industrial capacity is located below a line starting at Windsor, encompassing Toronto, and moving on to Montreal. This is industrial Canada; all other areas base their economies on key resources: in British Columbia, on wood, pulp and paper, with some hydro; in the Prairies, on gas, petroleum, potash, and wheat; in northern Ontario and Quebec, on mining, and pulp and paper, plus, again, hydro; in the Atlantic region, on pulp and paper, fish, and some coal, plus hydro in Newfoundland. These outliers feed the ''golden horseshoe'' and U.S. markets with their resources and, in turn, consume the finished products from there (1978, p. 100).

When considering the relative positions of the linguistic subsocieties in Canada (and of the regions as well) in terms of the distribution of different kinds of organizations and of their control, it is important to locate the subsocieties and regions in the total North American economy. This point was made quite convincingly twenty-five years ago by Faucher and Lamontagne. Their analysis dealt with the Quebec economy, but the basic point is applicable to all regions of the country:

> Quebec's industrial development has been North-American. Quebec's economy has never behaved in an autonomous and isolated way. On the contrary, it has always felt very deeply the impact of the North-American evolution. Its development has been mainly a response to change affecting the whole continent . . . (1953, pp. 34–35).

Different kinds of factors are involved in the determination of the position and role of a nation-state or a region in the continental and world economies. Faucher and Lamontagne emphasize the locational factors. They indicate that during the pre-industrial period Quebec was leading the way in Canada, its economic development being centred around Quebec City and Montreal. This development coincided with a phase of commercialism that gave great significance to the St. Lawrence waterway. The two main articles of commerce were wood and grain, and shipbuilding was an important industry. The passage from commercialism to industrialism saw the substitution of steel for wood, the construction of the railroads, and the introduction of the steam engine. Thus, there was a displacement of the ''centre of economic gravity in North America'' toward those regions rich in coal and steel, namely, the Appalachian region, the Pittsburg-Cleveland area, and southern Ontario.

A new era began for Quebec during the second decade of the twentieth century when occurred ''the depletion of certain resources and the insufficient availability of other factors in the United States,'' such as copper, pulpwood, iron, iron substitutes, and the substitution of coal by water as a source of electric power. ''This evolution involved deep changes in the relative importance of the locational factors and, this time, Quebec was strongly favoured by the new orientation of economic development'' (ibid., p. 31), which was characterized by rapid industrialization and growth in the province. This growth lasted until the late 1940s. The same growth also occurred in Ontario; both were developing in the same direction as they responded to the same U.S. impulse.

During the last twenty-five to thirty years, the Quebec economy seems to have experienced a decline relative to Ontario and to the rest of the country.[11] According to the Faucher-Lamontagne thesis, the shift of economic activity to the west of the country, associated with the exploitation of resources located there, would be a factor in this relative decline.

It is important to emphasize that the Faucher-Lamontagne thesis is not simply that the location of national resources is important in regional economic development, but that the locational factors take their importance from the role they play in the continental economy dominated by the United States. In other words, much of the evolution of different regions of Canada and of the disparities among them is due to the evolution of the U.S. economy and to the ways in which each Canadian region fits into that economy.

The role of Canadian economic interests in regard to regional development in Canada is also revealed in patterns of investments. Clement notes that

> As early as 1934, U.S. branch plants in Canada were highly concentrated geographically. Two-thirds of all U.S.-controlled plants were located in Toronto (32 per cent), Montreal (13 per cent), Hamilton (5 per cent), the Niagara Frontier (7 per cent), or nearby border cities (9 per cent). Of all manufacturing establishments in Canada in 1931, 42 per cent were in Ontario and 31 per cent in Quebec, but 66 per cent of the U.S.-controlled plants were in Ontario and 16 per cent in Quebec. Thus, the Ontario-centred branches of U.S. manufacturing firms tended even at this time to reinforce and aggravate the problems of regionalism in Canada (1978, p. 95).

This pattern persists today as shown by data on the distribution of non-financial industrial, and especially manufacturing, taxable income: U.S.-controlled firms obtain a disproportionate share of their taxable income from Ontario (relative to the importance of Ontario in terms of population in Canada). This is especially the case for income from manufacturing (see table 3.3.1). The taxable income of Canadian-controlled firms is distributed by region, more in accordance with the population than that of U.S.-controlled firms.

On the basis of these data, Clement observes that "if it were not for U.S. industrials, the problem of regionalism would not be as serious as it now is for the Atlantic provinces, Quebec, and British Columbia" (ibid., p. 101).

The hiring of executives by U.S.-owned firms is also interesting in regard to regional and linguistic factors. The Sales study conducted in Quebec in 1974[12] reveals certain patterns worth mentioning. Of the

---

[11] This is the case even though there may have been growth in absolute terms in many sectors and in the economy as a whole. On this question, see Fréchette (1977), Jouandet-Bernadat (1978), and Tremblay (1977).

[12] The results reported here are from part two of the article that appeared in *Le Devoir* (28 April 1977).

TABLE 3.3.1
DISTRIBUTION OF TAXABLE INCOME, BY REGION AND CONTROL, 1972

	PERCENTAGE					
CONTROL OF COMPANIES	Atlantic	Quebec	Ontario	Prairies	British Columbia	Total
Non-financial industrial						
United States	3.2	18.1	53.5	17.6	7.3	100.0
Canada	5.2	26.0	41.8	13.4	13.0	100.0
Manufacturing						
United States	2.7	18.9	62.2	9.6	6.7	100.0
Canada	3.6	28.8	43.2	9.8	14.4	100.0
Population	9.5	28.0	35.7	16.4	10.1	100.0

SOURCE: Clement (1978), pp. 101–2.

U.S.-controlled firms, 40.9% of executives were born in the United States; only 26.3% were born in Quebec—the lowest percentage of all foreign-controlled firms. European firms in Quebec hire even fewer Canadian-born executives (39.8%), but all from Quebec. In contrast, British firms in Quebec hire mostly Canadian-born executives (67.5%; 54.6% from Quebec). Sales also hypothesized that in the foreign purchase of a Canadian-owned firm, the language of the executives would tend to be English if it were purchased from Anglo-Canadians and French if purchased from Franco-Canadians. The hypothesis was verified in the first case, but not the second: firms purchased from French Canadians are now, at the rate of 85.9%, directed by executives of other regions. Finally, he also found that the executives of U.S.-controlled firms were much more likely than executives of British- or European-controlled firms to think that the imposition of French as the language of work would have very negative consequences for the Quebec economy.

One possible explanation for such behaviour is that while Canadian corporations have set up some organizational means in order to accommodate cultural and linguistic variations in different parts of the world, they have not done so for Canada since it was considered part of the culturally and linguistically homogeneous North American environment.[13] The French community in Quebec has been perceived more or less as an anomaly; it was an ethnic minority that was expected to adapt, like the other ethnic minorities, to the imperatives of economic enterprises.

Patterns such as these suggest that the practices of Canadian-controlled organizations, as well as processes within Canada, have an impact on the patterns of organizational stratification among regions and linguistic subsocieties in Canada. It should be mentioned, however, that U.S.

---

[13] Sales draws this possible interpretation from Mira Wilkins (1974).

enterprises played their role in Canada largely with the collaboration of important segments of the Canadian political and economic élites and of the population at large. This has been the case both among anglophones and francophones.

It is not our objective to go into a comprehensive analysis of the patterns and causes of regional and linguistic disparities in Canada. We wish to emphasize that an important dimension of such inequalities is concerned with the location of organizations and of their control.[14]

Moreover, it should be noted that up until the late 1950s, government policies in Canada were such as to interfere as little as possible with the "forces of the market" insofar as regions were concerned. There was preoccupation with regional inequalities, but largely in terms of compensation for the negative impacts of the "forces of the market" on individual incomes and social security. It is only in the late 1950s that the economic development of regions became a direct object of government policy. This occurred at both levels of government roughly at the same time, a phenomenon that was, and is, a source of considerable tension between them, as we will see in a subsequent chapter.[15]

Several attempts have been made, mainly through provincial government initiatives, to improve the conditions for the formation and growth of francophone-run enterprises. Generally, these have taken two forms: providing financial assistance to francophone private enterprises and the formation of State enterprises. The first type of measure was implemented through agencies, such as La Société générale de Financement, La Société de Développement industriel, and La Caisse de Dépôt et de Placement. The second type is exemplified by State enterprises such as Sidbec and Hydro-Québec. It is not clear, however, how much effect these governmental initiatives and non-governmental activities, such as those of the co-operative movement, especially Le Mouvement des Caisses populaires Desjardins, have had in reducing the degree of dependence of the francophone-controlled segment of the economy or in stopping further increases in dependence.

It has been hypothesized that phenomena such as the dissociation of economic power and social responsibility, the low integration of economic and socio-political power, and the structural dependence of the economy of a regional or linguistic community constitute one of the main sources of regionalism, "ethnic nationalism," and political independence movements in modern industrial societies.[16] That is to say, regional groups and élites emerge as countervailing forces to the distant centres of power. They tend to use political means (which are not restricted to governmental actions) to

---

[14] For a further discussion of this question, see Breton and Breton (forthcoming).

[15] For a detailed discussion of the attitudes of federal and provincial governments toward regional disparities and their evolution over time, see Careless (1977).

[16] See, for example, Hechter (1971).

incite these centres to be more responsive to the interests of the regional community. Sometimes, if they see the possibility, they will advocate taking over organizations in a domain of economic activity in order to be able to control the decisions made in them. Thus, regionalism, ''ethnic nationalism,'' and independence movements emerge in response to the fact that the interests of the regional or linguistic community are controlled by centres of power external to it, over which they have little influence, and whose interests are not strongly tied to what happens in that particular region. These movements are socio-political expressions of a questioning of the legitimacy of the institutions of the society, the distribution of economic power, and the way in which it is used.

This questioning has repercussions for the central government of the society. In some instances, the central government is perceived as incapable of dealing with the situation, of affecting significantly the decisions of the centres of economic power; its usefulness is then put in doubt. In other instances, it is seen as unwilling to do anything serious in this regard because the parties in power at the national level are perceived as tied to the nationally or internationally organized economic interests. In such instances, the legitimacy of the central government is under challenge.

CONCLUSION

Underlying the strains on the society that originate in political institutions are those that derive from the organization of the economy and the distribution of decision-making power within it. It may well be that the latter are more important than the former in terms of the seriousness of their impact and therefore in terms of required solutions. Of course, the two are interconnected: it would be a mistake to think of political solutions *or* economic solutions; the thinking must be geared toward solutions that pertain to or take into account the *interaction* between the two sets of institutions.

Three kinds of issues that can cause strains on the societal community were discussed in this chapter:

a. The legitimacy of the economic system of the society may be questioned when important segments of that system are not perceived as providing equal opportunity to the members of each of the linguistic communities in which it operates.

b. The legitimacy of the system of economic organizations may also be questioned whenever the decision-making centres of the system appear to consider the interests of a regional or linguistic community as secondary and especially if their attitude *vis-à-vis* it is exploitative, even if only mildly so. Such a dissociation may result from the cultural and linguistic cleavages between those who control the organization and the community. But more importantly, it is rooted in the fact that the interests of the controllers are only weakly linked with the conditions in a particular community. The problem of legitimacy is further accentuated by the fact that the dominant economic élite, whose interests are not primarily regional, is poorly connected with the social and political élites, whose interests are tied to the condition of the regional community.

c. The legitimacy of the economic organization may be further weakened by the fact that the economic organizations of the linguistic community are so located in the national and international economic structure that they find it difficult to grow. This may lead those who have an interest in those organizations to advocate serious transformations in the distribution of organizational power, transformations that would cause strain on the society.

We believe that these three issues are at the root of the crisis currently experienced in Canadian society.

Central Political Institutions and Citizens of Each Linguistic Community

For political institutions as for other institutions, legitimacy is something that needs to be acquired and maintained; that is to say, support from members of the political community is not automatic, and their identification with the institutions needs to be acquired and nourished. How is this achieved? What characteristics of, and behaviour by, political institutions result in support and identification? What results in unwilling support and rejection, indifference and antagonism? What issues and problems arise in attempts to establish legitimacy in the eyes of citizens?

This chapter addresses these questions with regard to the central government of the country, whose citizens are from two linguistic communities. In other words, what issues have to be dealt with if legitimacy is to be established and maintained with the two linguistic segments of the population? What circumstances would bring about support for, and identification with, the central government from the two groups of citizens? In dealing with these questions, it will be necessary to take account of the fact that each of the language collectivities shows considerable internal diversity economically, culturally, and regionally. The concern, then, is with a set of questions about the relationship between the State and citizens, as individuals or in groups, given that the citizens form two language communities. Moreover, the focus is only on those aspects of the State-citizen relationship that have implications for legitimacy and its different dimensions.

There are three general classes of issues or problems faced by a political institution and its agents in building and maintaining its legitimacy. Political institutions are decision-making centres for the formulation and implementation of policies. A first set of issues concerns the accessibility of those centres to the citizens of each linguistic community. Are there channels of influence from each of them? How are the chances of participation in decision-making processes distributed across collectivities? What are the actual patterns of participation? What characteristics of the institutions and of the two communities, in addition to the language factor, have an impact on accessibility and participation?

177

The political process involves interactions between the State and the citizens. It is a two-way process, although usually not symmetrical (the interactions from the State to the citizen are more numerous and significant than the reverse). Various decisions and activities emanate from the decision-making centres that may or may not meet the expectations of citizens. The second set of issues pertains to the political decisions and their impact (or lack of it) on the condition of citizens. In this study, we are concerned with the differential impact of policies on the condition of each linguistic community and of its members.

However, political institutions are not just instruments for achieving certain purposes; they embody certain values; acquire a distinctive character; are the expression of the culture of a community; and have a symbolic value. Objects such as flags and monuments may be important symbols; but institutions, whether political, religious, economic, or other, are far more significant as collective symbols. They incorporate much more cultural content than flags, and are a much more powerful expression of the collective identity.

Symbols can have positive, negative, or mixed connotations. For instance, certain aspects of our institutions symbolize positive values, such as liberty and security; others reflect the dominant culture of the society (the British parliamentary system);[1] others indicate a tie to a foreign power (the representative of the British Crown). Features of our institutions such as these have a bearing on their legitimacy; they affect the extent to which individuals support them and identify with them.[2] A third set of issues pertains to the symbolic dimension of institutions.

In a democratic society, accessibility of decision-making centres is important for establishing their legitimacy. If a political institution is perceived as deliberately making it difficult for a group to exert influence on it, then it is unlikely to receive willing support. Also, one can identify more easily with an institution that is under the authority and influence of one's own community. It is difficult for an institution to be perceived as an extension of the social and cultural personality of a group if that group has no input in the making of the institution, its functioning, or both.

Similarly, if the decisions and activities of a government are inequitous for a particular segment of the society, or are perceived to be so, there will be problems of legitimacy. Such problems may also result if contacts of

---

[1] The fact that the Quebec House of Representatives was named the *Assemblée nationale* in the early sixties is not an accident nor a collective quirk; it is a highly significant symbolic gesture.

[2] The personality of an individual is in part a social phenomenon; it represents a particular combination of the elements of the culture in which he was born. Given this basic socio-psychological proposition, we can say that identification is possible to the extent that there is a continuity between the social personality of individuals and the character of institutions. Conversion or acculturation is the transformation of the social personality of an individual in line with the cultural values and symbolic contents of institutions other than those of his community of origin.

government institutions with one linguistic community are more frequent and efficient than with the other. If it is the particular groups of people in authority that are perceived as the cause of the problem, attempts will be made to replace them through the mechanisms provided for this in democratic societies. However, if it is felt to be virtually impossible to replace the authorities, or if the source of the inequities or poor relationships is perceived to be not in the authorities themselves but in the institution, then it is the institution itself that people will seek to transform or reject. Our concern here is obviously with the legitimacy of the institution.

Finally, it must be noted that legitimacy is a matter of degree. In other words, certain groups may find the institution totally unacceptable, alien, and unworkable; others may question only certain of its features; others may find it acceptable; and finally, some may find it the best possible political system, both in terms of its accessibility and of the results it brings about.

ACCESSIBILITY OF CENTRAL GOVERNMENT

Political representation is a complex phenomenon. It can occur through different channels and mechanisms. This is the case whether we think of representation as the process whereby citizens voice their interests and political philosophies, or through which they contribute to the solution of problems or participate in the improvement of conditions in the society.

Representation through elected representatives. Among the most important mechanisms, at least in theory, are those through which representatives are selected for political decision making. How have these mechanisms worked insofar as francophones and anglophones are concerned? Have the two groups been represented in Parliament and in Cabinet in proportion to their size in the population? As can be seen from the accompanying tables, the representation of the two language groups in Cabinet has been fairly proportional, except for certain periods such as those under Conservative governments (table 3.4.1 and 3.4.3). Moreover, in comparison with other ethnic origins, the French representation has been particularly good. Tables 3.4.2 and 3.4.3 reveal a fairly proportional representation in Parliament, except again for certain periods. The other ethnic origins are underrepresented, both in Parliament and in Cabinet.

Another aspect of representation is the degree to which a region gives a majority of its votes to the governing party. Engelmann and Schwartz write that

in 17 general elections between 1921 and 1974, inclusive, . . . the governing party received at least 50 percent of the popular vote in 7 elections in the Atlantic provinces and in 10 in Quebec. . . . In Quebec, characteristically, support for the government has generally been even higher, with two notable exceptions. When the remainder of the country helped elect a Conservative government in 1957 and 1962, Quebec voters gave only grudging support of approximately 30 percent. While such rejections of the governing party are the exception in Quebec, they are the norm in western Canada . . . (1975, pp. 187−88).

TABLE 3.4.1
MAN-YEARS IN WHICH EACH ETHNIC GROUP REPRESENTED IN
CANADIAN CABINET BY POLITICAL PARTY IN POWER, 1867–1966
(%)

Period	Party	English	French	Scottish	Irish	Other	Total Man-Years
1867–1873	Lib.-Cons.	42	23	22	13	—	86
1874–1878	Lib.	52	30	10	8	—	63
1879–1896	Lib.-Cons.	44	21	13	23	—	255
1897–1911	Lib.	46	21	17	17	—	229
1912–1917	Cons.	46	16	0	38	—	108
1917–1921	Unionist	60	6	18	16	—	73
1922–1925	Lib.	27	27	27	20	—	75
1926	Cons.	71	—	14	14	—	7
1927–1930	Lib.	33	33	18	11	6	73
1931–1935	Cons.	43	16	31	11	—	95
1936–1956	Lib.	51	23	21	4	2	303
1957–1962	Cons.	60	14	9	13	5	133
1962–1966	Lib.	44	33	20	—	3	102

SOURCE: Breton and Roseborough (1968).

TABLE 3.4.2
ETHNIC ORIGIN OF NEW MEMBERS OF HOUSE OF COMMONS
BY PERIOD DURING WHICH FIRST ELECTED, 1867–1964
(%)

Period	French	English	Scottish	Irish	Other	Total	N
1867–1873	24.9	31.5	26.2	14.5	2.8	99.9	317
1874–1877	25.3	16.5	35.2	22.0	1.1	100.1	91
1878–1895	27.2	25.3	23.5	20.9	3.1	100.0	383
1896–1899	24.8	23.9	26.5	20.4	4.4	100.0	113
1900–1910	20.5	26.9	26.9	22.4	3.2	99.9	308
1911–1929	21.7	26.2	29.7	19.5	2.9	100.0	512
1930–1939	30.8	24.2	27.9	14.6	2.5	100.0	240
1940–1953	28.7	32.3	22.5	11.6	4.9	100.0	387
1954–1958	31.3	30.8	15.9	12.6	9.3	99.9	214
1959–1964	48.1	29.1	13.3	5.1	4.4	100.0	158
Total percentage of members of Parliament	27.0	27.6	24.9	16.6	3.8	99.9	
Total N	736	751	679	453	104		2,723

SOURCE: Manzer (1974), p. 250.
NOTE: Because of rounding of numbers, totals do not always correspond to sum of parts.

TABLE 3.4.3

PERCENTAGE OF CANADIAN POPULATION IN SELECTED ETHNIC CATEGORIES AT EACH CENSUS BETWEEN 1871 AND 1971

Ethnic Origin	1871	1881	1901	1911	1921	1931	1941	1951	1961	1971
English	20.3	20.4	23.5	26.0	29.0	26.4	25.8	25.9	23.0 ⎫	
Irish	24.3	22.1	18.4	14.9	12.6	11.9	11.0	10.3	9.6 ⎬	44.6
Scottish	15.8	16.2	14.9	14.2	13.3	13.0	12.2	11.1	10.4 ⎭	
French	31.1	30.0	30.7	28.6	27.9	28.2	30.3	30.8	30.0	28.7
Other	8.6	11.3	12.5	16.3	17.2	20.5	20.7	21.9	26.6	26.7
Total	100.0	100.0	100.0	100.0	100.0	100.0	100.0	100.0	100.0	100.0

SOURCE: 1871–1911: Urquhart and Buckley (1965), p. 18; 1921–1971: Statistics Canada (1973b), cat. no. 92–723.

On the basis of such observations, we would expect a fairly high degree of allegiance to, and identification with, the federal government on the part of both anglophones and francophones. Yet various expressions of disaffection are being voiced. These are expressed in various ways, but perhaps the strongest and most significant are the pro-independence feelings among francophones in Quebec, feelings that are not negligible:

> As of late 1977, support for the independence of Quebec stood at about 18 per cent . . . (a figure that) represents an average of the four polls taken during the last three months of 1977. If one were to consider only the French Canadians in Quebec, one would currently obtain figures about 3 to 4 per cent higher concerning the support for independence (Pinard forthcoming).

Table 3.4.4 provides information for the period between 1962 and 1977. The support for *souveraineté-association*, which is another indicator of the dissatisfaction with the existing political institutions, is much stronger than for independence. Table 3.4.5 shows that "since 1977, support for sovereignty-association in the total adult population would be somewhere between 25 and 40 per cent . . . Among French Canadians only, support in 1977 would have been from 3 to 6 per cent higher" (ibid.).

TABLE 3.4.4
TREND OF OPINION RELATIVE TO INDEPENDENCE, QUEBEC, 1962–1978

YEAR	ALL ADULT QUEBEC CITIZENS			
	% in Favour	% Opposed	% Undecided	N^a
1962	8	73	19	998
1965	7	79	14	6910
1968a	11	71	18	202
1968b	10	72	18	746
1969	11	75	15	367
1970a	14	76	10	820
1970b	11	74	16	1974
1972	10	68	22	778
1973	17	64	19	1006
1974	15	74	11	349
1976b	18	58	24	1095
1976c	12	66	22	1042
1977a to d[b]	19	66	15	1750
1977e and f	19	71	10	1100
1977g to j	18	70	12	3500
1978b	14	79	7	972
1978c	12	74	14	300
1978d	17	73	10	721

ADULT FRENCH CANADIANS ALONE[c]

YEAR	% in Favour	% Opposed	% Undecided	N^a
1962	8	71	20	880
1963	13	43	23[d]	987
1965	8	76	16	5488
1967	7	87[e]	6	502
1968a	13	65	22	165
1968b	11	68	21	624
1969	13	70	17	294
1970a	16	73	11	696
1970b	13	70	17	1513
1972	11	65	24	660
1973	19	60	21	860
1974	17	70	13	277
1976a	23	63	13	725
1976b	20	55	25	954
1976c	13	65	22	755
1977b	19	61	20	600
1977f	23	68	9	700
1977g	18	64	18	616
1978d	20	70	10	617

SOURCE: Pinard (1978). See appendix 3.A.1 for sources of data and questions asked.
NOTES: a. Whenever indicated, "no answer" category eliminated. Ns for 1965 study weighted. In a few cases
   (e.g., some 1977 polls, 1978c), N approximate due to lack of exact information.
   b. In 1977, following election of Parti Québécois in November 1976, no less than ten polls were made
   public in Quebec on independence and related issues. In first panel of table, rather than present all or
   sample, average of proportions for each category for polls from January to April (4), May to August
   (2), and September to December (4) are given. In second panel, results of 1977 and 1978 polls for
   which data were available separately are reproduced.
   c. Ethnicity variously defined by self-identification, mother tongue, language at home, and so on. In our
   experience, either one of these measures in Quebec yields same results.
   d. Total in this row, 79%; others (21%) said not aware of separatist activities.
   e. In that study, separation was one among other less radical options; 87% total for other options.

These data on the degree of support for political independence and for *souveraineté-association* among francophones in Quebec do not indicate a high degree of legitimacy and a strong sense of identification with the central political institutions. This is especially so if we take the undecided into consideration: this category of respondents may not support independence or *souveraineté-association*, but their indecision suggests that they are wavering in their allegiance to the central government. This is so, in spite of the fact that Quebec francophones have been fairly well represented in the federal Cabinet and Parliament. Formal representation does not appear to be sufficient to assure a high degree of loyalty. It is therefore necessary to examine other aspects of representation, that is, other features of the political institutions affecting the extent and quality of representation.

   Functioning of electoral system. Political parties want power; it is one of their essential *raisons d'être*. Getting votes is the mechanism to gain power. Some analysts have argued that given the nature of the Canadian

TABLE 3.4.5
Trend of Opinion in Quebec Relative to Sovereignty-Association, 1970 and 1977–1978

	ALL ADULT QUEBEC CITIZENS			
YEAR	% in Favour	% Opposed	% Undecided and No Answer	N
1970a (opinion)	35	53	12	820
1970b (opinion)	28	49	23	1982
1977b (vote)	32	52	16	742
1977f (vote)	38	44	18	823
1977f (opinion)	40	46	14	823
1977g (vote)	26	56	19	729
1977h (opinion)	40	50	10	1458
1977j (vote)	42	55	4	1000
1978a (vote)	25	58	17	714
1978b (vote)	33	53	14	972
1978b (opinion)	39	50	11	972
1978d (opinion)	35	48	17	721
1978e (vote)	31	53	16	856

	ADULT FRENCH CANADIANS ALONE[a]			
YEAR	% in Favour	% Opposed	% Undecided and No Answer	N
1970b (opinion)	33	43	24	1511
1977b (vote)	38	46	16	600
1977f (vote)	44	37	19	700
1977f (opinion)	45	40	15	700
1977g (vote)	29	51	20	617
1978a (vote)	28	55	17	593
1978d (opinion)	39	45	17	617
1978e (vote)	35	47	18	?

SOURCE: See table 3.4.4.
NOTE: For questions asked, see appendix 3.A.2.
    a. Limited to those polls for which results available to author.

electoral system (single-ballot, simple majority in each electoral district) and the fact that language groups are geographically segregated, there will be an interest on the part of each political party to present candidates that have appeal for the electorate of each district. One implicaion of this is that the candidates put forward by each party will tend to be recruited from the language group that they seek to represent. Therefore, since both candidates and electors belong to the same language group, the candidates will tend to avoid the issues that are of particular concern to the members of the other group. This would be less likely to occur if the electorate of the district and the candidate were of different language groups (Pinard 1976*a*). National parties would encourage allegiance to, and identification with, the central government because, on the one hand, they increase the chances of election of candidates from both language groups, and on the other, they lead to the avoidance of issues and electoral strategies that appeal specifically to the language communities and emphasize the differences between them.

Other analysts have argued that the Canadian electoral system operates in such a way as to exacerbate regional tensions and accentuate identities (which, to some degree, correspond to the territorial distribution of the language groups), and this precisely because it encourages the use of electoral strategies and themes based on regional identities and interests (Cairns 1968; Simeon 1975; Wilson 1974). Simeon, for instance, writes that

> party strategies might be very different if each province were a single constituency with proportional representation, or if we had a few large constituencies not coterminous with provincial boundaries, or if we had pure proportional representation and one national constituency. The assumption here is that one very important effect of institutional factors is to provide political leaders with different incentives . . . (1975, p. 505).

In the present system, the incentives lead politicians to seek votes by appealing to regional and linguistic identities and interests.

Unfortunately, no data providing a direct test of these hypotheses about the strategies actually used by political parties and their candidates were found. It should be noted, however, that it would be difficult to obtain evidence that could establish whether a different electoral system would result in the use of strategies that are more integrative in that they would focus the attention and feelings of the electorate on common issues and therefore on the performance of government with regard to these common concerns rather than on regional issues.

Much of the argument about the integrative role of national political parties, however, assumes that *all* the major parties behave in roughly the same way in these regards: all recruit candidates from the different regions and language groups, and all incorporate elements in their platforms that will win them votes in each region and language community. However, if the national parties come to be identified with a particular language community and articulate the interests and political views of that community, interparty competition will then tend to be along linguistic lines and thus have a divisive effect—and this even if each language group has fairly adequate representation in Parliament. Of course, if the number of representatives is less than adequate, the divisive effect will tend to be even stronger.

To emphasize this aspect of the issue, Pinard has suggested that

> *la formation de partis à base culturelle à l'échelle nationale, dans les pays où il y a ségrégation territoriale, devrait être considérée comme une stratégie naturelle de la part d'élites culturelles visant à la décentralisation ou la sécession d'un système politique fragmenté* (1976*a*, p. 50).

Conversely, it could be argued that a natural strategy for an élite bent on an integrated political system would be to attempt to develop a strong base for all parties in each of the language communities.

In this context, a critical question concerns the extent to which the national parties in Canada tend to identify, and to be identified, more with one of the language communities than with the other. The data on the Cabinet (table 3.4.1) indicates a certain identification of the Conservative Party with the anglophone community, while the Liberal Party is relatively more identified with the francophone community. It is also known that the more leftist parties (CCF and present New Democratic Party) have failed to establish a strong base in the francophone community. Meisel points out that no federal party can be thought of as having ethnic, linguistic, or communal aims: "the accommodation of linguistic interests thus concerns parties primarily within their internal life rather than as an element of the inter-party struggle" (1974, p. 14). But he goes on to indicate that

> it is nevertheless a fact of critical importance that during the present century the Liberals have become the party favoured by French Canada and that they have been its most effective spokesman in Parliament. The Conservative party, on the other hand, is identified with English Canada and continues to demonstrate its incapacity to alter its ambivalent posture towards francophone interests, despite efforts by some Conservative elements to do so (ibid.).[3]

Representation of interest groups. As we have seen, the importance of both parties having a base in the two language collectivities stems in part from the fact that if they do, interparty competition is less likely to turn into a competition between language groups. But that importance rests on another factor as well. One of the main reasons there is more than one political party is that an electorate consists of different interests with regard to the main issues that confront a society. Each party tends to articulate certain interests; each tends to recruit its support more from certain segments of the electorate than from others. This is the case within language communities as well as between them. Thus, if only one of the (national) parties has a base in a particular community, it is quite possible that the interests of certain of its subgroups are not well represented, at least during certain periods of time. In other words, even though a political party may represent the broad interests of a language community, it may ignore the interests of certain groups within it. And if there is no other national party with a base in that collectivity, these other interests may be left unrepresented. If this occurs over a fairly long period of time—with little hope of an improvement in the situation due to the weakness and/or unacceptability of the other parties—a certain degree of

---

[3] See also Engelmann and Schwartz (1975, pp. 196–200). They show, with data collected in 1963, 1965, 1968, and 1972, that the Conservative and New Democratic Parties have two-thirds of their supporters among Protestant English-speaking Canadians. No such pattern of polarized support is found for the Liberal Party.

alienation, or at least a failure of identification or allegiance, is likely to occur. It would be useful to know, for example, if the alienation or the lack of identification with the federal government in Quebec is found mostly among those who have voted Liberal, but would have preferred to vote for another party if there had been one articulating their views. The need for a party articulating alternate views is suggested by data such as the following: in October 1977, a survey by Pinard and Hamilton revealed that while 44% of the sample said they were satisfied with the Liberal government in Ottawa, 66% intended to vote Liberal at the next election. According to Pinard, this pattern has occurred fairly consistently over time in Quebec.[4] Another pertinent result is that the number of undecided voters tends to be high in Quebec. This suggests that certain interests are not provided with viable alternatives by the party system. In the anglophone community, western alienation is no doubt related to its inadequate representation in the governing party over a long period of time.[5]

The nature of the connection of the interest groups in each language community with the central government is also important. It is so for a variety of reasons. Firstly, it may compensate for the failure of the party system in representing certain interests. Interest groups whose leaders are well connected with the decision-making centres may feel less negative about the fact that they are not represented in the party organization and its platform. Secondly, it has been argued that the importance of political parties has declined in recent years as a mechanism of representation of interests and that it tends to be replaced by mechanisms that link interest groups directly with government bodies.

> Recently, a more involved process of legislation has evolved. . . . Before any law or important administrative decision is decided upon, an intense consultation between officials and representatives of various vested interests takes place. There has been a striking increase in lobbying by interest groups who have the resources and capacity to do so. Many important decisions are arrived at through private consultations between civil servants and spokesmen for various vested interests, during which politicians play no role (Meisel 1978, p. 123).

The linkages of various interest groups with centres of decision making are important not only because they allow influence to be exerted upwards but also because they permit a downward flow of relevant information. Information about various aspects of issues and decisions constitutes a valuable resource. Not having access to such a resource puts one at a disadvantage. Moreover, it generates the feeling of ''being out of things''—a

---

[4] We are grateful to professors Maurice Pinard and Richard Hamilton for making these data available to us.

[5] Between 1921 and 1974, ''only once have the prairie provinces contributed a majority of their votes to the government, while British Columbia has come no closer than 49 percent, both times helping to elect a Conservative government in 1930 and 1958'' (Engelmann and Schwartz 1975, p. 188).

situation conducive to alienation rather than identification with the institution.

Finally, the élites of interest groups can play a significant role in shaping political opinions and attitudes, at least within their groups if not in the population at large. It would seem that the messages they convey would be determined in part by the nature of their relationships with the decision-making centres. Also,

> depending on the basis upon which they are organized, pressure groups may serve to further integrate a federal society or to further fragment it. That is, groups organized on a local or regional basis will tend to strengthen local awareness, local loyalties and local particularism, thus reinforcing fragmentation. On the other hand, groups organized on a national basis will tend to strengthen the national awareness of their members, to create feelings of identification with the national institutions of government, to heighten feelings of efficacy and involvement with those institutions and thus promote national integration (Kwavnick 1975, p. 71).

There are two aspects to the linkages with decision-making centres: one is a matter of access and the other is one of response on the part of the decision makers. By response are meant contracts, regulatory decisions, economic and commercial policies, grants, and so on. It would seem worthwhile to examine the patterns of linkages between the interest groups of each language community and the federal decision-making and administrative bodies. To which interest groups is the central government related, to which ones does it respond, and how are these groups distributed among language communities?

Unfortunately, little systematic evidence could be found on the patterns of linkages between the central government and the interest groups of each linguistic community. There is a fair amount of research on interest groups, but little that would allow to be assessed the degree of connection between the central government and the interest groups in each subsociety.[6] This is surprising in view of the possible role of such groups with respect to the cohesion of a highly differentiated society. A number of authors (Kwavnick 1975; National Advisory Council on Voluntary Action 1978; Stein 1968) have stressed the importance of such groups in connection with the linguistic diversity of the country. It appears that it is an area worth exploring further in connection with matters of legitimacy and identification.[7]

The question of the central government's linkages with the interest groups in each language community is particularly crucial in periods of rapid social change such as the last twenty years or so in Canada. These periods are

---

[6] The National Advisory Council on Voluntary Action had two studies carried out: on English- and French-language associations. Data were collected on the amount of funds received from the federal government. In the report (1978, pp. 165–69), some of the results on funding are presented, but in such a way that comparisons are difficult to make between the two sets of associations.

[7] The differential relationships of federal and provincial governments with interest groups is discussed in the next chapter.

indeed characterized by the emergence of new interests (financial, industrial, commercial, professional, cultural, and so on) or by the better organization of already existing ones. In such situations, problems of legitimacy and identification may arise for the central political institutions as a result of their failure to react with sufficient speed to accommodate the new and better-organized interests. As a result, the groups who do not find satisfactory channels for the effective expression of their interests may well become alienated from the central government—or fail to develop an identification with it—and seek support and action from their provincial governments.

Selection of political candidates and ministers. Closely related to the question of the more or less selective representation of the various interest groups in each language community is the matter of the selection of electoral candidates. Two questions can be raised here: firstly, is the process such as to prevent the selection of candidates representing certain interests within a language community? Secondly, does the process select as candidates persons who are central to the cultural group or persons who are peripheral or marginal to it? The hypothesis has been put forward that those who are selected and especially those who get to occupy important posts are atypical of the community and therefore not representative spokesmen for its interests; or that they have been selected and allowed to move up precisely because they are accommodating and fairly undemanding. Such an hypothesis is very difficult to test empirically. It is mentioned because it has been formulated to explain why the apparently adequate numerical representation did not have as much effect as could have been expected.

The composition of the Cabinet is important since the executive is a critical body in political decision making. A certain underrepresentation of the francophone community in the Cabinet was observed earlier, although not a very large one. Some have argued, however, that an anlysis based on the total count of Cabinet membership hides a more severe underrepresentation, which is revealed when the language distribution is considered by type of ministry (Simeon 1972). The evidence available gives some support to this hypothesis: table 3.4.6 provides data on representation by ministries, which have been classified into five categories. As can be seen, an underrepresentation of the French relative to their size in the total population has occurred in what most would tend to regard as the important ministries: policy making and human capital. On the other hand, there has been a French overrepresentation in the support and co-ordinative ministries, which are usually thought of as involving less power. Within these categories, there are also important variations, under and overrepresentation being very pronounced in certain instances.

Composition of bureaucracy. An important part of any government is its administration. It is one of the principal means through which it reaches the citizens. Many decisions are made at that level. Moreover, the

TABLE 3.4.6
PERCENTAGE OF YEARS IN WHICH SPECIFIED MINISTRIES
HEADED BY REPRESENTATIVES OF ETHNIC GROUPS, 1867–1966

Ministries	English	French	Scottish	Irish	Other	N
Policy-making ministries						
Prime Minister	51	23	24	2	—	100
Finance	78	—	4	18	—	100
Agriculture	49	11	27	13	—	100
Fisheries	39	33	23	5	—	100
Mines	33	20	38	3	5	60
Northern Affairs	53	18	29	—	—	17
Trade and Commerce	69	—	26	—	5	74
Transport	40	16	18	26	—	88
National Defence	55	18	18	9	—	100
External Affairs	91	3	—	5	—	58
Total	55	15	20	9	1	797
Human capital ministries						
Interior	60	—	14	25	—	63
Indian Affairs	59	4	16	20	—	69
Veteran Affairs ⎱ Health and Welfare ⎰	56	23	19	4	—	79
Labour	49	5	23	15	9	66
Immigration and Citizenship	44	8	44	3	—	36
Total	55	9	21	14	1	313
Support ministries						
National Revenue	36	22	15	24	3	145
Receiver General	42	33	—	25	—	12
National Defence	82	—	—	18	—	28
Post Office	34	45	3	18	—	100
Public Works	30	49	16	5	—	100
Total	37	34	11	17	1	385
Co-ordinative ministries						
President of Privy Council	54	32	11	3	—	91
Justice	31	25	25	19	—	100
Solicitor General	17	54	26	3	—	35
Secretary of State	31	39	—	30	—	100
Total	36	34	14	16	—	326
Ministries without portfolio	45	14	28	13	—	135

SOURCE: See table 3.4.1.
NOTE: Total number of man-years varies by ministry, since each has not lasted same length of time.

composition of the bureaucracy conveys images of the government as to its effectiveness, equity, and trustworthiness. In important ways, the bureaucracy is indicative of whom the government really represents. For these reasons—decision making, relationship with citizens, symbolic aspects—the composition of the bureaucracy is a critical component of the political institutions. In this section, the relative presence of the two language groups in that segment of the government apparatus will be considered.

Figure 3.4.1 shows that francophones have been considerably underrepresented in the federal bureaucracy for a long period of time. It is only in recent years that their presence corresponds to their proportion in the population. The sharp drop that occurred starting in the 1920s corresponds to the introduction of the merit system in the federal civil service. In such a system, the French experienced an educational disadvantage that

> was compounded by the Commission's narrow view of merit and efficiency. . . . Its standards and procedures were fashioned to correspond with the educational systems of the English-speaking provinces. . . . Of even greater effect on Francophone participation was the way that the goal of bureaucratic efficiency was conceived by the Commission and the department chiefs. In a word it was an uncompromisingly *unilingual* conception of efficiency (Beattie, Désy, and Longstaff 1972, p. 5).

The situation with regard to the use of French some time after this change has been described as follows by Beattie, Désy, and Longstaff:

> . . .After 1935 there was another set of grievances to contend with: a wave of protests and demands on language questions from all parts of French Canada, chiefly involving the lack of facilities and services in French provided by the federal administration. Month after month numerous complaints of this order were laid at Lapointe's feet, and he worked tirelessly in pursuing them, despite the fact that most of his efforts came to naught. It was a time when even the most trivial concessions to the idea of biculturalism were considered by the Anglophone majority to be wasteful and perverse. . . .
>   In spite of strong resistance on the part of those in the higher bureaucracy, Lapointe actually did gain a few minor successes in the administrative area, but the resistance he encountered now seems incredible. In one instance it took over a year to get acceptance from the Cabinet and the higher reaches of the bureaucracy that Quebec offices of the Public Service be furnished with telephone directories in both languages instead of in English only. The senior officers in charge resisted because they felt chary of allowing a precedent of this nature (ibid., pp. 7 – 9).

The authors also indicate that the Royal Commission on Government Organization, appointed in 1960, considered the problem of bilingualism. Even though the conclusion was reached that the situation was inadequate, it made no recommendations to remedy it: ''Once again, the link between unilingualism and efficiency was allowed to remain substantially unchallenged'' (ibid., p. 12).

The significance of the historical situation is accentuated by the fact that the Quebec bureaucracy was, and still is, almost entirely francophone (about

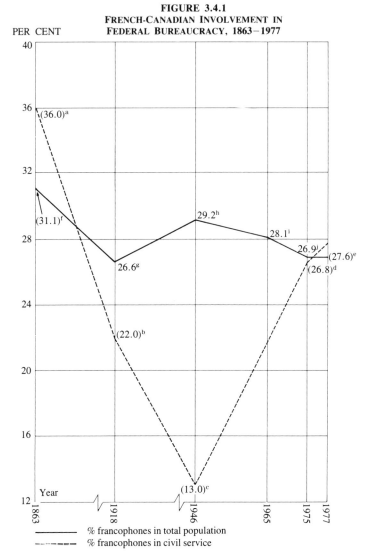

FIGURE 3.4.1
FRENCH-CANADIAN INVOLVEMENT IN
FEDERAL BUREAUCRACY, 1863–1977

PER CENT

——————— % francophones in total population
– – – – – – % francophones in civil service

SOURCE: a. Royal Commission on Bilingualism and Biculturalism (1969*a*), p. 98.
      b. Ibid., p. 101.
      c. Office of the Commissioner of Official Languages (1975), p. 1.
      d. Ibid.
      e. Ibid. (1977), p. 9.
      f. Royal Commission on Bilingualism and Biculturalism (1970), p. 19. Figure for "French ethnic origin" from 1871 census. Rest of figures for French mother tongue.
      g. Dominion Bureau of Statistics (1925). Figure for percentage French mother tongue from 1921 census. Figure for French ethnic origin is 27.9%.
      h. Dominion Bureau of Statistics (1944). Figure from 1941 census. Figure for French ethnic origin is 30.3%.
      i. Statistics Canada (1977). Figure from 1961 census. Figure for French ethnic origin is 30.4%.
      j. Ibid. Figure from 1971 census. Figure for French ethnic origin is 28.7%.

nineteen in twenty in the 1960s), in spite of the fact that one in five Quebec residents is non-francophone.

The changes brought about since the 1960s are substantial: in the civil service as a whole, the francophones are at present roughly in proportion to their numbers in the population. Moreover, if we look at senior civil servants, the situation also has improved considerably. Data collected in 1973 by Olsen on 224 federal bureaucrats ''who held positions of the rank of deputy minister or assistant deputy minister (or their salaried equivalents) in all the main state departments and agencies including Crown corporations, regulatory boards, and commissions'' (1977, p. 209) showed that 65% were of British origin, 24% of French origin, and 11% of ''other'' origins. This showed a marked increase for the French in comparison with what had been reported by Porter as the situation in 1953: 84% British origin, 13% French origin, and 3% ''other'' origins.

In contrast with the previous period, these changes have an almost dramatic character; when we consider that the changes also have involved a promotion of the use of the French language in the civil service, it is not surprising that they have been interpreted by many anglophones as a ''take over.''

Historically, a primarily anglophone bureaucracy in Ottawa and a primarily francophone one in Quebec have no doubt had an impact on the direction of the identification of francophone citizens in Quebec with each of the two levels of government. In a way, the situation contained both a ''pull'' and a ''push'' factor. It is difficult to tell, for lack of evidence, whether the recent changes at the federal level have had any effect in increasing identification with the federal government.

There is more to the bureaucracy than the composition of its personnel and representativeness of the language communities. There are also its internal rules, particularly those pertaining to language; the ways in which it symbolically represents itself; and the linkages it establishes and maintains with citizens, either individually or in groups. These various aspects will now be discussed.

Representation given socio-economic and numerical inequalities between communities. It is possible to argue that whatever the mechanisms for political representation, those segments of the society that are relatively weak will be underrepresented; that their interests will be less accounted for in policy formulation. The postulate is that centres of political decision making tend to be more responsive to the interests that wield more power. In other words, effective representation has a socio-economic basis that acts more or less independently of the formal institutional structures and procedures.

As seen in a previous chapter, the two language communities in Canada are unequal in terms of economic, numerical, and socio-political power. Because of this, the francophone subsociety and its various interest groups will tend to be in a position of relative weakness in attempts to influence policy making at the federal level. This may perhaps not be the case with respect to all issues. In addition, its position is one of relative, not absolute, weakness. Nevertheless, structurally speaking, it tends to be in the position of a permanent minority insofar as certain issues are concerned.

This situation of relative weakness has been a source of frustration for some francophones. A study conducted in 1965 showed that 49% of the respondents who identified themselves as French perceived the English as having the most influence in federal government decisions. (Note that 26% of those who identified themselves as English and 24% of those of other origins felt the same way about English influence on federal decisions.) The percentage of French respondents with that view was especially strong in electoral districts in which the majority was French (61%). On the other hand, most respondents of French origin did not feel this was an acceptable situation: only 9% felt that the English should have the most political influence. In contrast, 49% of the English respondents and 31% of those of other origins felt that the English should have the most political influence (Roseborough and Breton 1968, pp. 607, 610, and 628). Thus, it appears that the existence of inequalities is a source of frustration for francophones that is likely to be detrimental to societal cohesion unless there exist compensating mechanisms. Some of these are discussed later.

Another source of tension has been the issue of relative numbers and related natality and immigration policies. In any political system, especially a democratic one, numbers are an important political resource. Historically, the two language communities in Canada have been concerned with their gains and losses in population. The concern was equally important for both anglophones and francophones as long as the former were a numerical minority (up until around 1850) or at least as long as their numerical majority was not well established. The francophones, on the other hand, are still concerned with the question of numbers, especially since the considerable decline in their birth rate began in the late 1950s. In the minds of the Quebec élite, the birth rate was clearly related to *la survivance* and to the political situation of the French in the country. The Church systematically pursued policies of high natality. Quebec was also a strong supporter of family allowances, a matter that has been an object of contention between the Ottawa and Quebec governments.[8]

Immigration policies have been another source of controversy. Historically, anglophones have controlled immigration. First, the policies and

---

[8] The last time the issue emerged between Ottawa and Quebec, it was resolved by letting the Quebec government decide how the money was to be distributed among children, a smaller amount being given to the first child, with a progression for the second and third or additional children. Ottawa was still giving the allowances, but under a formula acceptable to the Quebec government, which obviously wanted to encourage larger families.

recruitment practices were definitely such as to favour the immigration of English-speaking people.[9] Second, events played in favour of anglophones: there were many more immigrants from English-speaking countries than from French-speaking ones. Moreover, the socio-economic situation in North America generally, and in Canada in particular, was such that non-English-speaking immigrants by-and-large assimilated themselves in the anglophone community. The effect of these circumstances was accentuated by policies of assimilation of immigrants in most of English Canada.[10]

In recent years, the interests of Quebec were seriously taken into account. The federal government adopted the principle that the policy should not upset the existing linguistic "balance" in the country, and special arrangements were negotiated giving the Quebec government *"le droit de sélectionner les immigrants qui exprimeront le désir de s'installer sur son territoire, et de refuser ceux qui ne répondront pas aux critères établis"* (*Le Devoir*, 21 February 1978).

Another phenomenon that added, and continues to add, to the imbalance of numbers is the linguistic assimilation of people of French origin outside Quebec.[11] As Joy (1972) points out, up until some time in the ninteenth century,

> assimilation in Canada tended to be in the other direction as French expansion engulfed many small colonies of Irish, Scottish and English origin and as French-Canadian families welcomed into their homes the orphans of Irish immigrants (p. 31).

Since then, assimilation of the French origin population occurs heavily "in those areas in which the French-speaking population is outnumbered by at least two-to-one" (ibid., p. 32). Using a measure of "apparent assimilation" based on the difference between ethnic origin and mother tongue for the youngest age group, Joy observes that over the thirty-year period 1931−1961, the proportion of French people retaining their language outside Quebec drops from 80% to 51%, a period that corresponds to rapid urbanization and the advent of radio and television (ibid., pp. 32, 35).[12]

---

[9] On this point, see Richmond (1967, pp. 3−28).

[10] See Rea (1977) for a discussion of such policies and practices in Manitoba at the beginning of the century. On assimilationist attitudes and policies in the past, see Kovacs (1978), Lower (1958), and Stamp (1970).

[11] Evidence on this is presented in chapters 3.5 and 3.6.

[12] On the question of linguistic assimilation in Canada, see also Maheu (1970). See Castonguay (1978) on the high rate of exogamy among young people living outside Quebec whose mother tongue is French: among the 15−24 year-old group, the percentage is 13% in New Brunswick, and varies between 35% and 68% in the other eight provinces; among the 25−34 year-old group, it is 12% in New Brunswick, and varies between 34% and 63% in the other eight provinces.

PROCESS OF POLITICAL DECISION MAKING

In addition to issues pertaining to the extent and quality of representation, there are those related to the character of government policies and their impact. These also can have an important bearing on the legitimacy of the political institutions and on the degree to which various groups of citizens identify with them. Firstly, policies must have some overall pattern of effectiveness. Some problems will not be dealt with, some policies will fail, and so on, but this is not likely to generate problems of legitimacy. However, if there is a systematic pattern of failure in some area of activity—and especially if such a pattern manifests itself in many areas—then the effectiveness of the institution may be questioned. Secondly, policies and policy making must reveal a pattern of fairness or equity. This study focuses on the pattern of equity with regard to the language communities. In other words, the legitimacy of the institution may be questioned if the policies it pursues are perceived as favouring one of the communities. Finally, a pattern of trustworthiness must be revealed. This refers to the fact that the political institution and its authorities can be relied upon to be effective and equitable without having to be monitored or constantly put under pressure.[13]

Four sets of issues having implications for effectiveness, equity, and trustworthiness will be considered in this section. The first pertains to the structures of decision making; the second to the operation of majority rule in policy making; the third to the structure and mechanisms through which the central political institutions reach the citizens of each of the language subsocieties; and the fourth to the content and outcomes of policy decisions.

Features of decision-making structures. A first consideration with regard to political decision making is the extent to which the structures and rules allow an adequate consideration of the interests of groups and individuals in the various regions and the related linguistic collectivities. Simeon argues that there are features of the Canadian national political institutions that render such a process more difficult:

> The logic of cabinet government, and the concomitant strict party discipline, sharply reduce the ability of the federal government to reflect within itself Canada's regional diversity. . . . Cabinet solidarity places severe limits on the ability of a minister to act as a regional spokesman. Party discipline does the same for MPs and inhibits cross-party regional alliances. . . . The organization of the departments both reflects and reinforces this tendency. With partial exceptions, like DREE, departments are structured along functional or economic lines rather than along regional lines . . .
> (1975, pp. 505−6).

As a result of the processes suggested by these hypotheses, the central government may not be seen as dealing with regional as well as national

---

[13] Gamson defines political trust ''as the probability . . . that the political system (or some part of it) will produce preferred outcomes even if left untended'' (1968, p. 54).

problems, and as a result, might command less allegiance and support than provincial governments.

This would suggest that the strength of regional and national identifications is not only a function of the geographical, cultural, and socio-economic differences among the various parts of a country, but also a function of characteristics of the political institutions. One dimension of this question pertains to federal-provincial relationships and decision-making structures. These are considered in chapter six. The questions raised here concern the ways in which federal decision making incorporates regional interests or the extent to which it has a tendency to function as the government of a unitary state; they also are concerned with whether the features of the federal decision making structures have any impact on their legitimacy *vis-à-vis* the citizens of each region of the country. These questions need to be explored further.

Majority decision making. Elsewhere in the report, inequalities in economic and numerical power and status between the language communities were presented and some of their implications for political decision making were discussed. In a democratic society, relative size has a peculiar importance that derives from the use of majority rule for decision making. Indeed, in a culturally or linguistically divided society where one of the communities is much smaller than the other, majority rule tends to institutionalize the disadvantages due to relatively small numbers. In other words, if on a number of issues each language group has a package of interests that are in varying degrees of contradiction with those of the other, majority rule will guarantee that the smaller group will always lose on those issues.[14] Moreover, this disadvantage can be compounded by circumstances of relative disadvantage in economic and social power.

It should be emphasized that the disadvantage based on differences of socio-economic power and institutionalized in majority rule is issue specific. It may occur over a large number of issues or over only a few. Moreover, certain issues, such as linguistic and cultural ones, may involve most members of the two language communities to some degree, while others may concern only certain segments of each of the language communities. Many economic issues are of this order, as in the case of a policy that favours industries located in the francophone region of the country while disfavouring others in anglophone regions. Thus, different groups may agree that the political institutions do not function well, but for different reasons.

The operation of majority rule, especially if compounded by a weak economic and social bargaining power, is not likely to lead members of the weaker group into believing that the system works to their advantage. Such a situation leads to demands for "self-regulation," at least with regard to those

---

14 On this question, see Lehmbruch (1974), Nordlinger (1972), and Steiner (1974).

matters for which one feels in a "permanent minority" situation.[15] Note again that since such matters may vary from one subgroup to another within a community, the demand for self-regulation may come from different directions and for different reasons.

In addition, several authors who have analysed conflict-regulation mechanisms in culturally segmented societies have noted that none of the mechanisms for conflict regulation that seem to work are based on majority principles; that on the contrary, majority mechanisms seem to accentuate the conflicts. Nordlinger summarizes Calhoun's (1953) basic reason for the ineffectiveness of pure majority thus:

> If governments are to regulate severe conflicts they must take into account the interests of the entire society, which means those of each segment. But "government of the numerical majority" is an "absolute government" in the sense that it only responds to one segment of the society—the majority segment (1972, p. 34).

What are the alternatives to majority principles? Self-regulation is one suggested by the above argument. Demands for provincial autonomy and partial or complete political independence have been heard quite forcefully during the last twenty years—mostly, but not exclusively, from francophone Quebec.[16] Many anglophones also feel that the solution to the tensions between the two language communities is in that direction. Some decentralization has taken place. It involves a decrease in the number of issues and problems dealt with at the national level, thus avoiding the majority-minority situation.

There are also measures of accommodation, Calhoun's "concurrent majority":

> If all segments are to be considered, then it becomes necessary to rely upon the broadly inclusive principle of the "concurrent majority." The adoption of the latter denotes a "constitutional government," which "takes the sense of the community by its parts....and regards the sense of all its parts as the sense of the whole." Otherwise the conflict "would continue until confusion, corruption, disorder, and anarchy would lead to an appeal to force—to be followed by a revolution in the form of government." (ibid.)

But Nordlinger points out that the principle of "concurrent majority" should not be embedded necessarily in the governmental structure. He indicates that non-majority mechanisms for accommodation are essential, but that there are others: stable government coalition between political parties,

---

[15] Salisbury (1968, p. 167) argues that groups "seeking self-regulation are likely to be small relative to the total polity and do not believe they could win in a redistributive game." He argues with professional and other economic groups in mind, but there seems to be no reason why his argument could not apply to cultural groups as well, at least with respect to those policies that affect them, directly or indirectly, as cultural groups.

[16] There have been regional independentist demands in western Canada as well in recent years.

practices based on the principles of proportionality,[17] mutual veto,[18] purposive depoliticization,[19] compromises, and concessions (ibid., pp. 21–30).

Over the years, a number of such non-majority principles have been used in Canada. They underlie some practices concerning, for example, the selection of leaders of political parties, the formulation of certain policies (such as language policies), and the relationships with provincial governments.[20] Frequently, these were strongly criticized as wasteful and generating inefficiencies in government operations. Some appear to argue that the minority should accommodate to the requirements of democratic-majority government rather than adapting the government structures and practices to the existence of two major linguistic segments in the society. In short, even though the non-majoritary principle has some basis in Canadian history and is progressively gaining wider acceptance, it still encounters resistance on the part of ardent supporters of the majority principle.

A third possibility lies in the segregation of activities, but without the decentralization of authority. In this way, members of each language group have their own domain of activity. Since there is minimal contact and budgets are allocated in proportion to the size of the groups, conflicts are avoided. The organization of the national radio and television networks is based on this principle. Solutions to problems are worked out for each subsociety in terms of the requirements of its own particular situation.

A fourth alternative consists of varying compensations to a subsociety for its economic or social disadvantages. The various types of redistributive measures fall in this category.

The first two types of practices (self-regulation and accommodation) involve the language collectivities as corporate entities, that is, as political communities with their own governing structures and authorities, a bargaining between élites or governments at the same or different levels. In Canada, the bargaining has been mostly between the central and provincial governments, but it has involved some degree of interprovincial relationships. The other types of practices involve relations between the central government and the citizens, either individually or in groups.

---

[17] Examples of practices relying on the principle of proportionality is the distribution "according to the proportionate population size of the segments or to their relative electoral strength" of elective and appointive government positions and of scarce resources (research grants, Crown corporations, and so on) (Nordlinger 1972, p. 22).

[18] The mutual veto "provides that governmental decisions cannot be taken unless they are acceptable to all major conflict organizations." (Nordlinger 1972, pp. 24–25).

[19] In purposive depoliticization, "conflict group leaders agree not to involve the government in public policy areas which impinge upon the segments' values and interests." This may involve, for example, the agreement "not to raise segmental issues during election campaigns" (Nordlinger 1972, p. 26).

[20] See Engelmann and Schwartz for a discussion of such practices (1975, chapter 14).

The examples given in the previous paragraphs suggest that the majority principle has not always operated in Canadian political institutions. Several non-majority practices have in fact been used; some have been institutionalized. But it appears that a systematic analysis of existing practices (and not only of those defined in formal terms) would be valuable.

Reaching individual citizens. The legitimacy of the political institutions, and the identification of citizens with them, depends on the way in which they reach citizens and on how they affect them. Channels exist to communicate with the population and to dispense services; they may be more or less elaborate, different for the two linguistic communities, or not give results for each of them. Political institutions also reach the population with concrete results: the implementation of decisions, information, and symbolic messages. Again, the set of impacts and messages may be more or less complex and may be different in the case of each of the linguistic communities.

The focus here is on the nature of the relationship of the political institutions and their élites with the citizens. In the present context, however, special attention is given to determine whether that relationship is different with the members of the two linguistic communities. Three aspects will be considered briefly: the administrative structures for reaching citizens, the provision of services in the official languages, and the content and impact of policies. Other relevant questions, such as the creation and diffusion of a national culture, and the nature and intensity of the competition between provincial and federal governments for the allegiance of citizens, will be discussed in the next chapter.

a. Structures for reaching individual citizens. Governments reach, or fail to reach, citizens through the content of their policies, which may have positive, negative, or no impact at all on the degree of allegiance and loyalty of citizens. Governments also establish various kinds of structures to link themselves with citizens: transmission of information and propaganda, delivery of services, collection of taxes, and so on. The character of such structures and the ways in which they are administered can also have an impact on the degree of legitimacy these political institutions enjoy in the eyes of the citizens and on the degree to which citizens identify with them.

A number of dimensions of such structures were discussed in the previous section, focusing on linguistic aspects and related issues and problems. We wish to consider briefly the extent of the links. To what extent is the central bureaucracy directly connected with citizens as individuals or as members of groups? What is the range of activities involved? What is the nature of the relationships in activities such as supervision, advice or technical assistance, financial aid, performance of a service, application of rules, granting of permits, and collection of fees? Do individuals have easy access to needed services and permits? What are the reactions of individuals to the relationships with government functionaries? What sort of an image do they form of the government in terms of effectiveness, equity, and trustworthiness? Do they get the feeling that they are dealing with ''their'' government?

No evidence could be found on the amount and character of the relationships between government officials and the citizens of each linguistic community. In 1969, however, a study was carried out on attitudes and perceptions of the federal government, with results presented by region and language.[21] In terms of information, attitudes toward information, and interest in political affairs, the following results are significant:

- Francophones are more knowledgeable of federal government involvement in various programmes and policy areas than anglophones (56% and 46%, respectively).
- The two language groups do not differ in their degree of exposure to federal advertising.
- Francophones are more likely than anglophones to believe that the government supplies honest information and that ''you usually know where you stand with it'' (27% in Quebec, 25% in Ontario, and 17% in Alberta—the lowest of all regions).
- Francophones show a higher level of interest in government affairs than do anglophones (48% in Quebec and 34% in Ontario, the Quebec percentage being the highest of all regions).

On the other hand, in terms of expectations, perceived treatment, and efficiency, the pattern of responses is different:

- Francophones are more likely than anglophones to score high on ''political provincialism.''[22]
- Francophones are more likely to feel that the federal government is unresponsive, or usually unresponsive, to their suggestions (42% in Quebec compared with 33% in Ontario. Other provinces, such as Alberta with 40%, are close to Quebec on this question).
- Francophones do not expect prompt treatment from federal government officials as frequently as anglophones do (55% expect slow treatment in Quebec and only 35% in Ontario; again, Alberta is the province that comes the closest to Quebec on this item with 46%).
- Francophones do not expect fair treatment by the federal government as frequently as anglophones do (52% expect fair treatment in Quebec and 66% in Ontario; in Alberta, the percentage is 57%; with Manitoba and Saskatchewan, it is the closest to that of Quebec).

---

[21] The study was conducted by the Institute for Behavioural Research, York University, Toronto, for the Task Force on Government Information (1969).

[22] ''Political provincialism'' is an index based on four items: (a) whether or not the respondent's province gets little attention from the federal government in comparison with other provinces; (b) whether or not the federal government does a poor job of handling complaints of people in the respondent's area; (c) whether or not the federal government has taken too much power away from provincial governments; and (d) whether there are many problems that a provincial government could still handle alone.

• With Alberta, Manitoba, and Saskatchewan, Quebec also shows the highest percentage of people who feel that the federal government is inefficient (50% in comparison with 43% in Ontario).

Patronage is another area where there is little known about government-citizen linkages. There appears to be no doubt that patronage is a source of political allegiances and loyalties, but how strong and lasting these would be is difficult to say. The question is how is patronage distributed among businesses, consulting firms, industries, and so on, from each of the language collectivities? No data could be found either on the extent of patronage and its distribution or on its effect on political allegiances.[23]

b. Provision of services in the official languages. In a society consisting of two language communities, the legitimacy of the central political institutions and the extent to which citizens will identify with them depend to a considerable extent on questions of language. Indeed, language being an instrument of communication, prevailing patterns of usage will affect the character of the relationship between government and citizens. Moreover, language being an embodiment of culture and symbols, it serves to shape the central institutions as objects of identification. Because of this, language is singled out as a special characteristic of the structures through which the central government reaches the citizens of each of the language communities.

As seen earlier, when linguistic changes began to be introduced in the early 1960s, the central government was overwhelmingly anglophone. Moreover, up to the time of the adoption of the Official Languages Act in September 1969, the legislative measure concerning language related to the federal government was Article 133 of the British North America Act, which required bilingualism during the debates of the House of Commons and the Senate, as well as bilingual archives, minutes, and parliamentary journals.

The situation began to change somewhat with the passage of the Civil Service Act of 1961 and of the Official Languages Act of 1969. The first

made the Civil Service Commission rather than the departments responsible for determining the language requirements for positions throughout the Public Service. Explicit requirements bearing on the staffing of regional offices serving a language minority were also laid down. Basically, these stated that, where there is a significant Francophone or Anglophone minority, an equivalent proportion among the staff in the regional office must be able to work in both French and English.

These developments were given further encouragement in a policy statement by Prime Minister Pearson on April 6, 1966 in the House of Commons. The statement reiterated the aim of providing better language services to the public, but also covered new ground. It included bilingual skills as an element of merit for positions judged to require such skills, and pressed for the encouragement of French as a language of work within the federal administration. Various mechanisms—expanded facilities for instruction in French, bonuses to clerical personnel who can work in both official languages, opportunities for senior officers of both linguistic backgrounds to immerse

---

[23] Additional aspects of the structures for reaching citizens are discussed in the next chapter.

themselves completely for a year in the other language and culture—were announced to support the development of French as a working language (Beattie, Désy, and Longstaff 1972, pp. 12–13).

The salient features of the Official Languages Act are as follows:
Bilingualism concerning the law
   i. The principle of equal authority of legislative texts regardless of the language in which they were written.
   ii. There is no question of giving priority to the language in which the law has been written or to the language used to debate that law in the House of Commons.
Bilingualism related to documents written for the public
   Any document emanating from Parliament or from the Government of Canada by a judiciary, quasi-judiciary, or administrative agency or a Crown corporation must be written in both official languages.
Bilingualism related to the tribunals
   i. Regulations concerning procedure must be written in both official languages.
   ii. Procedure concerning inquiry and hearing: testimonies can be given in either language, the choice being left to the person who has to testify.
   iii. Decisions of the tribunals: as far as judgements are concerned, they must be written in both official languages. As to oral decisions, either language can be used.
Bilingualism related to administrative agencies with the government
   Departments and agencies related to the Government of Canada must ensure that one can communicate with them in either of the two official languages, particularly if they are situated in the national capital or in their head office if their offices are situated in a bilingual district.
Aid to travellers
   Services should be provided in both languages if the demand justifies it.
Creation of special bilingual districts
   Bilingual districts must receive all services in both official languages. They can be created when the two following conditions are met:
   i. If both official languages are the languages spoken by the residents of the area.
   ii. If at least 10% of the residents speak one of the official languages as a mother tongue.
   Bilingual districts are to be supervised by a consultative committee.
Commissioner for official languages
   The role of the commissioner for official languages is to ensure that the status of each of the official languages is recognized and that the rationale of the present law is respected, as well as the intention of the legislator in the administration of government or parliamentary institutions. He is not a super administrative authority, but he has the power of persuasion coupled with the power to call for public opinion to judge the rightfulness of a particular situation.

The contemporary problems faced by the central government with regard to winning the allegiance of citizens in both language communities emerge in part from certain features of the government's historical background: legally, the federal institutions were defined in most respects as anglophone; the language of work was largely English; the presence of francophones and the use of French in the civil service were, to a considerable degree, resisted by anglophones.[24] Consequently, the policy adopted in the early 1960s, which aimed at creating conditions such that francophones could more easily participate in, and identify with, the federal institutions, had to overcome a history whose weight was largely in the opposite direction.

The residues of that history in contemporary Canada manifest themselves in the socio-economic interests entrenched in the existing institutional arrangements, and in a distribution of status that affects the way people think of themselves and of their relation with the other language community. Indeed, segments of the civil service and sets of career lines had come to be identified as anglophone domains and others as francophone ones. A policy whose aim, effect, or both was to change boundaries of these domains so as to "make room" for francophones was bound to generate a considerable amount of resistance; indeed it did. Perceptions of a French takeover are widespread; the perceived proportion of francophones in the civil service is exaggerated, many thinking that francophones are more numerous; perceptions of discrimination against anglophones are common, as well as the view that language has replaced the merit principle for recruitment and promotion in the federal government.

Even the best policy implemented in the best possible way would have generated resistance and conflicts since such a policy affects real interests and frustrates aspirations. This is still more the case, however, when the policy is found to have flaws, when its implementation is deficient in some respects, or both. If a piece of legislation is not controversial, problems in its application are fairly easily identified and solved. If it is controversial, however, the public debate becomes confused, and the flaws become weapons that opponents of the legislation can use to fight. Problems of that nature occurred in relation to the language legislation and the bilingualism programmes, and may well have had an effect in accentuating negative attitudes between the linguistic communities.

The implementation of the linguistic policy is affecting the distribution of career and related interests between anglophones and francophones. But it is also modifying the distribution of status among communities in the society as a whole. These changes in legislation and in actual practices give a new, explicit recognition to the francophone community and confer added status. The new allocation of status is further emphasized by a variety of symbolic

---

[24] Data on the linguistic composition of the federal civil service have been presented above.

elements: throughout the country, the federal presence is now signified in the two official languages; commercial labelling must reflect the bilingual character of the society; and so on. As could be expected, the change in the distribution of recognition or status also brought about considerable resistance, especially in parts of the country where francophones are a numerical minority. It is felt by many that the status awarded to the French is out of proportion to their importance in the country.

The controversy over the new dispensation of career advantages, power, and status—or at least over the attempts at a new dispensation—seem to involve three fundamental issues. The first pertains to the appropriateness of giving formal recognition to a linguistic minority, be it symbolic or through material support and legal provisions concerning language use. Our hypothesis is that the changes attempted are clashing with a strongly held value in anglo-Canadian (and anglo-American) society. This value, which had an important role in building Canada as a British society, is that if an ethnic, religious, or linguistic minority wishes to provide itself with certain institutions for its own cultural survival and development or for other purposes, it should do so entirely on its own. There should be tolerance of such activities—provided they do not expand to the point of interfering with an adequate integration in mainstream culture and institutions—but they should receive no material or symbolic public support. The Canadian public institutions—governments, schools media, businesses—should formally recognize only one culture and one language; minority cultures and languages, if they are to manifest themselves and persist, must do so in private or semi-private institutions, that is, those run and supported by the minority group itself.

Of course, minority languages and cultures have been frequently recognized in Canada; the basic principle has not systematically been applied. However, such ''concessions'' have been made for practical reasons, as accommodations to cope with concrete situations involving the minorities. It is only in recent years that this tenet of Canadian culture has been challenged: increased formal recognition has been awarded to the French language and community. Although there are many who still retain the traditional view, by and large it seems that the issue is no longer whether or not there should be formal recognition, but rather how far it should go and what forms it should take. For instance, one issue to have surfaced recently is whether or not minority language rights should be embedded in the Constitution. To some, this would be going too far; others see it as an essential step in making the central government the government of both linguistic communities.[25]

It should be pointed out that viewed in the context of the traditional anglo-Canadian culture, the recent changes are close to being of a revolutionary nature. Indeed, if they do not abort, these changes could have begun a fundamental transformation of the character of Canadian society and its institutions. While some see these changes as a landmark in Canadian history, others find the transformation unacceptable, or do not want to acknowledge its occurrence or importance. For instance, when, at their 1977 conference, the provincial premiers agreed to "make their best efforts to provide instruction in education in English and French wherever numbers warrant," the declaration was hailed as a great victory by the prime minister of the country. It was seen by some as "a bench-mark in Canada in that it implicitly reflects the common recognition that there 'are' two official languages in Canada and that they should both be respected, not only in principle, but in practice" (*Toronto Globe and Mail*, 20 August 1977). However, many anglophones found the new definition of the linguistic reality unacceptable, while others—mostly francophones—minimized its significance, seeing it as just a verbal commitment that may never manifest itself in concrete measures, and in any case, that was long overdue.[26]

The premiers' declaration was significant. As indicated above, this objective was already incorporated in the "bilingual districts" policy, but the premiers extended it to education, which is a field of provincial jurisdiction. In terms of the phenomenon discussed here, namely, the redistribution of recognition and status, it is part of a process of far-reaching change. There is, of course, the question of how far and how rapidly it will affect the actual functioning of institutions.

A second issue raised by attempts to bring about a new dispensation of status between the language communities concerns the traditional view among anglophones that the French are a minority like the other ethnic

---

[25] On the impact of "public legitimation," but in a different context (Catholic education), see Westhues (1976). He found that "*the success of the Catholic schools is greater, the more public legitimation it enjoys*" (p. 139). Public legitimation in this case means that "the Catholic school is regarded as legitimate and deserving of support by the society as a whole, Catholics and non-Catholics alike. . . . [It] is recognized by the legal system, financially supported through public channels, defended by governmental authority, and accepted as the proper place of instruction for all Catholic children" (ibid., p. 139). In the context of this study, the issue is whether French should be awarded public legitimation in schools, courts, health and social services, and so on. That is to say, should the provision of such services be given legal, financial, and authoritative support from the State? On the basis of the Westhues study, this would have a positive effect on the francophone community. But it is probably resisted precisely because many anticipate that it would have this effect.

[26] The controversy was accentuated by the fact that the Quebec government had passed legislation making French the official language of the province. Of course, the legislation contained several provisions for anglophones; but the English language was given a minority status by the legislation. This rendered the situation symmetrical to that of the other provinces (except New Brunswick) in which English is the official language. In this context, any attempt to deal with the "minority language" was bound to activate intense feelings and generate controversy.

minorities. Thus, if the demands of the French for special recognition were to be granted, other ethnic groups would soon make similar demands that also would have to be recognized. Given the number of ethnic groups in the country, such a policy would generate chaos: no public institution would be able to function efficiently.

The French perceived this tenet as an argument used by the English community and its élite to justify not giving the French the status they were claiming. They saw the other ethnic groups as being used by the English in their status conflict with the French. To a large extent, the perception of the francophones was correct: the tenet that all ethnic minorities should be treated in the same way was used, in fact, as an argument against granting "charter group" status to the francophones.

But the argument was partly justified: giving formal recognition to the French was likely to trigger similar demands by other ethnic groups, and it did. As the work of the Royal Commission on Bilingualism and Biculturalism was progressing during the 1960s, some members, particularly the élites of other ethnic groups, became anxious about the possible consequences of the views of the commission for their own status: some feared that they would come to be seen as "second-class citizens." Others reacted not so much out of status anxiety as in an intrepreneurial spirit: they saw the commission, and the activities and debates it was generating, as an opportunity to raise the status of their own community.

The formula of multiculturalism within a bilingual context was adopted by the federal government in order to accommodate the demands of both francophones and other ethnic groups for special recognition. To what extent such an approach has been, and will be, successful is difficult to tell with the evidence available. The point we wish to emphasize is that recent developments with regard to bilingualism and multiculturalism represent the beginning of the dissolution (in Canadian culture and institutions) of the tenet that the French constitute an ethnic group like the others.

A third issue raised by the legal and organizational transformations of recent years concerns the conception of anglophone and francophone Canada that should be adopted in shaping the societal institutions. The explicit recognition of the francophone community and the determination of its status relative to the anglophone raises the question of how it is to be defined. What are to be its boundaries? Two conceptions of the linguistic communities have been confronting each other. On the one hand, there is a pan-Canadian view that identifies the relevant francophone community as consisting of francophones in all parts of Canada and similarly the anglophone community.[27] On the other hand, a segmentalist view identifies Quebec as the

---

[27] Relevant for particular policy purposes.

homeland of the francophones and the rest of Canada as the homeland of the anglophones. In this view, these are the boundaries of the linguistic communities that should be recognized socially and politically.

In the pan-Canadian view, recognition must be given and institutional arrangements made for members of each linguistic community wherever they are in Canada. Specific arrangements may have to vary from one part of the country to the other, but only for practical considerations. There is no essential difference between the linguistic communities in the different regions. In the segmentalist view, in contrast, there are differences based on phenomena such as size and institutional structures. Thus, the communities that are to be given charter group status are the francophone community in Quebec and the anglophone one in the rest of Canada. The francophone and the anglophone ''minorities'' are seen by segmentalists as minorities like the other minorities.[28] The views of segmentalists, however, are not entirely consistent: some francophone segmentalists argue that it is the Franco-Quebec community that should be given political and social status and that the anglophones in Quebec should be considered a minority like the others. However, in many ways, their attitudes *vis-à-vis* the francophones outside Quebec is that of pan-Canadians: many reproach other provinces for not giving proper recognition to their French minorities. Anglophone segmentalists, on the other hand, agree that the francophones should have a special status in Quebec, a status somewhat parallel to that of anglophones in the rest of Canada, and that the francophones outside Quebec should be treated like any other minority. However, many feel that the anglophones in Quebec do not constitute a minority like any other.

For obvious reasons, the francophones outside Quebec and the anglophones in Quebec tend to hold strong pan-Canadian views.

This third issue regarding which conception of Canada should prevail is far from resolved. In many ways, the two conceptions are irreconcilable. A choice has to be made. A critical obstacle is that the controversy is not only one over ideas. Rather, each conception is articulated in defence of the existing distribution of opportunities and status or for the promotion of an alternate distribution.

In this section, we have seen how the language use for the provision of services by the central government to the citizens of each linguistic community can have an impact on the legitimacy it is given by those citizens and on the extent to which they will identify with it. It should be added that the use of different languages in the provision of services is also a matter of efficiency. The central government has to relate to citizens for a variety of reasons. How efficiently this is done depends in part on its ability to be understood by those to whom the service or message is intended. Frequently,

---

[28] This description represents an extreme formulation of each of these views.

the costs of institutional bilingualism are estimated, but without taking into account the yield in terms of effective communication. This represents inadequate social accounting. In other words, there are benefits as well as costs for the central government in policies of bilingualism.

We have discussed three issues that the central government has encountered in its attempts to become bilingual:

a. Extent and kind of formal recognition to be given to the two linguistic communities

b. Recognition to be given to other ethnic groups

c. Appropriate definition of the francophone and anglophone communities to be used for policy purposes

We have argued that the first two of these issues are in the process of being resolved in the sense that perspectives have been worked out and are increasingly becoming accepted, even though problems of application remain. The third, however, is far from resolved—a fact that constitutes a fundamental obstacle to the formulation of institutional models and policies that would generate a fairly widespread consensus.

The existence of a controversy over the definition of the boundaries of the francophone and anglophone communities supports our earlier observation that it is now largely accepted in Canada that the two linguistic communities must be recognized explicitly. The current issues pertain to the modalities of formal recognition. Those who at one time wanted Canada to be an entirely anglophone society appear to have lost their historical battle; the few of that vintage who remain seem to be marginal to what is now the central debate in the country. This does not mean that they have no influence on the evolution of that debate and its outcome. They could possibly succeed in reshaping the debate in the old terms: should Canada be an exclusively anglophone country?

The independentist movement in Quebec is in large part a response to past and continuing attempts to define the institutions supposedly common to both communities as *de facto* anglophone institutions.[29] Secession would take care of the issue by eliminating it: after secession, each country would have its own language, and bilingualism would not be an issue. The anglophones who want Canada to be an English-speaking country and the francophone independentists are both in favour of unilingualism and against

---

[29] A recent and fairly dramatic attempt is the "bilingualism-in-the-air" incident, which confirmed for many independentists that the central government and its various organizations would never adequately serve the interests of the two linguistic communities.

bilingualism.[30] The presence of these groups complicates the process of developing an institutional framework in which both communities can participate effectively.

In trying to deal with these issues, we have seen that the central government has transformed itself in a number of ways. A critical question is whether it reaches the citizens of the two linguistic communities more effectively as a result of the changes in its linguistic rules and practices. Some argue that not only did it not improve its relationship with the francophones in Quebec, who do not consider it their government any more than they did in the past, but that it has also generated feelings of estrangement among many anglophones. Such a situation could be seen as the inevitable features of a transitional phase. Systematic evidence that would allow the analysis of trends in these regards, both in the anglophone and francophone communities, seems to be unavailable.

The transformation of the federal institutions with regard to language must be considered in the wider context of federal-provincial relationships, economic conditions, and socio-cultural transformations.

CONCLUSION

In this chapter, we considered certain features of the vertical dimension of societal cohesion; that is to say, we considered some of the ways in which the members of each linguistic community are linked with the common political institutions. We saw that in certain regards, the formal links of representation have existed since the beginning of Confederation: representation in Parliament and in the Cabinet. Insofar as these indicators are concerned, we could say that the central government has been accessible to each linguistic community more or less in proportion to their respective sizes.

A second observation is that important changes have been made, or are in the process of being made, the most striking being the linguistic composition of the civil service and the attempts to provide services in each of the official languages. The situation today is in marked contrast with that of just twenty years ago. Also, the allocation of ministries among anglophone and francophone politicians appears to have changed: there seem to be more francophone man-years in the more important ministries than in the past.

Certain features of the system of representation, however, seem to have changed relatively little. This is especially the case of the political party system. First, there is the fact that the Conservative Party is still largely the party of English-speaking Protestants; it has not mobilized significant

---

[30] The Quebec white paper on language states: "*Il ne sera donc plus question d'un Québec bilingue. Que l'État canadien se définisse comme bilingue n'empêche nullement que les provinces de l'Ouest, l'Ontario et les Maritimes soient massivement anglophones (à la seule exception du Nouveau-Brunswick). Le Québec n'est donc pas tenu d'être bilingue du fait de son appartenance au Canada.*" (*Le Devoir*, 2 April 1977.)

support in Quebec. Second, while having more diversified support in terms of language, religion, and ethnicity, the Liberal Party is largely an eastern party. The underrepresentation of the West in the government for long periods of time no doubt nourishes anti-eastern feelings. The claims of the francophones, the demands of the Quebec government, the changes in the representation of the francophones in the federal government, the attempts to change the status of the French language and community in the country, and the assertive nationalism of the francophones in Quebec appear to have nourished the anti-Quebec feelings.

An hypothesis that can be formulated in light of the evidence presented in this chapter is that much of the anti-Quebec feeling in the West may be as much a protest against their own status deprivation as anything else. Relatively speaking, the western regions of the country have *lost* status in the national community in recent years. On the one hand, the West has also been experiencing economic, social, and political transformations of importance. A new consciousness has emerged there, too. There is no doubt a wish among its élite to count in the economic and political map of the country. On the other hand, there have been relatively little attempts to accommodate this desire for a new status and an improved recognition on the part of the central political institutions. In view of this, the "special treatment" given to French Quebec appears to "add insult to injury." It improves its status without a corresponding improvement in the status of the West. If all the regions perceived each other as receiving inadequate recognition by the central government, the reactions would be quite different than they are when one perceived another as receiving special treatment. In fact, why would anyone who feels he is not getting a fair deal want to make concessions to others, let alone be magnanimous in his dealings with them?

It appears that the so-called "Quebec problem" or "French problem" in regard to the central government would be solved in part by dealing with the inadequate status of other regions of the country in the central political institutions;[31] it would then be easier for Quebec to receive the proper recognition.[32] One of the areas of reform is the political parties and their internal functioning. The composition of the bureaucracy, especially in the upper echelons, may be another. Finally, the functioning of the decision-making structures could be modified.

---

[31] There is no intention here of implying that this is the only relevant aspect of the question; as the rest of this report shows, it a multifaceted issue. However, we feel it is important to raise the basic question: under what conditions will people give prerogatives, recognition, and status to others? Or in other words, when will a certain allocation or reallocation of status be accepted as legitimate? The legitimacy of the State is increased when it is perceived as justly allocating resources and status.

[32] It should be noted that the same situation, but in reverse, would be obtained if we experienced a long period of Conservative government. Certain regions of the country would probably make important gains; but then the francophones in Quebec would really feel estranged.

Another aspect of representation examined concerns the linkages of interest groups with the decision-making centres. In recent decades, new interest groups have emerged; social classes have become more differentiated. Moreover, the government structure has modified itself: the bureaucracy has acquired an increased role in decision making, and Parliament has decreased in importance. The question we raised, but were not able to deal with adequately for lack of data, is whether the interests in each language community are well connected with the decision makers in the central government. This is an important matter; it is through such linkages that much of the "real" representation takes place. The matter of the connection of interest groups with the government is taken up again in greater detail in the next chapter.

Changes in recent decades have raised a number of issues about how Canadians should think of English and French Canada: should any formal/legal recognition be given to the two linguistic communities, that is, should the "two-nation" concept be adopted? The French, at least in Quebec, no longer think of themselves as a minority group, but rather as a nation. How is this new identity to be accommodated in the political system? Should it be recognized formally or only informally? What are the probable consequences of each course of action? These are policy issues that need further consideration.

Relationships Between Federal and Provincial Governments

We saw in the previous chapter that the maintenance and strength of a political community is partly dependent on the nature of the relationship that exists between the central political institution and the citizens of each of the linguistic communities. Another important set of factors pertains to the relationship between the levels of government. This is especially important in Canada in view of the concentration of francophones in one province, Quebec; so that the government of that province tends to be defined as the government of the main segment of the francophone community. In a real sense, the central government does not relate to anglophones and francophones only as individuals and groups, but also as corporate entities with their own political institutions. In this chapter, we will consider some of the sources of strains and cohesion that may exist in the vertical relationships between those governments.

Insofar as intergovernmental relationships are concerned, the strength of the political community depends on two major classes of processes: (1) those pertaining to the division of powers and financial resources; (2) those leading citizens to relate and identify with one or the other level of government. The first set of processes affects the relationship between two organizational systems, the incidence of conflict, collaboration, and exchange. The second deals with the implicit or explicit competition between the two levels for the allegiance and support of citizens.

DIVISION OF POWERS

The division of powers is a complex matter that goes beyond constitutional questions to include a whole range of political processes. The debate on these questions is not a recent one in Canada, and the many different participants include constitutional lawyers, political scientists, economists, politicians, social analysts, businessmen, and so on. It is not the intention here to review every facet of this ongoing debate. Rather, we will focus on three issues that appear to be particularly relevant to the question of the cohesion of a political community, and we will examine their potentially cohesive or divisive aspects. The first is the centralization/decentralization issue and its relation to questions of efficiency and organizational and class conflicts. The second is the issue of interdependence between levels of government. Third, there is the question of the existence of one province with a francophone majority while there are nine with an anglophone majority. Each of these issues will be discussed in turn.

Centralization/decentralization issue. The degree of centralization/decentralization is a basic issue with respect to the division of powers. It is also highly pertinent to the question of maintenance of the political community. Indeed, at the extreme, complete decentralization means separate states. Complete centralization, on the other hand, usually occurs in societies that are quite homogeneous;[1] in the case of Canada, it would represent the negation of a sociological reality. Thus, while complete decentralization would mean the end of the political community, complete centralization would seriously threaten the social organization of the country in its regional and linguistic dimensions.

As a parenthesis, it should be noted that we are not dealing here with concentration or deconcentration, which refers to the distribution of activities and not of powers. For instance, the central government may spread its offices and agencies very widely across the country while the decision making remains at the centre: this is deconcentration. The degree of centralization/decentralization is concerned with the distribution of decision-making powers themselves.

a. Efficiency dimension. From a rationalistic perspective, the degree of decentralization is a question of efficiency: at which level should the provision of particular services be organized so that in terms of quantity and quality, the best results be obtained for a given level of expenditure? This first aspect of the question pertains to the ''economies of scale'' that may result from the organization of a service at a more inclusive level. For instance, will a certain level of expenditure provide more and better police protection if it is organized at the level of the municipal, regional, or provincial governments? What would be the results for education if organized at the national, as opposed to the provincial, or the provincial, as opposed to the local, level from an efficiency point of view? What about programmes in welfare, manpower training, industrial development, immigration, and so on?

The assumption of this approach is that a number of rational criteria can be identified for evaluating the yield in relation to costs of different levels of organization of an activity. To put it differently, are certain areas of jurisdiction more efficient than others and for which activities or services is this the case?

---

[1] Some heterogeneous countries have a unitary system of government. Our statement is about a tendency, not an all-or-none phenomenon.

A critical aspect of this question concerns public goods and services. A characteristic of a public good is that once it is made available to an individual, it can be made available to others at no extra cost. Another characteristic is that it involves "externalities" that refer to the costs imposed on others without compensation or to the benefits others derive without having to pay for them. That is to say, once a public good is supplied, those who do not want it, who want less of it, or who want it in a different form have to "consume" what is available without being compensated for the fact that their preferences are not met. Similarly, those who contribute nothing to the provision of the goods or services cannot be excluded from their use. Efficiency in the provision of public goods therefore involves the minimization of "externalities." It is a question of reducing the proportion of people who do not get what they want and the proportion of those who benefit without sharing the costs.

Since we are dealing with the diversity of the population, it seems that services must be provided in a quantity and of a kind that minimize the proportion of people who are dissatisfied with the service they have to "consume." It can be argued that this depends on the degree of homogeneity of those for whom the good or service is provided with regard to preferences in particular domains such as education, health services, or type of industrial activity. Insofar as the linguistic (and regional) communities in Canada have different patterns of preference in given areas, the provision of services should be decentralized. Indeed, the services offered will correspond to most of the various clusters of preferences if the decision making with regard to the services to be provided is carried out within the cluster.[2] The important empirical question is to establish the areas for which there are common preferences and desired objectives across the linguistic communities and those for which there are significant differences.

There are two aspects to the question of efficiency. Firstly, from a technical point of view, how can the best results be obtained for a given amount of resources? The size of the organization providing the service is an important factor in this regard, and since its size is related to the magnitude of the territory and of the population involved, efficiency is related to the area of jurisdiction, and thus to the extent of centralization/decentralization. Secondly, from a public good point of view, how can the fact that segments of the population differ from each other in their preferences be best taken into account? This question also has a bearing on the centralization/decentralization issue. The answers to such questions depend on the kind of service. Presumably, these are services for which there is a national constituency;

---

[2] This of course does not guarantee that the decision making will meet the preferences of citizens. The responsiveness of governments depends on many other factors.

there are others for which there are regional and linguistic constituencies; and others for which there are local constituencies.

In Canada, as in many societies with federal systems, the Constitution defines the constituency for a number of areas of activity, but it leaves many ambiguities, and of course does not deal with the areas of public activity that have emerged since it has been adopted. However, there have been a number of technological, socio-economic, and cultural changes in Canada that have altered either the distribution of preferences or the technical conditions for the provision of certain services. These new conditions raise questions as to what should be the proper role and authority of the federal, provincial, and municipal governments in regard to the various publicly provided services. New problems of efficiency have to be dealt with. According to the rationalistic view, the existing tensions in the country are the results of changing patterns of preferences and of the technical problems of providing services.

b. Narrowing the status differential. The politics of *status* are also involved in the conflicts over the division of powers between levels of government. These pertain to attempts by the francophone community to change its status *vis-à-vis* the anglophone community and to the resistance encountered. These attempts have increasingly involved the structure of the political institutions. This is not entirely surprising since the relative status of communities is partly reflected in the relative status of their organizations in general, and of their political organizations in particular.

Those concerned with the issue are "divided on whether it logically implies the necessity of political or structural changes beyond expanding the status of the French language generally and maintaining a place for English within Quebec" (Black 1975, p. 174). There are those who argue that the existing linguistic and cultural duality is basic to Canadian society and should be reflected in the structure of its political institutions. The bicommunal basis of the society, it is argued, is not formally embedded in any of the existing structures: representation in Parliament is on the basis of numbers; representation in the Senate is regional; from a formal point of view, the Cabinet is composed on the basis of expediency, efficiency, or both, although informally, linguistic representation has frequently been the case; and finally, formally speaking, Quebec is considered a province like the others.

The proposals to remedy this situation vary considerably.[3] All are based on the two-nation principle, but incorporate it differently. Of these institutional expressions of the two-nation principle, one is federal, another is confederal, and a third is in the nature of an alliance. For instance, there are

---

[3] For an excellent discussion of the dualist concept of federalism as well as of other views of federalism, see Black (1977).

the demands for a *statut particulier* within the federation, requiring that "certain federal powers . . . be reassigned to the Quebec government with respect to residents of that province while Ottawa continue[s] to exercise that jurisdiction over other Canadians" (ibid., p. 18).

In the confederal model, each province (or groups of provinces) is seen as a sovereign state. Any delegation of powers that occurs is then upwards—from the provincial or regional governments to the central one. All residual powers, that is, those not specifically delegated, remain with the provinces.

The associate-state proposal represents a third type of arrangement in which there is no central government. Administrative structures may be required for the implementation of policies worked out among the participating states, but all decision-making powers remain with each sovereign state. Political and economic alliances would be formed for certain purposes, but these are in the nature of treaties or "common market" arrangements.

These different types of arrangements are proposed with the expectation that the status differential between the francophone and anglophone communities would be narrowed.

Underlying the quest for a new status is a new kind of nationalism in Quebec. Dion (1975) argues that nationalism in Quebec has moved from a conservative, then a liberal, phaee to reach a socio-democratic configuration. There are two critical aspects of this new configuration. One is the link between the collective aspirations of the francophone community in Quebec and the State, which is seen as the instrument for the pursuit of collective goals and for dealing with the economic, demographic, and cultural problems encountered. The other element of the configuration is perhaps more fundamental: it is a change in identity from that of a minority group to that of a people. This is reflected in shifts in the terminology to refer to oneself as being a *Québécois*, rather than a French Canadian.

A new collective consciousness arose, characterized by assertiveness, as opposed to its past defensiveness, by the desire for power, as opposed to its traditional relative withdrawal, and by the quest for status, in contrast with its minority-group orientation. This new consciousness is articulated mostly by groups whose career interests are tied with Quebec organizations, of which one of the most important is the State apparatus.

c. Underlying conflicts of interest. In addition to the politics of status, there are the politics of power and economic interests that are at the core of the centralization/decentralization controversy. The rational aspects pertaining to efficiency are introduced in the debate as arguments for or against a certain stand in the controversy. But what is at stake are conflicts over status, power, and economic interests. This involves the politicians and functionaries in governments; it also involves organized groups in the society, their interaction with different levels of government, and the connections between their interests and those of the various government departments and agencies. These issues are taken up in the section on intergovernmental competition.

Interdependence and collaboration. It has been noted that ''traditional discussions of federalism emphasize the co-ordinate and independent powers of federal and regional governments rather than their interdependence'' (Smiley 1970, p. 1). The same author points out that it is not only the discussions of federalism that have been bent in that direction, but its practice as well: ''Prior to the Second World War the norms of Canadian federalism consisted of the federal and provincial governments carrying out their respective roles as delineated by the constitution in relative isolation from one another . . . '' Their relationships ''were for the most part dominated by isolated patterns of collaboration in particular programmes and functions and by the periodic renegotiation of the five-year fiscal agreements'' (ibid., pp. 85, 94).

Since then, the situation has changed enormously. In the previous section, some of the social forces that led to federal-provincial interactions, frequently conflictual in nature, were indicated. The basic phenomenon underlying these changing interactions and noted by several observers, including Smiley, is interdependence. It is argued that the evolving social, economic, and political reality is such that different communities, regions, and countries find themselves increasingly in relationships of interdependence. Moreover, different fields of activity, such as health, education, industrial development, immigration, are intimately interrelated. The view is that interdependence is now inevitable not because of the political institutions themselves, but because of ecological, technological, and economic forces. According to this view, the emphasis on the division of powers may not be entirely irrelevant, but misses the essentials of the socio-economic reality and the requirements of this reality for intergovernmental relationships. A corollary of its central tenet is that modifications in the formal divisions of powers, even of a very extensive nature, will not eliminate tensions, conflicts of interests, and confrontations that are likely to result. This is so because the tensions and conflicts of interest are rooted in the interdependece of communities and of their activities, such that the groups and organizations of each community inevitably come into conflict with each other.

In its extreme form, this view dismisses the importance of the divisions of powers. It is even used sometimes to justify the institutional *status quo*. But even though it draws attention away from the division of powers, this perspective nevertheless has implications for institutional structures and processes. Indeed, by focusing on the fact that each level of government will not be able to handle most issues alone, it directs the analysis to the structures and processes of intergovernmental collaboration and to the conditions under which such collaboration occurs. In addition, it draws attention to the importance of mechanisms for the resolution of conflicts that will inevitably arise.

Intergovernmental relations can occur through structures and interpersonal interaction. In Canada, federal-provincial ministerial conferences occur on a regular basis. There are also federal-provincial committees on various matters: in 1965, a study by the director of the Federal-Provincial Relations Branch of the federal Department of Finance listed about one hundred of these committees and subcommittees.[4] Such linkages among government organizations can be an important source of cohesion. Firstly, insofar as the levels of government provide each other with resources (funds, information, links with localities and groups, symbolic support, and so on) that they would not have in sufficient quantity otherwise, they can be occasions of mutual benefit and cohesion. Secondly, the agencies and committees for the analysis of problems, decision making, sharing information, co-ordinating activities, or administration of programmes can lead to the development of ''relatively autonomous communities of officials across jurisdictional lines'' (ibid., p. 89). Thus, the interorganizational cohesion would be supported by networks of relations among people working in the various levels of government.

Thirdly, the existence of networks of linkages between the provincial and central governments can have an important symbolic impact by signifying to members of the various communities not only how they relate to one another and benefit from those ties, but also how their own governmental organizations contribute to the improvement of the conditions in the society as a whole.[5]

Do the linkages in fact have these cohesive effects? Do they result in mutually beneficial ideas, information, or other resources? Do they bring about ''communities of officials''? Do they have symbolic impacts? The evidence to answer these questions is thin. For instance, no evidence could be found on the extent to which there are interpersonal networks among officials at different levels of government. Whether or not there are ''communities of officials,'' and if they exist, how extensive and cohesive they are, cannot be assessed.

As far as the symbolic impact is concerned, there is one piece of evidence that suggests it is weak. A survey carried out for the Task Force on Government Information attempted to assess the degree of knowledge citizens have of the responsibilities and involvements of their federal and provincial governments (1969, p. 49).

---

[4] Quoted in Smiley (1970, pp. 89–90).

[5] There are two main sources of attachment to a community. One is the benefits (material, social, symbolic) that people derive from their membership in the community. If a person's interests and aspirations are not satisfied, and *a fortiori*, if they are frustrated by his belonging to a particular community, his attachment to that community will be weak and his tendency will be to leave it. The other is derived from the contribution one makes to the community. The argument is that the more a person contributes to the life of a group or community in terms of time, effort, or money, the more he identifies with that group or community since it becomes an extension of himself, so to speak. It is this second source of cohesion to which we are referring here.

The sample was asked whether the Federal Government, the provincial government or both are involved in 17 programmes, and areas of government activity such as unemployment insurance, ARDA and foreign policy.

By far the most frequent mistake was to attribute a programme or area to a single level of government when, in fact, responsibility is shared.[6]

The extent of federal-provincial interaction and joint involvement in activities appears to be mostly unknown to the population; it cannot be said to have a symbolic impact.

Under what conditions is federal-provincial interaction likely to lead to cohesion rather than to tension and disharmony? A complete analysis of such conditions will not be undertaken, but a few conditions will be discussed in order to indicate the kinds of issues that need to be dealt with.[7] First, the terms of the interactions and the characteristics of the structures in which they take place must be such as to be mutually beneficial. If one party sees little benefit or a benefit not proportional to the efforts that the interaction requires, it is not likely to have cohesive effects. Some authors argue that such a condition is virtually impossible to meet in reality. For instance, on the basis of a study of joint federal-provincial activities, Corry has concluded that

collaborative arrangements were almost inherently deficient:

1. Officials of different bureaucracies find both their desires to express themselves through their work and their career prospects frustrated by entering into constructive intergovernmental relations. The capable and ambitious official will try to "master the uncertainties which interfere with his control of the situation." These uncertainties include the actions of the officials of the other jurisdiction and the official will thus strive to extend his control to all aspects of the joint activity. Further, if the official shows himself to be relatively passive in his relations with the other government he may convey to his superiors, who control his career prospects, that he has lost his originality. Conflicts in joint activities cannot thus be attributed to the "perversity of civil servants" but rather to inherent factors in such situations. Such conflicts are more likely than otherwise to occur when able and zealous officials are involved.

2. It is characteristic of most joint activities that federal and provincial officials will disagree on the objectives of particular public policies and the appropriate means by which these may be pursued. In his analysis of conditional grants Corry asserted, "Hope for harmonious and efficient cooperation depends largely on the discovery of clear-cut objective criteria for measuring the activity—criteria which command agreement by their clarity. Such criteria are almost impossible to find" (Smiley 1970, p. 86).[8]

Such an argument leads to a rather pessimistic prognosis of federal-provincial collaboration. However, since the Corry study, federal-provincial collaboration has increased enormously, which suggest that there may well

---

[6] Out of a total of seventeen answers, 51% of the sample had five or less correct ones.

[7] For a further discussion of the conditions under which contacts have beneficial effects, see chapter 3.7.

[8] See Corry (1940). The quote is from Smiley (1970, p. 86), who summarizes Corry's study.

be circumstances where functionaries do not see the activities of their colleagues in other jurisdictions as interference and agreement on criteria and objectives can be secured. Considerable research appears to be needed on this matter.

A second condition for positive results from joint structures and activities can be called "domain security." If the members of an organization in one or both jursidictions attempt to expand their domain of power and activity at the other's expense, tension will inevitably occur. Such attempts can take various forms: unilateral decision making, bypassing the co-ordinating body in pursuit of certain activities, or using one's authority and resources to impose one's will, rather than seeking mutually acceptable compromises.

A third condition is that the representatives of each level of government participating in the joint programmes or structures must be given enough authority by their respective governments to enter into effective planning and negotiations. The fear of moves that would jeopardize one's career is sufficient to guarantee a low degree of collaboration. Moreover, the system of values at each level of government must be such that being successful in arranging collaborative ventures is rewarded, rather than ignored or, worse, sneered at.

An illustration is provided by the experience of federal-provincial activities in the area of regional economic development. In his analysis of activities in this domain, Careless (1977) notes that toward the late 1960s, "the continuation of the co-operative and even consultative federalism of the early sixties has been relegated to a notably lower priority by the federal government . . . " One of the ways in which this manifested itself is in practices that

> consisted in deliberately bypassing the co-ordination apparatus at the provincial level (often created through earlier federal encouragement) to deal directly instead with provincial departments or the private sector of the provincial economy. Even then provincial departments usually had the choice only of accepting or rejecting federal packages. . . .

One reason for this change in priorities is

> the desire to control the growth and impact of federal expenditures in joint programs. . . . The close regulation of the various steps in policy making—from policy guidelines through strategy to final programs—meant, however, that there was little provision for variations according to extra-departmental or extra-governmental forces. Value was placed upon the system and ends of budgeting, not the process of inter-departmental negotiations (pp. 168, 175).

The budgeting process, in effect, diminishes the authority and flexibility of federal officials in their intergovernmental relations.

Another reason for a de-emphasis on collaboration was "a growing desire at Ottawa to secure a greater visibility of federal policies . . . " (ibid.,

p. 177). This approach signified to officials that the rewards would be given for creating visibility for federal activities rather than for generating effective collaboration. "In fact, what was intended often to be a joint federal-provincial planning exercise deteriorated into negotiations over the best ways of showing the federal funds at work" (ibid., p. 176).

A fourth condition for successful collaboration is a commitment on the part of the respective élites to make the joint ventures work. This condition is related of course to the three previous ones. It has been mentioned as critical by several researchers (Franck 1968; Lijphart 1968). Conflicts over the division of powers, and competition for the allegiance and support of citizens can lead governments to avoid collaboration with each other and take unilateral action without even consulting each other. In addition, the willingness to collaborate is part of the overall configuration of historical and contemporary events that define the relationship between the two collectivities. For instance, certain socio-political events in Quebec have contributed to a lesser willingness to collaborate among certain segments of the élite. These events are associated with the rise of a new nationalism articulated by a political and social élite "not particularly concerned with 'overarching co-operation' with the English Canadian élite . . . " (White, Millar, and Gagné 1971, p. 59) This is related partly to the changed cultural and political consciousness of francophones in Quebec and partly to the fact that these new élites rose in opposition to political arrangements that they saw as unsatisfactory. The slow response on the part of anglophone élites was also a factor; in fact, from many anglophone quarters, the response was negative—a phenomenon that tended to discourage the motivation to collaborate.

It could be argued that the willingness to collaborate on the part of anglophone élites has historically been fairly weak. They wanted the political system and the economy to work, but with the clear expectation that it should be primarily francophones who accommodate to their greater numerical, economic, and political power rather than the other way around.

Recently, things have begun to change. Segments of the anglophone élite seem more prepared to adopt an accommodating behaviour at the individual and institutional levels. A few manifestations of this willingness are evident in the area of bilingualism, especially in federal institutions and agencies. There are also a number of manifestations at the provincial level.[9] However, few creative solutions have emerged from anglophone political élites. By and large, their stance has been to respond to ideas from francophones. True, the response has been more positive than in the past; but few initiatives have been taken.

---

[9] See chapter 3.6.

Anglophones rely heavily on francophone political leaders to deal with the situation. There is no strong political leadership among anglophones on this matter; it would be difficult to single out political leaders who are championing within their own community certain solutions to the problem. It may be that the leadership is simply reflecting the attitudes of the community; or it is due perhaps to the social and political fragmentation of English-speaking Canada. Whatever its cause, this phenomenon does not lead people to focus on interdependencies or attempt to collaborate (as opposed to ferreting out compromises from the other party).

In concluding this section, however, we wish to note that collaboration and co-ordination should not be taken as panaceas to all problems between levels of government. Too frequently, collaboration or co-ordination, and the corresponding lack of conflict between organizations, is unquestionably taken as desirable. Collaboration and co-ordination may be excessive in the sense that they may stifle innovation and entrepreneurial activity. They may also restrict competition, which is beneficial for citizens, among those who are in positions of power. The division of power is the opposite of the concentration of power which, when it reaches a certain threshold, is detrimental to the proper functioning of democracy. A certain level of tension among those who wield power is desirable in any political system.

Quebec as one of ten provinces dealing with central government. At different points in this report, various dimensions of inequality between anglophones and francophones are discussed: socio-economic, demographic, and linguistic. Another one frequently alluded to refers to the political demography of the country: the francophone population is a majority in one province only, while the anglophone is a majority in nine.

Many francophones in Quebec perceive this situation as a definite disadvantage in intergovernmental negotiations. This perception is heightened by the fact that some of the anglophone provinces are very small. This additional dimension of inequality leads some to challenge the existing institutional arrangements; others go further and question the value of the membership of their subsociety in the Canadian political community. The claims for a special status or for an associate-state system mentioned earlier are partly meant as solutions to this situation of disadvantage. Similarly, one reason underlying proposals to reduce the number of provinces with an anglophone majority (to four, for example) are put forward in order to have a more "balanced" situation.

The perceived disadvantage in relation to the central government appears to be based on an assumption of considerable homogeneity of interests among anglophone provinces and consequently of political unanimity. Moreover, the federal government is perceived as being more responsive to the demands of the anglophone majority, and as a result, tends to align itself with the anglophone provinces or at least to be a poor arbiter whenever anglophone and francophone interests differ.

Presumably, this assumption could be tested empirically: has there been historically a solidarity among anglophone provinces in the sense that in situations of conflicting interests between Quebec and the federal government, they have tended to side with the federal government?[10] If so, being a minority of one is indeed a definite disadvantage and would constitute a powerful incentive to seriously modify the rules of the game or pull out entirely from the system. If neither of these is possible, the alternative is to be ready for a political confrontation whenever one anticipates to be the losing minority through the ''normal'' process of negotiation.

But if the assumption of homegeneity and solidarity among anglophone provinces does not hold on most issues of importance, a different approach is called for—an approach that could be labelled the ''moving coalition.'' This would consist of provinces with a similar interest seeking each other out and attempting to form a winning coalition in dealing with the federal government or with other provinces. (The label ''moving'' is used to denote that the coalition may change from one issue to another.) With such a strategy, the existence of many provinces is better than two. Indeed, the existence of two invariably leads to a confrontation whenever there is a divergence of interest either in relation with each other or with the federal government. A large number allows the possibilities of coalitions; so that over time one can be on the winning, as frequently as on the losing, side.

Whether the ''moving coalition'' strategy has been used by provinces in Canada and how frequently, or which provinces have used it and for what kinds of issues does not appear to have been investigated systematically. However, some informal evidence suggests that it is not the prevailing mode of operation. The following observation by Careless indicates the absence of coalitions (1977, p. 195):

> Commentators on Canadian federalism have failed to read both sides of the greater federal flexibility in dealing with provinces. While, indeed, bilateralism may indicate greater concessions won by individual provinces, it may also serve as an entry for ''divide and conquer'' techniques in intergovernmental relations. Rarely have provinces been aware of each other's special relationships with Ottawa in shared-cost programs. As the number of meetings between Ottawa and all the provinces as a group has been reduced or changed in nature (as has been the case with DREE and Manpower), provinces have lost the opportunity to discover the informal, bilateral relations that have been established between Ottawa and each participant within the uniformity of the national formal agreement. Such a process has apparently worked to the disadvantage of both poor and rich provinces; the former have signed new ARDA agreements that are less generous than Ontario's, and the latter have not been able to gauge the size of federal redistributions of wealth from high to low income regions. The often different nature of relations between Ottawa and each province and the reluctance of each to reveal its own particular arrangements have created a situation whereby the provincial regimes cannot comment upon national development patterns apart from what Ottawa—i.e., the *federal* government—wishes to say they are.

---

[10] The expression ''anglophone province'' is used to describe a ''province with an anglophone majority.''

INTERGOVERNMENTAL COMPETITION FOR SUPPORT AND IDENTIFICATION OF CITIZENS

Another way of looking at the relationship between levels of government is to examine the ways in which each level relates to citizens. Most Canadians experience dual loyalties, and frequently the loyalty is stronger to the provincial than to the central government. We saw in the previous chapter that francophones are more likely to score high on "political provincialism" than anglophones.[11] There is substantial "political provincialism" in all provinces: it is highest in Quebec (57%) and lowest in Ontario (25%), with the Maritime provinces close to Quebec on this score (50%). In the same vein, Pinard, after reviewing a considerable amount of evidence on this matter, concludes that the provincial component of the system of dual loyalties is stronger among francophones in Quebec than it is among any other group (forthcoming).[12]

Moreover, the strength of citizen connections with each level of government appears to have changed significantly in recent years. This is the case with both the francophone and anglophone populations, but especially with the former. The general trend since the early sixties has been for provincial governments to acquire an increased importance in relation to the central government, such that the latter has been experiencing a new order of problems in establishing its legitimacy and in securing the identification of certain categories of citizens.

There need not be any opposition between the two levels of government in this regard: both can have a high degree of legitimacy; both can have the socio-emotional and material support of the citizens. But there may be circumstances that lead to competition, allegiance to one being defined as opposition to the other or individual citizens identifying more intensely with one than with the other. These circumstances are the result of many changes that have occurred in Canadian society in the last two decades or so. Some of these changes are structural, others are socio-psychological and socio-political in nature. The structural changes that we will consider in this section are those that have taken place in governmental institutions or have appeared in the socio-economic classes, and in the configuration of interest groups of the two subsocieties and in their relationships with the provincial and federal governments. The next section will deal with some of the socio-psychological and socio-political processes associated with the recent evolution of the two linguistic communities. These changes have set in

---

[11] See chapter 3.4 for definition of "political provincialism."

[12] Pinard notes, however, that the evaluation of the degree of loyalty depends on the point of reference: "When loyalty to Canada is compared with loyalty to Britain and its symbols rather than with loyalty to one's province, French Canadians appear more loyal to Canada than English Canadians, who are strongly loyal to Britain, the Royalty, etc." (forthcoming).

motion a number of processes that have generated tensions and conflicts between levels of government.

Changes in governmental institutions. Conflicts over the division of powers occur when politicians and bureaucrats attempt to obtain the authority and resources they need to maintain or improve their organizations. Such attempts are made because the positions individuals occupy in the organization as well as the benefits they derive depend on the amount of authority and resources at the disposal of their organization. The governmental system, like any other institutional system, consists of a multiplicity of agencies, departments, governing bodies, and so on. Each of these units has a certain function to perform and in doing so interacts with other units in the system.

In defining and performing its role, an organization needs authority and resources, such as money and information. A critical aspect of interorganizational interaction bears precisely on the definition of their respective roles, on their relative authority with regard to various questions, and on the allocation of existing resources. The various units and levels of government are always engaged in bargaining and occasionally come into conflict over such matters.

Some areas of conflict have become particularly important because of recent trends in areas such as economic development and the demand for public services. One of the main bases of legitimation of governments in modern societies is economic growth and the distribution of its results. Citizens expect effective performance on the part of their governments in these areas and evaluate those in power accordingly.

Presumably, it is possible to identify a series of factors associated with economic development. Some of these factors are natural (resource location) and are thus given for the functioning of an economy. But several factors are man-made: they pertain to the features of the socio-economic institutions of a region or of a country (its capital markets, the state of its technology, and so on), to the behaviour of its population (patterns of demand), and to the nature of its relationship with the economy of other regions or countries. These factors can be manipulated in various ways (e.g., tax policies, incentives, tariffs) in order to affect the level or patterns of growth in certain desired ways.

To the extent that there are factors that can be manipulated, the location of the power to control them is a potential issue and a potential source of conflict. The basic hypothesis here is that in their attempts to manipulate factors related to growth, governments at different levels have come in conflict with each other over the authority and resources that each perceives is required.

Economic growth has several requirements. It needs human capital, provided through education, vocational training, manpower retraining, health services; a material infrastructure consisting of transportation, public utilities, housing, and the like; services, in the form of welfare programmes, unemployment insurance, for the care of those that the growth cannot absorb;

ties with the international capital market and the goods and services markets, and so on. In modern societies, the State plays an important role in the provision of these services.

It happens that these functions have been constitutionally assigned to the provinces, (i.e., education), or constitute areas for which there is ambiguity (i.e., manpower training), or overlap of jurisdiction (i.e., health, welfare, transportation, and housing). Economic growth is consequently partly responsible for the relatively greater importance of provincial governments in Canadian society.

A related phenomenon has been the growth of the resource industry, which is also under provincial jurisdiction. To a large extent—and this varies from one province to another—the prosperity of the residents of a province depends to a significant degree on the resource economy, which includes not only the resource industries themselves, but also their ramifications in other industries.

One consequence of these developments is that provincial governments face new or accentuated problems of legitimacy of their own due to their increasing role in regard to economic development. A statement by Black (1968, pp. 32–33) expresses it very well in relation to the political process in British Columbia; the statement, however, appears applicable to all provinces, albeit in varying degrees and in different ways:

> Two of the most important facts of life for this political leadership lie in provincial ownership of all natural resources and the controlling influence of the resource economy on voter prosperity. Primary industry provides a large and diverse base for other industries; it is the key to the development of new areas of exploitation; and it almost directly determines the economic climate of the province. Virtually all the resources on which primary industry depends belong to the people and the government is charged with prudent resource management. There is a wide and general appreciation among the population that a direct connection exists between the soundness of government policies and economic prosperity, and no government can escape the consequences of this connection.

The increased role of governments in economic growth and the related increase in demand for public services have resulted in a considerable expansion of governmental institutions, particularly at the provincial level. And, whenever there is a substantial expansion or reorganization in an institutional system, there is a tendency for tension to arise concerning the distribution of authority among the different units and/or levels in the systems, as well as the allocation of resources among them.[13]

One indication of the importance of this phenomenon is the growth of the public sector, particularly at the provincial level. On this matter, Bird (1978, pp. 28–29) writes that

---

[13] See Breton (1977) for a discussion of these and related changes in Canadian society.

over the postwar period as a whole, the federal government, initially the largest employer in the public 'sector,' . . . has declined sharply in relative importance, while the institutional sector (which includes for example hospital employees) has grown so rapidly that it has become by far the largest public sector employer. The provincial and municipal sectors, especially the former, similarly grew in relative terms over the period, while the educational sector declined slightly in importance.

His observations are based on a study by Foot and Thadancy (1978), which is the source of figure 3.5.1. It is clear from these data that provincial government organizations have been expanding considerably, an expansion that corresponds to the growth in various fields of activity.

In Quebec, this phenomenon is accompanied by a shift from the Church to the State as the leading institution of society. As Archibald and Paltiel (1977) indicate, four important decisions made by the State have contributed to weaken the position of the Church in society: the creation of a ministry of youth and welfare in 1958; the adoption of a state plan of hospital insurance in 1961; the formation of a ministry of cultural affairs, also in 1961; and finally, the establishment of a ministry of education in 1964.[14] One of the consequences of this shift from Church to State is significant: the Church sought accommodations with the federal government, but was not in competition with it; it operated in a different "social arena." However, now that the State has become predominant, we find federal and provincial governments, that is, two organizations of the same kind, in competition for a limited amount of power and resources (Breton and Breton forthcoming).

In recent decades, changes have occurred in government institutions that have accentuated the level of competition and conflict between levels of government. Such competition and conflict are not new; what we have been observing is an increased intensity involving both the political and bureaucratic arms of governments. Interorganizational competition is normal: it is concerned with the power and resources needed by those running the organizations for the success of their ventures and, by implication, for their own success. When opportunities for expansion of command over decisions and resources present themselves as a result of social, economic, or technological phenomena, the competition is bound to be accentuated.[15] Moreover, when one organization (in the present context, an organization at one level of government) attempts to expand its power and control of resources, the related organizations at the other level will usually feel threatened and react accordingly.

Government institutions and interest groups. The interaction between government and interest groups is also relevant for an understanding of

---

[14] Latouche (1974) argues with some empirical evidence that the "Quiet Revolution" of the early 1960s accentuated trends begun some fifteen years earlier and was the result of processes set in motion in that earlier period.

[15] For a discussion of social changes involving the redistribution of power in different sectors of Quebec society, see Breton (1972).

FIGURE 3.5.1
GROWTH OF PUBLIC EMPLOYMENT*

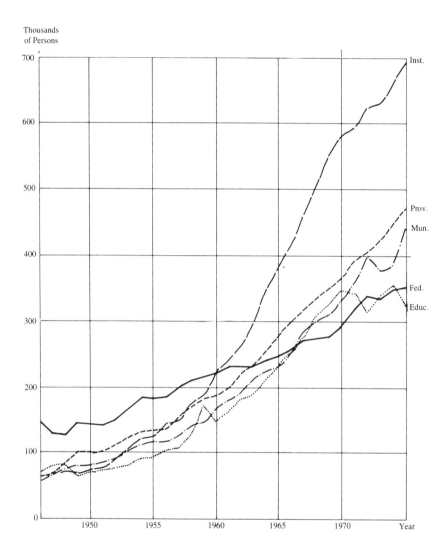

SOURCE: Foot and Thadaney (1978).

NOTE:* Based on taxation statistics data.

federal-provincial relationships. The advantages and disadvantages that governments and interest groups derive from the political process are interrelated in complex ways. It is not surprising to find that they attempt to influence, and are influenced by, each other's activities. In the previous chapter, the linkages of interest groups of each linguistic subsociety with the central government were considered; here, the concern is with the fact that interest groups are potentially affected by two levels of government.

Several authors have pointed out that governmental institutions and interest groups affect each other.[16] On the one hand,

> the distribution of power between the central and provincial governments influences the structure, cohesion and even the existence of interest groups. . . . Interest groups which are provincially based and which enjoy access to the provincial governments will be strong compared with nationally based groups enjoying access to the national government when the provincial governments enjoy a stronger position than the national government in the areas of concern to those interest groups, and vice versa. . . . In short, the pressure goes where the power is—and takes its organization with it (Kwavnick 1975, pp. 72, 77).

In other words, cohesive and well-organized interest group structures at the national level are in part dependent upon the presence of authority and resources at the federal level. Whenever this is the case, the questions raised in the previous chapter about the central government and its relationship with the members of the two language collectivities can also be raised for interest groups: to what extent is the decision-making body accessible to the members in different parts of the country, and through what mechanism does it reach them? Nationally organized interest groups can be a source of societal cohesion, but to what extent they have been so is difficult to establish with the available evidence.

However, if the power resides primarily at the provincial level, interest groups establish links at that level. For instance, although most economic functions are constitutionally under the jurisdiction of the federal government (e.g., rail and ship transportation, trade and commerce, money and banking, tariffs and agriculture), resources, as mentioned previously, fall under provincial jurisdiction. Thus, provincial governments have become important for the interests directly or indirectly associated with the exploitation of resources.

> Provincial jurisdiction over resources makes control over the provincial state apparatus important to certain sections of the bourgeoisie, and gives them an interest in strengthening the provincial state and providing it with the wherewithal to carry out its functions effectively. The increasing effectiveness and power of the provincial state, as well as its revenues from resource royalties, give it the means to assume new functions and acquire new assets. These in turn make it still more essential for the bourgeoisie—no longer simply those elements directly interested in resources—to

---

[16] See, for example, Bucovetsky (1975), Dawson (1975), Kwavnick (1975), and Stevenson (1977).

solidify their relationship with the provincial state on which they increasingly rely to promote their common interests. The process thus continues indefinitely (Stevenson 1977, pp. 78–79).[17]

The pursuit of interest at the provincial level leads interest groups to organize at that level. Insofar as this is the case, the society is characterized by a series of parallel organizations in various sectors of activity. This may be detrimental to linkages among interest groups across regions and linguistic communities, but not necessarily so. There may be conditions under which interest groups in different provinces would enter into exchanges or engage in common activities, thus contributing to societal cohesion. Little research appears to have been done on this matter.

On the other hand,

if the federal distribution of powers does have consequences for the strength and cohesion of the interest groups enjoying access to different levels of government, these groups may attempt to influence the distribution of powers between those governments. . . . rival groups representing the same interest but having access to different levels of government in a federal system will attempt to shift power to the level of government to which they enjoy access (Kwavnick 1975, pp. 72, 77).[18]

In this context, the critical question is what are the determinants of access? Under what conditions do interest groups become well connected with a level of government?

As Presthus points out, access is not so much a matter of "indirect attempts to influence governmental élites, e.g. letter-writing campaigns..."; it is more a matter of "direct intervention in the formal political process.... Here, interest group representatives can cash in political obligations built up in countless informal ways" (1973, p. 123). Access occurs through networks of political relationships. The networks, it can be argued, depend heavily on the cleavages in the social structure. As indicated earlier, the two language collectivities in Canada are segmented along social (and institutional) lines. This means that the networks of social relationships through which information and influence can flow tend to exist *within* each language collectivity.[19] To the extent that this is the case, we could argue that many francophone interest groups in Quebec, which are better connected with their provincial government, would have an incentive to promote or support an increase of the powers of that government.[20]

---

[17] On this question, see also Black (1968), Bucovetsky (1975), and Smiley (1976*b*).

[18] The actual cases analysed by Kwavnick gave strong support to his hypothesis.

[19] A similar argument could be made for regionally based socio-political networks involving political contacts at the provincial level.

[20] This is a matter of degree in the sense that an interest group may want an increase in powers at one level without wanting *all* powers at that level. There may be important advantages for an interest group, and not only inconveniences, to have two governments involved rather than a single one.

But there are also francophone interests that are well connected with the central government and, for the same reason, want to promote or support the powers of that level of government. Thus, federal-provincial relationships are complicated by the presence of rival interest groups in conflict with each other for a distribution of powers among governments that correspond to their lines of access.

The emergence of new interest groups or the transformation (growth or differentiation) of existing ones may be another source of pressure on governmental institutions, particularly concerning the division of powers. For instance, several authors have pointed out that the bourgeoisie in Quebec has transformed itself in a number of ways in recent decades. Analyses have been made of different types of enterprises and industries,[21] and of their changing importance in the economy.[22] The strength of the linkages of these different economic interests with the political parties and decision-making bodies at the federal and provincial levels is a matter of importance in the present context.

It appears that the interests of some segments of the bourgeoisie are pursued through the central political institutions and others through the provincial governments. There are a number of reasons for this. Firstly, the interests of some are more tied to the national economy, while those of others are rooted in the regional economy. Secondly, some segments of the bourgeoisie enjoy access to the provincial government, others to the federal.

A further process is that the government bureaucrats and politicians interested in maintaining or expanding their organizations will support groups that will find it in their interest to reciprocate. This occurs at the provincial as well as the federal level.

— An important question in this context is whether constitutional provisions have any bearing on intergovernmental competition. A constitution defines a certain distribution of authority and resources, and to that degree, sets the parameters within which the competition occurs. It will have an effect on the specific items over which levels of government compete; it may affect the strategies they use to increase the range of activity of their organizations; it may have an impact on the intensity of the competition.[23]

Equally certain is that no constitutional change will eliminate the competition between governments. It may change the character and the

---

[21] The small family firm, the foreign-owned monopoly firm, the Canadian-owned monopoly firm, and so on.

[22] See, for example, Bourque and Frenette (1970), Légaré (1977*a*, *b*), Niosi (1977), Racine and Denis (1970), and Sales (1976).

[23] Constitutions contain propositions that are general in nature and, because of this, are more or less ambiguous as to how they apply to given circumstances. Such ambiguities are frequently perceived as opportunities for organizational expansion on the part of bureaucrats and politicians at one level of government—usually at the bigger or wealthier level—while they are perceived as a danger by those at the other level—usually the smaller or less-wealthy level.

content of the competition, but it will not eliminate its existence since it is rooted in the functioning of organizations and in the process through which they relate to the other organizations in their environment.

Socio-cultural change and intergovernmental competition. One of the important institutions for the creation and diffusion of culture and social ideologies, namely, the education system, is under provincial jurisdiction. Moreover, because language is an instrument of communication, other institutions involved in the creation and diffusion of symbols, such as the media, are also under the control of people in each of the linguistic communities. But insofar as the provincial government controls more of the symbolic apparatus than the federal government, the former has an advantage in relating to individual citizens. That is to say, it controls some of the important instruments in the formation and maintenance of a political community.

The francophone cultural élite also grew, paradoxically enough, as a result of investments by the federal government in cultural activities: broadcasting, film-making, arts, theatre, humanities, social science research, and higher education. Federal involvement consisted in creating institutions such as Radio-Canada or l'Office national du Film and in giving grants to intitutions, groups, or individuals. These investments, those coming from the provincial government and the flowering of the popular arts and culture during the 1960s, encouraged a substantial growth of the cultural élite in Quebec.

Earlier in this chapter, the new nationalism and the accompanying changes in the collective consciousness were mentioned. These phenomena, together with the expansion and transformation of Quebec cultural institutions and the growth of its cultural élites, contributed to the intensification of interest in the Quebec institutions. Furthermore, the State was seen as instrumental in generating further socio-cultural development. These are among the most important factors in directing people's identification and ties with the provincial, rather than the federal, government.

Central government's ability to respond. There are certain factors that have prevented the central government from becoming a strong, countervailing pole of attraction. Several of these factors were discussed in the previous chapter in relation to the accessibility of the federal government and its capacity to reach citizens in each of the linguistic communities. These constitute "the burden of history" that in many ways still lingers on. Overcoming it is not an easy process since this past is now embedded in the collective memory, in ideological frameworks for the interpretation of current events, in mental sets for the imputation of motives, and in more or less established institutional identifications.

A number of authors have argued that the federal institutions are structured in such a way that they are incapable of incorporating the various "territorial particularisms." Smiley, for instance, argues

> that in the Canadian federal system territorial particularisms have come to find outlets almost exclusively through the provinces. This situation has come about largely as a result of the working of the institutions of the central government which from time to time operate so as to deny provincial and regional interests an effective share in central decision-making (1971, p. 328).

Regional interests are not systematically articulated in institutions such as the Senate, House of Commons, Cabinet, and the bureaucracy, even though some of these bodies are formally or informally constituted in terms of regional representation. It appears that representation in terms of the presence of persons from a region does not guarantee an effective representation of interests. The latter would require a different definition of roles and procedures for decision making.

Another institutional factor that has been hypothesized as relevant to account for the poor articulation of regional interests in federal institutions, particularly political parties, is the lack of integration or systematic linkages between federal and provincial parties. In many cases, the provincial parties are different from those at the federal level. When the same party exists at both levels, the ties between them appear to be fairly weak. There is no agreement on the hypothesis that a more systematic integration of parties at the two levels would facilitate the representation of regional interests in federal decision making.[24] Under what conditions would this be the case? Given the above observations about the functioning of institutions, it appears that linkages between federal and provincial parties would not have much effect unless the other institutions were also transformed.

There are also non-institutional factors affecting the capacity of the central government to incorporate regional interests. Some of these are in the realm of social attitudes. One of the conditions for involvement in an institution is that those concerned are made to feel that their involvement is welcome. Although attitudes are changing, this has not been the dominant message. It is again Smiley who writes that

> it has been too little stressed that during the first three years of the Quiet Revolution in Quebec there was in power in Ottawa a government less attuned to French-Canadian sensibilities than any other in Canadian history, with the exception of the administration emerging out of the conscription election of 1917 (ibid., p. 334).

In addition, the subsequent attempts by the federal government to become more "attuned to French-Canadian sensibilities" by adopting measures to change the status of the French language in Canada, by modifying the linguistic rules in federal institutions, and by responding to Quebec interests generated strong negative reactions among anglophones—a French take-over was taking place, "French was being rammed down anglophone throats,"

---

[24] See Pinard (1976*a*, pp. 48–50) for a discussion of this hypothesis, which was initially formulated by Riker (1964).

the French are "invading our turf," and so on. These reactions, by communicating the message that the francophones were intruders, that they were moving into somebody else's domain, certainly did not facilitate the task of incorporating those regional interests in central institutions.

These negative reactions have many sources, some of which were discussed earlier, such as the impact, or anticipated impact, on the careers, social indentities, and status of anglophones of various ethnic origins. An additional factor should be mentioned in the present context: the fact that attempts to incorporate western interests do not appear to have been as equally determined as attempts to incorporate francophone interests.[25] This certainly exacerbated the difficulties of regional representation in federal institutions. To many westerners, the attempts to increase the francophone presence in Ottawa was done at their expense; they could not see what was being done to increase their presence in the central government. Predictably, this fed the negative reactions and made regionalism a "problem" rather than a reality to be dealt with.

In short, recent decades have witnessed the emergence of circumstances that have strengthened the links of individuals and groups with the provincial governments, and of other circumstances that have made it difficult for the central government to maintain or strengthen its links with important categories of citizens, especially francophones in Quebec and westerners. These circumstances have brought about a situation in which the two levels of government compete for the allegiance of citizens. Of course, a situation of competition is inevitable with an independentist provincial government. But the competitive atmosphere was present before the election of the Parti Québécois.

One of the issues in this competition for the allegiance and support of citizens concerns which level of government should have direct linkages with citizens, either individually or in groups. In many instances the provincial government claims the resources from the central government so that it can provide services to citizens, while the central government wishes to organize those services itself so as to have a direct link with citizens. The competition is also manifest in the allocation of blame and credit for various social or economic problems. But whatever its manifestations, the competition is fundamentally over which level of government can best serve the interests of citizens in the different regional and linguistic communities, and therefore which one deserves their allegiance and support. The fact that the situation has come to be defined this way by important segments of the population is a clear sign of a crisis in the political community.

---

[25] Whether these attempts succeeded or not in the eyes of francophones is another matter.

SPECIFIC AREA OF COMPETITION: LANGUAGE LEGISLATION

Competition and conflict between the two levels of government manifest themselves in many different areas, such as economic development, assistance to small businesses, immigration, and communications. But one area of particular relevance is language. In terms of their stated, ultimate objective, there is no disagreement. Both want to improve the status of the French language and facilitate the improvement of the socio-economic condition of members of the francophone community.

But two different approaches have been adopted for the pursuit of this general goal: they are based on the pan-Canadian and segmentalist conceptions of Canadian society that were discussed in the previous chapter. Obviously, the former approach has been adopted by the federal government and the latter by the Quebec government, especially since the late 1960s.

The basic idea underlying the federal approach is that the well-being of citizens can be improved by providing conditions that facilitate individual socio-economic mobility. Legislation and agencies to prevent discrimination against individuals are therefore required. But it is also felt that the members of each language group will be able to avail themselves of existing opportunities if they can move anywhere in the country and ''feel at home.'' Thus, it is important that in all parts of the country, whenever numbers warrant it, services for the education of children in the language and culture of the family be provided; that other cultural facilities, such as radio and television stations, be available, and that they be able to use the services of at least the federal government in their own language. Moreover, if the two languages are accorded an equal social as well as legal status, mobility would be facilitated by making it easier for members of each group to be accepted when moving into a new community.

The approach adopted by the Quebec government rests on a different notion. It does not deny the importance of individual socio-economic mobility, but its basic concern is with the control of the economy in that part of the country it considers the ''homeland'' of the francophones. The preoccupation is with the condition of the community, with a greater cultural integration of economic organizations within the community, with the creation of a total cultural milieu. It is only within such a milieu in which institutions are run by and for the francophone community that adequate conditions for the improvement of individual well-being can really exist.

The advocates of each approach see numerous problems with the opposing view. They criticize the underlying assumptions, especially those that the policy makers at the other level apparently prefer to ignore. Several criticisms are levelled at the federal approach, one of which is the assumption that community facilities such as schools are sufficient for cultural maintenance and development. It implicitly denies, for instance, that the work environment is a powerful assimilating agency. It ignores the problem of the ''critical mass,'' namely, of the relative and absolute numbers required for cultural maintenance and development.[26] More fundamentally, it ignores the relationship between individual mobility and the distribution of the control of economic organizations in Quebec and New Brunswick, that is, in regions where francophones are concentrated. Finally, the critics of that approach point to the high rates of assimilation of francophones outside Quebec and especially to the relatively unresponsive posture of provincial governments.

Table 3.5.1 presents a few aspects of the legal status of the French language in the nine provinces with an anglophone majority, and of the English language in Quebec. A few observations should be made. Firstly, the situation in New Brunswick is significantly different, as it is the only province in which both French and English are official languages (since 1969). Therefore, the status of French in the provincial legislature and courts is greater than in the other provinces, and French educational facilities are more extensive. Outside Quebec, the percentage of French mother tongue is the highest in New Brunswick: 33% according to the 1976 census. Secondly, the formal status of the French language is still poorly established in the other eight anglophone provinces. Thirdly, changes have occurred, primarily since the late 1960s, in the field of education. The legal status has been improved and some education facilities have been provided, although not without resistance and conflict.[27]

In the area of education, the federal government has a cost-sharing agreement with the provinces for second-language instruction and mother-tongue instruction to Quebec's English-speaking minority and to the French-speaking minorities in the other provinces. However, more than half of the federal contributions go toward language instruction of the Quebec English-speaking minority. This appears to be due to the fact that Quebec has a larger English language school system than the other provinces have for their French-speaking minorities.[28]

There are political difficulties in giving increased official recognition and institutional services to the francophone population of many provinces. In all provinces except Quebec and New Brunswick, the francophones constitute a small percentage of the total provincial population. Moreover, the francophone population is smaller than several other ethnic groups, many of whose members do not see why the French should receive special treatment. Institutional recognition and services are usually given in the

---

[26] On the question of the linguistic security required for the development of a community and its members and for the minimization of conflicts, see Dion (1974) and Laponce (1975).

[27] The Fédération des francophones hors Québec (1977a) lists eighteen cities in four provinces where the conflict over French schools has been an object of controversy in recent years.

[28] See the *Toronto Globe and Mail*, 23 November 1977; also the Fédération des francophones hors Québec (1977b, pp. 69–70).

TABLE 3.5.1

SELECTED LANGUAGE PROVISIONS AT THE PROVINCIAL LEVEL, 1978

PROVINCE	POPULATION OF FRENCH MOTHER TONGUE (ENGLISH IN QUEBEC) 1976[a]	% OF TOTAL POPULATION 1976[a]	OFFICIAL STATUS OF MINORITY LANGUAGE	PROVINCIAL COURTS		LINGUISTIC PROVISIONS IN EDUCATION[c]
				Audition of Cases[b]	Possibility of Francophone Jury[b]	
British Columbia	38,635	1.6	—	Interpreters	No	No provisions in law. Discretionary.[d]
Alberta	44,810	2.4	—	Interpreters	Possibly	All courses, except English, may be offered in French. School boards are given authority to decide on use of French for instructional purposes in individual schools.
Saskatchewan	26,890	2.9	—	—	No	French may be used as a language of instruction, subject to regulations that determine the amount of time devoted to such instruction (regulations are set by provincial Cabinet.)
Manitoba	55,605	5.4	—	Interpreters	Right to a jury in French if judge is francophone	English and French have equal status as languages of instruction. A board must provide instruction in French if the parents of 28 pupils at elementary level and 23 at secondary level so request. Minister may authorize the setting up of classes for fewer students.
Ontario	467,540	5.6	—	Pilot projects in selected areas	Bilingual jury in pilot projects	The law requires special boards to establish French-language instructional units where numbers warrant.[d]
Quebec	796,665	12.8	—	In English, if all parties to the action agree	Yes	The law requires school boards to provide instruction in English for all children who are eligible under the law to receive this instruction.[e]
New Brunswick	226,695	33.5	Both English and French are official languages (1969)	Interpreters. Pleading in French at discretion of judge.	Yes	The chief language of instruction in a school is the mother tongue of the pupils. If school is mixed, classes are to be so arranged that the chief language of instruction is the mother tongue of each group.

TABLE 3.5.1 — Continued

PROVINCE	POPULATION OF FRENCH MOTHER TONGUE (ENGLISH IN QUÉBEC) 1976[a]	% OF TOTAL POPULATION 1976[a]	OFFICIAL STATUS OF MINORITY LANGUAGE	PROVINCIAL COURTS		LINGUISTIC PROVISIONS IN EDUCATION[c]
				Audition of Cases[b]	Possibility of Francophone Jury[b]	
Nova Scotia	37,300	4.5	—	Interpreters (in civil cases only)	No	No provision in law. Traditional.[f]
Prince Edward Island	6,590	5.6	—	Interpreters	No	No reference to language of instruction in law. Discretionary.
Newfoundland and Labrador	2,730	0.5	—	Interpreters (at Wabush, Labrador only)	No	No reference to language of instruction in law. Discretionary.

NOTES: a. Statistics Canada (1978).
b. Fédération des francophones hors Québec (1978, p. 51).
c. Council of Ministers of Education (1978).
d. Measures pertaining to language of instruction left to discretion of provincial minister.
e. Law 101 (Assemblée nationale du Québec 1977, p. 5) states following specifications:
   "...The following children, at the request of their father and mother, will be able to receive their instruction in English:
   (a) a child whose father or mother received his or her elementary instruction in English, in Québec;
   (b) a child whose father or mother, domiciled in Québec on the date of the coming into force of this act, received his or her elementary instruction in English outside Québec;
   (c) a child who, in his last year of school before the coming into force of this act, was lawfully receiving his instruction in English, in Québec, in a public kindergarten class or in an elementary or secondary school;
   (d) the younger brothers and sisters of a child described in paragraph c.''
   Also, under the law, government may exempt from instruction in French English-speaking children coming from a province that has concluded a reciprocity agreement with Québec and certain categories of persons staying in Quebec temporarily, or their children.
f. Traditional: School boards free to grant permission to use French as a language of instruction and traditionally have done so in predominantly French-speaking districts.

provinces in the name of the larger pan-Canadian context, but not without overcoming much resistance.

Also, the high rate of assimilation of people of French origin (outside Quebec and New Brunswick) does not strengthen the political will of the provincial élites toward adopting measures for the French; it may even weaken it. There appears to be a vicious circle: the minority situation and the high rate of assimilation do not encourage governments to give recognition and services, the lack of which encourages numerical weakness and assimilation. Such a situation has led a number of analysts to seriously question the viability of the pan-Canadian perspective.[29]

The relatively weak political will may also be related to the composition of the upper echelons of the provincial governments relative to that of the population. Table 3.5.2 gives the ethnic distribution of Cabinet ministers in four provinces between 1961 and 1973, and of high ranking civil servants in 1973. For purposes of comparison, the table also includes the percentage distribution by ethnic origin.

The composition of the élite is partly a cause and partly an effect of the weakness of the political will with regard to the status and services offered to the francophones.

Criticisms are also formulated against the Quebec approach: it assumes that enforcing a change in the language of work will result in a shift in the control of economic decision making, and that the change can be done rapidly without serious consequences to the population, ignoring the plausible hypothesis that only a fairly small segment of the middle-class will benefit from the legislation. It is based on a simple consensus view of the legal process: that since democratically elected governments express the will of the majority, the laws passed will be obeyed by virtually everyone. It does not seem to consider that laws are systems of constraints on behaviour, and as such, constitute incentives for those affected to avoid being submitted to them. The question of how people will react to the constraints imposed on them is especially important when a significant number of people are affected.

Much of the criticism is a response to the decreased status of English in Quebec. Up until 1974, English enjoyed the special status it had been given in Quebec by the British North America Act. Bill 22, adopted by the *Assemblée nationale* in 1974, changed this by declaring French the official language of the province. The *Loi sur la langue officielle* contained a number of specifications concerning French and English in public administrations, in industry and business, in education, and in the professions. In 1977 this law

---

[29] For example, Castonguay, on the basis of an analysis of the rates of endogamy among people of French mother tongue outside Quebec concludes: *"Que l'on se rende donc compte à quel point la foi en la résurrection des minorités hors-Québec est devenue aussi ridicule qu'illusoire"* (*Le Devoir*, 16 June 1978).

TABLE 3.5.2
ETHNICITY OF CABINET MINISTERS, HIGHER CIVIL SERVANTS
AND POPULATION IN FOUR PROVINCES

ETHNICITY	NUMBERS			
	Quebec	Ontario	Alberta	British Columbia
Cabinet (1961 −73)				
British	4	18	10	12
French	25	1	—	—
Other	1	—	4	6
Bureaucrats (1973)				
British	—	29	21	17
French	23	—	1	—
Other	—	—	1	2

	PERCENTAGES			
	Quebec	Ontario	Alberta	British Columbia
Population (1971)				
British	11	59	47	58
French	79	10	6	4
Other	10	31	47	38

SOURCE: Olsen (1977), pp. 205, 211; and Statistics Canada (1973*b*), table 2.

was replaced by Law 101, which re-establishes the new status of the French language in Quebec and attempts to deal with a number of problems that had arisen with the 1974 law.

Table 3.5.1 indicated the status of the English language in Quebec in comparison with the French language in the other provinces. As seen, in spite of its decreased status, the English language in Quebec is still well established.

The two approaches to the language issue are based on different views of reality and conceptions of the country. Each avoids what the other considers problematic. As a result, the solutions advocated differ. In both cases, opponents point to the unintended consequences that may be more important than the intended ones. A consequence of these circumstances is that each level of government considers that the problems it has to deal with are accentuated by the activities of the other level, a phenomenon that increases the intensity of the competition. The specific contents and forms of this competition in the area of language may be different when Quebec is involved as opposed to an anglophone province; but it is present with most of the provinces. It could be argued that it is in the interest of most provincial governments to be segmentalists as far as language is concerned, while it is in the interest of the federal government to be pan-Canadian.

CONCLUSION

In dealing with federal-provincial relationships and their significance for the relationships between anglophone and francophone subsocieties, we considered two general classes of issues: those pertaining to the division of powers between the two levels of government, and the related questions of competition for the allegiance and support of the members of each of the two collectivities.

Under division of powers, several questions were considered: the centralization versus decentralization of powers; the interdependence between levels of government and the propensity for collaboration; the anglophone majority in nine provinces and the francophone majority in only one.

Insofar as the issue of centralization versus decentralization is a rational one, that is, one of efficiency, we noted the need for systematic studies of the policy areas that would be more efficiently handled by one or the other level of government. It was emphasized that in considering matters of efficiency, the cultural and regional diversities of the Canadian population need to be taken into account. The goals and aspirations of citizens in different parts of the country and especially in the two linguistic subsocieties are not alike, and any consideration of efficiency that ignores these variations is bound to yield poor results.

One source of strain in federal-provincial relationships is the difference in status between the anglophone and francophone communities. Over the years, various kinds of constitutional solutions have been proposed which, if implemented, may not bring about that many changes in the day-to-day functioning of governments, and in negotiations and bargaining, but which would imply change in the status of the francophone, in relation to the anglophone, community. Solutions such as the associate-State model would have considerable impact in terms of symbolic recognition, even though it may not decrease the need for mechanisms of negotiation and accommodation required by the interdependence of the different regions.

It seems important that whatever the solutions ironed out, they take into account the status needs of both language communities, and attempt to accommodate the new identity that has emerged in Quebec in the last couple of decades. A relative decrease in the status of the anglophone community, however, cannot be easily achieved.

Whatever the constitutional model in existence, there will be interdependence between governments—an interdependence that will require exchanges, collaboration, and bargaining. We considered a number of conditions that would affect the propensity to collaborate among officials of different levels of government. First, the arrangements made must be mutually beneficial. Perhaps more important, however, is the feeling on the part of the officials at each level that their domain will not be invaded by the other. It is important that officials at each level be able to trust those at the other, a phenomenon related to the commitment on the part of each to "make the system work." If such a commitment does not exist and should the intent be to expand one's powers and resources to the detriment of the other, there will be strong tendencies to pull away from any kind of collaboration and go it alone.

On the question of the presence of one francophone *vis-à-vis* nine anglophone provinces, we suggested that the advantages of a moving coalition among provinces with similar interests would be a better strategy than the one that tends to define issues in terms of one against the nine others. We have suggested that it is rare to find issues where the alignment is one against nine; most issues involve more than one province favouring a particular alternative.

Attention was also given to the competition between levels of government. Such competition, it was noted, was greatly increased in recent years as a result of changes in the institutional structures of government, particularly at the provincial level. These changes were partly the result of social and economic transformations in the society: new patterns in the exploitation of resources, rapid economic growth during the 1950s and 1960s, and increased demand for services of various sorts from governments. One could argue that the increased competition is transitory, that with time new, mutually acceptable arrangements will be worked out. But since these changes were accompanied by an identity metamorphosis, it could be argued that they are the occasion for a profound transformation of the political institutions of our society.

The relationship of the two levels of government with the interest groups in society also was discussed. On the one hand, it was seen that government institutions have an impact on the structure of interest groups, their cohesion, and their activities, and by affecting what happens at the level of interest groups, may have some impact on the degree of cohesion of society. The modes of organization and functions of interest groups, whether they exist at the national or regional level, in turn can have an impact on societal cohesion. The conditions of a positive or negative impact, as well as the mechanisms through which such impacts occur, are poorly known. More research seems to be required on these questions.

On the other hand, interest groups may also have an impact on the structure of government institutions, and in this way, they may also have an impact on the cohesion of the society. It was noted that interest groups having greater access to a particular level of government will not only organize their activities at that level in order to promote their interests, but may also attempt to increase the power of the level of government to which they have access.

Moreover, there is an interaction between representatives of interest groups and the bureaucracies of each level of government. The support does not go only in one direction. That is to say, interest groups seek the support of a particular level of government in the pursuit of their interests, and bureaucrats at a given level of government seek the support of interest groups in the promotion of their organizational advantages and in their conflict with other levels of government. The dynamics of this interaction, and the factors affecting the degree of access of interest groups of each linguistic subsociety to the various levels of government require considerable research.

Finally, we discussed the issue of constitutional change. Some argue that constitutional changes involving the division of powers will have no effect on the degree of tensions between levels of government and therefore between the francophone and anglophone communities. The discussion in this chapter, however, does not support this view. Indeed, a particular distribution of powers provides both constraints and opportunities for bureaucrats and politicians at each level of government in the pursuit of their organizational objectives. Changes in the distribution of powers will affect the set of opportunities and constraints that they face. Such changes may well affect the level of tensions or conflict between the levels of government; it is certainly likely to affect the content of the bargaining or exchange between them. But perhaps more important is the fact that the distribution of powers, because of its possible effect on the organization of interest groups and their activities in regard to each level of government, may have important consequences for the cohesion of society. The division of powers between governments may affect the structure of interest groups and the ways in which they tie or do not tie the different parts of the country together. Moreover, the distribution of powers will act to orient the different interests in the direction of one government as opposed to another. We could argue that this is the reason why constitutional changes are so complex and difficult to achieve. The present division of powers is tied to an array of advantages and disadvantages for the various interest groups in the country. As a result, certain changes would no doubt be favoured by some, but would be strongly resisted by others. Constitutional changes may also affect the ways in which the interest groups in the francophone and anglophone subsocieties relate to each level of government.

Certain aspects of intergovernmental competition were illustrated by a discussion of the issue of language. The federal and Quebec governments have adopted different approaches in this regard that have led them into competition with each other. The dynamics of this competition were reviewed briefly and the role of the provincial governments, their actions, or inactivity in the area of language were considered as a factor in the evolution of the Ottawa-Quebec controversy.

Horizontal Relationships Between Francophone and Anglophone Institutions

Much of the recent work on national integration has focused upon the affective orientation of individuals toward the nation-state. The inappropriateness of using nationalistic feelings as the sole or most fundamental basis for explaining integration is in part due to the fact that such feelings are often the result, rather than the cause, of the processes that make for integration (Deutsch 1968; Smiley 1967). Within Canada there are a number of strong regional and provincial identities, making less intense the attachment of individuals to a national community. Theorists, wishing to circumvent the difficulties posed by the salience of regional and ethnic loyalties, and the lack of a strong national identity in Canada, have tended to explain the bonds of Canadian association largely in terms of a ''non-ethnic political nationalism'' (Smiley 1967), consisting largely of a common interest in the fulfilment of pragmatic goals such as economic progress and social security (Underhill 1938). Unless the particular forms through which a Canadian political nationalism is realized are specified, the assumption of a national community appears to remain at the normative level, advanced as a counterweight to the possibly disintegrative forces of regional and ethnic particularisms. Given the lack of explanatory power inherent in affective or idealist explanations of national integration, it would appear better advised to focus upon the pattern of ties between different segments established for material, political, and social benefits which accrue, although perhaps unequally, to different segments. In this chapter, we examine some of the processes of collaboration and interdependence that serve to link the two language communities more closely.

The nature of interdependence between the two language communities profoundly affects the extent and stability of national integration. If the transactions between the two collectivities are elaborate, involve large proportions of resources, and are perceived as upgrading their mutual interests, the resulting integration is likely to be fairly stable. If all these conditions are present except for the perception of mutually beneficial fulfilment of interests through the existing pattern of ties, there may be sentiments among one collectivity toward greater autonomy in certain spheres of action. However, extrication from the myriad ties between the two collectivities may be a very costly and difficult, if not impossible, process. In this context, we might note that even fairly extreme independentists within Quebec are aware of the advantages of economic transactions with the rest of Canada and formulate their alternative to the *status quo* in terms of a continued economic association coupled with political independence.

Earlier in the report, we discussed the conditions under which francophones and anglophones meet at the federal level—the degree of equity of their representation in the institutions of the central government, and the structure of federal-provincial relationships. In this chapter, we would like to examine those relationships that are direct and unmediated by the central government.

In analysing the pattern of horizontal relationships between the francophone and anglophone subsocieties, an important distinction can be drawn between those relationships involving individuals or aggregates of individuals, and those involving subsocieties as corporate entities or systems of organizations. While the next chapter will assess the former types of intergroup linkages, the present chapter will deal with the latter.

In the context of Canadian federalism, corporate relationships are best articulated through interprovincial relationships—the patterns of interaction between Quebec, where francophones form the majority and have held political control for over a century, and other provinces, where formal recognition of the francophone collectivity is relatively minimal.[1] It is a measure of the strength of the francophone collectivity in Quebec and the weakness of francophones elsewhere in Canada that corporate relationships between anglophones and francophones are much less developed and extensive outside Quebec.

As the nature of interaction between anglophone and francophone institutions involving Quebec on the one hand and the other provinces on the other is qualitatively different, further elaboration upon this distinction is warranted.

---

[1] The extent to which francophone interests are represented by provincial State institutions outside Quebec varies with their numerical strength, being highly visible in New Brunswick, where they comprise approximately 40% of the population, and practically non-existent in British Columbia, where they represent about 4%. Also, while certain of the French Canadian interests may be accommodated in *intra*provincial matters (e.g., in matters of language use in provincial courts and health facilities), it may be solely the dominant anglophone objectives that are involved in *inter*provincial affairs (e.g., in representation on boards dealing with interprovincial endeavours). We know of no studies that approach the question of francophone rights from this angle.

INSTITUTIONAL RELATIONSHIPS BETWEEN FRANCOPHONES AND ANGLOPHONES WITHIN AND OUTSIDE QUEBEC

Historically, French minorities outside Quebec developed their own institutions, as demographic density permitted, centred around the parish (Guindon 1968*a*). The future of the survival of the French language and culture, and thus of the French minorities themselves, and the nature of state intervention that was to aid their survival were ill-defined by the Confederation settlement and remain ambiguous to this day (Smiley 1967).

The extent to which francophone minorities have been able to retain their own set of institutions and avoid assimilation determines the quantity and type of corporate action in which they are able to engage. It also affects the nature of the integration between the two collectivities on a nation-wide basis. That is, the maintenance of the francophone linguistic and cultural bonds determines whether the bilingual and bicultural character of the country exists in some significant form, or whether Canada is in fact anglophone throughout, with a francophone appendage (which might possibly dissociate itself from the rest of Canada).

Thus the process of francophone and anglophone interaction at the corporate level is likely to have quite different implications for national integration depending on whether we are dealing with the relationships between Quebec and other provinces on the one hand, or those outside of Quebec on a more local basis on the other. In the case of interprovincial interaction involving Quebec, we are dealing with those economic, political, and socio-cultural relationships between English Canada and a francophone community with its own ''homeland'' and set of institutions. The assumption is that these relationships will bind the two collectivities and their corresponding regions more closely to each other. In the case of intergroup relations between francophone and anglophone collectivities outside Quebec, we are dealing with the issue of the survival of francophone social organization in the face of anglophone domination, and thus the viability of the persistence, and possible expansion, of a bilingual and bicultural reality on a national scale. Put in other words, the existence of a bilingual and bicultural Canada is predicated upon the existence of the ''French fact'' from one coast to another (see Fédération des francophones hors Québec 1977*a*). The alternative is further territorial segregation of the two ethnic collectivities.[2]

---

[2] It may strike the reader as odd that we are treating the persistence of francophone groups, and thus of the bicultural, bilingual nature of Canada, as the dependent variable, and the interaction of such groups with anglophone groups as the independent variable. This approach however has proven fruitful in previous research. Vallée (Vallée and Shulman 1969, p. 2), for instance, in his study of francophone groups outside Quebec, hypothesized that among the requirements for the persistence of francophone minorities was an optimum degree of conflict with groups. Jackson (1975), in his case study of a town in southwestern Ontario, describes the process by which French Roman Catholics became organized into groups only in face of conflict with English Roman Catholics and Protestants.

There is another reason why the preservation of French-Canadian culture and the francophone community, by implication the locus of reproduction of that culture, have been viewed as essential for the survival of Canada itself. It has long been argued that due to such factors as American cultural domination, American sway over the communication media, and increasing American presence in the Canadian economy, the uniqueness of anglo-Canadian culture is seriously undermined. As early as 1938, Ouimet noted that "the superficial difference between the average English-Canadians and their American neighbours is negligible." Thus, it has been reasoned that in order to preserve Canada's distinct character, a programme of binational development must be encouraged: "The French-speaking personality must achieve confidence in both its cultural security and its economic equality, not only within Quebec but in Canada as a whole" (Clarkson 1966, p. 139).

Later in the chapter, we will address ourselves to the question of whether francophones outside Quebec interact collectively with anglophones, and if so, what are the nature and extent of this interaction? Here we will examine the pattern of relationships existing between Quebec and other provinces.

INTERPROVINCIAL INTERACTION INVOLVING QUEBEC

We will begin by examining the corporate relationships between the francophone and anglophone collectivities in a situation where ethnic and territorial cleavages coincide. We will investigate the type and level of transactions between Quebec and the provinces that comprise English Canada. Our focus will be not only on the common interests shared by Quebec and other regions but also on the obstacles that impede interprovincial co-operation. To what extent does the ethnolinguistic boundary between Quebec and other provinces act as an obstruction to trade, socio-cultural exchange, and political collaboration?

In addressing ourselves to the question of interdependence between two regions commonly referred to as English and French Canada, we are well aware of highly salient and institutionalized cleavages in Canada that would align Quebec with other provinces. For instance, in the division of Canada into the "rich" and "poor" provinces, Quebec, Saskatchewan, Manitoba, and the four Atlantic provinces confront Ontario, British Columbia, and Alberta (Meisel 1974). A strong case has been made for viewing the major cleavage in Canada as that between the central industrial heartland or "metropolis" of Ontario and Quebec, and those regions east and west of this area that comprise the agricultural and resource-extraction periphery (Bercuson 1977, p. 2). Yet another model of Canada conceptualizes the country as a "loose collection of ten distinct political cultures," roughly corresponding to different stages of socio-economic development (Wilson 1974, p. 444). One need not accept Wilson's evolutionary model of development in order to recognize the very real political and socio-economic differences not only between English and French Canada but also among the provinces comprising English Canada.

The cleavages between the rich and poor provinces, the metropolis and hinterland, Quebec and English Canada, surface in the vertical relationships between the provincial and federal governments. However, to the extent that these cleavages serve to differentiate various regions, we would expect them to operate also in the horizontal aspect of intergovernmental relations. The boundaries defining a region would presumably be discernible by the modification of interprovincial collaboration and other relationships across those boundaries. Thus, our review of interprovincial relations will attempt to highlight not only the French-English contradiction that separates Quebec from the other provinces but the other regional cleavages as well.

In taking the province as our unit of analysis and centring our discussion on interprovincial relations, we do not wish to ignore the differences within provinces and the fact that the provinces are themselves ''additional sites for the accommodation of cleavages that do not necessarily coincide with provincial boundaries'' (McRae 1974a, p. 240). Our discussion of French-English relations outside Quebec will buttress this point. McRae qualifies his assertion about the significant variations within provinces by stating that Quebec is an immediate exception in that it evinces a greater degree of homogeneity than other provinces. To the extent that Quebec's population is predominantly French-speaking, this is true. However, within Quebec there exist enormous disparities between regions as far as ethnic mix, employment, productivity, and income are concerned.[3]

While recognizing that transactions between provinces will affect various groups and interests within provinces differentially, the systematic assessment of the distribution of benefits from interprovincial transactions is beyond the scope of this study and will be mentioned only briefly with reference to Quebec. Our discussion will attempt to assess the benefits (and costs) of co-operation between provinces and the collectivities that make up their constituencies. The arenas and mechanisms for interprovincial interaction and the areas of social activity covered by such interaction will be dealt with in this regard.

---

[3] The concentration of Anglo-American big business in Montreal, and consequently of anglophones in this urban centre, serves to differentiate Montreal, and its problems of ethnic relations and language policies, from the rest of Quebec (Morrison 1970).
Eastern Quebec stands out as a fairly underdeveloped region in the province: ''Per capita income in the area was little more than half the Quebec average in 1961, and approximately one third of the wage earners were unemployed for six months in the year'' (Brewis 1969, p. 208).

INTERPROVINCIAL RELATIONS: NEGLECTED AREA IN THEORY OR PRACTICE?

At the outset, we would like to note that the study of interprovincial relations in Canada has received little scholarly attention (Leach 1959; Smiley 1970, p. 101). To some, this gap in research on horizontal collaboration between provinces signals the actual neglect in horizontal relationships that could potentially serve as a cohesive force between disparate political and cultural communities (Black 1975, p. 99). To others, the fact that interprovincial co-operation has been such a neglected aspect of study is due to the paucity of formal, constitutionally based, and legally binding interprovincial arrangements such as those in other federations. It has also been suggested that the reason Canada has no independent secretariat for interprovincial relationships is the opposition of governments, federal as well as provincial, to the surrender of their vested authority and status to another level of government machinery (Aitchison 1963; Simeon 1972). Leach has attributed this lack of formal basis for interprovincial interaction to the effectiveness of informal contacts between provincial officials in providing liaison between provinces.

The most developed of the formal consultative processes between provinces appears to take place in the most specialized, professional, or administrative, and thus least politically sensitive, areas of activity. It is likely that in such areas the feelings of identification with the field of professional activity are greater than with governments (Institute of Intergovernmental Relations 1969). One frequently used forum for collaboration among administrators and professionals from different provinces are interprovincial meetings. Simeon notes that the most common type of intergovernmental conferences (including those involving the federal government) are meetings of public servants. Informal, day-to-day contact is similarly a prevalent method officials use to make interprovincial agreements dealing with administrative details.

The premiers of all provinces convene annually for the federal-provincial plenary conference. There is some disagreement in the literature as to what extent these conferences offer an opportunity for premiers to further horizontal relationships between the provinces. The focus of these conferences is matters of federal-provincial concern, and the federal government plays a dominant role in setting the agenda. One valuation of these conferences is that they are used by the federal government to present and ratify decisions that have already been made without previous consultation with the provinces. An opposite view is that although convened on federal initiative, federal-provincial conferences allow premiers and ministers to establish personal contact, exchange ideas, and share plans and programmes on purely provincial matters.

Since 1960, the premiers of provinces have met annually in conferences where federal government officials did not actively participate. The recent reinstatement and expansion of such purely interprovincial consultative bodies, as opposed to those of a federal-provincial nature, have been justified by the rapid growth of provincial interests. Stevenson (1977) sees the pattern in Canada of the growing activism of provincial governments as an exception to the general trend, in advanced capitalist countries, toward centralization and the erosion of local power. He attributes the assertiveness of provincial governments during the past few decades largely to the expansion of resource industries over which the provinces have jurisdiction.

Most interprovincial communication and collaboration does not include all ten provinces as participants, but rather occurs between two or three contiguous provinces (Institute for Intergovernmental Affairs 1969; Leach 1959; Simmons 1970*a*). Geographers who have done work on interprovincial flows of various types (for example, commodity flows, migration, phone calls, airline passenger movements) have pointed out that since each province, with the exception of Prince Edward Island and Newfoundland, has contacts with no more than two others, contiguity alone explains a great deal of transactions. However, not only contiguity but also ''regionalism'' of the type implied by the metropolis-hinterland model described earlier account for major patterns of interprovincial collaboration. Thus, there appears to be greater communication and joint projects, particularly of an economic nature, among the four Atlantic provinces, among the Prairie provinces, and between Ontario and Quebec. The provinces comprising each of the regions share to some extent a common economic base, with Ontario and Quebec forming an industrial heartland, and the Maritimes and the Prairies, two resource-based hinterlands. The common geographic position of provinces within a region is also important, as it means that provinces that are geographically clustered are more likely to share a common position in relation to their natural markets and sources of supply. A third element of similarity is the common historical experience of provinces within a region.[4] A combination of these and other factors has given the provincial populations and élites within a region a shared perception of Canada and Canadian federalism (Brewis 1969; Canadian Institute on Public Affairs and Mount Allison University 1965; Gartner 1977).

It is in response to dissatisfaction with representation of their interests at the federal level that much of the impetus for interprovincial collaboration has come about. For instance, what is now the Western Premiers' Conference was first assembled following discontent in the West with the results of the 1972 election, where the Liberal government in power was returned with only

---

[4] One could argue that these general statements conceal marked differences in economic activity, geographic location *vis-à-vis* markets, and historical experiences among the individual provinces. However, the selection of the boundaries of regions is always problematic, given that a region is an intellectual concept rather than an object given by nature (ibid., p. 45). The important point to note is that the provinces, through their governments and other organizations, have recognized and acted in accordance with the regional boundaries, giving or implying some of the reasons stressed by analysts delineating regions.

seven seats from the four western provinces. The institutions for western and Maritime provincial government co-operation, most developed in the Maritimes, provide sites for the working out of common regional viewpoints in dealings with the federal authorities. The major areas of effective co-operation in both regions have been economic—for example, in the fields of transportation, agriculture, industrial and resource development, trade, and fisheries.

Ontario and Quebec, perhaps due to their comparatively strong position with regard to population, economic wealth and benefits (such as the freight-rate structure), and representation in the federal government have been slowest to develop formal arrangements of co-operation with each other or with the other provinces. Both provinces have had a tendency toward separate action in the formulation of social and economic policy. One exception to the general tendency toward independent processes of development occurred in 1927 when Ontario and Quebec amalgamated fourteen pulp and paper mills in an effort to combat the influence of a U.S. firm (Morris and Lanphier 1977, p. 142). However, such examples of joint collaboration are relatively rare.

Interdependence consists not only of collaboration in joint projects, which presupposes at least some degree of similarity of values or outlook, but also transactions based on complementarity—on interlocking relationships of mutual resources and needs (Deutsch et al. 1968, p. 90). It is complementarity that forms the basis for trade. Within Canada, each province has

> differing endowments of raw materials, of the stock of physical capital, and of labour. . . . This means each province will have costs of production which, compared with other provinces, are more favourable for the production of some goods than others. The result is that each province will produce for trade a somewhat different range of products at any given time (Safarian 1974, p. 13).

Various reports on interprovincial trade flows indicate that this aspect of interdependence is highly evolved. In 1974, interprovincial trade accounted for one quarter of all Canadian manufacturing. Quebec and Ontario both dominate such trade, accounting for nearly 80 per cent of the interprovincial trade in manufactures (McKeough 1977). When considering overall trade surpluses—employment-creation effects of trade, estimated benefits received from the tariff, and advantages accruing to consumers in terms of lower prices and greater variety of goods—it appears that Quebec profits as much or more so than Ontario in trade between these two provinces. Moreover, Quebec and Ontario are the two greatest beneficiaries of interprovincial trade (Economic Council of Canada 1969; Fletcher 1977*b*; McKeough 1977; Safarian 1974).

Despite the apparently high level of trade flows that integrate Quebec closely to other provinces, there appears to be two sets of factors that negatively affect interprovincial economic integration. The first set of factors is those restrictions imposed by the independent action of provinces in formulating legislation. The second set is the alternative sources of capital and markets open to provincial enterprises.

Analysts have delineated various economic policies that impose direct and indirect costs to the free mobility of resources (goods, capital, and labour) across provincial jurisdictions. One of the major non-tariff barriers to interprovincial resource flows is the lack of uniformity among provinces in legislation and regulations pertaining to certification and licensing, transportation, mark-ups by product-marketing boards, government purchasing policies, and restrictions on non-resident landholdings, to name some of the major ones (Safarian 1974; Trebilock, Kaiser, and Prichard 1977). All of these policies tend to discriminate in favour of intraprovincial resources and place restrictions on internal free trade within Canada. It has been suggested that the relatively weak commitment of Canadian provinces to uniformity of legislation can be attributed to the fact that the Uniformity of Legislation commissioners are underresourced and have an invisible public profile.

Simmons (1970*a*), who measured a number of different types of interprovincial flows, including rail, ship, and truck commodity flows, concluded that in general Quebec was not linked to other provinces to the extent expected from its size and centrality. One inhibiting factor in interprovincial transactions between Quebec and provinces in English Canada is language. This manifests itself in such matters as Quebec's requirement that corporations wishing to raise capital in Quebec must file their prospectus in French in accordance with the Official Languages Act, thus facing additional costs in translation and added delay in transactions. The flow of professional labour between Quebec and other regions is also hampered by the failure of professional associations to incorporate both official languages into their standards (Trebilock, Kaiser, and Prichard 1977).

The alternative to interprovincial economic linkages has not necessarily been confinement of economic transactions to within each province. The fact that provinces and municipalities are free to operate in capital markets, domestic or foreign, has facilitated North-South integration on a regional basis (Institute of Intergovernmental Relations 1969). The postwar expansion of the resource industries by provincial governments was largely a response to U.S. needs and occurred with the aid of U.S. direct investment (Stevenson 1977).

Faucher and Lamontagne (1953) have advanced the thesis that Quebec's industrial growth and the exploitation of its natural resources were designed to complement the pattern of U.S. industrialization. For instance, since the 1950s when iron ore emerged as an important resource, the development of huge deposits of low grade ore north of the St. Lawrence River was prompted by the increased demand of the U.S. steel industry (McRoberts and Posgate 1976, p. 33). The economic policies of the Quebec government over the past two decades have furthered North-South integration. The mammoth James

Bay hydroelectric project, launched by the provincial Liberals and later endorsed by the Parti Québécois, was financed with U.S. capital (Stevenson 1977). At the end of 1972, Hydro-Québec contracted to export power for twenty years, beginning in 1977, to Consolidated Edison of New York (McRoberts and Posgate 1976, pp. 32—33).

The effect of the augmenting economic linkages between each of the provinces and the United States (including trade and U.S. investment in, and ownership and control of, enterprises situated in Quebec and other provinces) was summed up by Stevenson:

> Integration [of the Canadian economy with the United States] increased the balkanization of the national economy, as the provinces became more closely tied to corresponding regions in the United States and less integrated with one another (1977, p. 82).

NON-ECONOMIC RELATIONSHIPS BETWEEN QUEBEC AND OTHER PROVINCES

The discussion up to this point has indicated that there exists a substantial network of economic transactions linking Quebec to other provinces in English Canada, but that these transactions are limited by various practices that restrict the movement of resources to within provincial boundaries and the preference for forging economic liaisons with the United States. Although research specifically concerned with other forms of interaction among provinces appears to be fairly scanty, making it difficult to assess such relationships, it seems that interprovincial co-operation in social or cultural fields is relatively undeveloped both within and across regions (Bercuson 1977). Gartner (1977) points out that while provincial governments may have common interests, issues, and problems in such areas as social services, bilingualism, and school curriculum content, they often differ on questions of policy, objectives, and solutions.[5]

Quebec has taken a more vigorous role than other provinces in arguing that cultural and recreational programmes should be an exclusively provincial responsibility (Stevenson 1977). Quebec has also asserted itself in establishing direct contacts with French-speaking countries and with French-speaking communities of other nations. It maintains that such links, unmediated by federal (anglophone) authorities, are needed ''in order to strengthen the precarious position of the French Canadian group in Canada and of the French language in North America'' (Lalande 1973, p. 239). The corollary of this is that contacts with provinces where anglophones form the majority

---

[5] In some cases, the pursuit of common goals by francophones and anglophones in non-economic as well as economic fields occurs at the level of co-operation among voluntary associations rather than at the formal level of State institutions. The effects of French-English relations established within voluntary associations both with regard to the promotion of interethnic harmony and societal cohesion will be discussed in the following chapter.

would have the effect of weakening, or at least of doing nothing to develop, the French Canadian community and its language. In spite of the lack of benefits, perceived by certain groups within Quebec, of forging cultural links with English Canada, Montreal, the largest urban centre of Quebec, has hosted two of the most exciting cultural events in Canada—the world exposition of 1967 and the 1976 summer Olympics—events where other provinces were formally represented. However, regardless of the national and international prestige earned by the French Canadian hosts, the short duration of these events, and the fact that in financial terms they were extremely costly and left high deficits and disagreements as to who should cover them have meant that these cultural occasions may have been, in the long run, sources of tension between Quebec and the rest of Canada.

INSTITUTIONAL PATTERNS OF INTERACTION BETWEEN FRANCOPHONES AND ANGLOPHONES OUTSIDE QUEBEC

Within provinces outside Quebec, there are a number of compelling reasons why corporate relationships between anglophones and francophones are problematic and likely to be rare. In this section, we will examine to what extent collective and organizational interaction occurs between francophones and anglophones in regions other than Quebec. To what extent is such corporate interaction undermined by the assimilation and anglicisation of francophone minorities? In which institutional domains is such interaction likely to take place (political, economic, social, or cultural)? What is the effect of the existing patterns of interaction on societal integration?

In some regions outside Quebec, the survival of the francophone collectivity is itself dependent upon the largesse of the respective provincial governments, which are predominantly anglophone institutions. Such is the case of the Franco-Manitoban community, whose cultural centres depend upon funds from the provincial government for their programmes to keep French culture alive. This provincial support is likely circumscribed by the fact that there is presently not a single bilingual Cabinet minister within the Manitoba government, and that furthermore, this government must take into account the prevailing political milieu of widespread hostility toward Quebec and anything French (*Toronto Globe and Mail,* 21 January 1978). This relationship of dependence naturally limits the activities open to the francophone community to those not likely to alienate the source of funding—a government whose environment is anglophone and whose concerns are mainly those of the dominant anglophone community.

In their effort to depoliticize, and consequently mitigate, the conflict between anglophones and francophones, a general tendency of provincial governments in English Canada and of the federal government has been to divide into "watertight" compartments those issues that have cultural significance and those that do not (Kwavnick 1965; Ryerson 1972). These decision-making bodies have agreed to the limited maintenance of cultural duality and, in the spirit of anglo-American democracy, simultaneously refused political and economic duality. The result has been that francophone minorities outside Quebec have been most organized in the sphere of leisure activities and least so in the areas of political, and especially economic, life (Morris and Lanphier 1977, p. 49).

In creating linkages between two ethnocultural groups, those that aleady exist in terms of the dominance of one culture by another must be taken into account. Dominance of anglophone culture is very great outside Quebec, whereas within Quebec it is individuals from the English Canadian community who are increasingly feeling the dominance of francophone culture. An understanding of the distribution of power between the two collectivities in each region is crucial in comprehending the objectives and actions of francophone groups *vis-à-vis* the anglophone collectivity. For instance, whereas for francophones outside Quebec the idea of bilingualism is associated with the retention of their culture, for francophones in Quebec it is associated with its loss (ibid., p. 37). The Québécois regard bilingualism as the means and symbol by which francophones make the transition from the francophone to the anglophone culture, to which they finally assimilate. The objective of francophones within Quebec is therefore to create a situation of French unilingualism and domination by French culture to balance the dominance of the English language and culture elsewhere in Canada. Francophone groups outside Quebec, appraising the inevitable rights and necessity of the English language in their regions, desire equality of rights with anglophones, which in terms of linguistic policy means the promotion of bilingualism and the recognition of French in the institutional life of Canada (Choquette 1975; Jackson 1975; Morris and Lanphier 1977).

The movement of francophones within Quebec toward the formation of a Québécois nation-community has had a profound effect upon the identity and group activities of francophones in the rest of Canada (Lee and Lapointe forthcoming). The exclusion of francophones outside Quebec from the material and psychological benefits of events within Quebec has led to the emergence of new systems of solidarity. On the one hand, there appears to be a growing tendency toward structural differentiation of the French-Canadian nation into Québécois, Franco-Ontarians, Acadians, Franco-Manitobans, and so on. As the francophones in a province such as Ontario are well integrated into the occupational structure of the wider society, the Franco-Ontarian collectivity has lately strived to develop greater autonomy within institutional spheres, such as education, health services, and the courts. The more activist role, at the provincial level, of the State and the consequent growth of pressure group activity can account in part for the strengthened provincial basis of identification by francophone minorities (ibid.)

On the other hand, the French-Canadian (minus Quebec) system of solidarity lately has been consolidated at a new, more consciously political level. It was in response to the recognition that certain problems and interests were shared by all francophone communities outside Quebec that the nine provincial francophone associations were prompted to form a liaison structure in 1971 for the purpose of developing common objectives and in certain cases to undertake common actions. This interprovincial association evolved in 1975 into the Fédération des francophones hors Québec, with an explicit political role of reducing inequities faced by francophones in their linguistic and social rights. This interorganizational body views its role as the assurance of constant interprovincial communication between francophone associations and the creation of a common front among francophone communities for the purpose of solidary action (Fédération des francophones hors Québec 1977a). Despite the perception of its function as an activist liaison structure linking provincial francophone associations, which are in turn regarded as being the true political representatives of francophones in a minority position, the federation's source of funding (largely from government subsidies) and its lack of societal legitimation severely curtail the scope and effect of its political activity.

The nature of the Canadian electoral system (single-member plurality vote) entails that French-Canadian minorities outside Quebec who wish to obtain their collective interests through parliamentary action can only do this *successfully* by pursuing a coalition strategy with other groups. The limited size, and social and economic power of French minorities mean that a political strategy of organizing parties of their own that could then compete with like structures from the anglophone collectivity is bound to be ineffectual. The institutional structure of our parliamentary system is such that an ethnic minority, even one as large in relative terms as the Acadians in New Brunswick, that wishes to have its group interests represented must work through parties whose culture and principal actors are predominantly anglophone (Leslie 1969). Francophones in New Brunswick, who number about 40 per cent of the population, have indeed organized a Parti Acadien that explicitly affirms its Acadian nationalism in its socio-economic and socio-cultural programme. However, as Thériault (1977, p. 164) points out, the impact of this party up to now has not been strong.

In smaller geographical regions, for example, in towns where there is a substantial French-Canadian population, and in more delimited institutional areas such as education, it is possible for the French-Canadian minority to form organizations for the purpose of institutionalizing conflict with the English majority. The inequality between the two groups is accentuated by the fact that the organizations representing the dominant English collectivity in these conflicts are public, such as town councils and public school boards (Jackson 1975).

In terms of cultural activities, the francophone collectivity within Quebec has been quite introverted, a tendency aided by the structural bifurcation of the mass media into two linguistic broadcasting systems, and due also to the low priority assigned by francophones in Quebec to cross-cultural communication with anglophones. Francophone groups elsewhere recognize that they are living in an anglophone culture and that in order to preserve their culture and institutions, it is necessary to enlist the support of the dominant anglophone community and convince them of the validity of the francophone community's claim to distinctiveness (Vallée and Shulman 1969, p. 24). Thus, organizations such as the Fédération des francophones hors Québec have among their objectives the advancement of relations with all organizations that support the development of francophone communities outside Quebec (1977*a*). Their task of cross-cultural communication includes the promotion of French culture through such programmes as French-Canadian theatre played in anglophone schools throughout the country.

Outside Quebec, French-English corporate relationships are complicated by the existence of cross-cutting cleavages, a major one being religion.[6] It has been argued that in Canada the primary cleavage historically has been religious, and it is only recently that the pattern of institutional segmentation has shifted from religion to language (Choquette 1975, McRae 1974*a*, p. 243). However, the salience of one cleavage as opposed to another is to a large extent situational and determined by the particular issue of contention. Jackson (1975) demonstrated that conflict arose between the English Protestant and Roman Catholic groups (both French and English) when the issue was distribution of financial resources between the separate and public schools; and between French Catholics and English Catholics when the issue was distribution of resources between French and English panels within the separate school system.

Similarly, religion formed a basis for co-operation between the French in the West and other ethnic groups of Roman Catholic persuasion during the early part of the twentieth century. Since then, however, there has been a growing dissociation of francophones from other ethnic groups and avoidance of "ethnic" (meaning "immigrant") activities in an effort to establish the bilingual and bicultural framework formally advanced by the federal government during the late 1960s and by the Official Languages Act of 1969 (Painchaud 1976).[7]

---

[6] Note that in Canada religion did not represent a perfect case of a cross-cutting cleavage. Although the anglophone collectivity was split into Protestant and Roman Catholic factions, francophones were virtually of Roman Catholic faith only. However, the religious cleavage among anglophones served to prevent cohesion among them and offered a possible basis for solidarity between the two linguistic collectivities.

[7] Due to the articulation of dissatisfaction by some of the well-organized ethnic groups, the bicultural policy of the federal government was rescinded and replaced by a policy of "multiculturalism within a bilingual setting." This move left francophones with the feeling that they had been betrayed by the federal authorities acting in response to an "anglophone backlash," and also served to further alienate them from other ethnic groups (Painchaud 1976; Fédération des francophones hors Québec 1977*a*).

The presence of a cross-cutting cleavage such as religion may be a factor alleviating tensions caused by Canada's primary cleavage between francophones and anglophones (Jackson 1975). On the other hand, the existence of cross-cutting cleavages does not always produce a mitigating effect on interethnic conflict, and may heighten the dissension between two linguistic groups sharing the same religion. Such was the case in Ontario during the first quarter of the century, when there was intense conflict within Catholicism between the French and the Irish (Choquette 1975). One could argue that an important consequence of the presence of a cross-cutting cleavage was the diversion of francophone resources, which could have been used profitably to achieve greater equality with the dominant anglophone collectivity and a firmer establishment of the "French fact," to a conflict with a minority segment of the anglophone community, where the gain could not have been as advantageous.

As mentioned earlier, francophones as a collectivity are least autonomous in the economic realm. Although they are disadvantaged in comparison to anglophones in terms of income, occupational distribution, and ownership and control of industry, francophones are well integrated as individuals into economic organizations where anglophones predominate (Morris and Lanphier 1977, pp. 12–14; Royal Commission on Bilingualism and Biculturalism 1969*a*, *b*). In Jackson's study (1975), the similarity in interests of francophone and anglophone workers, created by relationships and joint participation in labour unions, provided an important situation of contact between the two collectivities. However, this contact took place between individuals (the type of interethnic relationships that will be considered in chapter 3.7) rather than communities as corporate entities, the class of relationships presently under discussion.

The regional distribution and strength of francophone collectivities as corporate entities outside Quebec, as well as their corporate activities with anglophone groups, have been neglected areas of study. The results of demographic surveys of Canada are fairly pessimistic about the survival of the "French fact" outside Quebec (Henripin 1975; Lieberson 1970; Maheu 1970). With the exception of French Canadians living in northern New Brunswick and in those parts of Ontario included in the "bilingual belt," French Canadians outside Quebec tend to experience a process of anglicisation. The trend over time shows that between the last two censuses a decrease occurred in the percentage of Canadians whose mother tongue is French in eight out of ten provinces, and of Canadians who speak French only in all provinces (table 3.6.1). As far as the distribution of the French population across the country is concerned, between 1941 and 1971, Canadians of French origin became more concentrated in the heartland of Quebec, British Columbia, and in the parts of Ontario that comprise the bilingual belt. Canadians who are French by language, however, became more concentrated only in the southern and western parts of Quebec, their number as a

TABLE 3.6.1
MOTHER TONGUE AND OFFICIAL LANGUAGE, CANADA AND PROVINCES, 1961–1971

| CANADA AND PROVINCES | MOTHER TONGUE | | | | | | OFFICIAL LANGUAGE | | | | | | | |
| | English | | French | | Other | | English Only | | French Only | | Both | | Neither | |
	1961	1971	1961	1971	1961	1971	1961	1971	1961	1971	1961	1971	1961	1971
CANADA	58.5	60.1	28.1	26.8	13.4	13.0	67.4	67.0	19.1	17.9	12.2	13.4	1.3	1.4
Newfoundland	98.6	98.5	0.6	0.7	0.8	0.7	98.4	97.9	0.1	0.1	1.1	1.7	0.2	0.1
Prince Edward Island	91.3	92.3	7.5	6.6	1.1	1.1	91.0	91.2	1.1	0.6	7.5	8.1	0.1	—
Nova Scotia	92.2	92.9	5.4	5.0	2.4	2.0	92.9	92.6	0.8	0.5	6.1	6.7	0.1	0.1
New Brunswick	63.3	64.6	35.2	34.0	1.5	1.3	62.0	62.5	18.7	15.9	18.9	21.4	0.2	—
Quebec	13.2	13.0	81.1	80.7	5.7	6.1	11.5	10.4	61.8	60.8	25.4	27.6	1.0	1.0
Ontario	77.5	77.5	6.8	6.2	15.7	16.2	88.9	87.2	1.5	1.2	7.9	9.3	1.5	2.2
Manitoba	63.4	67.0	6.6	6.1	30.0	26.8	89.6	89.2	0.8	0.5	7.4	8.1	2.1	2.0
Saskatchewan	68.9	74.0	3.9	3.4	27.2	22.5	93.5	93.6	0.4	0.2	4.5	4.9	1.4	1.2
Alberta	72.2	77.6	3.1	2.8	20.7	19.5	94.1	93.7	0.4	0.2	4.2	4.9	1.1	1.1
British Columbia	80.9	82.7	1.6	1.7	17.5	15.5	95.3	94.0	0.1	—	3.5	4.6	1.0	1.2
Yukon	74.3	83.4	3.0	2.4	22.7	14.0	93.5	93.2	0.2	—	5.6	6.5	0.5	0.2
Northwest Territories	35.5	46.8	4.3	3.3	70.2	49.8	58.9	73.2	0.4	0.2	7.0	6.0	33.5	20.3

SOURCE: Dominion Bureau of Statistics (1963), cat. no. 92–549; *idem* (1970), cat. no. 92–529; Statistics Canada (1973c), cat. no. 92–725; and *idem* (1973d), cat. no. 92–726.

TABLE 3.6.2
Distribution of French Population According to Origin
and Language, by Region, 1941 and 1971

	French by Origin (×1,000)		French by Language (×1,000)	
	1941	1971	1941	1971
Atlantic	100	137	61	41
Northern New Brunswick	153	208	151	192
Northern & Eastern Quebec	1,475	2,213	1,504	2,264
Southern & Western Quebec	1,220	2,546	1,213	2,607
Northern & Eastern Ontario	238	398	218	281
Southern & Western Ontario	136	339	71	72
Prairies	147	237	127	78
British Columbia	22	97	11	12
Canada	3,491	6,180	3,357	5,546
	% of Total for Canada			
Atlantic	2.9	2.2	1.8	0.7
Northern	4.4	3.4	4.5	3.5
Northern & Eastern Quebec	42.2	35.8	44.8	40.8
Southern & Western Quebec	35.0	41.2	36.1	47.0
Northern & Eastern Ontario	6.8	6.4	6.5	5.1
Southern & Western Ontario	3.9	5.5	2.1	1.3
Prairies	4.2	3.8	3.8	1.4
British Columbia	0.6	1.6	0.3	0.2

SOURCE: Joy (1975).
NOTE: Atlantic and Canada 1941 figures increased to reflect estimated French population of Newfoundland; "language" is mother tongue in 1941, home language in 1971.

proportion of the total French-by-language population decreasing in every other region (table 3.6.2).

One of the most telling measures of attrition of the French language (included for the first time in the 1971 census) is the extent to which Canadians of French origin speak French or English at home (see chapter 1.2). Again the pockets of French strength in northern New Brunswick and the fringe of Ontario that borders Quebec fare quite well in this regard, whereas other regions outside Quebec suggest an "irresistible march towards anglicisation" (Arès 1975, p. 130). There exists a large, though varying, gap between the number of Canadians of French origin and the number of Canadians who claim French as their mother tongue, and then again between those whose mother tongue is French and those who speak French at home (see table 3.6.3).

TABLE 3.6.3

NUMBER OF PERSONS REPORTING FRENCH AS ETHNIC ORIGIN,
MOTHER TONGUE, AND HOME LANGUAGE, BY REGION, 1971

Region	Total Population (×1,000)	French Ethnic Origin (×1,000)	French Mother Tongue (×1,000)	French Home Language (×1,000)
Atlantic	1,711	137	65	41
Northern New Brunswick	346	208	201	192
Northern & Eastern Quebec	2,350	2,213	2,257	2,264
Southern & Western Quebec	3,677	2,546	2,611	2,607
Northern & Eastern Ontario	1,228	398	330	281
Southern & Western Ontario	6,475	339	152	72
Prairies	3,542	237	139	78
British Columbia	2,185	97	38	12
Canada	21,568	6,180	5,794	5,546

% of Total Population in Each Region

Region				
Atlantic	100.0	8.0	3.8	2.4
Northern New Brunswick	100.0	60.3	58.0	55.4
Northern & Eastern Quebec	100.0	94.2	96.0	96.3
Southern & Western Quebec	100.0	69.2	71.0	70.9
Northern & Eastern Ontario	100.0	32.4	26.9	22.9
Southern & Western Ontario	100.0	5.2	2.3	1.1
Prairies	100.0	6.7	3.9	2.2
British Columbia	100.0	4.4	1.7	0.5
Canada	100.0	28.7	26.9	25.7

SOURCE: Joy (1975).

Despite the seemingly incontrovertible demographic trends, the inevitability of the disappearance of francophone communities outside Quebec can only be assumed if interventive processes initiated by government bodies have no effect upon the preservation of ethnic groups. However, research has demonstrated that the structure and language practices of institutions, such as educational, industrial, governmental, and mass media, are fundamental in determining whether a language will maintain its position and gain new speakers. Lieberson (1970) has singled out the amount of schooling in French available to French Canadians as one of the most crucial factors in French language retention. This finding is significant, given the importance theorists have attributed to language as a major pillar for the persistence of ethnic communities (ibid.; O'Bryan, Reitz, and Kuplowska 1975).

However, the capacity for governments to carry through programmes that would aid the retention of French and the preservation of francophone communities must be viewed in the context of the distribution of power between the two collectivities and the general political milieu. Government support, through the granting of funds, for programmes of one collectivity may be viewed by others as directly disfavouring their interests since they are in competition for scarce resources. This would explain the low level of French-language education available outside Quebec in areas where there are substantial numbers of francophones (Morris and Lanphier 1977). The introduction of French into the courts and other institutions on an equal basis with English has similarly been resisted because of the immense costs involved not only in financial terms but also in terms of the foreseen loss of political support given to the provincial governments by the anglophone majority (*Toronto Globe and Mail*, 10 June 1978). Nonetheless it seems possible that if anglophone élites could be convinced of the long-term interests of the preservation of viable francophone communities, in their capacity as opinion leaders, they could help structure the political environment; so that legitimation is given to the investment of funds for such perservation.[8]

CONCLUSION

French Canadians within Quebec and those in regions outside Quebec are similar on a number of dimensions. Many attitudes and socio-economic characteristics are shared by French Canadians wherever they live, and the same may be said for English Canadians. However, in terms of demographic factors, such as size and density of population, and in terms of their control of institutional structures, the two collectivities are internally differentiated, showing quite disparate patterns within, as opposed to outside, Quebec. The control that French Canadians have over the political institutions within Quebec has meant that many of the relationships that the francophone community has with the anglophone community are articulated through the horizontal interaction between Quebec and the provincial governments of English Canada.

Francophones outside Quebec have no comparable political structure through which to represent their interests in interaction with the anglophone collectivity. The small size of francophone minorities and the lack of power relative to the anglophone collectivity have meant that the institutional relationships with anglophones are fairly limited. The action of interorganizational associations, such as the Fédération des francophones hors Québec, is bounded by their source of funding from anglophone-dominated political institutions and their lack of formal mandate. Given the forecast made by demographers and socio-linguists of an overall trend toward decreasing numbers of francophones outside Quebec, resources for francophone institutional structures and thus for organizational interaction with the

---

[8] The effect that élites have as opinion leaders on cross-cultural communication will be taken up in the next chapter.

anglophone community are likely to diminish. Extensive funds and social support from the anglophone collectivity and its élites might be able to strengthen the francophone community throughout Canada, and thus lend credence to the model of a pan-Canadian bilingualism and biculturalism. The chances of such support being given must be viewed however in the context of the distribution of power between the two collectivities and the priorities of the anglophone collectivity, which are fashioned by other factors such as strong regional identities and interests.

Study of interprovincial relationships is most advanced at the economic level, where there are the most extensive interprovincial links. In terms of its social and economic development, Quebec has taken a fairly independent course and has engaged in few joint projects with other provinces. Focusing upon interprovincial trade, it seems that the province is well integrated: its tariff-protected industries enjoy substantial benefits, and a great number of jobs are created for francophones through such trade. However, an economic pull to the south complicates, and may even override, the cohesive effects of East-West trade links.

Although the small amount of attention given in the literature to non-economic types of interaction between Quebec and other provinces makes it difficult to make firm statements, it appears that interprovincial social and cultural relationships involving Quebec are relatively limited, and perhaps inhibited, by the language difference. Thus overall, Quebec's role in interprovincial relationships is ambiguous, being tied fairly closely to other eastern provinces in some cases and isolated in others.

It has been argued that the "Quebec problem" differs from the problems faced by other provinces in that it is an internal, rather than "regional," problem (Leslie 1977). For Quebec, it is not a matter of a distinctive economic interest being poorly or well served by federalism and trade with other provinces. Rather, Quebec's problem is that francophones are not in economic control and resent the dominant economic role of "les Anglais." According to this view, no amount of economic linkages with other provinces is likely to alleviate French-English conflict, as such links are not forged between the two language communities, but between the dominant interests of the anglophone collectivities from Quebec and other regions.

The implications of this hypothesis are that economic conflicts within Quebec between anglophones and francophones take on increased importance, and are not likely to be offset by horizontal relationships in the political and cultural spheres over which francophones have institutional control.

Relationships Among Individual Members of the Two Linguistic Communities

In evaluating the extent to which interindividual relationships across the francophone and anglophone subsocieties increase cohesion, both the attitudes of individuals concerning the other subsociety and the patterns of interaction need to be considered. Two distinctly opposed hypotheses have been put forward concerning the effect of individual attitudes and behaviour on integration in segmented societies. The first, the "contact" hypothesis, asserts a positive effect of intergroup contact or interaction on intergroup tolerance and harmony. Such a view assumes that lack of knowledge and familiarity of the other group is the cause of individual intolerance or prejudice. The co-variance of knowledge and sympathy for the other group's problems was found in a study conducted at the time of the "Quebec crisis" of 1970. Although the direction of causality could not be established, attitudes of English Canadians concerning the separatist movement were more favourable as information about separatism increased (Rothbart 1970).

In contrast with the contact hypothesis, the "isolation" hypothesis regards conflict as inevitable within societies divided by language, ethnicity, or religion. Increased contact will only accentuate the differences along which the larger society is divided and thus lead to an exacerbation of conflict between subsocieties. Obversely, when the number of intergroup contacts at the non-élite level is kept to a minimum, the likelihood of intergroup antagonism being acted out is sharply reduced (Nordlinger 1972). According to this hypothesis, the major mechanism for conflict regulation is élite co-operation at the national level.[1] Only the élites from the two collectivities,

---

[1] The isolation theorists or "consociationalists" posit a number of conditions that facilitate the success of overarching co-operation at the élite level in divided societies. These include highly homogeneous subcultures, fairly persistent cleavages between subcultures, approximate equality in size and power of subsocieties, and the existence of foreign threats (Lijphart 1971; McRae 1974b; Noel 1974). The effect of each of these conditions on integration through élite accommodation is touched upon in this and other sections. It is interesting to note that some of these variables, for example, equality in power, are roughly equivalent to conditions that are viewed as conducive to interethnic harmony by the contact theorists, whereas others, such as the persistence of deep cleavages, are seen by the contact theorists as counter-productive.

265

through their overarching co-operation, are able to play a direct and positive role in combatting the dangers of fragmentation. The non-élites are seen as too numerous, scattered, fragmented, and weak to make a significant, direct, and positive contribution to integration of the two collectivities. All that is required of the masses is "that they be committed to their own sub-cultures and that they trust and support their respective élites" (Noel 1974; see also Nordlinger 1972).

The extent to which support is garnered from the masses for the élites is largely dependent upon the accommodation by the élites of a multiplicity of interests. The policies of recent governments in Quebec have attempted to take into account the demands of the middle classes by the government's commitment to planning and state enterprise (De Wilde 1977), of the nationalists by language policies, and of the working class by the Parti Québécois government's proposed "anti-scab" legislation, programmes for guaranteed annual income, and better working conditions. (De Wilde 1977; Légaré 1977a). This support is desired by the Parti Québécois government for the purpose of negotiating with the federal government for political sovereignty rather than for a stronger integration of Quebec within Confederation.

Various aspects of élite contribution to societal cohesion have been discussed in previous chapters, including the extent of participation of francophone and anglophone élites in the federal institutions and their important role in the regulation of conflict between subsocieties, which is often articulated at the larger societal level. Simeon (1972) has pointed out the primacy of the bargaining process between political leaders at the federal and provincial levels, which has resulted from the centralized structure of Canadian government.

Another facet of élite behaviour, which élite theorists (e.g., Clement 1975; Laumann and Pappi 1976; Porter 1965) have stressed as important for cohesiveness among élites and which is likely to play a part in the success of negotiations, is the pattern of interpersonal relationships between members of the francophone and anglophone élites. As summed up by Laumann and Pappi (1976, p. 159): "The crucial feature . . . is the impact of informal social ties on the influence structure. Politically relevant information and persuasion tend to flow along friendship ties."

There is an astonishing lack of information in the literature about the personal ties between élites from the subsocieties. Porter (1965), in his study based on 1951 data, found that French and English élites did not have a high rate of intermarriage, a pattern that he attributed to both language and religious differences, as well as to the underrepresentation of French Canadians in the national economic élite. He ascribed the relative lack of interaction to their separate educational experience—the anglophone élite in the private, fee-paying schools of eastern Canada and the francophone élite in classical colleges in Quebec. The segregation at the level of educational institutions, which was also found to prevail in Clement's (1975) study of the 1971 corporate élite, is crucial for later friendship ties, given that the connections with other élite members forged at school continue long after formal education ceases. Clement also found that in another important realm of social life, that is, in club life, there is a high degree of separation between French and English élites outside Quebec, although they do come together in the Montreal clubs (p. 244–47). The segregation in interpersonal and kinship ties between francophone and anglophone élites parallels their structural separation—in Quebec, the French Canadian economic élite is in non-monopolist industries; the English Canadian economic élite controls monopolist enterprise (Légaré 1977*a*); and the media is split into the two charter languages (Clement 1975). At the formal and informal level, these two modes of separation create a profound obstacle to élite accommodation and the resolution of conflict between the two subsocieties.

The proponents of the isolation hypothesis thus hold that it is the behaviour of the élites, those at the uppermost levels of various institutional structures rather than individuals at large, that determines the outcome of conflicts between subsocieties and the future of societal cohesion. In addition, they have correctly pointed out that in many cases intergroup contact has *not* led to a reduction of intergroup conflict or intolerance and has often *increased* tension and caused outbreaks of violence (Amir 1969; Billig 1976). This empirical evidence, which appears to refute the simplistic version of the contact hypothesis, has lead to attempts to formulate the conditions under which contact between groups leads to intergroup harmony (Allport 1954; Amir 1969; Nordlinger 1972). Among the dimensions that have been specified as affecting the nature of the contact are: (a) the personal versus impersonal nature of the contact; (b) the voluntary or "forced" nature of the contact; (c) the degree to which the contact is one of equal status between groups; (d) the common versus conflictual nature of goals; (e) the extent of institutionally provided opportunities and support for intergroup contact; (f) the direction and intensity of initial attitudes; and (g) the élite versus non-élite status of participants. It should be pointed out that none of these factors act in isolation in conditioning the nature of the contact or of its effects upon cross-cultural amity and societal integration.

The following discussion will attempt to outline the effect that each of these variables has on integration at the interpersonal level and more importantly on societal cohesion. A review of Canadian studies investigating interpersonal relationships between francophones and anglophones will provide us hopefully with some basis to evaluate the relative merits of the contact and isolation hypotheses in understanding the nature of the links between the two collectivities. The present stage of research dealing with our *problématique* obligates us to offer only tentative and suggestive conclusions.

PERSONAL VERSUS IMPERSONAL NATURE OF CONTACT

Contacts of the same proximity and frequency can have quite different effects upon attitudes depending upon whether they are of a personal or impersonal character (Amir 1969). Personal relationships are defined as those in which the individual personalities form a crucial part of the rationale for the relationship. Impersonal relationships refer to contacts that are established for primarily instrumental reasons and where individual personalities enter in only to the extent that they facilitate or hinder the attainment of particular goals. Research has demonstrated that instead of leading to greater tolerance and understanding, impersonal forms of contact tend to harden negative stereotypes and increase prejudice against individuals perceived to be part of an ''out-group.'' In contrast, more personal forms of contact improve intergroup relations due to the creation of positive attitudes toward members of the other group.

Social interaction of French and English Canadians at the mass as well as élite level has rarely been studied in a systematic fashion. We would like to know the pattern of interpersonal ties and interaction both within (e.g., within Quebec) and across regions (e.g., between Quebec and other provinces). Studies by geographers mentioned earlier have provided us with some notion of the extent of individual interaction (MacKay 1958; Simmons 1970a,b; Yeates 1975). MacKay's study identified a significant ''boundary effect'' on long distance telephone traffic due to the language barrier between Quebec and Ontario and between Quebec and the United States. He concluded that for telephone messages from Quebec cities, ''English-speaking cities behave as if they were five to ten times as far away as Quebec cities of the same size and separation and those in the U.S. as if they were 50 times distant.'' Since MacKay's data did not allow him to distinguish between business and personal calls, his measure mixes interindividual and interorganizational contacts. In a recent replication however, Simmons, who was able to separate business from residential calls, found a similar decrease in interaction due to the linguistic and cultural boundary between Quebec and Ontario. He also found that residential calls, which is one rough indicator of personal, as opposed to impersonal, relationships, were more sensitive to ''distance decay,'' that is, they were more likely than business calls to decrease in frequency with greater distance. This finding is not unexpected, given that individuals usually maintain friendship ties with those who are in close proximity and accessible (Freedman, Carlsmith, and Sears 1974, pp. 63–68).

A survey study of Quebec residents commissioned by the *Toronto Star* (1977) found that the proportion of francophones who reported having friends or relatives (although not necessarily anglophone) living in some province other than Quebec was about 60%. One fundamental question posed by researchers (e.g., Yeates 1975) is whether the boundary effect on interaction in the case of Quebec and Ontario was due primarily to politico-juridical or linguistic-cultural factors. The finding of the *Toronto Star* study that the proportion of unilingual French who said that they had friends or relatives living in other provinces was about half the proportion reported by the entire francophone population (33% vs. 60%) lends support to the latter interpretation.

An unpublished study by the Social Research Group (1965) using interview data from a national survey of randomly selected Canadians provides a portrait of friendship and kinship ties between French and English Canadians and attitudes concerning such interethnic ties. Both English and French Canadians were much more likely to express a desire to have members of the other group among their best friends and close relatives than to actually have such ties. For example, nearly half of the English Canadians said that they would like to have French Canadians among their best friends, but only 17% actually had such close ties. The gulf between expressed desire to have English Canadian friends and actually having them as close friends is even greater for French Canadians (57% and 15%). The large percentage of members from both charter groups who expressed willingness to engage in fairly close personal contacts with members of the other group appears to augur well for integration at the individual level, quite apart from the effect that this might have on integration at the societal level.

A replication of the Social Research Group study was done recently by the Centre de recherches sur l'opinion publique (*Maclean's*, 6 February 1978). In general, it was found that English and French-Canadian attitudes about each other and close relationships with individuals from each other's group had not altered substantially since the original study reported thirteen years earlier. More francophones (19%) now reported having Anglo friends, although fewer (46%) said they actually *wanted* Anglos as friends. The pattern of attitudes and relationships was much the same for English Canadians in both studies, although the proportion of those opposed to having francophones as close relations decreased from 19% to 15%.

A recent nation-wide survey (Berry, Kalin, and Taylor 1977) found that British Canadians and French Canadians tended to rate each other as very "familiar" to each other when presented with a list of ethnic groups. They also gave each other favourable ratings on various attitudinal dimensions. The ratings given by British Canadians to French Canadians were less positive than the reciprocal ratings, but nonetheless were more positive than those given to the other ethnic groups. The authors interpreted this structure of British- and French-Canadian attitudes as evidence of a "charter-group" phenomenon, such that both British- and French-Canadian respondents make a clear distinction between themselves on the one hand and groups of non-British or non-French origin on the other. The authors also attributed importance to the "multicultural" context of the survey that brought forth the "charter-group" profile. In previous experimental studies (e.g., Lambert et al. 1960; Larimer 1970), where English and French Canadians were asked to compare each other in a context that involved only these two collectivities, the ratings given to the subject's group and to the other group were far less similar and generally disfavoured the French Canadians.

Thus, in comparison to the other ethnic groups, British and French Canadians recognize certain positively evaluated similarities between individuals from their own and the other "charter group." However, when rating is confined to the two collectivities, a hierarchy is recognized by *both* British and French Canadians whereby the latter are judged to be inferior along some stereotyped dimensions. The likely explanation for the negative ratings given to the French by the British and to the French by themselves in the Lambert et al. and Larimer studies would be in terms of factors such as the subordinate socio-economic position of French Canadians and the political socialization of individuals from both collectivities. Also, in accounting for the discrepancy between the findings of these two studies on the one hand and the Berry, Kalin, and Taylor (1977) study on the other, one should not discount the possibility that the political events within Quebec during the first half of the 1970s produced an increased self-confidence among French Canadians, resulting in higher ratings given to the French in the more recent study done by Berry, Kalin, and Taylor.

The relatively low level of personal contacts individuals have across subsocieties compared to the mutually favourable attitudes may be a factor of the language barrier, the discrepancy in social status, or the lack of institutionally provided opportunities and support for intergroup contact. The effect that these variables have on interpersonal relations across subsocieties will be discussed subsequently.

Of all forms of personal contact, intermarriage has been viewed as the most accurate index of the degree of intergroup tolerance within a society. Also, intermarriage that involves partners from different regions in the country, by building kinship networks across the country, might be conducive to mass support for national integration. Unfortunately, we are not aware of any research that investigates the extent of intermarriage between individuals from different regions. It must also be kept in mind that intermarriage involving individuals of French and English origin is not always a sign of tolerance and acceptance of the other culture, but may be an indication of assimilation of the minority group individual, particularly in an environment where the minority is numerically small and dispersed. In a study conducted in Montreal, it was found that in French-English marriages, the English-Canadian culture dominated in most aspects of the marriage, especially if the male was English Canadian. Truly bilingual and bicultural marriages appeared to be a rarity, and instead, accommodation in these mixed marriages would occur to the cultural detriment of one of the spouses. In those areas of behaviour that have been recognized as most crucial in preventing assimilation, such as the language used in the home, it was found that the French spouse was more likely to yield to his or her English partner (Carisse 1971).

One study (Royal Commission on Bilingualism and Biculturalism 1970, pp. 274−79), which reported on the rates of intermarriage by ethnic origin, found that while males and females of French origin in 1961 had the second and third highest national rates of endogamy, the rate of intermarriage was by far the highest to persons of British origin. The British, who were also highly endogamous (more so for males than females), reciprocated in having the highest rate of intermarriage to individuals of French origin. There were substantial regional differences in rates of endogamy and intermarriage across the two subsocieties. In Quebec, the rate of endogamy for persons of French origin was extremely high; in provinces where there are substantial French minorities (New Brunswick, Manitoba) this rate was still quite high; in provinces where the proportion of persons of French origin was lower and where institutional support for the retention of the French language and culture was minimal (e.g., Newfoundland and British Columbia), the rate of exogamy, particularly to persons of British origin, exceeded the rate of endogamy. Analyses of intermarriage data for Montreal and Toronto illustrate the importance of the regional factor. Whereas in Montreal the rate of endogamy was highest for family heads of French origin, in Toronto this category evinced the lowest endogamy rate (Richard and Campbell 1978, p. 5). The regional differences were far less pronounced for the rates of British endogamy and intermarriage with persons of French origin. Only in Quebec was this latter figure considerably (about three times) higher than for the national average.

Richard and Campbell (ibid., p. 8) note that the higher rate of intermarriage for the British-origin group in Montreal as opposed to Toronto is largely explicable in terms of its relative size *vis-à-vis* the rest of the population. Controlling for size of ethnic population, the propensity for ethnic intermarriage is in fact nearly identical for males of British origin in both cities. The authors speculate that the reason for the high rate of endogamy of especially the native-born Protestant anglophones in Montreal is best explained by their attempt to perpetuate their socio-economic dominance. One might note that this regional pattern manifest in intermarriage rates was also found for kinship ties in the Social Research Group (1965) study, where British Canadian respondents reported a substantially higher rate of French Canadians among their close relatives in Quebec than in other provinces.

Regional variations in demographic ratios of francophones to anglophones offer varying opportunities for interethnic contact and thus for the establishment of closer, more personal ties. Cultural exchange programmes actively attempt to foster personal ties between individuals from the two collectivities by recruiting persons to participate in interprovincial exchanges. One such programme, sponsored by the Canadian Council of

Christians and Jews and running for twenty-four years, arranges for the exchange of francophone students from Quebec and anglophone students from Ontario, and since 1976, from other provinces. The aim of this programme is explicitly stated in terms of the contact hypothesis—to develop understanding between francophone and anglophone students, to ''build bridges'' between the two linguistic communities, and to maintain a ''harmonious intermingling of Canada's major language groups'' (Canadian Council of Christians and Jews 1977*a*). From a questionnaire survey of Ontario students participating in the 1977 student exchange, one finds that almost all students felt that the exchange helped to improve their French, an effect that presumably, given further opportunity, would facilitate cross-cultural communication. A very large percentage of the respondents (86%) said that the aspect of the exchange they enjoyed most was meeting new and different people. Moreover, almost 70% of the participants said that they planned to maintain contact with their partner. Unfortunately, data do not exist that assess the extent to which one of the stated objectives of this project—the development of a network of friendships based on common understanding and appreciation of the other's cultural heritage—has been fulfilled. The questionnaire survey does give evidence however of a large gap in articulation between personal liking for francophones by anglophones and anglophone understanding of political problems of the francophone collectivity. Whereas the Ontario respondents voiced their enjoyment of meeting francophones from Quebec, almost one-half simultaneously said that the exchange did not make them more aware and understanding of the current political climate in Quebec (Canadian Council of Christians and Jews 1977*b*). This lack of correspondence between integration at the interpersonal level and at the level of understanding of the political problems and objectives of the other group, which has also been found in other studies (Social Research Group 1965), ought to be an important consideration in cultural exchange programmes that have the explicit or tacit aim of advancing intergroup harmony.

Furthermore, the promotion of an interprovincial exchange of francophones and anglophones on any large scale would involve astronomical costs, given the population ratios of the two groups in Quebec and other provinces and the geographic expanse of the country. In light of the actual and possible patterns of non-élite interpersonal contacts across subsocieties, it would seem judicious to place less weight on this mode of horizontal integration in the achievement of societal consolidation.

VOLUNTARY OR FORCED CONTACT

Economic constraints and networks of obligation tying an individual to his kin and religion are some of the factors that compel individuals to remain in a situation where contacts are of an involuntary nature (Clark 1971;

Nordlinger 1972). The unavoidable contacts with individuals from the other subsociety that can result from such constraints are likely to intensify feelings of hostility. In contrast, voluntary choice of contact with individuals from the other subsociety is likely to be conducive to cohesion or at least to a reduction of conflict (Nordlinger 1972).

For proponents of the isolation hypothesis (Lijphart 1968), the issue is not so much one of the benefits of voluntary contact, which are either discounted or denied in their writing, but rather one of the aggravating effects of forced contact on interethnic conflict. Given the built-in predisposition toward hostility against the other group conditioned by centuries of intergroup conflict, these theorists appear to assume that voluntary contact with members of the other group will not be sought out. The most fruitful solution for the resolution of conflicts is therefore the isolation of the collectivities in terms of where people live and work, in the schools, and over the mass communications network. It is assumed that this compartmentalization of social relationships would reduce the number of sites for conflict and thus contribute to the predominance of élites, a condition that is viewed as facilitating the regulation of conflict. It does not seem likely that the isolation theorists would object categorically to free-choice contacts across collectivities, as these would not seem to have the same exacerbating effect on conflict as would involuntary contacts (Nordlinger 1972, pp. 104–10). However, as will be discussed later, if opportunity is not provided by institutional arrangements, the likelihood of interpersonal contacts being established across subsocieties is reduced significantly.

The study by the Social Research Group analysed the pattern of voluntary and involuntary contacts between francophones and anglophones.[2] It was found that when contacts at school and church were included as instances of involuntary contacts, French Canadians had about the same (approximately 53%) number of voluntary and involuntary contacts with English Canadians. When contacts at school and church were excluded from involuntary contacts, French Canadians had less voluntary contacts (53%) than involuntary ones (60%).

English Canadians had more voluntary contacts (56%) than involuntary ones (41% when schools and churches are included, and 46% when excluded) with French Canadians. The authors note however that the frequency of involuntary contacts (in stores, restaurants, etc.) may have been underestimated, since the English-Canadian respondents may not have known that those addressing them in English were French Canadians.

---

[2] The distinction between voluntary and involuntary contact is somewhat arbitrary. This was recognized by the authors of the Social Research Group study who classified voluntary contacts as contacts at home and at social gatherings, and involuntary contacts as interaction in stores and restaurants, the work place, and business meetings. The difficulty of classifying contacts at school and at church lead the authors to perform two analyses—one where contacts at school and church were included in involuntary contacts and one where they were not.

Both voluntary and involuntary contacts of French Canadians are sensitive to regional differences. French Canadians outside Quebec are far more likely to have contacts with English Canadians, whether these contacts are voluntary or involuntary. The involuntary contacts of English Canadians with French Canadians are also sensitive to region; so that English Canadians are much more likely to interact with French Canadians in stores and restaurants in Quebec than in other regions. Contacts at home or at social gatherings increase only slightly in Quebec compared with other regions, intimating that English-Canadian social ties with French Canadians are limited by the structure of preference of English Canadians. The factors that predetermine this structure of preference will be discussed later in this chapter.

DEGREE TO WHICH CONTACT IS ONE OF EQUAL STATUS

Evidence from studies of race relations in the United States has tended to point to the positive effect on attitudes of contact between individuals of equal status and to the negative effect of contact between individuals of unequal status (Allport 1954; Amir 1969; Stouffer et al. 1949).

The relative status of the two collectivities refers both to the economic, political, and social position of francophone *vis-à-vis* anglophone individuals, and to the standing of one community in relation to the other. In any particular instance, these two levels of status may interact; so that, for instance, the fact that the English language is accorded greater recognition, an example of group status, may adversely affect the socio-economic mobility of an otherwise qualified francophone individual, lowering his individual status. In interests of conceptual clarity, it is useful however to distinguish the two levels—individual and group status—in order to assess the extent of equality between the two collectivities.

In chapter 3.2, we discussed the disadvantaged position of francophones in terms of income, career opportunities, economic benefits of education, and general socio-economic status. The consistently lower income of French Canadians and the common pattern of ethnic division of labour whereby French Canadians are disproportionately concentrated in lower-level jobs, and English Canadians, in higher-level jobs have deleterious effects upon intergroup contact. Specifically it reduces the possible proportion of contacts that can occur between individuals of equal status from different sub-societies. This reinforces the stereotyped view of inferiority held by English Canadians of francophones on a number of dimensions, including intelligence, importance, and complexity (Gardner, Taylor, and Feenstra 1970). It also serves to create widespread resentment among francophones. A survey of Quebec residents found that one-third of francophone Quebecers felt that they were looked down upon and considered inferior by English Canadians (*Toronto Star* 1977).

In chapter 3.2, the collective or organizational inequalities between francophones and anglophones were also discussed. Ownership and control of industry and management of major economic organizations are all dominated by anglophones, with francophones being relatively disfavoured. This pattern serves to reproduce the present inequalities in economic opportunity between francophones and anglophones. The fact that the information network created by the large enterprises whose stockholders and management are anglophone has not integrated the French Canadian labour market has meant that francophones have had less success in obtaining top management positions, and the most specialized and prestigious jobs (Migué 1970).

The lower status of the French language is determined by the interplay of a number of factors, such as anglophone predominance in top organizational levels, the more frequent use of English as the language of technology, and the greater international status of English. The disadvantaged status of the French language may predispose anglophones to view negatively communications across communities, which involve the use of the "inferior" French language. Given that motivation is such an important prerequisite for successful acquisition of a second language (Lambert 1967; Simon 1974), emotional resistance of anglophones to learning a language they consider subordinate to their own is likely to further impede beneficial cross-cultural communication.

In addition to the various objective indices of the relative status of the two groups, the subjective assessment of how francophones and anglophones fare in an overall distribution of status must also be considered (Pineo 1977). Horizontal relationships between francophones and anglophones are governed not only by objective indices of equality but also by individuals' perceptions of the degree of equality. A change in perception of the relative statuses of the two groups may behave as a motor for change in the relationships between them.

It has been argued (Berry, Kalin, and Taylor 1977; Kwavnick 1965; Milner and Milner 1973; Pineo 1977) that at the root of the present French-English conflict is the change in the French Canadians' perception of their status *vis-à-vis* the English Canadian collectivity and the immobility of the perception of English Canadians of the relative social standing of the two collectivities. Experimental studies performed in the late 1950s and early 1960s by Lambert and his laboratory found that the ratings made on various personality traits by *both* English and French Canadians were far less favourable to French Canadians than to English Canadians (Lambert et al. 1970). The resistance on the part of the dominant linguistic group to acceptance of equal status with the subordinate linguistic group appears to be so trenchant that it extends to a negative assessment of performance of a French-Canadian individual despite the positive, objective measure of efficiency of his performance (Taylor and Gardner 1970).

The negative ratings by French Canadians of their own group was thought to be due to an internalization of their minority-group status. Other studies found this preference for English Canadians to be a developmental phenomenon that surfaced at about twelve years of age (Lambert 1967, p. 98). Recent surveys (Berry, Kalin, and Taylor 1977; Pineo 1977) have indicated that a transformation in the self-identity of French Canadians has occurred toward a greater assertiveness and an assessment of their own standing as equal to that of English Canadians, a change that has been attributed to the ideological ferment of the Quiet Revolution, the more positive role of the State in Quebec, and the growing representation of French Canadians in previously unoccupied prestigious occupations and élite positions (Morrison 1970). In contrast, the assessment by English Canadians of their objective social standing in relation to all other groups, including the French Canadians, presents a picture of Anglo-dominance (Berry, Kalin, and Taylor 1977; Pineo 1977). Thus, this lack of congruence in perception of social standing of the two collectivities is perhaps a critical source of tension between French Canadians and English Canadians.

PURSUIT OF COMMON GOALS

The development of tolerance and cohesion between groups necessitates that the goals pursued be common rather than competitive (Allport 1954). Cross-cultural collaboration on joint projects usually requires some degree of organization and is undertaken either by subsocieties as corporate entities (e.g., through provincial governments) interacting directly with each other or through the mediation of societal institutions. The paucity of interprovincial, and consequently cross-cultural, endeavors has previously been discussed.

The pursuit of common goals by individuals with persons from the other collectivity is usually dependent upon their common membership in an organization. The fact that French Canadians have a lesser tendency to belong to any kind of association than English Canadians, with the exception of work associations, and that they also express less desire for such memberships means that they are somewhat more restricted in possible concerted action with English Canadians in multiethnic associations. Also while English Canadians expressed a greater preference for associations whose membership was open to various ethnic groups, French Canadians have a greater preference for voluntary associations where the members are recruited strictly from their own ethnic group (*Maclean's*, 6 February 1978; Social Research Group 1965). This expressed preference of French Canadians to compartmentalize their voluntary associational activities is in accordance with the recommendations of isolation theorists who would view this segregation of activities as a positive move reducing the number of opportunities for interethnic conflict.

The greater reluctance of French Canadians to participate in a multiethnic association appears to be attributable to the uneven distribution of advantages—benefits, minus costs of participation, accruing to English and French Canadian members—rather than to reluctance of engaging in contact with English Canadians *per se* (Meisel and Lemieux 1972). The advantages of membership in a multiethnic association and thus the satisfaction gained from interethnic contact made within the association is largely affected by its organizational structure. There are a number of structural arrangements adopted by Canadian associations that represent the objectives and cultures of French and English Canadians to different degrees. At one extreme exists a single pan-Canadian structure, which is composed of individual members or local chapters, is most likely unilingual, runs according to English-Canadian models of operational efficiency, and caters to the needs of the anglophone majority group. At the other, one finds two parallel pan-Canadian associations, one for each language group, with a tenuous link between the two. Since such a dualist structure reduces the problems of domination of language, culture, and objectives of one group (anglophone) over the other (francophone), it is perhaps the most conducive to membership satisfaction. However, the drawback to such a structure is precisely that the two associations function in complete, or almost complete, isolation from one another and therefore the members cannot benefit from cross-cultural contact (ibid., p. 297).

Controversy over the ideal structural pattern for voluntary associations with francophone and anglophone members not surprisingly runs parallel to the debate over the optimum political arrangements for Canada. Although voluntary associations exist independently of the State, they are sensitive to changes in the political environment in which they function, particularly if their objectives are of a controversial nature and are directed toward influencing public policy. Meisel and Lemieux single out the growth of political nationalism in Quebec as one of the most critical developments that triggered the ethnic crises in most Canadian multiethnic associations. The rapidity of change within Quebec brought new francophone leaders to the fore, who sought to attain goals incompatible with those of the older generation of anglophones who exercised power at certain levels within voluntary associations. The resulting frictions in some cases were so serious that the only solution was to split the associations in two. Joint programmes designed to mutually benefit two structurally separate organizations are difficult to carry on at the best of times; in a climate of political tension, it would seem that such joint enterprises would require extraordinary dedication to better relations between the two linguistic communities.

Projects specifically designed to promote greater understanding between anglophones and francophones have been undertaken by bodies such as the Canadian Council of Christians and Jews. Bringing together anglophones and francophones from all provinces, the hope of such conferences as The Acadian District of Clare Forum held in 1977 is to establish a mechanism for cross-cultural communication. Given the short length of these conferences and the small number of participants, the impact on interethnic harmony is not likely to be very significant.

A fundamental question posed by the contact hypothesis is whether contact that involves co-operation in order to achieve a common goal can have a beneficial effect on interethnic attitudes when participant groups are of unequal status. It is fairly evident that if the contact between two groups is perceived by one to be to its disadvantage, the relationship may not only not reduce prejudice but may even intensify intergroup tension (Amir 1969). However it has been suggested (Coleman 1959) that if the perception of an organizational goal is salutary for all participants, the fact that they have unequal statuses in pursuit of that goal is secondary. The evidence concerning this question is fairly inconclusive and requires further study. However, the findings of the Meisel and Lemieux (1972) study and of more recent research undertaken by the National Advisory Council on Voluntary Action (1978) indicate that francophones, although used to enduring linguistic and cultural costs for so many years, are becoming less satisfied with the subordinate status allotted to them by such Anglo-dominant arrangements within voluntary associations. Secondly, ostensibly similar goals among anglophone and francophone components of voluntary associations may in fact be in fundamental conflict and incompatible with one another (Meisel and Lemieux 1972, p. 293).

INSTITUTIONALLY PROVIDED OPPORTUNITIES AND SUPPORT FOR INTERGROUP CONTACT

Through the regulation of recruiting practices and the running of day-to-day business, organizations have the capacity to provide opportunities for interethnic contact or alternatively to segregate ethnic groups and inhibit contact. Moreover, organizations are able to control the quality of contact on a number of dimensions that have been outlined as affecting the outcome of contact. For example, by exercising some type of quota system, an organization can ensure that francophones and anglophones are equally represented at all levels of the organization; so that they may meet each other on an equal-status basis. Organizations can provide recreational facilities and programmes; so that francophones and anglophones are more easily able to meet each other on an informal and more personal level.

Institutional support for interethnic contact can also be furnished by more formal mechanisms such as laws. At one extreme of deliberate, constitutionally provided segregation, intended for the separation and perpetuation of both cultures, is the dual nature of the institutional structure of education in Canada. As well as inhibiting interaction among individuals across subsocieties, this segregation in education of the two linguistic communities appears to have had extremely important repercussions for cross-cultural understanding. Nation-wide studies of secondary-school education and textbooks have shown the extent to which a wide divergence in approach to Canadian history and Canadian studies occurs between the two linguistic communities, such that there exists an almost total neglect or a distorted consideration of the other community's contributions (Hodgetts 1968; Trudel and Jain 1970).

The dualistic institutional structure of education, religion, and mass media helps maintain distinctive views of life characteristic of the anglophone and francophone cultures, which for the isolation theorists are the *raison d'être* for preserving organizational segmentation (McRae 1974*b*, p. 6). The apparent circularity of the argument made by isolation theorists whereby a cleavage partially created by a certain organizational system justifies the preservation of that system can be circumvented only if it can be demonstrated that an integrated institutional structure would heighten, rather than alleviate, interethnic tensions. We are not familiar with any research that provides such substantiation to the isolation hypothesis. However, we can speculate that to the extent that integrated institutional structures threaten the representation of the languages and cultures of the two communities, they are likely to create tensions between them.

Contact between linguistic groups requires institutional backing for the use of both languages. However, the extent to which bilingualism is instituted in economic organizations follows more the motives of profit and interests of efficient operation than the principles of national unity or interethnic harmony. This is demonstrated first of all by the fact that French-English contact in business or industry is not affected by regional differences, which one would expect to exert varying opportunities for contact: "At work, an average of about one third of the French Canadians do not have contacts with English Canadians, either in Quebec or outside of Quebec" (Social Research Group 1965, p. 248).

Secondly, the extent to which a particular enterprise is bilingual depends upon the efficient operation of the communication network. The pattern that has resulted is not one of individual bilingualism, which is regarded as far too costly to achieve, but rather one of coexistence of two languages without bilingualism (Fishman 1967; see also Laponce 1975). The tendency in Quebec's large manufacturing firms seems to be for an organization to be characterized by one language, usually English, at the upper-managerial level, and the other language, most often French, at the wage-roll level. Individual bilingualism usually exists only between the two areas; this "bilingual belt," in the past involving relatively small numbers of people, ensures communication (Morrison 1970). Due to such factors as the Quebec government's recent language legislation, French Canadians' increased assertion of their language rights, direct influence of the provincial government as a major buyer and supplier, increasing availability of French Canadians for higher levels of work in industry, and increased purchasing power, language requirements have been changing in Quebec's industrial firms; so that the bilingual belt has been moving upward over the years and has widened to some extent. This has improved the employment chances for bilingual francophones in the higher reaches of industrial firms, and consequently brought a greater number of francophones in contact with anglophones at least within these higher levels.

The importance of institutional support for interethnic contact can cogently be seen in the case of the Canadian Armed Forces. The military has been noted as a locus for interethnic tolerance in studies of race relations in the United States. Studies have pointed out how individuals, closely associated together under conditions of combat, are more favourably disposed to each other (Allport 1954; Stouffer et al. 1949). The Canadian Armed Forces deserve special attention as they account for roughly a quarter of all federal government personnel. However, historically they have evolved within the language and culture of the anglophone subsociety, with the army having been somewhat more receptive to the problems of recruiting and retaining francophone personnel than the navy and air force (Royal Commission on Bilingualism and Biculturalism 1969*a*). As a result, the proportionate representation of French Canadians in the Armed Forces has not been achieved. Moreover, until recently, contacts between francophones and anglophones (with the exception of a few francophone enclaves in the army) have generally been an experience of assimilation of the former to the language and culture of the latter rather than an experiment in interethnic contact.

Since 1972, however, there has been a conscious effort on the part of the National Ministry of Defence to redress the balance between francophones and anglophones in the Armed Forces (Ministère de la Défense nationale 1975). This has taken the form of a fifteen-year programme whose objectives have been (1) to guarantee within the Armed Forces the equality in status for the French and English, as well as the existence of equal rights and privileges in the utilization of both languages; and (2) to reflect within the Armed Forces the linguistic and cultural values of both anglophones and francophones. Various measures have been implemented in pursuit of these goals: in 1972 an intensive effort began to recruit francophones at all levels and categories of the Armed Forces; the number of courses taught in French increased from four to forty-seven between 1969 to 1973; more attention has been given to the French language; so that twenty-one French-language units exist, seventeen of them in Quebec; within these units French is favoured as the language of work, and francophone military personnel are given a chance to accede to superior posts, an impossibility for unilingual francophones in other units.

The complexity of attaining a bilingual Canadian Armed Forces throughout Canada reflects the dilemma of this model for Canadian society as a whole. For instance, this objective involves not only allowing francophones to work at all levels in their own language but also extensively teaching a second language to all military personnel. As the situation now stands, the majority (11,315 out of 17,015) of bilingual military personnel are francophones (ibid.). Since bilingualism among the minority group often signifies the intermediary step toward linguistic assimilation, the increase in francophone bilinguals does not necessarily imply a stable bilingual institution.

The navy and air force, where francophone personnel is poorly represented, reproduce in institutional form the regional situation that prevails outside Quebec in varying degrees. In provinces where the francophone population is small in numbers, scattered (Morris and Lanphier 1977), and lacking in institutional completeness, the most important effect of interaction of francophones with anglophones is assimilation:

> In British Columbia and Newfoundland, where less than 2% were of French mother tongue in 1961, the apparent assimilation rate was about 90%. In the Prairies, Ontario, Nova Scotia and Prince Edward Island, those of French mother tongue formed between 3% and 8% of the population, and apparent assimilation rates ranged between 49% and 70%. In New Brunswick, francophones formed 35% of the population and their assimilation rate was only 14%. In Quebec, where francophones formed over 80% of the population, there was no apparent assimilation (p. 47).

This demographic situation of the diminishing importance, percentage-wise, of francophones outside Quebec and of their augmentation within Quebec, with a possible realization of a unilingual province (Maheu 1970), appears to suggest a growing costliness and impracticality of integration at the individual level and the increasing importance of institutional relationships for the maintenance of national unity.

DIRECTION AND INTENSITY OF PRE-CONTACT ATTITUDES

The proficiency of contact in promoting intergroup harmony is largely contingent upon both the direction and intensity of the attitude prior to contact. Studies of intergroup contacts have found that positive attitudes tend to become more positive with contact whereas negative attitudes tend to become more negative. Moreover, initial attitudes that are intensely hostile toward the other groups are not likely to be modified by intergroup contact (Amir 1969).

Both the nature and vigour of pre-contact attitudes are conditioned by the internal dynamics of each of the collectivities. The contact individuals have with the culture and image of the other subsociety, provided by the major socializing institutions of their own subsocieties, is fundamental in structuring the response to interpersonal contacts. Although cross-cultural communication would no doubt be aided by widespread bilingualism, attention must also be drawn to the degree to which the content of the message in socializing institutions is sympathetic to the other linguistic community.

One of the basic requirements for maintaining isolation at the mass level, according to the consociational theorists, is that the cleavage dividing the two subsocieties be sufficiently intense and durable so as to give members of the two segments distinctive outlooks or cultural orientations that are not capable of assimilating each other (McRae 1974*b*, p. 6).

Hodgetts (1968) has delineated the manner in which educational institutions of the anglophone and francophone subsocieties have contributed to the tensions between the two collectivities. Stereotyped notions of the other collectivity have evolved through the often bitter and resentful historical interpretation of English-Canadian domination taught in French-Canadian, Roman-Catholic schools, and the somewhat patronizing and self-assured attitude toward French Canada disseminated in English-Canadian schools. This same study demonstrated that English-Canadian students have equivocal ideas about French-English differences, and that students from both collectivities do not consider, or have knowledge of, important developments in each other's community. Material from the other's culture is sadly neglected in school libraries, thus reinforcing reading preferences found in the homes of high school students and teachers—which in English Canada is overwhelmingly for U.S. periodicals, and in Quebec, for French-language literature.

Like education, the mass media is bifurcated both linguistically and ideologically. Commentators on the performance of the national radio and television network, the Canadian Broadcasting Corporation, have noted that while it has fulfilled many of its nationalist aims—providing coverage to sections of the country that would otherwise be neglected, helping in the development of Canadian talent, and so on—it ''has not been noticeably successful in increasing understanding between French- and English-speaking Canadians'' (Peers 1966, p. 263). Over the years, there has been little interaction or co-ordination between the two linguistic production groups, referred to as the anglophone *CBC* and the francophone *Radio-Canada*. The linguistic isolation of Quebec, reinforced by the monopolistic position held during the 1950s by Radio-Canada, promoted uniquely Québécois forms of culture, including the Quebec *chansonnier* phenomenon and *téléromans* and public affairs programmes. The latter played an important role in the dissemination of new and critical ideas, and has since been criticized for overfostering Québécois nationalism (Schwartz 1967, pp. 51−52; *Toronto Globe and Mail*, 19 November 1977).

A number of organizations and trade associations representing particular media interests claim to have an all-Canada orientation.[3] In practice,

----

[3] Among these organizations are the CTV Televison Network Ltd., the Institute of Canadian Advertising, the Magazine Advertising Bureau, the Canadian Public Relations Society, the Association of Canadian Advertisers, Inc., Broadcast News, the Canadian Daily Newspaper Publishers Association, the Canadian Cable Television Association, and the Canadian Advertising Advisory Board (Elkin 1975, p. 240).

however, many of them are representative (in terms of programme content, hiring, etc.) only of English-speaking Canada (Elkin 1975, p. 240). A study that examined mass-media consumption among Montrealers found that diffusion techniques of a bicultural content through a unilingual channel that could potentially serve as instruments for reciprocal knowledge of anglophones and francophones were not being utilized. Moreover, even bilingual individuals, other than "equilinguals," restricted their consumption of mass-media products—television and newspapers—to the language they knew best (Mousseau-Glaser 1972).

The linguistic affinity of English Canada to the United States has enabled the easy penetration of U.S. mass culture and the disregard for French Canadian content. In addition the value of Canadian unity and identity, which has been affirmed by numerous royal commissions and parliamentary committees investigating the state of the mass media in Canada, has apparently been overriden by the North American media ideology of free choice. The results in terms of Canadian consumption of mass media are described by Elkin (1975, p. 232):

> When the choice is free, Canadians are likely to choose American movies, magazines and television shows. For the popular movies, Canadians offer little competition. For magazines, Canadians buy almost four times as many American as Canadian magazines, including *Playboy*, *Life*, *True Story*, *National Geographic*, *Time* and *Reader's Digest* and others.

Ironically, the growing overlap in popular culture has not meant the building of bridges between French and English Canada since it has consisted predominantly of the greater availability of dubbed American programmes in Quebec (*Toronto Globe and Mail*, 19 November 1977).

Advertising in Quebec, which did not fall within a formal structure controlled by an established élite as did other aspects of the mass media and the educational system, was a forum for the same messages, styles, and values geared toward selling the products of multinational companies as those broadcast in English Canada, with only peripheral variations. The Quiet Revolution brought resistance, mainly among members of the new middle class employed in advertising agencies, to the diffusion of English-Canadian culture in advertising, which was often literally and awkwardly translated from English. English-language companies have adapted their advertising in the direction of increasingly distinctive French-Canadian symbols and language in order to maintain their market. These modifications over the years have been more in the presentation than in the substance, but they have served to reduce the volume of North American anglophone culture and simultaneously to reinforce the contemporary francophone culture (Elkin 1973).

Thus the changes that have occurred in Quebec during and since the Quiet Revolution, initiated by the activist provincial government with support from almost all segments of the population and imbued with a spirit of neo-nationalism, have mitigated the acceptance of anglophone culture within Quebec.

Government agencies, mass media personnel, educators and numerous other groups attempted to improve the spoken language, revive French-language culture and limit the infusion of English-Canadian and American influences (ibid., p. 218).

Contrary to the expectations of many, the growing similarity in materialistic values, technological sophistication, pattern of urbanization, and other concomitants of modernization that has occurred between Quebec and English Canada has not lead to a growing *rapprochement* in culture or increased cross-cultural understanding (Kwavnick 1965). On the contrary, these similitudes have made more cogent for francophones the inequalities they suffer in their relationships with anglophones.

ÉLITE VERSUS NON-ÉLITE STATUS OF PARTICIPANTS

The favourable impact on attitudes produced by interpersonal contacts across subsocieties can occur either through aggregation or diffusion. The former refers to the cumulation of positive feelings between francophones and anglophones that take place with an increase in the sheer number of contacts. The latter assumes that the consequences of contact are not confined to the attitudes of participants, but extend to the attitudes of others through communication with actual participants. If the predominant effect of contact were aggregation, it would matter little whether individuals entering into relationships with persons from the other collectivity were élite or ordinary citizens. However, certain factors suggest that in terms of sheer volume and recurrence of contact, diffusion is a more important vehicle for cross-cultural attitudes than aggregation.

Firstly, given the vast size of Canada, travel is usually restricted to the contiguous provinces (Simmons 1970a). Few francophones from Quebec have travelled to any province other than Ontario, and of the unilingual French population, only one-third has travelled to other parts of the country (*Toronto Star* 1977). Secondly, socializing institutions, such as schools, church, and mass media, are important mechanisms in attitude formation, and have a more continuous impact upon individuals than interpersonal contacts, especially those made when travelling.

Assuming the ascendant role played by diffusion, it would seem that contact between élites rather than ordinary citizens is more essential in creating interethnic harmony. The model of a segmented society as drawn by the isolation theorists envisages two separate segments and an overarching structure of élite co-operation (McRae 1974b, p. 7). The assumption is that in view of the irreconcilable cleavages existing at the mass level, integration will occur only at the élite level. However, by virtue of their position at the top of the organizational structures that comprise each subsociety, the élite are able largely to control the content of the image of the other subsociety and its political culture. Thus, the élites, in their capacity as opinion leaders, are capable of promoting integration at all levels of society far more than could be achieved through mere interpersonal contact.

The part played by élites in the diffusion of information and valuations of the other collectivity appears particularly important in light of the fact that research has shown that there is no necessary correspondence between integration at the individual level (friendship and kinship relationships) and attitudes relating to the political and social interests of each group (Canadian Council of Christians and Jews 1977*b*; Social Research Group 1965). It is the latter type of attitudes and awareness of the dissatisfactions felt by each collectivity with its place in Confederation that appear to be especially pertinent to the question of societal integration.

The fact that potential vehicles for cross-cultural communication have been underutilized for the promotion of societal cohesion, or used in a diametrically opposed fashion to reinforce ethnic stereotypes and create enmity between francophones and anglophones appears to be at least partly attributable to the vested interests of élites in preserving their separate institutional domains, and a mobilized population willing to sustain them in pursuing this objective. The tendency for élites to *support* cultural fragmentation becomes more pronounced when major élites of one subsociety, as in Quebec, no longer see the advantages in maintaining the Canadian system and are dedicated in their goal of independence.

In the view of the isolation theorists, this proclivity of élites to actively maintain the cleavage between subsocieties (while forging accommodationist solutions at the federal level) is fairly predictable behaviour in all cases of segmented societies. If this tenet proves to be true, then the isolation theorists are realistic in their appraisal of the likelihood that cross-cultural contact at the mass level will not be a significant positive factor in integration of the two linguistic communities. Against a background of strain or grievance felt by one or both of the collectivities, such contact might tend in fact to have a negative impact.

CONCLUSION

From the discussion in this chapter, we can identify three important issues pertaining to the relationship between interpersonal contact across subsocieties and societal cohesion. These issues can be posed in the form of questions:

1. Under what conditions is contact between individuals from different subsocieties likely to have a positive effect on individual attitudes and behaviour toward the other subsociety?
2. What factors affect the implementation of favourable contact between the French and English communities?
3. What is the relationship between amicable interpersonal relationships and societal cohesion?

Contact between individuals from the French and English communities can have either positive or negative consequences on individual attitudes concerning members of the other group. The likelihood that the effects of contact will be positive is contingent upon a number of conditions outlined in this chapter. The most favourable types of contacts are those of a personal and voluntary nature occurring between status equals. The interaction across communities should involve the pursuit of common, as opposed to independent or conflicting, goals. Moreover, opportunities for interpersonal contact should be furnished by institutional practices and supported by various organizational structures and rules. Much of the outcome of contact depends on pre-contact attitudes, which should therefore be formed by prior socialization. Given the greater impact in terms of sheer volume that diffusion has over aggregation, it also seems that élite contact across subsocieties is of greater consequence than non-élite contact.

It is one thing to stipulate those conditions that are likely to facilitate a more favourable outcome of contact. It is another to deal with the factors that determine the conditions having a favourable impact on contact. Some of these factors are capable of being regulated by the governmental decision-making bodies at all levels. Mechanisms exist, for example, whereby the collective rights of francophones can be increased; so that equal-status contact is more likely to occur. The structure and rules of institutions can be changed so as to provide more opportunities for contact between francophones and anglophones. However, despite the theoretical possibility of improvement in many of these areas, one must not lose sight of the real obstacles that prevent the full implementation of the conditions favourable to interethnic tolerance and liking. The majoritarian basis for decision making, institutionalized in our governmental system, and the Anglo-American philosophy of individual rights are formidable barriers to eliminating many of the existing social and economic inequalities. Strongly anchored initial antagonisms toward each other's collectivity are not the result of accident, but are due at least partially to the vested interests of élites in control of socializing institutions in maintaining the loyalty of their constituencies. The sheer expanse of the country is yet another impediment that makes continuous interpersonal relationships involving participants from Quebec and, for example, British Columbia very difficult to maintain. Thus, the parameters that in each case influence the conditions identified as favourable in contact situations must be an important consideration.

Often the assumption is made that interpersonal liking and extensive interpersonal ties between the two language communities provide a conducive political climate for the cohesion of the two communities. Although research on this question is rather unsystematic and incomplete, the evidence seems to indicate that there is no necessary correspondence between these two levels of integration. Factors other than interpersonal ties (such as prior socialization and economic interests) seem to be more fundamental in structuring the political attitudes of citizens.

Conclusion

The objective of this study was to identify the factors that are conducive to the cohesion of Canadian society and those that may act as forces of disintegration. In many instances it is difficult to assess the impact of a particular factor or process because of the complex interaction of factors affecting societal cohesion and the lack of knowledge in this area. We did identify several areas in which additional research would be useful to understand the sources of strains and of possible cohesion. It is even more difficult to establish the relative importance of the different factors and processes considered. However, in spite of the inconclusiveness of much of our analysis, some general observations can be made about the way these phenomena and events impinge on the degree of societal cohesion.

INEQUALITIES AS SOURCE OF TENSION

The two linguistic subsocieties are unequal in terms of numbers, wealth, and status, and these inequalities are reflected in the distribution of organizational control. Much of the control of the economic institutions of the francophone subsociety is in the hands of anglophones in Canada or in the United States. In many ways the inequalities between the anglophone and francophone subsocieties parallel the inequalities between the United States and Canada: differences in numbers, wealth, status, and the distribution of organizational control, which is in many instances located in the United States. A given state of affairs may be accepted for long periods of time because there is no choice, but this does not mean that the institutional system underlying this state of affairs is considered legitimate.

Inequalities among subsocieties generate tensions through at least two related sets of factors: one pertains to the location of economic control, and the other to the nature of the linkages between social and political elites on the one hand, and economic élites on the other.

We noted that much of the regionalism and nationalism in Canada is largely a response to a distribution of economic control that leaves the locality, region, or subsociety wanting in a number of regards. When the members of a community feel that the decisions that affect their well-being in some significant way are being taken elsewhere and not necessarily with their interests in mind, the legitimacy of such a system may be put in question.

Moreover, the political institutions that tolerate or support such a system may also be put in question.

In this context, the role of the central government in building regional economies should be examined carefully. Since the early 1960s, provincial governments in Canada have taken an increasingly active role in economic development. This was partly the result of developments in areas that are constitutionally the responsibility of provincial governments, as in the field of natural resources. However, part of the provincial involvement with economic development may have stemmed from federal inactivity, in the sense that the federal government was concerned with the "national" economy and not with each regional economy. The federal stance was frequently given a negative connotation: being concerned with a "national" economy was perceived by many as a concern for the economy of central Canada, and among francophones in Quebec, as a concern with anglophone interests in Ontario and Quebec. In fact the central government may not be the only one to blame; many political élites and economic interests in the various regions were benefiting from the policies geared to the "national" economy. The historical determinants of this situation are no doubt very complex, but the result appears to be that the central government is perceived by many in different parts of the country as having been inactive, and perhaps even detrimental to the development of their region or linguistic subsociety. Many feel that if the responsibility for economic affairs remains in the hands of the central government, the loss of control over their own economies will persist. This issue is one of the main sources of tension in Canadian society today—a tension that not only opposes federal and provincial governments, francophone and anglophone interests, western and central Canadian interests, but also opposes groups within the linguistic and regional subsocieties.

We also noted that the class that is economically dominant in Quebec (mostly anglophone) is not the class that is socially and politically dominant (mostly francophone). This is another source of tension. Élites from different institutional spheres usually seek each other's support for running their organizations. The ethnolinguistic cleavage, which is accompanied by weak interpersonal networks among the élites, renders the exchange and collaboration quite difficult. Moreover, instead of seeing the pursuit of their respective interests as mutually supportive, the dominant classes in each institutional sphere frequently come to see them as opposed. Some social scientists argue that the tensions stemming from such situations are resolved only when the same social class becomes dominant in all important institutional spheres.

Both of these sources of tension—the location of economic control and the related linguistic dissociation between institutional élites—underline the importance of two phenomena: (a) the presence of a strong economic élite in each linguistic (and regional) subsociety—an élite that is indigenous to the subsociety and therefore well integrated into it; and (b) linkages between the indigenous élites of each collectivity, and the nationally and internationally based élites in different institutional spheres.

CHANGES IN RELATIVE STATUS OF THE TWO LINGUISTIC COMMUNITIES

Many events of the last ten to fifteen years have consisted in attempts to improve the status of the francophone community and its language or have had implications in this regard. These events have been quite varied: legislation defining the official status of the two languages; legislation and administrative decisions concerning their use in education, courts, legislative assemblies, work, labelling and advertising, public services; steps concerning the linguistic composition of the federal civil service and the language practices in it; various measures aimed at dealing with the "independentist threat"; different forms of assistance to, and recognition of, the francophone communities outside of Quebec; a multiplicity of manifestations of sociopolitical and cultural assertion on the part of francophones, together with the media coverage that these usually entail.

These events, which are partly the result of the social changes mentioned in a subsequent section, have had a number of consequences, a few of which will be reviewed here. For instance the linguistic dualism of Canadian society has been accentuated. It should be mentioned parenthetically that a number of demographic processes discussed in the report have contributed significantly to the accentuation of this dualism. This in turn has led to a paradoxical situation: it has increased the need to make choices concerning the language regime that should prevail in Canada while at the same time making it more difficult to make the choices. We have seen that two conceptions of Canadian society—the pan-Canadian and the segmentalist—were confronting each other, and that the confrontation involved groups and categories of people having an interest in one conception more than the other. This interest, it should be noted, can be symbolic, ideological, economic (e.g., a career line), or political (especially among the élites). We have seen that the confrontation involved political parties and governments as well as socioeconomic and cultural groups.

A basic issue in the confrontation is the way in which Canada will be bilingual. (Although there are still some who believe that Canada is a "one-language country," that is, English, the majority of Canadians appear to willingly accept the existence of two language communities.) In the segmentalist conception, bilingualism means that Quebec is francophone and the rest of Canada, anglophone. But then what happens to the language minorities—the anglophones in Quebec and the francophones outside of Quebec—becomes problematic. This problem is further complicated by the fact that the sociological and numerical situation of francophones varies enormously from one part of the country to another. In the pan-Canadian conception, bilingualism means that English and French have an equal status everywhere in the country. In this case, it is the situation of francophones in regions where they constitute less than 5 per cent of the population that is at issue. Obviously, the task is to find a workable compromise between these views, but it is far from obvious what the compromise should be. It must respect the rights of minorities, be administratively feasible, and be politically acceptable to groups with contradictory interests in this matter.

Since status is a relative phenomenon, improving the status of one group invariably involves a loss for another. Much of the resistance to the promotion of the French language is a reaction to the relative loss of status that it represents for anglophones. Bilingualism in the federal institutions has been perceived by many anglophones as an attempt to better represent the two linguistic communities and to improve the level of services for the two language groups, but at the detriment of their own language and culture. For many anglophones, the francophones are another minority group that should accommodate itself to the language, culture, and institutions of the majority.

Some members of the non-British ethnic groups experience this loss of status in a particular way: many of them perceive that increasing the status of the French in Canada defines them as second-class citizens. This is especially the case in those parts of the country where the French constitute a very small percentage of the population, frequently smaller than the percentage for some of the other ethnic groups.

Many negative attitudes found in the West, for instance, toward the steps taken to improve the status of the francophone subsociety constitute a response to the lack of recognition by the institutions and population of the central region of the country. We could argue that if parallel attempts had been made to increase the status of western Canada, its culture, its way of life, and its institutions in the eyes of the rest of the country, there would be less resentment against an increase in the status of the francophones and their language. A similar argument could be made for the Atlantic provinces. The basic point is that it is not easy to give status to somebody else when deprived of status and recognition oneself.

In this connection it is worthwhile recalling the observations made about the representation of the West at the national level. It was noted that because of the functioning of the national political parties, given the territorial distribution of the population, the party forming the government at the federal level has not been, in most elections during a long period of time, the choice of the majority of voters in the West. This phenomenon can be seen as a sort of status deprivation that would make it even more difficult to accept increases in the status of the francophones.

People will not necessarily reject a relative loss of status. On the contrary, it is frequently accepted for monetary gains or for the sake of social solidarity. The question is when do people accept and when do they reject a loss of relative status. It seems that this question has been neglected both by researchers and by those who have undertaken and managed institutional changes. A simple proposition is that those who are already experiencing status deprivations will have difficulty in accepting further losses. Such a proposition could lead to a wide range of applications, starting with fundamental reforms within the national political parties, such that each give proper recognition to the different regions of the country when they either form the government or the opposition. The role of the media and the educational systems of the country should be examined with regard to the allocation of status.

In short it is imperative for the cohesion of Canadian society that adequate recognition and status be given to the francophone subsociety, its language, culture, and institutions. But it is also equally important that adequate status and recognition be given to the other segments of society. In this sense, societal cohesion, like the cohesion of any social entity, is a two-way process.

CENTRAL GOVERNMENT LINKAGE WITH CITIZENS

Much of the debate on the topic of national unity is concerned with the structure and role of government institutions at both the federal and provincial levels. A basic question is whether the formal structure of government has any impact on the cohesion of our society. Does it have any significant effect on the tensions that exist between the anglophone and francophone subsocieties? And if the formal aspects of government have an impact, can specific features relevant to societal cohesion be identified?

We saw that over the years francophone and anglophone representation has been fairly adequate in the federal Cabinet and Parliament. There appears to have been, however, hidden underrepresentation in the Cabinet in the sense that anglophones predominate in the important ministries. Nevertheless, the overall picture is not one that would lead us to see formal structures and mechanisms for political representation as being problematic for the cohesion of the society. This is especially the case if we note that if anything the situation has improved for francophones in the last fifteen to twenty years. Yet the legitimacy of the federal governmental institutions has been increasingly put in question. On the basis of such observations, it would seem that additional changes in the formal mechanisms of representation would not have much of an impact.

On the other hand, representation occurring through less formal or institutionalized mechanisms may well have a significant impact on the ways in which issues are brought up and defined in Cabinet and Parliament, the allocation of people to the various positions in these bodies, or their linkages with the various groups in each linguistic community. Given the existence of formal representation, these other processes may be the critical ones. It would be interesting to speculate about the tensions and problems of legitimacy that would have resulted in the absence of formal representation.

For instance, it was noted that because of the way in which the political parties have functioned, the West has rarely contributed the majority of its votes to the government. It is easy to surmise that if such a situation had occurred with Quebec, we would be much closer to a political secession than we are today. The importance of formal representation, then, should perhaps not be dismissed too easily. It appears to be a necessary, but not sufficient, condition for legitimacy.

The composition of the civil service was another important element of representation considered. It was observed that at one time the situation was rather dismal as far as francophone representation was concerned; not only was their participation low but the use of French was actively resisted by the civil service. However, important changes have occurred since the early 1960s in this regard. Some argue that this improvement has not had much of an impact because the change came too late, because of the way in which it was managed, and because they were not successful in connecting the federal civil service with the francophone interest groups.[1] We noted with the evidence available that it is difficult to assess the impact of the changes in the composition of the civil service. However, we can again imagine what the situation would be had such changes not taken place. Moreover, counter-hypotheses are also reasonable: that at the symbolic level for the francophone and anglophone communities, the changes indicate a significant and relatively new francophone presence in the federal institutions; that at the political level there are now a substantial number of francophones with a vested interest in the central government; that at the networks level some beginnings have been made in establishing new linkages.

An adequate representation in the federal service is critical: the symbolic elements, vested interests, and networks of contacts that it involves is the stuff of which societal cohesion is made. Its importance will be further emphasized in connection with the division of powers discussed in the next section.

Adequate representation within the national political parties, which was already indicated in the previous section, is also important with respect to the linkages that citizens in different parts of the country establish with the central government and therefore with respect to the cohesion of society. The analysis suggested that the electoral system and the political parties in their internal structure and functioning may be the components of the formal political institutions that are in greatest need of reform if the various segments of our society are to be more effectively linked with the central government.

---

[1] For instance some argue that the francophones from outside Quebec are disproportionately represented in the civil service relative to those from Quebec. Informed evidence suggests that there may be a basis for this proposition. Such evidence would directly support the hypothesis that the changes have not had as much effect as they could in connecting Quebec groups with the central government.

Finally it seems almost unnecessary to repeat that it is very difficult to imagine a high degree of loyalty to societal institutions on the part of members of a linguistic subsociety unless they can deal with that institution, or function in it, in their own language. Otherwise that institution will retain an element of foreignism to them.

DIVISION OF POWERS BETWEEN LEVELS OF GOVERNMENT

Another aspect of governmental structure is the division of powers between levels of government. There are several perspectives on this question: one stresses rationalistic decision making; one focuses on interdependencies among levels of government; another looks at relationships among levels of government as interorganizational relationships; another draws attention to the inequalities between the subsocieties' functioning in the political system; and yet another emphasizes the dynamic interaction between interest groups and each level of government. These various perspectives are not mutually exclusive, but each identifies a different set of processes. In the rationalist perspective, some functions are seen as performed more effectively and efficiently at one, rather than another, level of government. An underlying idea is that insofar as the demand for services and regulation varies by regional or linguistic subsocieties, provincial governments are in a better position to devise and administer policies and programmes in accordance with the preferences and interests of the population in each subsociety.

According to this perspective, loyalty to the central government depends on it assuming only those responsibilities that it can effectively carry out with regard to all the subsocieties, thus gaining legitimacy in each of these. Alternatively it could attempt to devise regional policies and programmes or show flexibility in applying national policies in different sections of the country. One danger in this approach is that it may give, or appear to give, preferential treatment to certain regions, a circumstance that may lead the others to question its legitimacy. Finally if certain functions are best performed by a provincial government, the central government is likely to gain loyalty by giving it assistance in carrying out its responsibilities. Collaboration between levels of government that increases effectiveness and efficiency is likely to reinforce the legitimacy of the entire State. The basic proposition is that insofar as there are interdependencies between parts of a country and among policy areas, collaboration between levels of government is likely to increase citizens' loyalty to both levels of government.

This perspective assumes that the division of powers could be settled on the basis of an analysis of the various advantages and disadvantages of a particular dispensation; that what is required is systematic research on the basis of which the optimal pattern of centralization/decentralization can be established. If this were possible, the matter of the loyalty of the citizens from each linguistic subsociety to the central government as well as the competition between levels of government could be resolved. Many argue however that the rationalist view is idealistic. Some counter that the interdependencies between parts of a country as well as between policy areas are such as to preclude a neat division of powers, except in a limited number of areas; that the exercise of powers by one level of government invariably involves the areas of jurisdiction of the other levels. In this view, regular and frequent bargaining is required. The central question, then, is the adequacy of the rules and mechanisms through which bargaining occurs. They must be such as to require compromises and generate benefits for each of the parties involved. The legitimacy of the political institutions depends on the effectiveness and fairness of the bargaining mechanisms, whatever the division of powers.

Closely related to the view that stresses interpendencies is the approach that locates the sources of tension and cohesion in the relationships between bureaucracies at different levels of government. Firstly, it was noted that the importance of the bureaucracy in policy making relative to that of Parliament and Cabinet has increased enormously in recent decades, both at the federal and provincial levels. Secondly, even though the absolute size of the bureaucracies has increased at both levels, it has increased proportionately more at the provincial level.

The significance of the first institutional change is that many federal-provincial relationships now occur at the level of the bureaucracy rather than that of Cabinet and Parliament. This gives increased importance to the circumstances leading to competition, conflict, and collaboration between government bureaucracies. In many ways the division of powers between levels consists of a distribution of prerogatives, status, and funds between two bureaucracies. Each set of bureaucrats has its own aspirations; each also has to respond to expectations and demands from the public through the politicians. The acquisition of the means to respond to expectations and demands may lead to tensions or collaboration. The attempts toward expansion however usually lead to conflict. The politics of bureaucratic aggrandizement may be one of the important sources of tension in the society and of a weakening of the legitimacy of the political institutions. It is also in relation to these interorganizational dynamics that the more rapid expansion of the provincial bureaucracies takes on its significance. The expansion led to demands for more resources and authority, which in turn brought about resistance from the other level of government. A redistribution of organizational power is in process and it will take some time before it is resolved.

In this interorganizational perspective, tensions and problems of legitimacy arise whatever the formal division of powers. This does not mean that the division of powers is irrelevant. What the approach emphasizes is that the internal dynamics of a bureaucracy, as well as those of the relationships between bureaucracies, are so as to increase the likelihood of conflict. The issue is again to establish mechanisms for effective negotiations and to provide the conditions for exchange and collaboration, rather than to attempt to undermine each other's position.

Another perspective focuses on the demographic, socio-economic, and ecological inequalities between the subsocieties. The view is that the actual differences in power are more a reflection of these inequalities[2] than of a formal division of powers: extensive formal powers are meaningless if one controls little resources. In this view, a redistribution of formal powers would have little effect on the outcome of the political bargaining. On the other hand, it could be argued that to a certain extent formal institutional arrangements, including the division of powers, can alleviate the liabilities of inequality. The argument is that unless they do so the legitimacy of the political institutions will tend to be weak. Thus, the division of powers can increase the loyalty of citizens from unequal subsocieties to political institutions by compensating for the inequalities.

Finally, there is an approach that focuses on the interaction between the division of powers, and the structure and functioning of interest groups. It seems that the division of powers between levels of government has an effect on the structure, cohesion, and functioning of interest groups. Reciprocally interest groups are also concerned with the jurisdiction of each level of government, since it affects benefits that they can obtain. They may even be inclined to support actively a particular division of powers, or to attempt to modify it in such a way that it can better serve their own interests. One factor that may lead to such behaviour is the networks of access of interest groups to each level of government. One component of the linguistic segmentation is the existence of two parallel networks of social contacts, which ramify through the social, political, and economic spheres. As a result, interest groups may be better connected with one level of government than with the other, and thus tend to favour the maintenance of, or an increase in, the powers of that level of government.

According to this perspective, problems of legitimacy arise when the groups who are potentially, or in fact, affected by the powers of the central government do not have adequate access to those who exercise these powers. In such a case, loyalty will go to the more accessible level of government. It was noted that such a phenomenon has happened in Quebec and in other parts of the country, primarily in the West. The problems of legitimacy arising from such circumstances tend to be relatively serious in periods of rapid

---

[2] We are not referring to individual inequalities in income and wealth across subsocieties. The individuals of two subsocieties or countries could be equally rich, yet one subsociety could be more powerful if it was much larger than the other or had large quantities of a highly desirable national resource. Of course, the power of a subsociety and the wealth of its members are not unrelated. The concern here is with the former. The question of *reducing* inequalities was discussed in the first section of this conclusion.

social change, that is, when new interest groups emerge or when existing ones grow in size or become better organized.

The alternative in dealing with such problems of legitimacy is on the one hand to redistribute powers so that the dispensation is made in line with the linguistic and regional division social networks, and on the other to devise mechanisms that will contribute to the eventual formation of bridges between the interest groups in each subsociety and the central political institution.

The impact of the division of powers on the legitimacy of the political institutions and thus on the cohesion of the society is complex. A multiplicity of factors and processes are involved. The existence of interdependencies gives considerable importance to collaboration and bargaining, whatever the formal division of powers. The exercise of power in any area entails interorganizational competition and possible conflicts that have implications for institutional legitimacy. Moreover, there are important interactions between the division of formal powers and the distribution of demographic, socio-economic, and ecological sources of power. There is also a complex interaction between the division of powers and the functioning of interest groups in the society, which has implications for the legitimacy of the different levels of government. In short the division of powers is not simply a matter of deciding which level of government can more effectively and efficiently do the job in different areas, given the existence of two linguistic subsocieties, as the rationalistic approach would lead one to believe. Rather, it always interacts with other processes involved in intergovernmental relations, and it is this interaction that has relevance for the cohesion of society.

RELATIVE IMPORTANCE OF HORIZONTAL VERSUS VERTICAL LINKAGES AMONG INSTITUTIONS

There are two kinds of linkages through which the parts of a society can hold together: connected to a centre and thus indirectly to each other, or linked directly, the centre acting as a co-ordinating agency. Of course both types of linkages are not mutually exclusive; they may even support and reinforce each other.

We have observed that horizontal linkages between provincial governments have been less important than the vertical relationships with the federal government. The Canadian Confederation is not an alliance of partners pursuing a common objective and ironing out problems, but more a series of units connected to each other through a common centre of policy making. The provinces do have relationships with each other: conferences of premiers, councils of ministers, and committees of various sorts, but these do not appear to have high prominence in the eyes of citizens. The conferences that receive a lot of attention are the federal-provincial ones, which again are more symbolic of the provinces relating with the federal government than with each other.

There are several factors that frustrate horizontal relationships in Canada and thus hinder the strengthening of that basis of societal cohesion. For instance, it is not in the short-run interest of the central government to encourage horizontal relationships among the various provinces: this may appear to weaken the importance of its role in policy making, to decrease the amount of initiatives that it can take, and generally to give the provinces opportunities to increase their own powers relative to those of the central government. Geography is another factor, with the vast distances between the various parts of the country. Differences in the historical background and evolution among the various regions are also of importance in this context, as well as the extensive social and institutional segmentation between the linguistic and regional subsocieties.

Horizontal relationships of an economic nature serve to link together the different regions of the country. In the case of Quebec, the most extensive trade flows and other economic transactions have been with Ontario. The effects that this interprovincial trade has on such factors as the creation of jobs are considerable for both Quebec and Ontario; so that the consequences of severing such links would indeed be serious. At the same time, however, any analysis of the importance of trade between Quebec and other provinces for societal cohesion must not neglect the fact that it is conducted primarily between anglophone-owned and -controlled enterprises within each province. Thus the economic links are partly a reflection of the economic dominance of anglophones within Quebec, which is a source of resentment for francophones since, as seen in a previous discussion of issues pertaining to organizational control, it is perceived as frustrating many of their collective goals.

In addition, it seems that relationships between individuals have had more salience in the public consciousness and in government programmes than relationships among organizations in different parts of the country. The possibilities and limitations of interpersonal relations for the cohesion of the society is discussed later—a discussion that indirectly emphasizes the importance of interorganizational relationships. It was indicated earlier that subsocieties consist of systems of organizations and that the cohesion of the society depends on the transactions and collaboration that occur between organizations of the different subsocieties. The argument is that the more extensive the mutually beneficial transactions and the more these involve different types of organizations, the more the cohesion of the society rests on a solid basis.

It seems that the preoccupation of policy makers and researchers with the cohesion of society has centred on vertical relationships with the central government and on horizontal relationships among individuals, with a relative neglect of horizontal relationships among the organizations of the different subsocieties. The reasons for this relative neglect and the possibilities that interorganizational relationships offer should be explored further: the historical reasons why horizontal relationships have not acquired the prominence of vertical ones in the Canadian political system; the ideological and structural reasons for this situation; the existing transactions (political, economic, cultural) and their impacts; the limitations imposed by distance and cultural differences; and the conditions and means of cross-cultural communication.

There are many obstacles to the strengthening of horizontal relationships, but this does not mean they should be neglected. In fact one could argue that those relationships have as much, if not more, importance for the cohesion of society than the vertical ones. A group whose members are well connected with each other and have profitable exchanges among themselves is perhaps more cohesive than a group whose members are only indirectly linked to each other through their connection with a leader. Such a statement can be applied to the cohesion of the various segments of a society: their direct interconnections are perhaps a greater source of cohesion than their indirect connections through the political centre.

COMPETITION BETWEEN LEVELS OF GOVERNMENT FOR SUPPORT OF CITIZENS

Both the central government and provincial governments interact with citizens; both are concerned with establishing their legitimacy. As a result, competition may arise between the two levels of government for the allegiance and support of the citizens of a particular constituency. The functionaries at each level of government may claim more legitimacy than the others; they may claim that their level of government is the true government of that population, that it knows better what the population needs, and so on.

From the citizen's point of view, such competition may not be detrimental: it may increase the level and quality of services that he receives and it may make him less dependent on a particular government. On the other hand, the conflict between the two levels may become such that the legitimacy of the entire State is put in question: if élites of the two sets of organizations are constantly in conflict over who has the authority, who should be doing what, whether the distribution of powers is right, it is quite possible that citizens will either lose interest in the political institutions or start believing that there is something profoundly wrong with them.

The competition between the levels of government is also a competition for the support of interest groups. Many of the linkages between governments and citizens occur through intermediary organizations that articulate the views, preferences, and problems of different categories of citizens and attempt to improve their conditions through negotiations with governments. The competition for the allegiance and support of the population may take the form of a competition between governments as to which one can best accommodate particular interest groups.

Another issue is whether the legitimacy of the central government depends more on its linkages with individual citizens or on its linkages with the other level of government. This is especially important when a lower level of government corresponds with regional and linguistic cleavages in society. In other words, the more the population of a linguistic subsociety considers its government as dealing with its problems and thus gives it its loyalty, the more the central government would put its own legitimacy into question if it attempted directly or indirectly to challenge the legitimacy of the lower level of government. In that sense, the central government's relationship with the provincial governments is essentially a relationship with a set of institutions that is actuallyhan extension of the social personality of the subsociety in question.

SOCIAL CHANGE WITHIN LINGUISTIC COMMUNITIES

The cohesion of Canadian society is affected not only byhwhat occurs between the linguistic societies but also by phenomena and events that occur within them. A number of social, economic, and political phenomena that have occurred in each linguistic subsociety, especiallyhthe francophone one, have been identified in the study: changes in the dominant classes in each subsociety; changes in identity; socio-polptical mobplization; demographic changes.

The structure of the dominant classes in the different parts of the country has been changing, leading to conflicts among some of the segments of these classes. These segments include those whose interests are connected with foreign corporations; those whose interests are connected with the national economy; those whose interests are primarily located in the regional economy. The latter in particular have been trying to protect the emerging regional cconomy and change certain conditions; so that it becomes less dependent on external decision-making centres.

Each segment of the dominant classes is aligning itself with a certain level of government (although not necessarily to the exclusion of the other), a process that is a source of some of the tensions in Confederation. For instance, in western Canada certain economic interests have grown and, in allegiance with the provincial governments, are fighting against eastern domination. In Quebec a new bourgeoisie has emerged within the francophone population and, with the assistance of the provincial government, is fighting against anglophone domination. It appears that in both cases the more traditional bourgeoisie is better connected with the central government than the new rising bourgeoisie, which is tied with the provincial government. Hence in the Canadian Confederation there is a major source of strain that is rooted in the changing structure, particularly of the dominant economic classes, of Canadian society.

The changes in the composition of the dominant economic class and in the relative importance of its segments are related to changes in the world economy and in the role that the Canadian economy as a whole, as well as the various regional economies, play in it. The impacts are asymmetrical: world economy affects the national and regional economies, and even though there is a reciprocal impact, it is much smaller; similarly the national economy affects the regional ones and again the reciprocal impact is less significant. In order to promote and protect their interests in such a system, the various economic actors attempt to use one or another level of the State apparatus. In this process, those with regional interests in conflict with those whose interests are primarily national may bring about tensions between levels of government. Or in attempting to gain advantages from one level of government, certain interests form alliances with political élites at another level of government. All these are sources of tension in the political institutions.

We discussed the socio-economic changes that have led to an increase in the bureaucratic élites and to a change in the relative size of the bureaucracy at the two levels of government, and commented on these phenomena as sources of strain in the political system.

In addition to changes in the economic and State bureaucratic élites, there have been important socio-psychological transformations, particularly in the francophone subsociety. There has been a fundamental shift in identity: from that of a minority group to that of a people or nation. This is a critical shift underlying many of the other changes that have been taking place within the francophone subsociety as well as in its relationship with English-speaking Canada.

This shift in identity has critical implications for the mode of incorporation in the society as a whole. Indeed, the critical issue for a minority group is to learn to function within the institutional system of the society and to achieve the best possible level of well-being in it. For a collectivity defining itself as a people or nation, the critical issue is to be able to run its own institutional system, to shape it in terms of its own cultural imperatives, whether these be language, values, or customs. Thus, the problem facing Canadian society and its economic and political institutions is whether it can accommodate this new identity.

Accompanying the change in identity has been extensive social mobilization. There has been a high level of participation in the nationalistic movement in Quebec, made possible by the formation or renewal of a wide range of organizations with either political or cultural goals.

In part, the significance of this socio-political mobilization, as far as the cohesion of Canadian society is concerned, relates to the competition between the levels of governments. In its initial phases, at least, such mobilization can be channelled in many directions. The élites of organizations frequently come into competition with each other in attempting to orient it in their favour. Understandably that part of the élite that tied its career to the provincial institutions is attempting to channel the social participation in its direction. On the other hand the élites whose interests are tied to the national or federal institutions attempt to orient the socio-emotional energies toward the support of Confederation. Also those whose objectives consist in attempting to locate more of the control of the economy of their region or linguistic community away from external centres toward their own region or linguistic community capitalize as much as possible on the new nationalism or regionalism as a weapon in this endeavour.

There have also been demographic realities to deal with: an important decrease in the birth rate among francophones; the traditional propensity of immigrants to assimilate into the anglophone community; migrations away from Quebec toward the rest of the country; the assimilation of francophones outside of Quebec; these are phenomena that have brought about a renewed concern for the demographic health of the francophone subsociety. A threat of further diminishing of numbers is felt with some intensity—its seriousness may have been exaggerated by some and used by others for their own political purposes. However, given the importance of numbers both politically and economically in our society, the demographic trends mentioned are of significance in the relationships between the two collectivities. In fact, they constitute one factor leading to the recent language legislation in Quebec.

INTERPERSONAL CONTACTS ACROSS LINGUISTIC COMMUNITIES

One perspective on the problem of integration suggests that a greater volume of contacts between individuals from the two subsocieties would promote societal cohesion. It is assumed that continuous interaction with members of another group advances understanding and sympathy for the other group's goals and aspirations. This is particularly apt to be the case if interaction is between individuals of the same status, if it is of a voluntary and personal nature, and if it occurs within the context of the pursuit of common goals. Moreover, its effects are likely to be more enduring if contact is recurrent rather than occasional, and supported by institutional practices rather than merely left to the discretion of individuals.

While this ''contact'' hypothesis may have some merit, one can specify two major problems that would attenuate the likely impact on integration of interpersonal interaction. The first problem lies in the fact that the conditions under which interpersonal interaction would lead to positive results frequently cannot be objects of public policy, may take generations to implement, or are likely to be resisted by the interests affected. This is certain to be the case when the distribution of economic and political power and social status favours one group to the detriment of another. Moreover, the feasibility of the most favourable types of contacts between francophones and anglophones occurring in a sustained manner is contingent upon geographical proximity, a condition that prevails only in a few regions of the country.

A second problem concerns the basic assumption that interpersonal linking will encourage political stability in a particular society by advancing a basic comprehension of, and possibly even agreement with, the other group's objectives. Although much more research is warranted on this question, the available evidence indicates that there exists a hiatus between interindividual harmony and societal cohesion. This may be due to a variety of factors including the greater role that each subsociety's institutions play in political socialization, and the overriding importance of each collectivity's social and economic interests. The fact that only a small proportion of each subsociety's population has a significant and direct input into political decision making suggests that interpersonal contact may be more important for integration among the élites of the two linguistic communities than among the population at large.

ABSENCE OF COMMON CULTURE AND SET OF SYMBOLS

One of the bases of cohesion in a society is the presence of a common culture and a common set of symbols—common in the sense that the symbols and elements of culture evoke essentially the same meanings and the same kinds of emotions in people, whatever their position in the society. Also the common culture and set of symbols are usually supported by channels of communication among the different parts of the country.

In Canada there are few elements of culture (other than U.S. culture) and few, if any, symbols that are generative of solidarity between francophones and anglophones. There are many reasons for this, most of which are related in one way or another to the segmented character of Canadian society discussed at various points in this study. Most of the institutions for the creation and diffusion of culture are linguistically segregated. This is inevitable due to the importance of language as an instrument of communication. For instance whether they be organized by the federal government, provincial governments, or the private sector, the mass media are segregated linguistically. There is some translation, but by and large there exist two more or less independent systems of mass communication and cultural expression. The educational system is also largely segregated along linguistic lines at all levels.

Together with the absence of "nationalizing agencies" overarching the two linguistic subsocieties, there has not been, nor is there today, a truly national, that is, bicultural, élite in Canada. There have been a number of individuals, but there does not exist a class consisting of people from each linguistic community who can function and be fairly at ease in each of the cultures. To be completely bicultural is probably an impossibility; but without being perfectly bicultural, one can move a long way in that direction. Bicultural individuals of course would be bilingual; they would have contacts and friends in each linguistic community; they would be able to experience in a meaningful way the cultural activities peculiar to each community; they would be able to communicate effectively with members of each community, whether it be in situations of work, politics, recreation, or other.

Because of the existing institutional segmentation, there have been few opportunities for the emergence of such a class of people. Also there are few areas in the country where anglophones and francophones are physically close to each other. In addition, historically the central government—an institution that is supposed to be common to both collectivities—has not been a milieu for the formation of bicultural individuals. It remains to be seen whether recent changes will have an effect in that direction.

Among the factors hindering the emergence of a common culture and set of symbols, one cannot ignore the weight of the past, the historical points of tension from the conquest onward, which are embedded in the collective memories. To a large extent, they have formed the attitudes held by members of the two collectivities toward each other and have shaped the mental set through which current events are interpreted. Many other historical circumstances, in addition to points of tension, could be listed: the role of the relatively large immigration of Loyalists from the United States, the ''importation'' of certain institutions—the political system in particular, the strong orientation toward Britain among Canadians of British origin, and so on. These events and several others did not facilitate cross-cultural communication and their presence in the collective memories maintain their effects over time.

There is also the immense appeal of American culture for Canadians, the greater capacity of U.S. industries of mass culture to generate a continuous flow of production, and the control by U.S. interests of a number of mass-culture organizations in Canada. This American presence does not facilitate the emergence of a Canadian culture, although it may indirectly facilitate cross-cultural communication by bringing about a certain degree of homogeneity between francophones and anglophones.

Finally the difference in size between the two subsocieties, together with the fact that English is the dominant language on the North American continent, is a condition conducive to a certain cultural insecurity among francophones, which causes some hesitation with regard to large scale cross-cultural communication. Indeed, cross-cultural communication is virtually impossible unless the groups in contact are strong and do not see each other as a threat to their own cultural survival and development.

In such a sociological and historical context, it seems very difficult indeed for a common culture and set of symbols to develop, and for cross-cultural communication to flourish. In fact, some authors have argued that in segmented societies it may be wise, from the point of view of the cohesion of society, not to emphasize the importance of a national culture and symbols; and that an emphasis on such elements almost inevitably stimulates negative feelings by bringing the past back to the collective consciousness.

It seems that unless a truly bicultural élite recruited from both linguistic subsocieties emerges, it is not realistic to expect much from various *ad hoc* attempts at cross-cultural communication at the mass level. Unless this happens seriously at the level of the élite—political, economic, cultural—it is difficult to envisage that it would happen in any significant way in the rest of the society.

Sources and Questions Asked for Results Presented in Table 3.4.4

Sources and Questions Asked

For data from 1962 to 1976a, sources and questions asked, as well as other details, can be found in Pinard and Hamilton (1977, p. 247–48). Sources of subsequent data are given below, followed by questions asked.

1976b	Hamilton-Pinard Quebec Provincial Election Study (pre-election wave)
1976c	Hamilton-Pinard Quebec Provincial Election Study (post-election wave)
1977a,d,e,i 1978c	Gallup Poll by Canadian Institute of Public Opinion (February, April, July, and November)
1977b	SORECOM Poll for CBC (February)
1977c	CROP Poll (March)
1977f	CROP for Reader's Digest (August)
1977g	Hamilton-Pinard Study for CBC (October)
1977h	Centre de sondage, University of Montreal, for Radio-Canada (October)
1977j	Gallup Special Quebec Study (December)
1978a,d	IQOP for Dimanche-Matin (February and September) (February data in table 3.4.5.)
1978b	INCI for Radio-Canada (May-June)
1978e	CROP for La Presse (October) (See data in table 3.4.5.)

1976b	"Personally, do you favour or not Quebec becoming an independent *country* which would no longer be a part of Canada?"
1976c,g	"If tomorrow there were a referendum to decide the future of Quebec, would you vote *for* or *against* Quebec becoming an independent *country* which would no longer be a part of Canada (1977g: . . . a province of Canada?")
1977a,d,e,i 1978c	"There has been quite a bit of talk recently about the possibility of the province of Quebec separating from the rest

of Canada and becoming an independent country. Would you yourself be in favour of separation or opposed to it?''

1977b ''Personally, do you favour or not Quebec becoming an independent country which would no longer be a province of Canada?''

1977c ''Do you think Quebec should be an independent country or should not be an independent country?''

1977f ''Since the Parti Québécois came to power on November 15 last, we hear more and more about a referendum in which the people of Quebec will be asked to vote on the political future of Quebec. I am going to suggest four possibilities regarding the future of Quebec. For each of these possibilities, tell me whether you personally would be very much in favour, reasonably in favour, not particularly in favour, or not at all in favour of . . . independence for Quebec?'' (First two and last two categories added together.)

1977h
1978b ''The following are a number of constitutional options open to Quebec. Are you very much in favour, more or less in favour, not particularly in favour or not all in favour of . . . independence for Quebec (i.e., a total political and economic independence)?'' (The part in parentheses was omitted in the English version of the questionnaire in 1977h. The results presented add up the first two and last two categories.)

1977j ''And if a vote (on the future of Quebec) offered these options, which one would you choose: Quebec to become independent; Quebec to remain within Canada.''

1978d ''Could you tell me if you are in favour or not in favour of each of the following constitutional options: . . . The separation of Quebec from the rest of Canada?'' (Our translation.)

Questions Asked for Results Presented in Table 3.4.5

1970a	"Do you favour Quebec becoming separate politically from the rest of Canada while remaining in an economic union with it?"
1970b	"It has been suggested that Quebec become an independent country *politically*, while retaining *economic* links with Canada. Are you personally for or against political independence with economic association with Canada?"
1977b	"The Parti Québécois wants Quebec to become an independent country, economically associated with the rest of Canada. If the government of Quebec were able to arrange such an economic association with the rest of Canada, would you then vote in a referendum *for* or *against* Quebec becoming an independent country?"
1977f 1978e	"The solution presently favoured by the Parti Québécois Government is that of sovereignty-association, which is to say that Quebec would become a politically independent country with an economic alliance with Canada. If a referendum were to be held today on this question, would you vote *for* or *against* sovereignty-association? (In 1978e, the word *solution* was replaced by the word *option*.)
1977f	"Since the Parti Québécois came to power on November 15 last, we hear more and more about a referendum in which the people of Quebec will be asked to vote on the political future of Quebec. I'm going to suggest four possibilities regarding the future of Quebec. For each of these possibilities tell me whether you personally would be very much in favour, reasonably in favour, not particularly in favour, or not all in favour of . . . sovereignty-association, in which a politically independent Quebec would have an economic alliance with Canada?"
1977g	"The Parti Québécois option is sovereignty-association, that is, it wants Quebec to become an independent country which would propose an economic association to the rest of Canada.

If tomorrow there were a referendum on this subject, would you vote for or against Quebec becoming an independent country which would propose to the rest of Canada an economic association?''

1977h   Same introduction as in 1977h, table 3.4.4, then: '' . . .
1978b   sovereignty-association, in which a politically independent Quebec would have an economic alliance with Canada?'' (First two and last two categories added together.)

1977j   ''If a vote on the future of Quebec offered these options, which one would you choose: Quebec to become independent; Quebec to remain within Canada; Quebec to become independent, but have an economic association with the rest of Canada?'' (The results for the first and third options are added together as ''for'' sovereignty-association.)

1978a   ''If a referendum were held tomorrow in Quebec to propose sovereignty-association, that is, political independence for Quebec and an economic association with the rest of Canada, would you personally say 'yes' or 'no' to sovereignty-association?''

1978b   ''The Parti Québécois presently advocates sovereignty-association, that is, political independence for Quebec with an economic association with Canada. Would you vote for or against sovereignty-association if a referendum were held today on this matter?''

1978d   Same introduction as in 1978d, table 3.4.4, then '' . . . the political independence of Quebec and an economic association with the rest of Canada?'' (Our translation.)

References and Bibliography

Aitchison, J.H.
1963 "Interprovincial Cooperation." In *The Political Process in Canada: Essays in Honour of R. MacGregor Dawson*, edited by J.H. Aitchison, pp. 153–70. Toronto: University of Toronto Press.

Akian, Gail Grant, and Breton, Raymond
Forthcoming *Évolution de la francisation dans le monde du travail au Québec*. Montreal: Institute for Research on Public Policy.

Albinski, Henry S.
1967 "Politics and Biculturalism in Canada: The Flag Debate." *Australian Journal of Politics and History* 13: 169–88.

Allport, Gordon W.
1954 *Nature of Prejudice*. Cambridge, Mass.: Addison-Wesley Publishing Co.

Amir, Yehuda
1969 "Contact Hypothesis in Ethnic Relations." *Psychological Bulletin* 71: 319–42.

Anisfeld, Elizabeth, and Lambert, Wallace E.
1964 "Evaluational Reactions of Bilingual and Monolingual Children to Spoken Languages." *Journal of Abnormal and Social Psychology* 69: 89–97.

Archibald, Clinton, and Paltiel, Khayyam Z.
1977 "Du passage des corps intermédiaires aux groupes de pression: la transformation d'une idée illustrée par le Mouvement coopératif Desjardins." *Recherches sociographiques* 18, no. 1: 59–91.

Arès, Richard
1972 *Nos grandes options politiques et constitutionnelles*. Montreal: Les éditions Bellarmin.
1975 "Les minorités franco-canadiennes: étude statistique." In *Mémoires de la Société royale du Canada*, Fourth Series, vol. 13. Ottawa: Société royale du Canada.

Association des économistes québécois
1977 *Économie et indépendance*. Montreal: Éditions Quinze.

Averitt, Robert T.
1968 *The Dual Economy: The Dynamics of American Industry Structure*. New York: W.W. Norton & Co.

Barth, Fredrik, ed.
1969 *Ethnic Groups and Boundaries: The Social Organization of Culture Difference*. Boston: Little, Brown & Co.

Beattie, Christopher
1975 *Minority Men in a Majority Setting*. Toronto: McClelland and Stewart.
Beattie, Christopher; Désy, Jacques; and Longstaff, Stephen
1972 *Bureaucratic Careers: Anglophones and Francophones in the Canadian Public Service*. Ottawa: Information Canada.
Bercuson, David Jay, ed.
1977 *Canada and the Burden of Unity*. Toronto: Macmillan Co. of Canada.
Berghe, Pierre van den
1969 "Pluralism and Polity: A Theoretical Exploration." In *Pluralism in Africa*, edited by Leo Kuper and M.G. Smith, pp. 67–81. Berkeley and Los Angeles: University of California Press.
Bernard, Jean-Paul, and Desrosiers, Richard F.
1971 "Le Québec et le fédéralisme, 1950–1970: chroniques des débats idéologiques et des événements politiques." In *Fédéralisme et nations*, edited by Roman Serbyn, pp. 87–125. Montreal: Les Presses de l'Université du Québec.
Berry, John W.; Kalin, Rudolf; and Taylor, Donald M.
1977 *Multiculturalism and Ethnic Attitudes in Canada*. Ottawa: Supply and Services Canada.
Billig, Michael
1976 *Social Psychology and Intergroup Relations*. London: Academic Press.
Bird, Richard
1978 "The Growth of the Public Service in Canada." In *Public Employment and Compensation in Canada: Myths and Realities*, edited by David K. Foot, pp. 19–44. Scarborough, Ont.: Butterworth & Co. (Canada) for Institute for Research on Public Policy.
Black, Edwin R.
1968 "British Columbia: The Politics of Exploitation." In *Exploiting Our Economic Potential; Public Policy and the British Columbia Economy*, edited by Ronald Alexander Shearer, pp. 23–41. Toronto and Montreal: Holt, Rinehart and Winston of Canada.
1975 *Divided Loyalties: Canadian Concepts of Federalism*. Montreal: McGill-Queen's University Press.
1977 "What Alternative Do We Have If Any?" In *Must Canada Fail?*, edited by Richard Simeon, pp. 152–68. Montreal: McGill-Queen's University Press.
Boulet, Jac-André
1977 "Évolution dans la distribution des revenus de travail des groupes ethniques et linguistiques sur le marché montréalais de 1961 à 1971." Mimeographed. Ottawa: Economic Council of Canada.

Bourque, Gilles, and Frenette, Nicole
1970 ''La structure nationale québécoise.'' *Socialisme québécois* 21−22: 109−56.
Brazeau, Jacques
1964 ''Quebec's Emerging Middle Class.'' In *French Canadian Society*, edited by Marcel Rioux and Yves Martin, vol. 1, pp. 296−306. Toronto: McClelland and Stewart.
1975 ''L'usage des langues dans les activités de travail.'' In *Multilingual Political Systems: Problems and Solutions*, edited by Jean-Guy Savard and Richard Vigneault, pp. 303−15. Quebec: Les Presses de l'Université Laval.
Breton, Albert, and Breton, Raymond
Forthcoming *Why Disunity? An Analysis of Linguistic and Regional Cleavages in Canada*. Montreal: Institute for Research on Public Policy.
Breton, Albert, and Mieszkowski, Peter
1975 *The Returns to Investment in Language: The Economics of Bilingualism*. Discussion Paper no. 7512. Toronto: University of Toronto.
1977 ''The Economics of Bilingualism.'' In *The Political Economy of Fiscal Federalism. International Institute of Management*, edited by Wallace E. Oates, pp. 261−73. Lexington, Mass.: Lexington Books.
Breton, Raymond
1964 ''Institutional Completeness of Ethnic Communities and the Personal Relations of Immigrants.'' *American Journal of Sociology* 70: 193−205.
1972 ''The Socio-Political Dynamics of the October Events.'' *Canadian Review of Sociology and Anthropology* 9: 33−56.
1977 *The Canadian Condition: A Guide to Research in Public Policy*. Montreal: Institute for Research on Public Policy.
1978 ''The Structure of Relationships Between Ethnic Collectivities.'' In *The Canadian Ethnic Mosaic: A Quest for Identity*, edited by Leo Driedger, pp. 55−73. Toronto: McClelland and Stewart.
Breton, Raymond, and Roseborough, Howard
1968 ''Ethnic, Religious and Regional Representation in the Federal Cabinet, 1867−1966.'' Unpublished. Toronto: University of Toronto.
Brewis, T.N., ed.
1969 *Regional Economic Policies in Canada*. Toronto: Macmillan Co. of Canada.
Brunet, Michel
1958 *La présence anglaise et les Canadiens; études sur l'histoire et la pensée des deux Canadas*. Montreal: Librairie Beauchemin.

Bucovetsky, M.W.

1975 "The Mining Industry and the Great Tax Reform Debate." In *Pressure Group Behaviour in Canadian Politics*, edited by Paul Pross, pp. 87–114. Toronto: McGraw-Hill Ryerson.

Cairns, Alan C.

1968 "The Electoral System and the Party System in Canada, 1921–1965." *Canadian Journal of Political Science* 1: 55–80.

Calhoun, John C.

1953 *A Disquisition on Government*. New York: The Liberal Arts Press.

Canada, Dominion Bureau of Statistics

1963 *1961 Census of Canada*. Vol. 1 (Part 2), *Population: Official Language and Mother Tongue*. Cat. no. 92–549. Ottawa: Queen's Printer.

1970 *1961 Census of Canada*. SP-5, *Population: Mother Tongue*. Cat. no. 92–529. Ottawa: Queen's Printer.

Canada, Ministère de la Défense nationale

1975 "Les Canadiens-français et leur langue au sein des Forces canadiennes: situation passée, présente et à venir." Paper presented to the Biennale de la francophonie canadienne, Chicoutimi, Que. Mimeographed.

Canada, Office of the Commissioner of Official Languages

1975 *Information* 1, no. 1 (September-October).

1977 *Revised Official Languages Policies in the Public Service of Canada*. Ottawa: Treasury Board, Official Languages Branch.

Canada, Royal Commission on Bilingualism and Biculturalism

1969a *Report*. Book 3A, *The Work World*, parts 1 and 2. Ottawa: Queen's Printer.

1969b *Report*. Book 3B, *The Work World*, parts 3 and 4. Ottawa: Queen's Printer.

1970 *Report*. Book 4, *The Cultural Contribution of the Other Ethnic Groups*. Ottawa: Queen's Printer.

Canada, Statistics Canada

1973a *Canada Year Book 1973*. Ottawa: Information Canada.

1973b *1971 Census of Canada*. Vol. 1 (Part 3), *Population: General Characteristics—Ethnic Groups*. Cat. no. 92–723. Ottawa: Information Canada.

1973c *1971 Census of Canada*. Vol. 1 (Part 3), *Population: General Characteristics—Mother Tongue*. Cat. no. 92–725. Ottawa: Information Canada.

1973d *1971 Census of Canada*. Vol. 1 (Part 3), *Population: General Characteristics—Official Language and Language Most Often Spoken at Home*. Cat. no. 92–726. Ottawa: Information Canada.

1978 *1976 Census of Canada*. Vol. 2, *Population: Demographic Characteristics—Mother Tongue*. Cat. no. 92–821. Ottawa: Supply and Services Canada.

Canada, Task Force on Government Information
1969 *To Know and Be Known.* Vol. 2, *Research Papers.* Ottawa: Queen's Printer.
Canadian Council of Christians and Jews
1977a "Annual Report: 1976–77." Mimeographed. Toronto: Canadian Council of Christians and Jews.
1977b "Student Exchange Evaluation: Ontario Region (1977)." Mimeographed. Toronto: Canadian Council of Christians and Jews.
Canadian Institute on Public Affairs, and Mount Allison University
1965 "The Idea of Maritime Union." Report of conference at Mount Allison University, Sackville, N.B. Mimeographed.
Careless, Anthony
1977 *Initiative and Response: The Adaptation of Canadian Federalism to Regional Economic Development.* Montreal: McGill-Queen's University Press for the Institute of Public Administration of Canada.
Carisse, Colette
1971 "Cultural Orientations in Marriages Between French and English Canadians." In *Minority Canadians.* Vol. 2, *Immigrant Groups,* edited by Jean Leonard Elliott. Scarborough, Ont.: Prentice-Hall of Canada.
Carlos, Serge
1973 *L'utilisation du français dans le monde du travail.* Quebec: Éditeur officiel du Québec.
Castonguay, Charles
1978 "La montée de l'exogamie chez les jeunes francophones hors Québec." *Le Devoir,* 16 June.
Cheffins, R.I.
1969 *The Constitutional Process in Canada.* Toronto: McGraw-Hill Ryerson.
Choquette, Robert
1975 *Language and Religion: A History of English-French Conflict in Ontario.* Ottawa: University of Ottawa Press.
Clark, S.D.
1971 "The Position of the French-Speaking Population in the Northern Industrial Community." In *Canadian Society: Pluralism, Change and Conflict,* edited by R.J. Ossenberg, pp. 62–85. Scarborough, Ont.: Prentice-Hall of Canada.
Clarkson, Stephen
1966 "A Programme for Binational Development." In *Nationalism in Canada,* edited by Peter Russell, pp. 133–52. Toronto: McGraw-Hill Ryerson.
Clement, Wallace
1975 *The Canadian Corporate Elite: An Analysis of Economic Power.* Toronto: McClelland and Stewart.

1978 "A Political Economy of Regionalism in Canada." In *Moderniza-tion and the Canadian State*, edited by Daniel Glenday, Hubert Guindon, and Allan Turowetz, pp. 89–110. Toronto: Macmillan Co. of Canada.

Clement, Wallace, and Olsen, Dennis
1974 "Official Ideology and Ethnic Power: Canadian Elites 1953–1973." Paper read to American Sociological Association, Montreal, Que. Mimeographed.

Coleman, James S.
1959 "Academic Achievement and the Structure of Competition." *Harvard Education Review* 29, no. 4: 330–51.

Cook, Ramsay
1966 *Canada and the French-Canadian Question*. Toronto: Macmillan Co. of Canada.

Corry, J.A.
1940 *Difficulties of Divided Jurisdiction*. Royal Commission on Dominion-Provincial Relations Study. Ottawa: Queen's Printer.

Council of Ministers of Education
1978 *The State of Minority Language Education in the Ten Provinces*. Toronto: Council of Ministers of Education.

Croisat, Maurice
1970 "Centralisation et décentralisation au sein des partis politiques canadiens." *Revue française de science politique* 20: 483–502.

Dawson, Helen J.
1975 "National Pressure Groups and the Federal Government." In *Pressure Group Behaviour in Canadian Politics*, edited by Paul Pross, pp. 27–58. Toronto: McGraw-Hill Ryerson.

Deutsch, Karl W., et al.
1968 *Political Community and the North Atlantic Area: International Organization in the Light of Historical Experience*. 1957. Reprint. Westport, Conn.: Greenwood Press.

Deutsch, Morton
1973 *The Resolution of Conflict: Constructive and Destructive Processes*. New Haven, Conn.: Yale University Press.

De Wilde, James
1977 "The Parti Québécois in Power." In *Must Canada Fail?*, edited by Richard Simeon, pp. 15–27. Montreal: McGill-Queen's University Press.

Dinsmore, John
1975 "Éléments d'une position du Québec dans ses relations économiques avec les États-Unis." In *Le nationalisme québécois à la croisée des chemins*, Choix Series, no. 7. Quebec: Centre québécois de relations internationales.

Dion, Léon
1974 "French as an Adopted Language in Quebec." In *Sounds Canadian: Languages and Cultures in Multi-Ethnic Society*, edited by Paul Migus, pp. 42–58. Toronto: Peter Martin Associates.
1975 *Nationalisme et politique au Québec*. Montreal: Éditions Hurtubise—H.M.H.

Dion, Léon, and de Sève, Micheline
1974 "Quebec: Interest Groups and the Search for an Alternative Political System." *American Academy of Political and Social Science Annals* 413: 124–44.

Dofny, Jacques, and Garon-Audy, Muriel
1969 "Mobilités professionnelles au Québec." *Sociologie et sociétés* 1: 277–301.

Driedger, Leo, and Peters, Jacob
1977 "Identity and Social Distance: Towards Understanding Simmel's 'The Stranger'." *Canadian Review of Sociology and Anthropology* 14: 158–73.

Dumont, Fernand, and Montminy, Jean-Paul, eds.
1966 *Le pouvoir dans la société canadienne-française*. Quebec: Presses de l'Université Laval.

Durocher, R., and Linteau, A., eds.
1971 *Le "retard" du Québec et l'infériorité économique des Canadiens français*. Montreal: Éditions du Boréal express.

Economic Council of Canada
1969 *Interim Report on Competition Policy*. Ottawa: Queen's Printer.

Elkin, Frederick
1969 "Advertising Themes and Quiet Revolutions: Dilemmas in French Canada." *American Journal of Sociology* 75: 112–22.
1973 *Rebels and Colleagues: Advertising and Social Change in French Canada*. Montreal: McGill-Queen's University Press.
1975 "Communications Media and Identity Formation." In *Communications in Canadian Society*, 2d rev. ed., edited by Benjamin D. Singer, pp. 229–43. Toronto: Copp Clark Publishing.

Engelmann, Frederick C., and Schwartz, Mildred A.
1975 *Canadian Political Parties: Origins, Character, Impact*. Scarborough, Ont.: Prentice-Hall of Canada.

Faucher, Albert, and Lamontagne, Maurice
1953 "History of Industrial Development." In *Essais sur le Québec contemporain; Essays on Contemporary Quebec*, edited by Jean-Charles Falardeau, pp. 23–37. Quebec: Les Presses universitaires Laval.

Fédération des francophones hors Québec
1977a "La Fédération des francophones hors Québec: son origine, son orientation, ses membres, ses objectifs." Mimeographed. Ottawa: Fédération des francophones hors Québec.

1977b *Les héritiers de Lord Durham*. Vol. 1. Ottawa: Fédération des francophones hors Québec.

1978 *Deux poids, deux mesures: les francophones hors Québec et les anglophones au Québec: un dossier comparatif*. Ottawa: Fédération des francophones hors Québec.

Fishman, Joshua A.

1967 "Bilingualism With and Without Diglossia; Diglossia With and Without Bilingualism." *Journal of Social Issues* 23, no. 2: 29–38.

Fletcher, Frederick J.

1977a "Public Attitudes and Alternative Futures." In *Must Canada Fail?*, edited by Richard Simeon, pp. 28–41. Montreal: McGill-Queen's University Press.

1977b "The View From Upper Canada." In *Must Canada Fail?*, edited by Richard Simeon, pp. 93–106. Montreal: McGill-Queen's University Press.

Foot, David K., and Thadaney, Percy

1978 "The Growth of Public Employment in Canada: The Evidence From Taxation Statistics, 1946–1975." In *Public Employment and Compensation in Canada: Myths and Realities*, edited by David K. Foot, pp. 45–62. Scarborough, Ont.: Butterworth & Co. (Canada) for the Institute for Research on Public Policy.

Fortin, Gérald

1969 "Le nationalisme canadien-français et les classes sociales." *Revue d'histoire de l'Amérique française* 22: 525–37.

Franck, Thomas M., et al.

1968 *Why Federations Fail: An Inquiry Into the Requisites for Successful Federalism*. Studies in Peaceful Change, no. 1. New York: New York University Press.

Fréchette, Pierre

1977 "L'économie de la Confédération: un point de vue québécois." *Analyse de politiques* 3: 431–40.

Freedman, Jonathan L.; Carlsmith, J. Merrill; and Sears, D.O.

1974 *Social Psychology*. 2d ed. Englewood Cliffs, N.J.: Prentice Hall.

Gamson, William A.

1968 *Power and Discontent*. Homewood, Ill.: Dorsey Press.

Gardner, R.C.; Taylor, D.M.; and Feenstra, H.J.

1970 "Ethnic Stereotypes: Attitudes or Beliefs?" *Canadian Journal of Psychology* 24: 321–34.

Gartner, Gerry T.

1977 "A Review of Cooperation Among the Western Provinces." *Canadian Public Administration* 20: 174–87.

Gibbins, Roger

1977 "Models of Nationalism: A Case Study of Political Ideologies in the Canadian West." *Canadian Journal of Political Science* 10: 341–73.

Globe and Mail, Toronto
1977 "Quebec Goes Searching for Its Roots and Finds Them in Television." 19 November.
1978*a* "French Language Crusade Hinges on Parking Ticket." 10 June.
1978*b* "Province Polarized Over the Francophones." 21 January.
Guindon, Hubert
1968*a* "Social Unrest, Social Class, and Quebec's Bureaucratic Revolution." In *Canada: A Sociological Profile*, edited by W.E. Mann, pp. 157−62. Toronto: Copp Clark Publishing.
1968*b* "Two Cultures: An Essay on Nationalism, Class, and Ethnic Tension." In *Contemporary Canada*, edited by R.H. Leach, pp. 35−59. Toronto: University of Toronto Press.
Haas, Ernst B.
1961 "International Integration: The European and the Universal Process." *International Organization* 15: 366−92.
Hargrove, Erwin C.
1970 "Nationality, Values, and Change: Young Elites in Canada." *Comparative Politics* 2: 473−99.
Hechter, Michael
1971 "Towards a Theory of Ethnic Change." *Politics and Society* 2: 21−45.
Henripin, Jacques
1975 "L'avenir des francophones au Canada." In *Mémoires de la Société royale du Canada*, Fourth Series, vol. 13. Ottawa: Société royale du Canada.
Hodgetts, A.B.
1968 *What Culture? What Heritage? A Study of Civic Education in Canada*. Toronto: Ontario Institute for Studies in Education.
Hodgetts, J.E.
1967 "Canada." In *Decisions and Decision-Makers in the Modern State*, edited by J.E. Maynard. Zurich: UNESCO.
Hughes, Everett C.
1972 "The Linguistic Division of Labor in Industrial and Urban Societies." In *Advances in the Sociology of Language*, vol. 2, edited by Joshua A. Fishman, pp. 296−309. The Hague: Mouton, Imprint of Humanities Press.
Hughes, Everett C., and McDonald, Margaret L.
1941 "French and English in the Economic Structure of Montreal." *Canadian Journal of Economics and Political Science* 7: 493−505.
Institute of Intergovernmental Relations
1969 *Intergovernmental Liaison on Fiscal and Economic Matters*. Ottawa: Queen's Printer.

Jackson, John D.
1975 *Community and Conflict: A Study of French-English Relations in Ontario*. Edited by Gordon B. Inglis. Toronto: Holt, Rinehart and Winston of Canada.

Jocas, Yves de, and Rocher, Guy
1957 "Inter-Generation Occupational Mobility in the Province of Quebec." *Canadian Journal of Economics and Political Science* 23: 57–68.

Jouandet-Bernadat, Roland
1978 "Un diagnostic de l'économie québécoise." *Le Devoir*, 1 June.

Joy, Richard J.
1972 *Languages in Conflict: The Canadian Experience*. Toronto: McClelland and Stewart.
1975 "Language Trends Shown by the Census Figures." Paper read at Concordia University, Montreal, Que. Unpublished.

Kovacs, Martin Louis
1978 *Ethnic Canadians: Culture and Education*. Regina, Sask.: Canadian Plains Research Center.

Kwavnick, David
1965 "The Roots of French-Canadian Discontent." *Canadian Journal of Economics and Political Science* 31: 509–23.
1975 "Interest Group Demands and the Federal Political System: Two Canadian Case Studies." In *Pressure Group Behaviour in Canadian Politics*, edited by Paul Pross, pp. 70–86. Toronto: McGraw-Hill Ryerson.

Lalande, Gilles
1973 "Quebec and International Affairs." In *Quebec Society and Politics: Views From the Inside*, edited by Dale Thompson, pp. 239–50. Toronto: McClelland and Stewart.

Lambert, Wallace E.
1967 "A Social Psychology of Bilingualism." *Journal of Social Issues* 23, no. 2: 91–109.

Lambert, Wallace E.; Hodgson, R.C.; Gardner, R.C.; and Fillenbaum, S.
1960 "Evaluational Reactions to Spoken Languages." *Journal of Abnormal and Social Psychology* 60: 44–51.

Lamy, Paul
n.d. "Language Conflict and Language Planning in Canada." Paper read at Canadian Sociology and Anthropology Association Annual Meeting, Laval University, Quebec, Que. Mimeographed.

Laponce, J.A.
1975 "Relating Linguistics to Political Conflicts: The Problem of Language Shift in Multilingual Societies." In *Multilingual Political Systems: Problems and Solutions*, edited by Jean-Guy Savard and Richard Vigneault, pp. 185–207. Quebec: Les Presses de l'Université Laval.

Laporte, P.

1974 *L'usage des langues dans la vie économique du Québec: situation actuelle et possibilités de changement*. Commission d'enquête sur la situation de la langue française et sur les droits linguistiques au Québec. Synthèse S7. Quebec: Éditeur officiel du Québec.

Larimer, George S.

1970 "Indirect Assessment of Intercultural Prejudices." *International Journal of Psychology* 5: 189–95.

Latouche, Daniel

1974 "La vraie nature de . . . la Révolution tranquille." *Revue canadienne de science politique* 7: 525–36.

Laumann, Edward O., and Pappi, Franz U.

1976 *Networks of Collective Action: A Perspective on Community Influence Systems*. New York: Academic Press.

Laurin, Camille

1977 "La politique québécoise de la langue française." White paper deposited in the National Assembly. *Le Devoir*, 2 April.

Leach, Richard H.

1959 "Interprovincial Co-operation: Neglected Aspect of Canadian Federalism." *Canadian Public Administration* 2: 83–99.

Lee, Danielle, and Lapointe, Jean

1979 "The Emergence of Franco-Ontarians: New Identity, New Boundaries." In *Minority Canadians*. Vol. 3, *Two Nations, Many Cultures. Ethnic Groups in Canada*, edited by Jean Leonard Elliott, pp. 99–113. Scarborough, Ont.: Prentice-Hall of Canada.

Légaré, Anne

1977a *Les classes sociales au Québec*. Montreal: Les Presses de l'Université du Québec.

1977b "Les classes sociales et le gouvernement péquiste au Québec." Paper read at University of Toronto, Ont. Mimeographed.

Lehmbruch, Gerhard

1974 "A Non-Competitive Pattern of Conflict Management in Liberal Democracies: The Case of Switzerland, Austria and Lebanon." In *Consociational Democracy: Political Accommodation in Segmented Societies*, edited by Kenneth D. McRae, pp. 90–97. Toronto: McClelland and Stewart.

Leslie, Peter M.

1969 "The Role of Political Parties in Promoting the Interests of Ethnic Minorities." *Canadian Journal of Political Science* 2: 419–33.

1977 "Ethnic Hierarchies and Minority Consciousness in Quebec." In *Must Canada Fail?*, edited by Richard Simeon, pp. 107–35. Montreal: McGill-Queen's University Press.

Leslie, Peter M., and Simeon, Richard

1977 "The Battle of the Balance Sheets." In *Must Canada Fail?*, edited by Richard Simeon, pp. 243–48. Montreal: McGill-Queen's University Press.

Lieberson, Stanley
1970 *Language and Ethnic Relations in Canada*. Toronto: John Wiley and Sons (Canada).

Lijphart, Arend
1968 *The Politics of Accommodation: Pluralism and Democracy in the Netherlands* Berkeley and Los Angeles: University of California Press.
1971 "Cultural Diversity and Theories of Political Integration." *Canadian Journal of Political Science* 4: 1–14.
1974 "Consociational Democracy." In *Consociational Democracy: Political Accommodation in Segmented Societies*, edited by Kenneth D. McRae, pp. 70–89. Toronto: McClelland and Stewart.

Lower, Arthur R.M.
1958 *Canadians in the Making*. 2d ed. Toronto: Longman Canada.

Mackay, J. Ross
1958 "The Interactance Hypothesis and Boundaries in Canada: A Preliminary Study." *Canadian Geographer* 2, no. 11: 1–8.

McKeough, W. D'Arcy
1977 "Interprovincial Trade Flows, Employment, and the Tariff in Canada." Mimeographed. Supplementary material to the 1977 Ontario Budget. Toronto: Treasurer of Ontario.

Maclean's
1978 "Can't We Be Friends? A Special Report." 6 February, pp. 20–21.

McNaught, Kenneth
1966 "The National Outlook of English-Speaking Canadians." In *Nationalism in Canada*, edited by Peter Russell, pp. 61–71. Toronto: McGraw-Hill Ryerson.

McRae, Kenneth D.
1974a "Consociationalism and the Canadian Political System." In *Consociational Democracy: Political Accommodation in Segmented Societies*, edited by Kenneth D. McRae, pp. 238–61. Toronto: McClelland and Stewart.
1974b Introduction to *Consociational Democracy: Political Accommodation in Segmented Societies*, edited by Kenneth D. McRae. Toronto: McClelland and Stewart.

McRoberts, Kenneth, and Posgate, Dale
1976 *Quebec: Social Change and Political Crisis*. Toronto: McClelland and Stewart.

Maheu, Robert
1970 *Les francophones du Canada, 1941–1991*. Montreal: Éditions Parti pris.

Manzer, Ronald A.
1974 *Canada: A Socio-Political Report*. Toronto: McGraw-Hill Ryerson.
Meisel, John
1970 *Working Papers in Canadian Politics*. Montreal: McGill-Queen's University Press.
1974 *Cleavages, Parties and Values in Canada*. London and Beverly Hills, Calif.: Sage Publications.
1978 "The Decline of Party in Canada." In *Party Politics in Canada*, 4th ed., edited by H.G. Thorburn. Scarborough, Ont.: Prentice-Hall of Canada.
Meisel, John, and Lemieux, Vincent
1972 *Ethnic Relations in Canadian Voluntary Associations*. Royal Commission on Bilingualism and Biculturalism, document no. 13. Ottawa: Information Canada.
Migué, Jean-Luc
1970 "Le nationalisme, l'unité nationale et la théorie économique de l'information." *Revue canadienne d'économique* 3: 183–198.
1971 "L'industrialisation et la participation des Québécois au progrès économique." In *Le Québec d'aujourd'hui; regards d'universitaires*, edited by Jean-Luc Migué. Montreal: Éditions Hurtubise—H.M.H.
Milner, Sheilagh Hodgins, and Milner, Henry
1973 *The Decolonization of Québec: An Analysis of Left-Wing Nationalism*. Toronto: McClelland and Stewart.
Morris, Raymond N., and Lanphier, C. Michael
1977 *Three Scales of Inequality: Perspectives on French-English Relations*. Don Mills, Ont.: Longman Canada.
Morrison, Robert N.
1970 *Corporate Adaptability to Bilingualism and Biculturalism*. Royal Commission on Bilingualism and Biculturalism, document no. 5. Ottawa: Queen's Printer.
Mousseau-Glaser, Monique
1972 "Consommation des mass media: biculturalisme des mass media ou bilinguisme des consommateurs." *Canadian Review of Sociology and Anthropology* 9: 325–46.
National Advisory Council on Voluntary Action
1978 *People in Action*. Ottawa: Supply and Services Canada.
Nationalisme québécois à la croisée des chemins, Le
1975 Choix Series, no. 7. Quebec: Centre québécois de relations internationales.
Newman, Peter
1977 "The Establishment Has Abandoned Quebec to Its Own Dark Devices." *Financial Post*, 30 April.

Niosi, Jorge
1977 "Le gouvernement du P.Q., le capital américain et le capital canadien." Paper read at University of Toronto, Ont. Mimeographed.
Noel, S.J.R.
1974 "Consociational Democracy and Canadian Federalism." In *Consociational Democracy: Political Accommodation in Segmented Societies*, edited by Kenneth D. McRae, pp. 262–68. Toronto: McClelland and Stewart.
Nordlinger, Eric A.
1972 *Conflict Regulation in Divided Societies*. Studies in International Affairs, no. 29. Cambridge, Mass.: Harvard University, Center for International Affairs.
O'Bryan, K.G.; Reitz, J.G.; and Kuplowska, O.M.
1976 *Non-Official Languages: A Study in Canadian Multiculturalism*. Ottawa: Supply and Services Canada.
Olsen, Dennis
1977 "The State Elites." In *The Canadian State: Political Economy and Political Power*, edited by Leo Panitch, pp. 199–224. Toronto: University of Toronto Press.
Orban, Edmond, ed.
1976 *La modernisation politique du Québec*. Sillery, Que.: Éditions du Boréal express.
Ouimet, Roger
1938 "The Preservation of French-Canadian Culture Within Confederation." In *Problems in Canadian Unity*, edited by Violet Anderson, pp. 50–66. Toronto: Thomas Nelson & Sons.
Painchaud, Robert
1976 "The Franco-Canadians of Western Canada and Multiculturalism." In *Multiculturalism as State Policy: Conference Report, Second Canadian Conference on Multiculturalism, Government Conference Centre, Ottawa, February 13–15, 1976*. Ottawa: Supply and Services Canada.
Parkin, Frank
1976 "System Contradiction and Political Transformation." In *Power and Control: Social Structures and Their Transformation*, Sage Studies in International Sociology, vol. 6, edited by Tom R. Burns and Walter Buckley. London and Beverly Hills, Calif.: Sage Publications.
Peers, Frank
1966 "The Nationalist Dilemma in Canadian Broadcasting." In *Nationalism in Canada*, edited by Peter Russell, pp. 252–70. Toronto: McGraw-Hill Ryerson.

Pelletier, Réjean, ed.
1976 *Partis politiques au Québec.* Montreal: Éditions Hurtubise—H.M.H.

Pinard, Maurice
1976*a* "The Moderation and Regulation of Communal Conflicts: A Critical Review of Current Theories." Paper read at Workshop on the Politics of Multicultural Societies, Louvain, Belgium. Mimeographed.
1976*b* "Pluralisme social et partis politiques: quelques éléments d'une théorie." In *Partis politiques au Québec*, edited by Réjean Pelletier, pp. 37—52. Montreal: Éditions Hurtubise—H.M.H.
1978 "Ethnic Segmentation, Loyalties, Incentives, and Institutional Options in Quebec." Paper presented at Canada-Israel Workshop, Sde Boker, Israel. Mimeographed.
Forthcoming "Loyalties, Incentives and Constitutional Options Among French Canadians in Quebec." In *French-English Relations in Canada*, edited by Paul Lamy and Danièle Lee. Toronto: McClelland and Stewart.

Pinard, Maurice, and Hamilton, Richard
1977 "The Independence Issue and the Polarization of the Electorate: The 1973 Quebec Election." *Canadian Journal of Political Science* 10: 215—59.

Pineo, Peter C.
1977 "The Social Standing of Ethnic and Racial Groupings." *Canadian Review of Sociology and Anthropology* 14: 147—57.

Porter, John
1965 *The Vertical Mosaic: An Analysis of Social Class and Power in Canada.* Toronto: University of Toronto Press.

Pratt, Larry
1977 "The State and Province-Building: Alberta's Development Strategy." In *The Canadian State: Political Economy and Political Power*, edited by Leo Panitch, pp. 133—62. Toronto: University of Toronto Press.

Presthus, Robert
1973 *Elite Accommodation in Canadian Politics.* London: Cambridge University Press.

Quebec, Assemblée nationale du Québec
1977 *Bill 101.* Charter of the French Language. Assented to 26 August 1977. Quebec: Éditeur officiel du Québec.

Quebec, Commission d'enquête sur la situation de la langue française et sur les droits linguistiques au Québec (Commission Gendron)
1972 *La situation de la langue française au Québec: rapport.* Livre 1, *La langue de travail: la situation du français dans les activités de travail et de consommation des Québécois.* Quebec: Éditeur officiel du Québec.

Racine, Luc, and Denis, Roch
1970 "La conjoncture politique depuis 1960." *Socialisme québécois* 21−22: 17−78.

Raynauld, André
1961 *Croissance et structure économiques de la province de Québec.* Quebec: Ministère de l'Industrie et du Commerce.
1973 "The Quebec Economy: A General Assessment." In *Quebec Society and Politics: Views From the Inside*, edited by Dale Thompson, pp. 139−154. Toronto: McClelland and Stewart.
1974 *La propriété des entreprises au Québec: les années 60.* Montreal: Les Presses de l'Université de Montréal.

Raynauld, André; Marion, Gérald; and Béland, Richard
1975 "Structural Aspects of Differences in Income Between Anglophones and Francophones: A Reply." *Canadian Review of Sociology and Anthropology* 12: 221−27.

Rea, J.E.
1976 "My Main Line Is the Kiddies . . . Make Them Good Christians and Good Canadians, Which Is the Same Thing." In *Identities: The Impact of Ethnicity on Canadian Society*, edited by Wsevolod Isajiw, pp. 3−11. Toronto: Peter Martin Associates.

Reitz, Jeffrey G.
1975 "Trends in Occupational Inequality Among Ethnic Groups in Canada, 1961−1971." Unpublished. Toronto: University of Toronto, Department of Sociology.

Richard, Madeline A., and Campbell, Douglas F.
1978 "The Differential Effects of Religion and the Cultural Setting on Ethnic Intermarriage in Toronto and Montreal, 1971." Paper read at Population Association of America Annual Meeting, Atlanta, Ga., 14 April. Mimeographed.

Richmond, Anthony H.
1967 *Post-War Immigrants in Canada.* Toronto: University of Toronto Press.

Riker, William Harrison
1964 *Federalism: Origin, Operation, Significance.* Boston: Little, Brown & Co.

Roseborough, Howard, and Breton, Raymond
1968 "Perceptions of the Relative Economic and Political Advantages of Ethnic Groups in Canada." In *Canadian Society*, 3d ed., edited by Bernard R. Blishen et al., pp. 604−28. Toronto: Macmillan Co. of Canada.

Rothbart, Myron
1970 "Assessing the Likelihood of a Threatening Event: English Canadians' Evaluation of the Quebec Separatist Movement." *Journal of Personality and Social Psychology* 15: 109−117.

Ryerson, Stanley B.
1972 "Quebec: Concepts of Class and Nation." In *Capitalism and the National Question in Canada*, edited by Gary Teeple, pp. 211-28. Toronto: University of Toronto Press.
Safarian, A.E.
1974 *Canadian Federalism and Economic Integration*. Constitutional Study Prepared for the Government of Canada. Ottawa: Information Canada.
Sales, Arnaud
1976 "Les industriels au Québec et leur rôle dans le développement économique: rapport préliminaire de recherche." Groupe de recherche sur les élites industrielles du Québec. Montreal: Éditeur officiel du Québec.
1977 "La question linguistique et les directions d'entreprises." *Le Devoir*, 27-29 April.
Salisbury, Robert H.
1968 "The Analysis of Public Policy: A Search for Theories and Roles." In *Political Science and Public Policy*, edited by Austin Ranney, pp. 151-175. Chicago, Ill.: Markham Publishing Co.
Sauvé, Maurice
1976 "Les Canadiens-français et la direction des entreprises au Québec." Mimeographed. Montreal: École des Hautes études commerciales.
Schwartz, Mildred A.
1967 *Public Opinion and Canadian Identity*. Scarborough, Ont.: Fitzhenry and Whiteside.
1974 *Politics and Territory: The Sociology of Regional Persistence in Canada*. Montreal: McGill-Queen's University Press.
Shoup, Carl S.
1977 "Interregional Economic Barriers: The Canadian Provinces." In *Intergovernmental Relations*, edited by Ontario Economic Council, pp. 81-100. Toronto: Ontario Economic Council.
Simeon, Richard
1972 *Federal-Provincial Diplomacy: The Making of Recent Policy in Canada*. Toronto: University of Toronto Press.
1975 "Regionalism and Canadian Political Institutions." *Queen's Quarterly* 82: 499-511.
1977 "Scenarios for Separation." In *Must Canada Fail?*, edited by Richard Simeon, pp. 189-203. Montreal: McGill-Queen's University Press.
Simeon, Richard, and Elkins, David J.
1974 "Regional Political Cultures in Canada." *Canadian Journal of Political Science* 7: 397-437.

Simmons, James W.
1970*a* "Interprovincial Interaction Patterns in Canada." Mimeographed. Toronto: University of Toronto.
1970*b* "Patterns of Interaction Within Ontario and Quebec." Mimeographed. Toronto: University of Toronto, Centre for Urban and Community Studies.

Simon, Walter B.
1974 "A Sociological Analysis of Multilingualism." In *Sounds Canadian: Languages and Cultures in Multi-Ethnic Society*, edited by Paul Migus, pp. 3–22. Toronto: Peter Martin Associates.

Smiley, Donald V.
1967 *The Canadian Political Nationality*. Toronto: Methuen Publications.
1970 *Constitutional Adaptation and Canadian Federalism Since 1945*. Royal Commission on Bilingualism and Biculturalism, document no. 4. Ottawa: Queen's Printer.
1971 "The Structural Problem of Canadian Federalism." *Canadian Public Administration* 14: 326–43.
1976*a* *Canada in Question, Federalism in the 70s*. 2d ed. Toronto: McGraw-Hill Ryerson.
1976*b* "The Political Context of Resource Development in Canada." In *Natural Resource Revenues: A Test of Federalism*, edited by A.D. Scott. Vancouver: University of British Columbia Press for B.C. Institute for Economic Policy Analysis.

Social Research Group
1965 "A Study of Interethnic Relations in Canada." Unpublished. Montreal: Social Research Group.

Stamp, Robert M.
1970 "Education and the Economic and Social Milieu: The English Canadian Scene From the 1870s to 1914." In *Canadian Education: A History*, edited by J. Donald Wilson, Robert M. Stamp, and Louis-Philippe Audet. Scarborough, Ont.: Prentice-Hall of Canada.

Stein, Michael B.
1968 "Federal Political Systems and Federal Societies." *World Politics* 20: 721–47.

Steiner, Jung
1974 "The Principles of Majority and Proportionality." In *Consociational Democracy: Political Accommodation in Segmented Societies*, edited by Kenneth D. McRae, pp. 98–106. Toronto: McClelland and Stewart.

Stevenson, Garth
1977 "Federalism and the Political Economy of the Canadian State." In *The Canadian State: Political Economy and Political Power*, edited by Leo Panitch, pp. 71–100. Toronto: University of Toronto Press.

Stouffer, S.A.; Suchman, E.A.; DeVinney, L.S.; Star, S.A.; and Williams, Jr., R.M.
  1949 "Adjustment During Army Life." In *The American Soldier*, Studies in Social Psychology in World War II, vol. 1. Princeton, N.J.: Princeton University Press.
Taylor, Donald M., and Gardner, Robert C.
  1970 "Bicultural Communication: A Study of Communicational Efficiency and Person Perception." *Canadian Journal of Behavioural Science* 2: 67–81.
Thériault, Léon
  1977 "Cheminement inverse des Acadiens et des anglophones des Maritimes (1763–1955)." In *Mémoires de la Société royale du Canada*, Fourth Series, vol. 15. Ottawa: Société royale du Canada.
Toronto Star
  1977 *What Quebec Really Wants*. Toronto: *Toronto Star*.
Trebilock, M.J.; Kaiser, G.; and Prichard, R.S.
  1977 "Restrictions on the Interprovincial Mobility of Resources: Goods, Capital and Labour." In *Intergovernmental Relations*, edited by Ontario Economic Council, pp. 101–22. Toronto: Ontario Economic Council.
Tremblay, Rodrigue
  1977 "Le Québec a besoin d'une nouvelle révolution tranquille, mais cette fois de nature économique." *Le Devoir*, 5 August.
Trudeau, Pierre E.
  1965 "Federalism, Nationalism and Reason." In *The Future of Canadian Federalism. L'avenir du fédéralisme canadien*, edited by P.-A. Crépeau and C.B. Macpherson, pp. 16–36. Montreal: Les Presses de l'Université de Montréal.
Trudel, Marcel, and Jain, Geneviève
  1970 *Canadian History Textbooks: A Comparative Study*. Royal Commission on Bilingualism and Biculturalism, document no. 5. Ottawa: Queen's Printer.
Underhill, Frank H.
  1938 "Some Observations Upon Nationalism and Provincialism in Canada." In *Problems in Canadian Unity*, edited by Violet Anderson, pp. 67–78. Toronto: Thomas Nelson & Sons.
Urquhart, M.C., ed., and Buckley, K.A., ass. ed.
  1965 *Historical Statistics of Canada*. Toronto: Macmillan Co. of Canada.
Vaillancourt, François
  1977 "Un aperçu de la situation économique des Anglophones et Francophones du Québec, de 1961 à 1971, et de l'impact possible sur cette situation: du projet de loi 1." Paper presented to the Commission parlementaire étudiant la charte de la langue française au Québec, University of Montreal, Que. Mimeographed.

Vallée, Frank G.
1969 "Regionalism and Ethnicity: The French-Canadian Case." In *Perspectives on Regions and Regionalism and Other Papers. Proceedings of the Tenth Annual Meeting of the Western Association of Sociology and Anthropology*, edited by B.Y. Card, pp. 19–26. Edmonton, Alta.: University of Alberta Printing Services.

Vallée, Frank G., and DeVries, John
1975 "Data Book for Conference on the Individual, Language and Society." Mimeographed. Ottawa: Department of Sociology, Carleton University.

Vallée, Frank G., and Shulman, Norman
1969 "The Viability of French Groupings Outside Quebec." In *Regionalism in the Canadian Community 1867–1967, Canadian Historical Association Centennial Seminars*, edited by Mason Wade, pp. 83–99. Toronto: University of Toronto Press.

Veilleux, Gérard
1971 *Les relations intergouvernementales au Canada, 1867–1967; les mécanismes de coopération*. Montreal: Les Presses de l'Université du Québec.

Veltman, Calvin J.
1976 "Les incidences du revenu sur les transferts linguistiques dans la région métropolitaine de Montréal." *Recherches sociographiques* 17:323–39.

Watts, Ronald L.
1977 "Survival or Disintegration." In *Must Canada Fail?*, edited by Richard Simeon, pp. 42–60. Montreal: McGill-Queen's University Press.

Westhues, Kenneth
1976 "Public vs Sectarian Legitimation: The Separate Schools of the Catholic Church." *Canadian Review of Sociology and Anthropology* 13: 137–51.

White, Graham; Millar, Jack; and Gagné, Wallace
1971 "Political Integration in Quebec During the 1960s." *Canadian Ethnic Studies* 3: 55–84.

Wilkins, Mira
1974 *The Maturing of Multinational Enterprise: American Business Abroad From 1914 to 1970*. Studies in Business History, no. 24. Cambridge, Mass.: Harvard University Press.

Wilson, John
1974 "The Canadian Political Cultures: Towards a Redefinition of the Nature of the Canadian Political System." *Canadian Journal of Political Science* 7: 440–83.

Yeates, Maurice
1975 *Main Street: Windsor to Quebec City*. Toronto: Macmillan Co. of Canada.

Part Four

Immigrants, Their Descendants, and the Cohesion of Canada

by

Jeffrey G. Reitz

Chapter 4.1

Introduction

PRELIMINARY REMARKS

How is the cohesion of Canadian society affected by the fact that over a quarter of its population consists of immigrants and their descendants? Compared to problems posed by French-English relations in Canada, any impact of the so-called "other" ethnic groups on societal cohesion seems insignificant. French-English relations have raised the serious prospect of Quebec separation. By contrast, ethnic groups composed of immigrants and their descendants have launched no secessionist movements. They make no claims to sovereignty over a territory in Canada. Land claims, such as those asserted by the small native population concentrated in remote, but resource-rich, hinterland regions, have no relevance in the "other" ethnic groups.

Ethnic groups formed by immigrants may have more important effects on societal cohesion if that concept is defined more broadly, and not only in terms of continued sovereignty of a central government over territory. Societal cohesion in a general sense refers to the ability of members of society to get along together. In a cohesive society, individuals and groups share a common identity, recognize common leadership, and are able to pursue common goals effectively. Lack of societal cohesion may show itself in many ways. A separatist movement is only one. Chronic conflicts, alienation, withdrawal, and social apathy also reflect lack of cohesion. Such symptoms of social debilitation and malaise—the weakening of the social fabric—may be as costly, ultimately, as political separation. By the same token, preventing separation is not the only way to foster societal cohesion. A group may contribute by encouraging a common identity and basis for co-operation.

Among the various ways in which Canadian cohesion may be affected by the "other" ethnic groups, movements for political separation are probably the least likely. Political sovereignty is not a feasible option for ethnic groups composed of immigrants and their descendants. These groups are dispersed geographically and institutionally throughout Canadian society. Unlike the British, French, and native peoples, they have never constituted autonomous societies or "nations" dominant over a territory within Canada. Instead they exist largely as informal and associational communities established by individual immigrants within the framework of Canadian society dominated by the British and French groups. These ethnic communities do have to varying degrees institutions parallel to those of the British and French. But they are always limited in terms of the number and diversity of the institutions involved, and in terms of their actual or potential political autonomy. They are also limited in their capacity to mount any threat of collective action against other groups. When comparisons are made between various types of ethnic and linguistic groups facing such radically different situations, the use of a broad definition of societal cohesion is particularly important.

How can the impact of the ''other'' ethnic groups on societal cohesion be identified and analysed? What framework is appropriate? In Canada as in other countries where nineteenth and twentieth century immigration has had a major demographic impact, such as the United States and Australia, very general speculations and arguments have been voiced (Fine 1960; Lermer 1955; McKenna 1969; McNaught 1966; Matthews 1965; Royal Commission on Bilingualism and Biculturalism 1970; Wangenheim 1966; Wrong 1955). These discussions have made various claims about overall effects.

One view is that if immigration produces ethnic groups that remain socially isolated, experience little economic mobility, and have cultural patterns clashing with the dominant culture, then these groups undermine societal cohesion because they engage in constant and disruptive conflict with the rest of the society, or else withdraw and remain marginal with little social participation.

A second argument holds that ethnic groups formed by immigrants may actually promote social harmony because ethnic loyalties provide cohesive ties across social classes, regions, or other lines of conflict in society, because ethnic identity satisfies a need for communal feeling in a bureaucratic society, and because cross-cultural communication enriches every group.

Finally, there are those who argue that any positive or negative implication of ethnic heterogeneity for national cohesion is often transitory, since more or less complete assimilation is in store for many groups.

There is probably some truth in all these arguments, depending upon specific circumstances. What is needed, and what the following discussion seeks to provide, is a framework within which relevant social processes can be examined empirically in their implications for specific aspects of societal cohesion.

One feature of this whole issue, which is of particular interest to Canadians, is the position of the ''other'' ethnic groups in the French-English conflict. Again there are alternative views of the impact these groups have on that conflict. Some argue that the main conflict in Canada is linguistic, and that linguistically the ''other'' ethnic groups are disposed toward the anglophone community and have ethnic interests in common only with that community. This precipitates French-English conflict over immigration policy. Within Quebec, it causes an English-French dispute over whether to allow immigrant children to be educated in English rather than French. Elsewhere in Canada, it leads to conflict over whether emphasis on ancestral languages by the "other" ethnic groups has the consequence of displacing efforts to promote French-English bilingualism.

A more sanguine view is that the "other" ethnic groups, as cultural groups, have interests in common with both linguistic communities, reducing the dangers of polarization. The French-English relationship creates a context making ethnic diversity more acceptable, generating an ideology of multiculturalism. In turn cultural diversity, particularly within the anglophone community, helps moderate French-English conflict. At issue here is the complex relation between language and culture, and the relative status of official and "non-official" languages.

The French-English conflict also affects the very context in which the "other" groups find themselves, and the kinds of relationships that they have within Canadian society. To some extent the other groups are a "third party" with their own distinctive interests. A third party may benefit from conflict between the other two. But if it lacks power, it may be ignored by the two other groups if they assign greater priority to their conflict with each other.

The following analysis suggests elements needed for a framework within which to locate concrete issues, evaluate relevant information, and identify significant gaps. The analysis is intended to be tentative rather than definitive. It will stress questions, problems, and political choices, as much as findings and conclusions.

FRAMEWORK FOR ANALYSIS

A tentative framework for analysis can be provided by listing the major dimensions to be taken into account. Each dimension will be reviewed here as an introduction to issues considered to be most important. Some of these are common to analysis of all types of interethnic relations, while others refer specifically to the case of ethnic groups composed of immigrants and their descendants.

First, societal cohesion is seen as varying in two aspects: the degree of legitimacy ascribed to social and political institutions by various groups in the population, and the degree to which members of these groups identify with the national society. For the "other" ethnic groups, as already mentioned, no political structure exists to compete for legitimacy with the Canadian State (as the Quebec government does for the French, and the traditional bands do for native peoples). But the existence of the ethnic community suggests a possible alternative cultural identification. This may make the withdrawal of legitimacy or national identification a more immediate response to difficulties.

Secondly, the analysis will focus on two aspects of interethnic relations potentially affecting societal cohesion: inequality and conflict on the one hand, social contact and communication on the other. Inequality and conflict generate tension, may undermine institutional effectiveness, and lead to the withdrawal of legitimacy. Contact and communication shape the structure of conflict and affect the emergence of a common identity. There is agreement among social scientists that these two types of processes are important to cohesion. But social scientists do not agree on exactly how or why. Whether a given degree of conflict actually threatens institutional functioning and legitimacy is controversial. So, too, is the extent of the need for common cultural values. The analysis must attempt to examine the implications of conflict, accommodation, communication, and isolation for societal cohesion without even hoping to resolve the more general theoretical quandaries.

Most attention should be given to interethnic relationships between the dominant English and French groups and the various other ethnic groups. Relationships among the smaller groups, say between Ukrainians and Jews, may also be important. This is partly because they affect the relation each group has with the dominant groups. One issue here is the extent to which the various smaller groups may act in concert with one another to form a so-called ''third force'' in Canadian politics to balance the English and French groups.

Thirdly, interethnic relationships potentially affecting societal cohesion must be examined at the individual level and at the ethnic community level. Relationships at both levels may affect societal cohesion. Institutional development among ethnic groups composed of immigrants and their descendants is very limited by comparison with that among English, French, and native peoples. Parallel institutions do exist, but they do not encompass a significant proportion of the social lives of a very many of the group members. Thus, in the case of the other ethnic groups, relationships to other groups in Canadian society exist primarily at the individual level. Although each ethnic community as a corporate group has a relationship with other groups in the society, negotiating this relationship is less important to societal cohesion than it is in the case of the English, French, and native peoples. As a matter of fact, one issue is how intergroup relationships at the individual level, as well as intraethnic relationships among various sub-groups, subcultures, social class levels, or factions within an ethnic community, may either intentionally or unintentionally affect organizational strength at the level of the ethnic community itself, with subsequent potential effects on societal cohesion. In other words, group survival itself is a key variable in the case of the ''other'' ethnic groups.

Fourthly, the relationships among ethnic groups should be analysed in the context of other important intergroup relationships in society. These include primarily the linguistic and regional groupings in Canada. Mention has already been made of the implications of linguistic conflict. With respect to region, each of Canada's major regions has its own distinctive ethnic composition. Ethnic groups within each region have specific relationships to one another. How do interethnic relationships within one region affect the relation between that region and the rest of the society? More generally, what is the connection between interethnic relations in various subgroups of the society, and the integration of each subgroup into the total society? To what extent do ethnic, linguistic, regional, and other divisions overlap one another, intensifying conflict and obstructing intergroup communication?

Fifthly, interethnic relations vary from one institutional sphere to another, and each may have its own impact on societal cohesion. Problems in different institutions are interrelated, but each gives rise to somewhat different types of ethnic conflict. The issue of equality of opportunity, and proposals for dealing with it, arise primarily in economic institutions. The issue of the linguistic and cultural status of groups arises primarily in socio-cultural institutions such as educational institutions, the media, religious and various other social organizations. Political institutions are called upon to deal with unresolved problems in other areas. Moreover, federal political institutions control overall immigration and foreign policies of concern to ethnic groups, and are the focus for sentiments of legitimacy and identity. Each set of institutions requires separate consideration.

And sixthly, the analysis must attend to the great variety of ethnic groups in Canadian society. Ethnic groups vary in size, proportion of native born, social class composition, culture, historical experiences, and race. Background characteristics such as these affect the kinds of issues likely to become important in interethnic relations. For example, large and well-established middle-class groups of European origin may be concerned with cultural acceptance and retention, while the smaller non-European groups, both well established and recently arrived, may as often raise the issue of racism and discrimination in economic institutions. A study such as this cannot provide all the pertinent details on all groups or even on all the major groups (for a broad overview, see Royal Commission on Bilingualism and Biculturalism 1970; a wide variety of historical information on specific groups is available). But it would be a mistake to attempt to generalize about the impact that these groups may have on societal cohesion without taking account of at least the most import differences among them.

These six dimensions can be visualized as in figure 4.1.1. Societal cohesion (1) is at the top and all other dimensions are considered in relation to it. Societal cohesion may be affected by aspects of interethnic relationships (2) at both the individual and group levels (3) and by other intergroup relationships (4) in which they are embedded. Any of these relationships may differ from one institutional sphere to another (5). And finally each dimension is affected by the characteristics of the groups involved (6).

Linkages among all dimensions are possible. For example, inequalities experienced by individuals of a particular ethnic origin may reinforce

FIGURE 4.1.1
Dimensions of the Problem

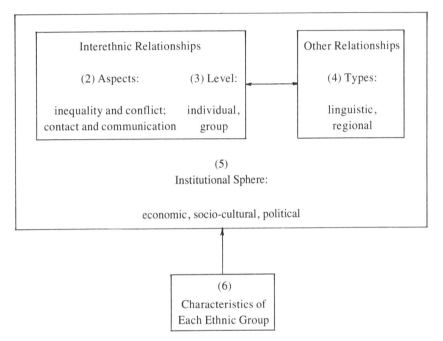

ethnic-group boundaries (2→3); intergroup contact and communication thereby may be reduced (3→2); attention may shift toward these inequalities and away from other problems such as regional conflict (2 and 3→4); economic inequalities among ethnic groups may lead to inequalities of cultural or political status (5→2→5); and so on. Such linkages are important in identifying complex effects on societal cohesion.

These six dimensions will be incorporated in the discussion as follows. Throughout the discussion the focus is on societal cohesion (1). Chapter 4.2 will present an overview of the main background characteristics of the various "other" ethnic groups in Canadian society (6), and describe their interethnic relationships within each linguistic group and region, and their patterns of ethnic community formation and survival (2, 3, 4). Chapters 4.3, 4.4, and 4.5 will discuss problems in ecomonic, socio-cultural, and political institutions (adding 5). In chapter 4.6 some additional empirical data bearing on overall interethnic cohesion will be examined (1). Finally, chapter 4.7 will draw conclusions and attempt to highlight some of the choices relevant to cohesion facing Canadians today.

Immigration and Interethnic Relationships in Canada

The impact of ethnic groups composed of immigrants and their descendants on societal cohesion depends very much on the background characteristics of each group and their relationships to other groups in Canadian society. This chapter presents an overview of Canadian immigration history. It then describes three aspects of intergroup relations identified earlier as relevant to societal cohesion: the distribution of ethnic groups across the two linguistic communities and various regions of Canada; their relationships with the dominant British and French groups; and their own patterns of intragroup organization and communal life. As these aspects are described, possible implications for societal cohesion can be suggested. It will become apparent that while each aspect has been studied in Canada, the impact on national identity and political legitimacy cannot always be assessed by using existing research.

IMMIGRATION AND ETHNIC GROUP BACKGROUND CHARACTERISTICS

Each of the more than fifty ethnic groups arising from immigration has its own unique configuration of characteristics. These include patterns of immigration and settlement in various regions of the country, the proportion who are now native-born Canadians, the economic and other resources of the group, its culture (language, religion, general social values, and historical experience), and its racial character. These ''raw materials,'' considered in relation to the characteristics of Canadian society, shape experiences and opportunities in Canada. Each group is different. Its place in the overall Canadian situation should be considered separately. The collective impact of all the groups is important too, as well as the consequences of the ethnic ''mix'' as created in Canadian society as a whole and as it varies from region to region.

Canadian immigration policy was, and is, part of a broader government strategy of nation building. Immigration was planned to meet manpower requirements of business and to populate vast areas of arable land in the Canadian West. Workers were needed to clear and cultivate the land, build railways and roads, extract resources, and build cities. Canadian immigration policy is one of pragmatic and managed responses to economic needs and goals.

> Canadian immigration history can be read as a series of pragmatic reactions to relatively short-term interests and pressures, influenced by the emergence of the concept of Canada's "absorptive capacity" for immigrants at any given time (Department of Manpower and Immigration 1974, p. 2).

Canada has required a steady flow of immigrants since Confederation in 1867.

Immigration flow into Canada as a percentage of the total population over the period between 1851 and 1971 is shown in table 4.2.1. Immigration was most salient during the 1850s, 1880s, the first thirty years of this century, and the period since the Second World War. These were years of greatest economic expansion in Canada. The 1880s saw construction of the Canadian Pacific Railway and the opening of the West. The present century began with an overall economic recovery and renewed agricultural development. The post-World War II period has been a period of economic expansion and increasingly urban development.

Immigration policy has pursued economic objectives, but was also influenced by social and political pressures. Selection procedures have been highly sensitive to culture and race, particularly in the early years. Preference was given to immigrants most like the native Canadian population. This in

TABLE 4.2.1

TOTAL DECADE IMMIGRATION AS PERCENTAGE OF AVERAGE POPULATION CANADA, 1851–1861 TO 1961–1971

Intercensal Decade	Decade Immigration as Percentage of Average Population	Average Population[a]
1851–1861	12.3	2,832,965
1861–1871	7.5	3,459,445
1871–1881	8.7	4,007,034
1881–1891	14.9	4,579,024
1891–1901	4.9	5,102,227
1901–1911	24.6	6,288,979
1911–1921	17.5	7,997,296
1921–1931	12.5	9,582,367
1931–1941	1.4	10,941,720
1941–1951	4.4	12,577,334[b]
1951–1961	9.6	16,123,838[c]
1961–1971	7.2	19,903,279[c]

SOURCE: Kalbach and McVey (1979), p. 46.
NOTES: a. Arithmetic mean of the two successive census populations.
    b. Excludes Newfoundland in 1951.
    c. Includes Newfoundland in 1951 and 1961.

turn influenced the ethnic composition of Canadian society. A policy report in 1910 announced that

> the policy of the Department [of Interior, responsible for immigration] at the present time is to encourage the immigration of farmers, farm labourers, and female domestic servants from the United States, the British Isles, and certain Northern European countries, namely, France, Belgium, Holland, Switzerland, Germany, Denmark, Norway, Sweden and Iceland (ibid., p. 9).

This report also indicated the government intention to do "all in its power to keep out of the country undesirables" including "those belonging to nationalities unlikely to assimilate and who consequently prevent the building up of a united nation of people of similar customs and ideals" (ibid., p. 10). Exclusion of non-whites was most blatant in policies adopted toward Asian immigrants. Cheap Chinese labourers were used in western railway construction and mining as a purely pragmatic convenience. When these labourers were no longer needed, strong pressure was exerted to restrict and then end Asian immigration. Government policy reflected the view that too much ethnic diversity poses a threat to societal cohesion. Quebec tended to oppose all immigration as being advantageous only to the anglophone community (ibid., p. 2).

In the World War II period, immigration policy still was highly selective in terms of race and culture (Hawkins 1972). Efforts to preserve Canadian cultural uniformity continued. "British and American immigrants were the most favoured. Northern Europeans were relatively well received. Other Europeans were accepted if no one else was available. Non-whites were not welcome" (Department of Manpower and Immigration 1974, p. 17). Too much Asian immigration, in the official view, "would be certain to give rise to social and economic problems of a character that might lead to serious difficulties in the field of international relations" (ibid., p. 19). In 1955, the minister of Citizenship and Immigration, J.W. Pickersgill, stated that too many immigrants from the wrong sources would cause "a problem within Canada." Speaking of the sizeable numbers coming from Italy at the time, he went on to say that: "We want those Italians who come to be Canadians, and to be welcome and to fit into our society, and only so many can come from any country and fit in and be welcomed into our society at any one time" (Parai 1975, p. 453). During this period, restrictions based on country of birth, employability, and family connection severely curtailed immigration by non-whites or by those whose culture was seen as quite different from native Canadian culture.

Liberalization of immigration policy began seriously in the 1960s (ibid.). New regulations in effect by February 1962 greatly de-emphasized nationality as a criterion of selection and gave more importance to employability. In 1967, these new regulations were formalized in a "points" system summarized in table 4.2.2.[1] The sponsorship rule, under which "points" are not required, allowed all residents of Canada to sponsor their spouses, parents, grandparents, fiancés, and unmarried children under twenty-one years of age, regardless of nationality. Canadian citizens could sponsor their children of any age or fiancés, again regardless of their nationality. The 1962 regulations did much toward replacing previous racial, ethnic, and geographic discrimination. They stressed educational and occupational qualifications, which can be assessed objectively. Table 4.2.2 shows that under the points system, half of total assessment units are applied to satisfy manpower needs of the economy.

TABLE 4.2.2
UNITS OF ASSESSMENT, CANADIAN IMMIGRATION REGULATIONS, 1967

	MAXIMUM ASSESSMENT UNITS	
FACTORS	Economic[a]	Socio-economic
1. Education and training	8	12
2. Personal assessment by the immigration officer		15
3. Occupational demand[b]	15	
4. Occupational skill[b]	10	
5. Age		10
6. Arranged employment (or designated occupation)[c]	10	
7. Knowledge of English and French		10
8. Relative in Canada		5
9. Employment opportunities in the area of destination	5	
Total	48	52

SOURCE: Parai (1975), p. 458.
NOTES: a. Assessment units are distinguished here as to whether factor is essentially and clearly economic or whether other socio-aspects are also involved. In the case of education and training, only those years beyond high school are shown as being essentially economic in nature; for simplicity, assessment by immigration officer has been assigned to socio-economic column.
b. In event that an applicant intends to establish a business or retire in Canada, he/she may be given credit of twenty-five units instead of being assessed under factors (3) and (4) above, provided that he/she has sufficient financial resources to so establish him/herself and that immigration officer is satisfied that proposed business has reasonable chance of being successful.
c. Introduced in February 1974, this factor recognizes that an occupation in which workers are particularly in short supply is almost certain to provide employment to a worker qualified in that occupation. Provided jobs in question offer continuous employment, and accepted standards of wages and working conditions, occupations in which shortages exist in a particular location may be "designated" by minister of Manpower and Immigration. Applicant qualified in such an occupation, destined to an area of certified shortage, and able to meet required licensing or regulatory requirements receives ten units.

[1] Independent applicants need fifty points, nominated relatives need twenty or thirty points from the first five factors, and sponsored applicants need no points, as long as they are not excluded for reasons of poor health, criminal involvement, or subversive activity.

Not all discriminatory features have been eliminated from selection policies, however. When weight is given to language and formal education, there are inherent cultural biases. Moreover, the system provides for a ''personal assessment'' by the immigration officer. Finally, although Canadian immigration offices are now more numerous in countries all around the world, they are still most numerous in Britain, northern Europe, and the United States, thus paving the way for prospective immigrants from those areas.

Throughout the history of Canadian immigration, there has been a steady increase in the ethnic and cultural diversity of the population. Table 4.2.3 shows the steady increase in the proportion of the non-British and non-French component of the population to a total of 26.7% in 1971. Furthermore the so-called third element itself has become progressively more diverse, as shown in figure 4.2.1 and table 4.2.4. Prior to 1901, the ''other'' ethnic groups included primarily Northern Europeans (the highly visible Chinese group was numerically quite small). By the end of the first three decades of the twentieth century, East Europeans (Ukrainians and Poles) and Jews were present in large numbers, and there were smaller, though significant, numbers of Russians and Italians. The post-war immigration wave has been by far the most diverse, with all groups represented, and the Italian group far more significant than before.

TABLE 4.2.3
POPULATION OF BRITISH ISLES, FRENCH, AND OTHER ORIGINS
CANADA, 1871, 1881, AND 1901–1971

Ethnic Origin	1871[a]	1881	1901	1911	1921	1931	1941	1951	1961	1971
					($\times 1,000$)[b]					
British Isles	2,111	2,549	3,063	3,999	4,869	5,831	5,716	6,710	7,997	9,624
English	706	881	1,261	1,871	2,545	2,741	2,968	3,630	4,195	6,246
Irish	846	957	989	1,075	1,108	1,231	1,268	1,440	1,753	1,581
Scottish	550	700	800	1,027	1,174	1,346	1,404	1,547	1,902	1,720
Other	8	10	13	26	42	62	76	92	146	86
French	1,083	1,299	1,649	2,062	2,453	2,928	3,483	4,319	5,540	6,180
Other	292	477	659	1,146	1,466	2,068	2,308	2,981	4,702	5,764
Total	3,486	4,325	5,371	7,207	8,788	10,377	11,507	14,009	18,238	21,568
					(%)					
British Isles	60.6	58.9	57.0	55.5	55.4	51.9	49.7	47.9	43.8	44.6
English	20.3	20.4	23.5	26.0	29.0	26.4	25.8	25.9	23.0	29.0
Irish	24.3	22.1	18.4	14.9	12.6	11.9	11.0	10.3	9.6	7.3
Scottish	15.8	16.2	14.9	14.2	13.4	13.0	12.2	11.0	10.4	8.0
Other	0.2	0.2	0.2	0.4	0.5	0.6	0.7	0.7	0.8	0.4
French	31.1	30.0	30.7	28.6	27.9	28.2	30.3	30.8	30.4	28.6
Other	8.4	11.0	12.2	15.9	16.7	19.9	20.0	21.2	25.8	26.7
Total	100.0	100.0	100.0	100.0	100.0	100.0	100.0	100.0	100.0	100.0

SOURCE: Kalbach and McVey (1979), p. 195
NOTES: a. Four original provinces only.
b. Due to rounding of figures, totals do not always correspond to sum of parts.
c. Exclusive of Newfoundland prior to 1951.

TABLE 4.2.4

POPULATION BY ETHNIC ORIGINS OTHER THAN BRITISH ISLES AND FRENCH,
CANADA, 1871, 1881, AND 1901–1971

Ethnic Group	1871	1881	1901	1911	1921	1931	1941	1951	1961	1971
					(×1,000)					
Other European	240	299	458	945	1,247	1,825	2,044	2,554	4,117	4,960
Austrian, n.o.s.	—	—	11	44	108	49	38	32	107	42
Belgian	—	—	3	10	20	28	30	35	61	51
Czechoslovak	—	—	—	—	9	30	43	64	73	82
Finnish[a]	—	—	3	16	21	44	42	44	59	59
German	203	254	311	403	295	474	465	620	1,050	1,317
Greek	—	—	—	4	6	9	12	14	56	124
Hungarian[b]	—	—	2	12	13	41	55	60	126	132
Italian	1	2	11	46	67	98	113	152	450	731
Jewish	—	1	16	76	126	157	170	182	173	297
Lithuanian	—	—	—	—	2	6	8	16	28	25
Netherlands	30	30	34	56	118	149	213	264	430	426
Polish	—	—	6	34	53	146	167	220	324	316
Roumanian[c]	—	—	—	6	13	29	25	24	44	27
Russian[d]	1	1	20	44	100	88	84	91	119	64
Scandinavian	2	5	31	113	167	228	245	283	387	385
Ukrainian	—	—	6	75	107	225	306	395	473	581
Yugoslavic	—	—	—	—	4	16	21	21	69	105
Other	4	6	5	7	18	9	10	36	88	195
Asiatic	—	4	24	43	66	85	74	73	122	286
Chinese	—	4	17	28	40	47	35	33	58	119
Japanese	—	—	5	9	16	23	23	22	29	37
Other	—	—	2	6	10	15	16	19	34	129
Other	52	174	177	158	153	158	190	354	463	519

SOURCE: Kalbach and McVey (1979), pp. 198–99.
NOTES: a. Includes Estonian prior to 1951.
     b. Includes Lithuanian and Moravian in 1901 and 1911.
     c. Includes Bulgarian in 1901 and 1911.
     d. Includes Finnish and Polish in 1871 and 1881.

Revised immigration regulations of the 1960s produced a substantially increased flow of immigrants from Asia, the West Indies, Africa, and Central and South America. Blacks and Asians have been in Canada for generations. Best known of the long-established communities are the black community in Nova Scotia, dating from the seventeenth century, and the Chinese community in Vancouver, dating from the nineteenth century. But since the early 1960s, the number of Blacks and Asians has swelled considerably. Census data do not distinguish racial groups and in any case are not collected frequently enough to keep up with the rapidly changing situation. Table 4.2.5 shows the shift toward non-white immigration to Canada by 1968, and particularly by 1973. By 1968, Hong Kong had become the first non-European country (other than the United States) to be among the top ten sources of immigrants. By 1973, Jamaica, India, and Trinidad were also among the top ten. Estimates of the number of Blacks and members of other non-white groups now residing in Canada vary widely. In cities such as

FIGURE 4.2.1
Population Trends, Selected Ethnic Origins, Canada, 1901–1971

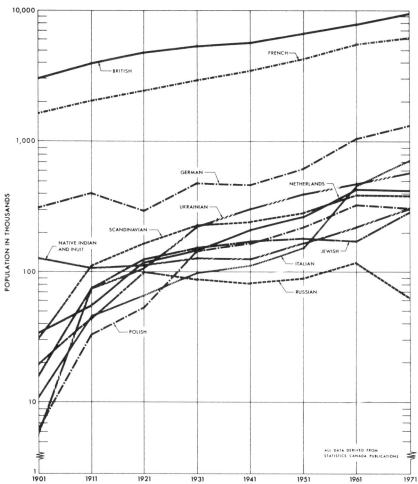

SOURCE: Kalbach and McVey (1979), p. 197.

Toronto, estimates of the number of Blacks today range from 50,000 to 200,000.

Various patterns of immigration over time imply group differences in the proportion of Canadian-born today. In groups having significant immigration before World War I, including Germans, Scandinavians, and Ukrainians, the proportions of Canadian-born are highest. Among other groups, such as Jews, Poles, and Dutch, there are somewhat higher proportions of immigrants today. The proportions of immigrants are highest among new groups, such as the Portuguese, Greeks, West Indians, and other groups concentrated in Toronto and Montreal, and among long-established groups,

TABLE 4.2.5
TEN LEADING SOURCE COUNTRIES OF IMMIGRANTS FOR SELECTED YEARS

1951	1960	1968	1973
Britain	Italy	Britain	Britain
Germany	Britain	United States	United States
Italy	United States	Italy	Hong Kong
Netherlands	Germany	Germany	Portugal
Poland	Netherlands	Hong Kong	Jamaica
France	Portugal	France	India
United States	Greece	Austria	Philippines
Belgium	France	Greece	Greece
Yugoslavia	Poland	Portugal	Italy
Denmark	Austria	Yugoslavia	Trinidad

SOURCE: Kalbach and McVey (1979), p. 49.

such as the Chinese and Italians, which have increased immigration very substantially in recent years. (The Chinese group also is affected by earlier efforts to keep the male-female ratio high.)

Immigrants often differ from their descendants in their orientations toward Canada and the ethnic homeland, and these differences can produce conflict both within and between groups. Generational conflict within families is a special instance of intragroup conflict. Conflicts among groups can arise if some groups are preoccupied with problems of immigrant adaptation, while others become concerned with cultural recognition and long-term cultural survival.

Economic and social resources possessed by immigrants upon arrival in Canada, including levels of education, knowledge of English (or for those going to Quebec, French), occupation experience, financial security, organizational skills, and so on, are very important in determining ''entrance status'' and the general relation between the ethnic group and other groups in Canadian society. There are variations both within and between groups in this respect, as well as major changes over time. These complex patterns are crucial to an understanding of the position occupied by each group today.

Early North and East European immigrants, destined to the agricultural sector of the Canadian economy, were very often of peasant background with little formal education. Subsequent waves of immigrants from these countries were more highly educated and tended to settle in urban areas.

Italian immigrants, both the pre-war group and the much larger post-war group, were relatively uneducated and obtained jobs as manual labourers through community contacts in the major cities. Their ''entrance status'' was as a fairly sizeable group near the bottom of the occupational hierarchy. The situation of recent Greek and Portuguese immigrants is similar.

Chinese immigrants in the past, including those employed as railway construction labourers, tended also to be uneducated. But the more recent flow from Hong Kong has a very high average educational level and occupies a relatively high position on the job status ladder. Similarly, immigrants from the West Indies appear to be divided into two groups: a professional or semi-professional class educated in British schools and able to secure relatively high status jobs, and an uneducated lower class of urban or rural origin. Many women in this latter group have come to Canada to obtain jobs as domestics.

The enormous diversity among and within the ethnic groups arising from immigration has the consequence that these groups have little capacity for collective action as a cohesive third force in Canadian society. The various groups do have some interests in common, and they may benefit in some ways from being regarded as a cohesive third force; but their very different immigration histories, regions of settlement, economic position, culture, and racial character separate them from one another, perhaps as much as they are separated from the dominant British and French groups. Place of origin, recency of immigration, social-class position, and cultural orientation also vary within, as well as among, groups. This internal diversity reduces the degree of common interest and capacity for collective action of each separate group.

LINGUISTIC AND REGIONAL LOCATION

Members of the other ethnic groups are not represented equally within the two major linguistic communities, nor are they evenly distributed across the regions of Canada. Instead, linguistic and regional boundaries overlap to a significant degree with ethnic-origin boundaries. Linguistic and regional conflicts may develop into, or reinforce, ethnic conflicts, and these latter may affect the former.

Immigrants and their descendants are oriented primarily to anglophone society in Canada, principally because of anglophone control over economic opportunity. The anglophone orientation is reflected first in patterns of settlement. Immigrants have been attracted mainly to anglophone areas of Canada. Most have settled outside Quebec and New Brunswick. Within Quebec they have settled mainly in Montreal, where there is a substantial and influential anglophone minority.

The anglophone orientation of immigrants and their descendants is reflected also in the social contact and linguistic assimilation that occurs. The minority groups experience far more contact with English Canadians than with French. English Canadians have more face-to-face contact with members of the ''other'' groups than they do with French Canadians (Social Research Group 1965, p. 235). Language transfer in the small ethnic groups is toward English. Language choice is salient in Montreal—the 1961 Census shows that among the other groups in Montreal, 69.9% of mother tongue shifts were toward English and 30.4% toward French (Commission of Inquiry on the Position of the French Language and on Language Rights in Quebec 1972, pp. 166−7). Of the two most visible "other" groups in Montreal, Jews are much more oriented toward the anglophone community than are Italians. In 1961, 60.9% of Montreal Jews used English only, 0.9% used French only, and 36.2% used English and French. Among Montreal Italians, 13.9% used English only, 27.4% used French only, 34.7% used both English and French, and 24.0% used neither (ibid., pp. 163, 165). This Jewish-Italian difference is explained at least in part by social class stratification among French, English, Jews, and Italians in Montreal. An immigrant group becomes oriented toward the linguistic community most dominant at its own social class level and with which it has more contact. The relative degree of linguistic proximity to English and French may be important, too. It is easier for an Italian to master French than English.

Minority ethnic groups are concentrated in particular regions even within anglophone areas. The regional distribution of ethnic groups is shown in figure 4.2.2 (for 1961) and table 4.2.6 (for 1971). Few members of non-British and non-French groups have settled in any of the Atlantic provinces. They tend to be concentrated in the areas from Ontario westwards. Concentrations are particularly high in the Prairie provinces. In Ontario and British Columbia, about one-third of the population is neither British nor French in origin. In the Prairie provinces of Manitoba, Saskatchewan, and Alberta, the proportion is about one-half.

Each region has a different ethnic composition. In the Prairie provinces, there are large proportions of Germans and Ukrainians. These two groups alone make up about one-quarter of the Prairie population, while making up only 11.9% of the population of British Columbia, and 8.3% of the population of Ontario. Scandinavians, Poles, and Dutch, too, are well represented in the Prairies.

In Ontario the ethnic composition is more diverse. Five groups most significant in the Prairies—Germans, Ukrainians, Scandinavians, Poles, and Dutch—constitute less than half of the non-British and non-French population. Ontario contains more South Europeans (Italians, Greeks, Portuguese) and non-Europeans (Chinese, West Indians, East Indians, Japanese). This reflects to a large extent the greater significance of recent immigration for Ontario. The ethnic composition of British Columbia is also more like that in Ontario—there are more South Europeans (particularly Italians) and non-Europeans (particularly Chinese)—but there is also a larger Scandinavian population.

Urban areas tend to be more ethnically diverse. Greeks, Jews, Portuguese, and Italians have tended to settle almost exclusively in urban areas. But regional differences in ethnic composition affect both urban and rural areas. For example, the ethnic composition of Winnipeg and Edmonton includes heavy representation of Ukrainians and Germans, in comparison

TABLE 4.2.6

PERCENTAGE DISTRIBUTION OF POPULATION BY ETHNIC GROUP, CANADA AND PROVINCES, 1971

Ethnic Group	Canada	Nfld.	P.E.I.	N.S.	N.B.	Que.	Ont.	Man.	Sask.	Alta.	B.C.	Yuk.	N.W.T.
British Isles	44.6	93.8	82.7	77.5	57.6	10.6	59.4	41.9	42.1	46.8	57.9	48.7	25.2
French	28.6	3.0	13.7	10.2	37.0	79.0	9.6	8.8	6.1	5.8	4.4	6.7	6.5
Other	26.7	3.3	3.6	12.3	5.3	10.4	31.0	49.3	51.8	47.4	37.7	44.6	68.3
Other European	23.0	1.3	2.8	9.9	3.7	8.8	27.6	42.7	45.8	41.6	30.1	27.5	12.9
German	6.1	0.5	0.9	5.2	1.3	0.9	6.2	12.5	19.4	14.2	9.1	8.5	3.8
Netherland	2.0	0.1	1.1	1.9	0.8	0.2	2.7	3.6	2.1	3.6	3.2	2.8	1.0
Scandinavian	1.8	0.2	0.2	0.5	0.6	0.1	0.8	3.6	6.4	6.0	5.1	5.4	2.6
Polish	1.5	0.1	0.1	0.4	0.1	0.4	1.9	4.3	2.9	2.7	1.4	1.3	0.8
Russian	0.3	0.0	0.0	0.0	0.0	0.1	0.2	0.4	1.1	0.6	1.1	0.4	0.2
Ukrainian	2.7	0.1	0.1	0.3	0.1	0.3	2.1	11.6	9.3	8.3	2.8	3.3	1.8
Italian	3.4	0.1	0.1	0.5	0.2	2.8	6.0	1.1	0.3	1.5	2.5	0.9	0.7
Jewish	1.4	0.1	0.1	0.3	0.2	1.9	1.8	2.0	0.2	0.4	0.6	0.2	0.1
Other	3.9	0.2	0.2	0.8	0.4	2.0	6.1	3.8	4.1	4.1	4.5	4.7	1.9
Asiatic	1.3	0.3	0.3	0.6	0.4	0.7	1.5	1.0	0.8	1.6	3.6	0.8	0.5
Other & not stated	2.4	1.7	0.5	1.8	1.2	1.0	1.9	5.6	5.2	4.2	3.9	16.4	54.9
Total	100.0	100.0	100.0	100.0	100.0	100.0	100.0	100.0	100.0	100.0	100.0	100.0	100.0

SOURCE: Kalbach and McVey (1979), p. 204.

FIGURE 4.2.2
Ethnic Composition of Canadian Population by Province, 1961

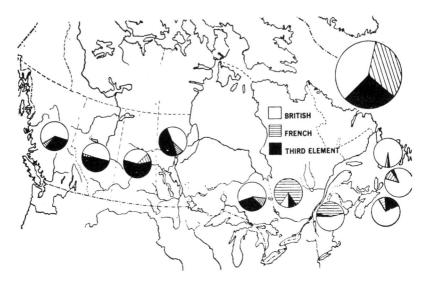

SOURCE: Yuzyk (1973), p. 28.
NOTE: Percentages are as follows:

Province	% in Each Ethnic Group		
	British	French	Other
British Columbia	61	4	35
Alberta	45	6	49
Saskatchewan	40	7	53
Manitoba	43	9	48
Ontario	60	10	30
Quebec	9	81	10
New Brunswick	55	40	5
Nova Scotia	71	12	17
Prince Edward Island	80	17	3
Newfoundland	94	4	2
Canada	44	30	26

with Toronto or Vancouver, reflecting the situation in each province as a whole (O'Bryan, Reitz, and Kuplowska 1976, p. 32).

Within both urban and rural areas, the various "other" ethnic groups display several patterns of residential segregation. Studies by Richmond (1972) in Toronto, and Driedger and Church (1974) in Winnipeg show that at least some members of many groups, particularly South Europeans, Jews, and Chinese, live in ethnically very homogeneous communities. Other non-European groups from South Asia and the West Indies may follow this pattern, though detailed, descriptive studies are not yet available.

The linguistic and regional location of the minority ethnic groups very much affects their relation to Canadian society. The anglophone orientation leads many francophones to see the ''other'' ethnic groups as a cultural threat; it may make British Canadians more tolerant of ethnic diversity. The impact of regional variations is probably complex. The alienation of the West from central Canada often has anti-French overtones. There is a belief that Ontario is preoccupied with its relation to Quebec and gives correspondingly less importance to the other ethnic groups. But there may be an anti-British aspect as well because western Canada is also less British than Ontario. Ontario's non-British and non-French population has interests overlapping with those of parallel groups in the West, but differences are created by the greater recent immigration and the different ethnic composition (South European and non-European as opposed to North European and East European). Issues seen as important by second and third generation Ukrainians and Germans in the West may be different from those important to immigrant Italians, Greeks, Chinese, and West Indian Blacks in Ontario. More generally, regional variations in interethnic relations may be affected not only by the linguistic conflict in Canada, but also by differences among the ''other'' ethnic groups themselves. These and other possible implications are explored further in the next section and in subsequent chapters.

INTERETHNIC RELATIONSHIPS

Interethnic cohesion depends upon the kinds of relationships existing between each particular ethnic group and other groups in society. Two aspects of interethnic relationships are important: the degree of inequality, conflict, and problems of conflict resolution; and the extent of contact and communication providing a basis for an acceptance of a common national identity. Variations across the two linguistic communities and the major regions of Canada should be examined, as these affect societal cohesion.

Ethnic-status inequality. Studies have been done in Canada to show the social status or standing of each ethnic group in the eyes of the two dominant groups. The ethnic status of a minority group reflects majority-group perceptions of cultural similarity, common historical experience, and a sense of familiarity. Ethnic-status inequality experienced by members of a minority group indicates the potential for inequality and conflict within particular institutional settings, and also may reflect to an extent actual inequalities and conflicts. An ethnic group of very low status is likely to encounter prejudice and discrimination; ethnic inequality and conflict are likely to lead to negative ethnic stereotypes and low ethnic status.

The existence of ethnic-status inequality in Canada is beyond doubt. A recent national study by Pineo (1977) reported data on how English and French Canada see the ''social standing'' of a variety of groups (see table 4.2.7). In both linguistic communities, the British and French Canadians

TABLE 4.2.7
HIERARCHY OF ETHNIC AND RACIAL GROUPS IN ENGLISH AND FRENCH CANADA

English Canada (N = 300)		French Canada (N = 93)
English Canadians (83.1)	83	
English (82.4)	82	
British (81.2)	81	
	80	
	79	
	78	
	77	French Canadians, English Canadians
	76	Catholics (77.6)
Protestants (75.3) Scots (75.2)	75	
My own ethnic background (74.4)	74	My own ethnic background (73.7)
	73	
	72	French (72.4)
	71	English (71.0)
Catholics (70.1)	70	
Irish (69.5)	69	
	68	
	67	
	66	British (66.0)
	65	
	64	
	63	
	62	
	61	
French (60.1)	60	
	59	
Dutch (58.4)	58	
Swedes (56.6)	57	Scots (56.5)
French Canadians (56.1) Swiss (55.7)	56	
Norwegians (55.3)	55	Irish (55.2) Protestants (54.8)
	54	
	53	
Danes (52.4)	52	
	51	Italians (51.3)
People of Foreign Ancestry (50.1)	50	Dutch (49.7)
Austrians (49.6) Belgians (49.1)	49	
Germans (48.7) Finns (47.6)	48	
	47	
Jews (46.1) Icelanders (45.6)	46	
	45	Belgians (45.3) Swedes (44.8)
Ukrainians (44.3)	44	Swiss (44.4)
Italians (43.1) Hungarians (42.6)	43	Jews (43.1)
Poles (42.0) Romanians (42.1)	42	
Lithuanians (41.4) Czechoslovaks	41	
(41.2) Greeks (39.9)	40	Germans (40.5) Ukrainians (40.0)
	39	People of Foreign Ancestry (38.9)
	38	Hungarians (38.4) Poles (38.0)
	37	Norwegians (38.0) Austrians (37.5)
Russians (35.8)	36	
Japanese (34.7)	35	
	34	Romanians (33.9) Greeks (33.5)

TABLE 4.2.7 *(Continued)*

English Canada (N = 300)		French Canada (N = 93)
Chinese (33.1)	33	Russians (33.2) Icelanders (32.9)
	32	Canadian Indians (32.5) Czecho-
	31	slovaks (32.4) Finns (32.3)
	30	Danes (32.2)
	29	Lithuanians (29.1)
Canadian Indians (28.3)	28	Japanese (27.8)
	27	Coloureds (26.5)
Coloureds (26.3)	26	
Negroes (25.4)	25	Chinese (24.9) Negroes (23.5)

SOURCE: Pineo (1977), p. 154.
NOTE: Respondents asked to place group names into one of nine ranked categories according to their "social standing." Mean rankings converted to scale of 0 to 100.

have the highest status (although in French Canada, the French Canadians are seen as equal with the English Canadians, while in English Canada, the French Canadians are seen as having significantly lower status). Other Europeans, particularly East and South Europeans, have lower status, and racial minorities (Japanese, Chinese, East Indians, and Blacks) have lowest status.

Similar inequalities were reported in a second national study by Berry, Kalin, and Taylor (1977, pp. 99–108). A somewhat different method was used; members of the sample rated each group on six different evaluative criteria (see table 4.2.8). Only nine groups were evaluated by the entire sample; others were evaluated only by respondents who mentioned them most prominently as groups of which they were aware.[2] Again the British and French were rated most highly, followed in rough order by North Europeans, East Europeans, South Europeans, and non-whites (except that in this study the Japanese received a relatively high evaluation). Again the British and French Canadians evaluated one another more highly than they evaluated any of the other ethnic groups (ibid., p. 113).

The fact that English and French Canadians give higher status to one another than to any of the other ethnic groups is an important one. Its meaning, however, must be carefully interpreted. The low status of the "other" ethnic groups by comparison both to English and French does not mean they are involved in conflicts more serious than the English-French conflict. In some cases, serious inequalities may be accepted as legitimate, at

---

[2] The authors caution: "We cannot place the same degree of confidence in the data derived from the nominated groups as we can from the standard ones. Some respondents may nominate a group because they are particularly attracted to or familiar with that group, others because they dislike the group, and still others because in their geographic region there are many members of that particular group." However, the opposite point could be made that expressions of opinion on the groups most familiar to a respondent are a particularly valuable guide to his overall outlook.

TABLE 4.2.8
MEANS OF EVALUATIONS OF VARIOUS ETHNIC GROUPS

Standard List of Ethnic Groups	Mean	N	Rank	Respondent Nominated Ethnic Groups	Mean	N
English	.52	1801	1			
			2	Scottish	.49	186
French	.47	1786	3			
			4	Dutch	.46	138
			5	Scandinavian	.39	94
			6	Irish	.37	142
			7	Belgian	.35	48
			8	Japanese	.13	111
			9	Hungarian	.10	93
			10	Polish	.08	230
Jewish	.04	1717	11			
German	.02	1716	12			
			13	Czech	.02	47
			14	Russian	−.07	79
			15	Yugoslavian	−.09	54
			16	West Indian	−.11	48
Immigrants in general	−.12	1736	17			
Ukrainian	−.13	1601	18			
Italian	−.20	1719	19			
			20	Portuguese	−.25	112
Chinese	−.26	1736	21			
			22	Spanish	−.31	39
			23	Greek	−.36	127
Canadian Indian	−.46	1786	24			
			25	Negro	−.52	51
			26	East Indian	−.95	102

SOURCE: Berry, Kalin, and Taylor (1977), p. 106.
NOTE: Ratings based on extent to which each group perceived as "hardworking," "important," "Canadian," "clean," "likeable," and "interesting."

least on a temporary basis. At the same time, the small groups lack power and resources to cause a significant struggle. Acceptance of inequality, either with optimism for future change or with resignation in the face of obstacles to change, explains why serious inequalities experienced by some of the "other" ethnic groups may not produce a serious threat to national cohesion.

Status inequalities experienced by the "other" groups are different in each linguistic group in Canada. French Canadians tend to rank the non-English, non-French ethnic groups lower than do English Canadians. In the Pineo study, for example, English Canadians give "people of foreign ancestry" a rating of 50.1, while French Canadians give them a lower rating of only 38.9. Pineo notes that "French Canada is not a nation of new immigrants, and foreign ethnicities are somewhat downgraded" (1977,

p. 155). But the smaller number of new immigrants in French Canada, making them less familiar to French Canadians, is certainly not the only factor. Many French Canadians see their own status relation to English Canadians as problematic. As a consequence, they tend to see the anglophone-oriented small ethnic groups both as an economic threat and in particular as a cultural threat. Cappon (1978) showed that in encounters between French Canadians and Italians, communication focused on the relation of each group to the dominant anglophone group rather than to each other.

There is a general tendency for lower-status groups in a society to feel greater hostility toward minorities. This is sometimes attributed to their lower level of education. However, in the French Canadian case, it is clear that immigrant groups are seen as a threat to the disadvantaged French position. In fact, Cappon's study suggests that among French Canadians themselves, it is the higher-status groups that are most hostile to minority ethnic groups because of their cultural concerns, while the lower-status French Canadians are more tolerant and concerned with the economic position of their group.

Significant regional differences in minority ethnic status were reported by Berry, Kalin, and Taylor (1977, pp. 108−11, 126). "Immigrants in general" were more favourably viewed in Ontario and British Columbia (where they are more numerous) than in the Prairies (where the descendants of immigrants are more numerous) or in the Atlantic provinces (where neither are very numerous), although in each anglophone region they were viewed more favourably than in Quebec. Ukrainians and Germans were viewed more positively in the Prairies and British Columbia; Italians tended to be viewed most positively in Ontario.

The position of non-whites in Canada is receiving increased attention. The very low status of non-whites, and in particular of East Indians and West Indian Blacks, is a matter of serious concern because of the rapid increases in the size of these groups in recent years. As the non-white population in Canada grows, there is increasing evidence of open hostility toward these groups as well as of attempts to minimize, control, or eliminate such hostility. Racist and ethnocentric diatribes against European immigrants of the kind quoted by Porter (1965, pp. 61−68) from early-twentieth-century publications are alien to the current public climate of opinion. This gives rise to hopes that Canada today can give a tolerant welcome to large numbers of non-European immigrants. But the current evidence on status inequality indicates that racism and ethnocentrism are there beneath the surface and are far from dead in Canada today.

An interview study in Toronto by Henry (1978) showed that about one in six white residents was willing openly to express racist views. Canadians of East Indian and Pakistani origins seem to have replaced West Indian Blacks as the primary target. Racist views are more commonly expressed by less well-educated, older, and more religious persons, and by housewives. Among various white ethnic groups, racist views are more commonly expressed by those whose own ethnic status is relatively low, such as South Europeans. These findings parallel those produced in other North Atlantic countries; they warn that Canadian experiences in race relations may be not unlike those in other countries.

One manifestation of racism in Canada is interracial violence in schools, transportation systems, and public places generally. The importance of recent violent interracial incidents reported in the mass media may or may not be exaggerated (Pitman 1977), but they are certainly not "isolated" incidents. They reflect a significant degree of racism in Canadian society as a whole. According to one unpublished study cited by a voluntary organization concerned with race relations, interracial incidents are almost daily occurrences in some Toronto schools.

Implications of ethnic-status inequalities for societal cohesion will be examined in specific institutional contexts before general conclusions are drawn. At this point, two observations can be made. Ethnic status inequality represents a problem for societal cohesion, whether it is openly resisted or passively accepted. Any surface acceptance of major inequalities such as those experienced by Blacks and East Indians ultimately may prove illusory. A second point is that English and French Canadians do differ in the status they assign to the "other" groups, and any analysis of potential contributions by these groups to a reduction of English-French conflict should take account of this fact.

Social contact and communication. Interethnic social isolation tends to be associated with interethnic inequality. Both may affect the emergence of cohesion. The study by Berry, Kalin, and Taylor (1977, p. 126) showed that individuals tend to have greater contact and familiarity with members of groups toward which they have the most favourable attitudes. Thus, low levels of intergroup contact affect primarily the lowest status groups. There is relatively little contact between francophones and members of the "other" ethnic groups, as was mentioned above in the discussion of regional and linguistic location.

In some cases it appears that increased intergroup contact may be one factor leading to improved cohesion. There are examples of the correlation between contact and positive intergroup evaluation also in the regional variations. As mentioned earlier, German and Ukrainian Canadians are most favourably viewed in the West, where they are relatively more numerous and presumably have more contact with Anglo-Saxons. Italians and other immigrant groups are more favourably viewed in Ontario, where again they are most numerous.

But there is no simple relation between increased intergroup contact and greater intergroup cohesion when there are underlying inequalities and conflicts. It was once felt that increased interethnic contact and communication always improved interethnic understanding, and attitudes and relations generally (Allport 1958; Deutsch and Collins 1951). Each side benefited culturally and socially. This, as much as reduced inequality, was a rationale behind the American movement for racial integration in schools, housing, and other areas. But recent American research (Armor 1972) argues that contact may also be the occasion for expressions of pent-up hostility. The context and content of communication is also crucial. Contacts that occur in situations threatening to one group or another may increase, rather than decrease, alienation.

Possible evidence that increased contact may actually threaten cohesion can be seen in data on non-white groups, presented by Berry, Kalin, and Taylor (1977, p. 126).

> If there were a positive relationship between contact and ethnic attitudes we would expect that Canadian Indians would be rated more favourably in the western provinces and the Chinese would be evaluated more positively in British Columbia. The fact that this did not occur systematically indicates that attitudes are specific to certain conditions of contact.

Presumably these "conditions of contact" include inequality and the extent to which the minority group is perceived as posing an economic or cultural threat. Contact between English Canadians and European-origin ethnic groups may lead to greater cohesion because these groups today are integrated locally in ways not threatening to either side. The same may not be true of non-white groups. Means (1969) observes that the degree of discrimination encountered by Asians and Blacks in Canada increases with their size in a particular location. Blacks suffer discrimination more in Nova Scotia and Ontario than in Quebec; Asians suffer discrimination more in British Columbia than in other provinces.

Similarly, increased contact between French Canadians and members of the "other" ethnic groups would not necessarily help reduce tensions by itself; the study by Cappon (1978) illustrates this. Encounters between French Canadians and Italians provided an occasion for expressions of, rather than reductions in, hostility.

The hypothesis that greater cultural differences between an immigrant group and the host society creates greater problems for intergroup contact and communication should be considered also. Whether interethnic communication really is becoming more difficult in Canada because of increased ethnic and cultural diversity is an open question. Some groups, such as Mennonites, Hutterites, and Doukhobors, are so eager to pursue their own very distinct life-styles that they form isolated communities in rural areas. Interaction with the outside society is infrequent and always may be problematic.

In future research on interethnic contact and its effects, attention should be paid to various forms of contact and to different kinds of effects. Contact at work, in neighbourhoods, and in various planned and unplanned contexts may be compared. Instances of cultural cross-fertilization that increase the scope and richness of common culture may be identified. Participation in ethnic festivals and enjoyment of "food from many lands" may be popular, but effects on intergroup relations may be more apparent than real.

At the present time, there is no evidence that English Canadians are either more or less ethnocentric because of their contacts with other groups. As a matter of fact, English conflict with, and isolation from, the French is sometimes cited in Canada as creating a context conducive to greater ethnic tolerance, presumably leading to less inequality and greater societal cohesion. All these speculations deserve more careful study than they have so far received.

ETHNIC COMMUNITY FORMATION AND SURVIVAL

One of the central topics pervading all discussions of ethnic groups composed of immigrants and their descendants concerns the formation of an ethnic community life, and the survival of such communities and their culture over time. Two issues arise here with important implications for societal cohesion.

One issue is created by the argument that assimilation is likely. What assimilation means is still extremely controversial, but it may be defined as a process by which immigrants, or at least their descendants, eventually abandon most significant ties to an ethnic-origin group and become part of the dominant cultural group. Intraethnic cohesion disappears. To the extent that an ethnic group assimilates in this sense, the whole problem of its positive or negative impact on societal cohesion becomes one of passing significance or of significance only so long as immigration continues. The pace of assimilation is relevant, of course; if assimilation takes several generations, then the time involved is a century or more. Any social phenomenon lasting over a century is significant, even if it is a "passing phase."

A second issue concerns the long-term relation between inter- and intraethnic cohesion. Unassimilated ethnic groups may be involved in interethnic relationships favouring societal cohesion, but such relationships ultimately may tend to undermine ethnic cohesion. Conversely, it may be that many types of interethnic relationships that reinforce ethnic cohesion, such as ethnic inequality or lack of interethnic contacts, tend to undermine societal cohesion. Porter (1972) argued that maintenance of ethnic cohesion in Canada is linked to inequality and conflict, with negative implications for the society as a whole. A degree of institutional isolation may be required for the maintenance of language and other aspects of ethnic culture, and such isolation in some cases may inhibit the formation of national identity and the effective functioning of societal institutions. A counter-argument would be that at least some ethnic groups would never accept the legitimacy of institutional arrangements likely to weaken the ethnic community. Attempts to impose assimilation may lead to a breakdown of interethnic cohesion.

Further, conditions supportive of long-term ethnic group survival are not necessarily disruptive, and legitimacy is enhanced when these conditions are provided.

In the context of these two issues, research has examined prevailing patterns of change over time in ethnic group cohesion. Evidence on European-origin groups in Canadian cities shows that over time and from one generation to the next, individual attachments to an ethnic community weaken considerably. Figures 4.2.3 and 4.2.4 show that by the third generation all aspects of group ties become less salient than they were for earlier generations. A sharp decline in the degree of ethnic cohesion over three generations is unmistakable. To be sure, these ties do not disappear entirely. Whether they will do so in the future is a matter for speculation and further study.

Each ethnic group displays a somewhat different pattern. Generally, ethnic groups having experienced the greatest degree of inequality in Canadian society, either in the past or in the present, tend to maintain the strongest group ties. At one extreme, there can be no doubt that among Canadians of North European or Scandinavian origin, ethnic group attachments weaken most rapidly. East and South Europeans seem to maintain stronger ties than North Europeans (Reitz 1980). Comparable evidence on Jews (not included in the data just cited) undoubtedly would show relatively strongly persisting group ties. Non-white groups in Canada for several generations, such as the Blacks in Nova Scotia, have maintained a distinctive community life. These group variations correspond to patterns of ethnic inequality and economic segregation in Canada. Participation in ethnic community life also reduces interethnic contact and communication for most people, at least quantitively. Reduced contact is one of the important reasons why ethnic communities are formed in the first place. Immigrants, particularly those who speak neither of Canada's official languages, frequently must find ways to organize their lives with a minimum of contact with other groups. Once established, such communities do serve to maintain a degree of ethnic isolation.

Specific features of ethnic communities that foster their own survival also tend to reduce contact with outsiders. One of these is residential segregation. Such segregation works two ways; it makes in-group contacts more likely and out-group contacts less likely. Another example is ethnic religious institutions. Membership in an ethnic community church almost automatically excludes comparable contact outside the ethnic community. Even in social spheres where multiple ties are more likely, there is a tendency for increased contacts in one ethnic community to reduce contacts in another. Thus, while it is possible for an individual to extend his network of personal friendships widely both in his own ethnic community and outside as well, research suggests that social pressures make this unlikely. The more deeply involved in an ethnic community, the fewer friendships one has outside the

FIGURE 4.2.3
Language-Related Ethnic Characteristics by Generation

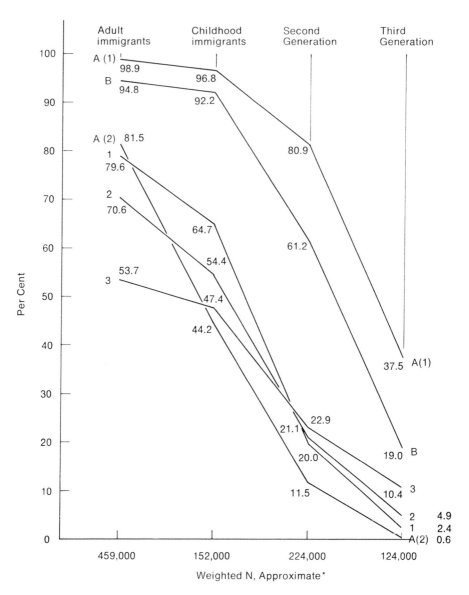

SOURCE: Reitz (1974), p. 112.
NOTES: Italians, Germans, Ukrainians, and Poles are combined.

    * Actual *N*s used to calculate percentages vary as a result of missing data. Total unweighted *N* = 1317.

    A(1): Percentage having at least some knowledge of ethnic language.

    A(2): Percentage fluent in ethnic language.

    B: Percentage whose mother tongue is ethnic language.

    1:   Percentage speaking ethnic language "every day."

    2:   Percentage having read any ethnic newspaper or bulletin written in ethnic language during previous
          year.

    3:   Percentage associated with a church in which ethnic language is used in services.

FIGURE 4.2.4
Other Ethnic Characteristics by Generation

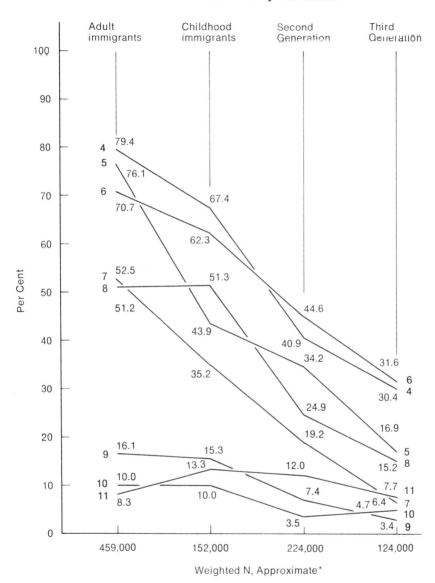

SOURCE: Reitz (1974), p. 113.

NOTES: Italians, Germans, Ukrainians, and Poles are combined.

* Actual *N*s used to calculate percentages vary as a result of missing data. Total unweighted *N* = 1317.

4: Percentage identifying with ethnic label (e.g., Italian, Italian-Canadian, Canadian of Italian origin).

5: Percentage having spouse in ethnic group.

6: Percentage maintaining close ties with ethnic group.

7: Percentage whose three closest friends are all in ethnic group.

8: Percentage associated with a church in which more than half of members are in ethnic group.

9: Percentage living in a neighbourhood in which residents are mostly in ethnic group.

10: Percentage whose main organizational membership (other than religious- or occupation-related organizations) is in organization in which more than half the members are in ethnic group.

11: Percentage having read any ethnic newspaper or bulletin written in English or French during previous year.

community (other things being equal). This is not only because an individual's energies are limited. Tension between groups or personal preferences mean that membership in one group's social circle tends to exclude membership in others. Driedger and Peters (1977) showed in their sample that strong ethnic identification is related to greater sense of ''social distance'' from other groups.

High levels of education in the second immigrant generation is one means to improve social status and at the same time establish contacts outside an ethnic community. But there is a negative effect on the maintenance of ethnic group ties. English-language public schools transmit primarily the culture of the dominant Anglo-Celtic group in Canada; they provide opportunities for the children of immigrants to establish extensive contacts outside their own ethnic community. (In most areas of Canada, residential segregation is not so severe as to create ethnically homogeneous schools in immigrant-group neighbourhoods.) Research evidence (e.g., Borhek 1970) clearly shows that increased years of education result in weaker ethnic identification and community ties. In other words, public educational institutions as they operate in Canada today help integrate individuals into at least one of the linguistic subsocieties of Canada, but at the same time they also tend to draw them away from their own ethnic community. Similar processes may occur in other institutions of the dominant society: the economy, the media, recreational facilities, the military, and so on. These institutions are important in effecting political resocialization, at the same time offering opportunities for upward mobility and increased interethnic contacts. Each specific institutional sector should be examined separately.

These observations support the view that at least some conditions favouring *intra*ethnic cohesion and community survival, namely, ethnic inequality and social isolation, are precisely the same conditions potentially undermining *inter*ethnic cohesion. This means there may be to some extent an inverse relation between ethnic cohesion and interethnic cohesion.

Other social processes may have an opposite effect, however. At least certain forms of ethnic solidarity can be stable while interethnic solidarity is supported. Ethnic solidarity is maintained not simply as a response to past or present inequality and isolation. Upward mobility is often possible within social domains controlled by a minority ethnic community; norms favouring Canadian identity and political legitimacy can be strongly enforced within ethnic community groups and institutions; the ''middle-man minority'' is one pattern in which interethnic contacts are maintained only if intraethnic ties are maintained also; ethnic cohesion fulfils a positive need for communal ties in bureaucratic and technological society.

Ideas along these lines are in the early stages of empirical exploration in Canada. Nagata (1969) observed that in the Greek community, many persons become interested in ethnic organizations only after they have become securely integrated into the host society. Ethnic community organizations in many cases may also function in a way that promotes a form of integration into Canadian society. Richmond (1969) presented data he interpreted this way. He found that immigrants whose native tongue was English were slower to become naturalized citizens. Organizations established in ethnic communities to assist the learning of English may actually promote Canadian society and influence immigrants to develop feelings of loyalty to Canada. Persons having the highest status within the community in many cases may tend to be those who maintain strong ethnic identification, but who are also strongly committed to Canadian society. If these persons become role models, persons who maintain ties to their ethnic community will for that reason become more committed to Canadian society. In a study of Toronto Italians, Neice (1978) suggested that becoming a Canadian citizen is an important step toward becoming accepted by the Italian-Canadian community. These and similar processes should be studied systematically across a number of different small immigrant groups. A comparative study in Canadian cities (Reitz 1980) shows that ''middle-class ethnicity'' itself varies from group to group according to the degree of economic segregation and isolation experienced by the group, either currently or at least in the past.

In short, it can be concluded that at least some of the conditions historically associated with, and supportive of, ethnic solidarity, namely, ethnic inequality and social isolation, pose at least potential problems for societal cohesion. But other conditions in ethnic communities, such as agencies promoting political, economic, or cultural links to other ethnic groups, may favour both intraethnic and interethnic solidarity.

SUMMARY

The purpose of this chapter has been to provide a broad overview of the origins and position of ethnic groups composed of immigrants and their descendants in Canada and to suggest implications for societal cohesion. This overview has stressed several themes.

Firstly, there is enormous diversity among the ''other'' ethnic groups, ranging from well-established multigenerational groups of North-European origin, to East-European groups with comparable immigration histories, to South-European groups dominated by fairly recent immigrants, and to a growing number of non-European groups having most social distance from the dominant cultural groups. This great and increasing diversity has meant that each group holds a somewhat different perspective on Canadian society. Each group experiences a different treatment within specific institutions. Increased ethnic diversity has not had the obvious negative effect on societal cohesion once anticipated. On the other hand, rapid changes are underway, and a complacent attitude toward the future may not be justified. Interracial relations of the future may not parallel interethnic relations of the past.

Secondly, the ''other'' ethnic groups are oriented primarily toward the anglophone community. The ways in which these groups are affected by, or in turn affect, linguistic and regional conflict in Canada are very complex. One hypothesis is that French-English conflict increases tolerance of ethnic cultural variations in the anglophone community, raising the status of the "other" groups. Whether or not this is true, French-English conflict may also raise expectations for cultural retention in the "other" groups, expectations that may not be realized. Thus, whether the French-English conflict reduces ethnic tension *within* the anglophone community is debatable. Similar hypotheses that the presence of the "other" ethnic groups helps reduce French-English conflict are debatable for similar reasons. Anglophones may, or may not, become more tolerant of francophone feelings, but francophones may oppose improved status for the "other" groups. The general pattern of intergroup interaction and the regional isolation of groups to some extent places the British group in the position of intermediary between the small ethnic groups and the French Canadians. This situation presents obstacles to improved understanding between the francophones and the small ethnic groups. Despite much discussion of these matters in Canada, there is little research on which to base conclusions. Comparisons with unilingual societies would be useful.

Thirdly, the weakening of ties to ethnic community groups and institutions over time and through generations tends to be associated with high ethnic status and high intergroup contact. However, the conclusion should not be drawn that ethnic community survival, associated with low status and low intergroup contact, always and necessarily undermines societal cohesion. To some extent, ethnic community institutions themselves may serve as agents promoting Canadian identity and institutional legitimacy. The relations between inequality, ethnic group survival, and governmental legitimacy are sensitive topics that will be discussed further in subsequent chapters.

In the absence of comprehensive research on the impact of the "other" ethnic groups on societal cohesion, it seems advisable to turn to a discussion of aspects of intergroup relations in specific institutions on which information is available. This will provide a necessary context for interpreting general information and formulating tentative conclusions about societal cohesion.

Relationships in Economic Institutions

Economic institutions are a fundamentally important arena of interethnic interaction. Cohesion in economic institutions is affected by the nature of economic exchange relationships (whether they are based on interethnic equality, and if not, the degree of inequality), the way in which these relationships are perceived and evaluated (either as legitimate or illegitimate), the steps taken in response to the situation (individual action, collective action, or no action), and the manner in which any conflicts are managed (affecting perceived legitimacy and the adequate functioning of the institutions). Inequality is the basic issue affecting cohesion, not conflict; without conflict, inequality can affect institutional legitimacy because individuals may be alienated by the feeling that economic institutions are relatively inaccessible to them. Conflict, on the other hand, may be important in generating social cohesion when it is successfully managed.

The issue of ethnic economic inequality has received considerable research attention in Canada. Related issues of response to inequality, and the reasons for such responses and their implications for social cohesion, have been accorded perhaps somewhat less attention in systematic research. Both topics are reviewed here with the intention of drawing conclusions where warranted and identifying gaps in existing information.

ECONOMIC INEQUALITY AMONG ETHNIC GROUPS

Economic inequality among ethnic groups may be described in terms of the position of each ethnic-origin group in the economic hierarchy, and in terms of differential opportunities for mobility to higher levels. Quantitative information exists primarily on the recent situation in Canada. Changes over time since the early twentieth century can be identified in rough qualitative terms. The reasons for inequality are relevant here. A key issue is whether economic mobility is obstructed by efforts to maintain ethnic cohesion. Ethnic representation in the economic élite is important, not only as an indication of mobility in itself, but also of the effects on lower-level mobility of influence at high levels.

Trends in occupational status. The existence of ethnic inequalities of job status and income in Canada is well known. Porter's classic analysis in *The Vertical Mosaic* (1965) showed that Canadian males of British and

Jewish (and, by 1961, Asian) origins tended to be overrepresented in high-status professional and financial occupations (see table 4.3.1). On the other hand, Canadians of Italian, French, and "other European" origins, and native Canadians, tended to be overrepresented in low-status primary and unskilled occupations. Other studies have used different occupational classifications and measures of inequality, but the results differ only in detail. For example, the study by André Raynauld, Gérald Marion, and Richard Béland (Royal Commission on Bilingualism and Biculturalism 1969, pp. 16, 36) showed that the Jews have higher mean-job status than the British; other groups are at the same disadvantaged level as the French, or below (see table 4.3.2).

Porter also analysed trends over the period 1931 to 1961. He concluded that the relative positions of ethnic groups changed very little (1965, p. 86). Jews and Asians improved their position at the higher levels to a greater extent than other groups; Italians and native Canadians became more underrepresented.

Ethnic inequality in jobs has declined in the more recent past. A comparison of data from the 1961 and 1971 censuses (see table 4.3.3) shows that the overall occupational distribution for each ethnic origin group became more like the national average (this holds for British, French, and native peoples, as well as for other ethnic groups). The only significant exception is the Asians, whose position jumped to a relatively higher level. Overall, this more recent analysis shows a clear and substantial trend toward reduced ethnic inequality.

The economic position of each group as it changes over time is affected by continuing patterns of immigration and by opportunities for economic mobility. First, let us consider immigration trends. Recent immigrants to Canada have a significantly better position than immigrants arriving before World War II (Kalbach 1970). The economic situation in Canada has improved dramatically since World War II, and immigrants have been more carefully selected to meet demands in the Canadian labour market. The slowly improving position of some ethnic groups may be due in part to such changes in immigration patterns. The vastly improved position of Asians is certainly attributable in part to the very high education and occupational qualifications of Asian immigrants in the 1960s and 1970s.

The economic situation of recently arrived racial minorities has yet to be studied systematically. The Canadian black population comes from many sources. Many black immigrants in Canada are highly educated. However, the average level of job status appears to be below that in any of the white groups. The overall position of East Indian and Pakistani groups may be similar.

Inequality of job opportunity. Inequality of opportunity is the critical issue. It was one of Porter's hypotheses in *The Vertical Mosaic* that ethnic groups in Canadian society maintain "entrance status" over time, and that

TABLE 4.3.1

ETHNIC ORIGIN AND OCCUPATIONAL CLASSES, MALE LABOUR FORCE, CANADA, 1931, 1951, AND 1961

PERCENTAGE OF OVERREPRESENTATION IN OCCUPATION BY ETHNIC GROUP

	British Total	British English	British Irish	British Scottish	French	German	Italian	Jewish	Dutch	Scandinavian	East European	Other European	Asian	Indian and Eskimo	Total Male Labour Force
1931															
Professional and financial	+1.6	+1.6	+1.0	+2.2	−.8	−2.2	−3.3	+2.2	−1.1	−2.9	−3.9	−4.4	−4.3	−4.5	4.8
Clerical	+1.5	+1.8	+1.0	+1.4	−.8	−2.2	−2.5	+.1	−1.9	−2.7	−3.4	−3.5	−3.2	−3.7	3.8
Personal service	−.3	0.0	−.5	−.7	−.3	−1.2	+2.1	−1.2	−1.5	−1.5	−1.1	−1.7	+27.8	−3.1	3.5
Primary and unskilled	−4.6	−4.4	−4.9	−4.8	+3.3	−5.3	+26.1	−14.5	−4.8	+1.4	+12.4	+35.8	+10.2	+45.3	17.7
Agriculture	−3.0	−6.1	+2.7	−1.5	+.1	+21.1	−27.6	−32.4	+18.5	+19.8	+14.5	−5.8	−20.9	−4.9	34.0
All others	+4.8	+7.1	+.7	+3.4	−1.5	−10.2	+5.2	+45.8	−9.2	−14.1	−18.5	−20.4	−9.6	−29.1	36.2
Total	0.0	0.0	0.0	0.0	0.0	0.0	0.0	0.0	0.0	0.0	0.0	0.0	0.0	0.0	100.0
1951															
Professional and financial	+1.6	+1.0	+.9	+2.5	−1.5	−2.2	−3.1	+4.2	−1.7	−2.1	−2.9	−2.4	−2.8	−5.2	5.9
Clerical	+1.6	+1.8	+1.3	+1.4	−.8	−2.5	−1.7	0.0	−2.4	−2.8	−2.8	−2.5	−2.9	−5.2	5.9
Personal service	−.3	−.2	−.4	−.5	−.2	−1.2	+2.0	−1.4	−1.2	−1.0	+.6	+2.0	+23.9	−.6	3.4
Primary and unskilled	−2.2	−1.7	−2.2	−3.2	+3.0	−3.7	+9.6	−11.5	−1.7	+.5	+2.3	+5.7	−1.9	+47.0	13.3
Agriculture	−3.2	−5.5	+.5	−1.6	−.3	+19.1	−14.7	−18.7	+17.3	+14.7	+11.2	+3.4	−8.7	−7.8	19.4
All others	2.5	+4.0	−.1	+1.4	−.2	−9.5	+7.9	+27.4	−10.3	−9.3	−8.4	−6.2	−7.6	−28.2	52.1
Total	0.0	0.0	0.0	0.0	0.0	0.0	0.0	0.0	0.0	0.0	0.0	0.0	0.0	0.0	100.0
1961															
Professional and financial	+2.0	—	—	—	−1.9	−1.8	−5.2	+7.4	−.9	−1.9	−1.2	−1.1	+1.7	−7.5	8.6
Clerical	+1.3	—	—	—	−.2	−1.8	−3.2	−.1	−1.7	−2.4	−1.7	−2.0	−1.5	−5.9	6.9
Personal service	−.9	—	—	—	−.2	−.7	+2.9	−2.4	−.5	−1.1	+.9	+5.1	+19.1	+1.3	4.3
Primary and unskilled	−2.3	—	—	—	+2.8	−2.1	+11.5	−8.9	−2.0	−.2	0.0	+1.8	−3.6	+34.7	10.0
Agriculture	−1.5	—	—	—	−1.4	+8.8	−9.5	−11.7	+10.3	+10.6	+6.9	+.6	−6.5	−6.9	12.2
All others	+1.4	—	—	—	+.9	−2.4	+3.5	+15.7	−5.2	−5.0	−4.9	−4.4	−9.1	−29.5	58.0
Total	0.0				0.0	0.0	0.0	0.0	0.0	0.0	0.0	0.0	0.0	0.0	100.0

SOURCE: Porter (1965), p. 87.

TABLE 4.3.2
INDEXES OF OCCUPATIONAL STATUS AND INCOME FOR MALE LABOUR FORCE
BY ETHNIC ORIGIN, CANADA, 1961

Ethnic Origin	Job-Status Index (British = 1.00)	Income Index (All groups = 100.0)
Jewish	1.312	166.9
British	1.000	109.8
Others	0.933	98.2
French	0.925	85.8
German	0.913	103.1
Ukrainian	0.892	86.8
Italian	0.892	81.0

SOURCE: Royal Commission on Bilingualism and Biculturalism (1969), pp. 16, 36.
NOTE: Job-status index expresses "distribution of the labour force among various occupational categories ranked according to the average income they command" (p. 36). Income index is ratio of average incomes in each ethnic-origin group to Canadian average, multiplied by 100.

TABLE 4.3.3
OCCUPATIONAL STATUS INDEX FOR ETHNIC-ORIGIN GROUPS IN CANADA,
1961 AND 1971

Ethnic Origin	1961	1971
Jewish	2.42	1.92
British	1.28	1.15
Scandinavian	0.91	0.87
Asiatic	0.90	1.19
German	0.85	0.87
Polish	0.83	0.86
Dutch	0.82	0.84
Other European	0.80	0.79
French	0.79	0.89
Ukrainian	0.78	0.84
Italian	0.47	0.57
Native peoples	0.15	0.41

SOURCE: Reitz 1980.
NOTE: Generally, index values may be interpreted as relative probabilities of obtaining higher-status jobs. Index value of 1.00 indicates average probability of obtaining high-status job. For detailed description of index, see Reitz (1977).

this pattern is related to the maintenance of ethnic cohesion. The evidence shows complex patterns; there are many gaps. Some upward mobility occurs in most, if not all, of the other ethnic groups. A prime example is the Jews. Despite discrimination, they have achieved high rates of mobility in the retail trades, and for the second generation, in the professions. To what extent are Jews an exceptional case? New research is slowly providing relevant facts. Census data analysed by Kalbach (1970) suggest a significant degree of upward mobility in most major minority ethnic groups (cf. Tepperman 1975). The Raynauld, Marion, and Béland study (Royal Commission on Bilingualism and Biculturalism 1969) showed that most of the differences in occupational status among ethnic groups can be attributed to differences in levels of schooling, rather than differences in opportunity. The highest level of schooling was attained by Jews, followed by the British. North and East Europeans were roughly at the same level as the French, and Italians had relatively low levels of schooling. In other words, inequalities of job status follow inequalities of educational attainment more than inequalities of opportunity for those with the same level of education (cf. Darroch 1979).

At the same time, the existence of varying degrees of unequal opportunity is not in doubt. A study in Toronto by Goldlust and Richmond (1973) clearly shows significant inequality of income opportunity among immigrant men. Given equivalent social origin, years of education, present occupation status, age, years of residence in Toronto, and years of post-secondary education, immigrant men of English and Jewish origins earned about one thousand dollars a year more than those of West European or Italian origins, who in turn earned about one thousand dollars more than those of Slavic, Greek, and Portuguese origin, and two thousand dollars more than Asians or Blacks (cf. also Li 1978). Better and more comprehensive data are needed, as well as information from other areas to compare various immigrant groups with the French.

Ethnic cohesion and job opportunity. Is ethnic cohesion a serious impediment to mobility, as Porter and many others have suggested? Does the desire to maintain close ethnic group ties obstruct the pathway toward economic success? Various reasons are sometimes given. Ethnic ties may impose demands conflicting with those of the labour market; they may reinforce commitment to an "old-world" value system, placing less emphasis on individual economic success; they may be less useful as economic resources than ties to other groups in society; they may lead to intensified discrimination at the hands of the dominant cultural groups; and so on. Evidence for a causal link between cultural or social "assimilation" and advancing economic position is almost completely lacking (see Yancey, Erickson, and Juliani 1976 for a review of U.S. research). The effect of ethnic cohesion, if it exists at all, is likely to vary depending on characteristics specific to each group.

Ethnic cultural retention may affect discrimination against some groups more than others. Northern European groups appear to encounter little discrimination, whatever their cultural orientation. Other groups, such as Jews, Italians, or racial minorities, obviously have encountered discrimination, at least in some contexts. However, abandonment of ethnic community ties is not necessarily an effective means to avoid such discrimination.

In certain instances, upward mobility may be facilitated by group cohesion. Jews are a possible example. In Canada, Jews have achieved high status without abandoning the Jewish community. High-status Jews in Toronto and Montreal have remained residentially segregated (in very affluent neighbourhoods), and do maintain community and religious ties. The history of the Jewish community shows that at the time of immigration, Jews became segregated in the garment industry and retail trades because of discrimination and other reasons (Kage 1962). But financial success was possible in part because the group as a whole could exercise control over economic opportunities. Success permitted subsequent generations to become well educated, and to achieve high status in medicine, law, and other professions, where there may be less institutionalized discrimination than exists in more bureaucratic settings. Within the professions, group segregation in particular organizations such as law firms or hospitals serves as a group resource and a shield against discrimination more than as an obstacle to mobility.

Many Italians, too, have found ways to achieve significant occupational success without abandoning ethnic community ties. Initially Italians became concentrated in the Canadian construction industry. Over the years, and partly as a result of their large numbers and the rapid expansion of construction, they acquired a great deal of power and control in that industry. According to Spada (1969, p. 273), more than half of the construction trades at all levels of development are now in Italian hands. This in turn has created opportunities for Italians outside bureaucracies dominated by Anglo-Saxons.

Smaller groups such as racial minorities may experience more limited possibilities for group control. Whether the abandonment of group ties contributes to upward mobility in such groups is not known. The Chinese historically encountered racist practices, such as disenfranchisement (until the 1940s), exclusion from licensed professions, and access to other jobs (Davis and Krauter 1971, pp. 75–76). They insulated themselves to a degree within "Chinatowns" and defended their communities against encroachment by outsiders. On the other hand, many younger Chinese men and women have now moved toward university-trained positions in technical fields and medicine (Lai 1971), following to some extent the Jewish pattern. The situation of the Japanese is very different. After the war-time incarceration, they made a conscious effort to blend into the Canadian community; so that their Japanese background would be as invisible as possible. A Japanese community still exists in Canada, albeit not residentially segregated. The more recent non-white immigrant groups encounter a new set of circumstances. The economic climate for small business is not what it once was. Whether these groups will find occupational niches promising mobility with some protection from discrimination remains to be seen.

Access to élite status. Mobility within the occupational structure does not necessarily imply access to élite status. Access to the upper echelons of business, where economic power is concentrated and major decisions are made, indicates economic acceptance and may also help guarantee equality of opportunity at lower levels.

Clement (1975) analysed ethnic representation among 775 directors and senior executives of 113 dominant corporations in Canada in 1972, and compared his results with Porter's (1965) analysis for 1951. He found that ethnic groups other than British and French are very much underrepresented.

> Although over one quarter of Canada's population is made up of ethnic groups other than the two charter groups (26.7 per cent), they have almost no representation in the economic elite, except for Jews. From the non-charter groups, there are only 32 Jewish-Canadians (4.1 per cent) and 10 from other "third" ethnic groups (1.3 per cent). In 1951 there were only six Jews (.78 per cent) in the elite thus indicating they have made significant inroads into the elite over the past twenty years (p. 237).

The overrepresentation of Jews is explained by their positions in family firms having grown to national stature in a single generation. "Six families [account] for 25 of the 32 Jewish members of the elite" (ibid.). Clement notes that these Jews are still socially isolated from the majority group, which restricts their real economic power. Other groups are underrepresented, more so even than the French.

Kelner (1970) studied ethnic representation in "strategic élites" (a second-echelon group whose status is restricted to one of six particular sectors: corporate, labour, political, civil service, communications, and academic) in Toronto in 1961. Non-Anglo-Saxon representation was increasing, but still small. There were interesting variations from one institutional sector to another. The labour, political, and academic élites were more open to non-Anglo-Saxons than were the corporate, media, or civil service élites. Jews were prominent in the academic élite, Italians and Ukrainians in the labour élite. Kelner concluded that rapid advance for minority groups occurs where there is room for innovation and entrepreneurial action outside stable, established corporate and bureaucratic structure. According to Kelner, non-Anglo-Saxons are still excluded from the social élite, restricting their access to the "core élite," the central group dominant over the various strategic élites.

These data reflect real differences in economic power, though not necessarily differences in opportunity for economic power. One cannot conclude that the small ethnic groups have been excluded from élite status, though this may have been true for some groups. Whether greater representation in the élite would help reduce the disadvantage experienced by members of the minority groups at lower levels remains a matter of speculation. Members of small ethnic groups who achieve élite status may be no more inclined than others to defend the interests of persons of similar origins in the labour force—perhaps even less so.

In sum, ethnic inequality does exist in Canada. It appears to be decreasing for some groups, but because of continuing immigration the overall degree of ethnic economic inequality in Canada is probably not decreasing and may be increasing. To a significant extent, ethnic community ties cut across the occupational hierarchy, and in many cases group members have found ways to avoid discrimination associated with ethnic cultural retention. Ethnic diversity is not restricted to the working class, and ethnic communities tend to be occupationally diverse.

RESPONSES TO ETHNIC INEQUALITY

A degree of ethnic inequality does not necessarily produce a proportional degree of ethnic conflict. There are several potential intervening conditions: perceptions of inequalities, their legitimacy, the diversity of interests within groups, modes of defensive adaptation, the capacity of a group for organized action. The impact on societal cohesion raises two other issues as well: whether interethnic inequality and conflict always hamper social-class solidarity, militancy, and conflict; and whether these affect political institutions, and support for left-wing ideologies and parties.

Pre-World War II immigrant response. Consider first the responses of immigrant groups during the early part of this century. Ethnic groups experiencing the greatest degree of inequality tended to respond defensively rather than offensively. A defensive group withdraws into particular occupations or marginal segments of the labour market. For example, the early Chinese immigrants who helped build the transcontinental railway often were forced subsequently to retreat into domestic service, laundry work, or other "feminine" occupations where competition with white males could be avoided, or into retail sales catering to other Chinese. Groups such as Italians and East Europeans tended to concentrate in certain occupations to enhance their chances to defend their own interests.

A defensive response was dictated by several conditions. Many native-born Canadian workers strongly resented the importation of "rate-busting foreigners." Each minority ethnic group had its own problems. Some were better off than others. Thus any one group could find few allies elsewhere in the population. A defensive response would also be likely if there were divisions and conflicts within a particular group.

Offensive action or instances of interethnic violence have been rare because they offer little hope for a reduction of inequality. Mass collective response has occurred only under extreme conditions of provocation. In one case in Montreal at the turn of the century, a mass of 10,000 new Italian immigrants found themselves without employment promised prior to arrival. Groups idle in the streets became involved in serious clashes with the police. A "Royal Commission Appointed to Inquire Into the Immigration of Italian Labourers to Montreal and the Alleged Fraudulent Practices of Employment Agencies" (1905) recommended measures to prevent a recurrence. This government action helped defuse an explosive situation without in itself changing the basic position of the Italians at the bottom of the occupational hierarchy.

Participation of immigrants and ethnic minorities in worker's unions may be one means to pursue group interests. But many minority groups were excluded from unions dominated by Anglo-Saxons. Thus minority participation in such unions may reflect prior progress toward a reduction of interethnic inequality and conflict. Some components of the early Ukrainian, Polish, Jewish, and other communities did participate in left-wing, working-class organizations. This was particularly evident in mining areas (Seager 1977). Whether such activities constitute a form of, or relative absence of, ethnic conflict remains controversial.

A study by Avery (1975) examined minority-group participation in militant labour activity. He regarded such participation as reflecting both ethnic and class conflict.

> Although it has been customary to regard Slavic and other European industrial workers as an obstacle to the formation of trade unions, more detailed studies have indicated that once these workers became accustomed to North American economic and social conditions they manifested a pronounced sense of class consciousness (p. 57).

To support his view, Avery listed numerous instances of minority group labour mobilization across Canada. He concluded that

> ...serious class and ethnic tension which developed between the "foreign" worker and the Anglo-Canadian business community, especially during the First World War and the "Red Scare" of 1919. Indeed, in response to the apparent radicalism of many immigrant workers the Immigration Act was dramatically altered in the spring of 1919. Immigrants who advocated Bolshevist ideas were not only excluded from the country, but were also subject to rapid deportation (p. 53).

The use of immigration policy in this way to control ethnic conflict shows the extreme weakness of minority groups in conflicts within Canadian institutions.

Whatever the degree of interethnic conflict in economic institutions, such conflict has not led to ethnic political polarization or to overwhelming ethnic-group support for leftist political movements. The reluctance, at least initially, of immigrants in rural areas to participate in political efforts to alleviate inequality has been stressed by most analysts. Lipset's (1968) classic study, *Agrarian Socialism: The Coöperative Commonwealth Federation in Saskatchewan*, noted that Ukrainian, German, French, and Polish settlers in Saskatchewan tended to form "distinct ethnic enclaves. . . . [and] have not participated as much in rural community organizations as have English-speaking farmers" (p. 52; see also p. 68). Lipset analysed voting statistics to show that the socialist CCF vote in the 1934, 1938, and 1944 elections tended to come from Anglo-Saxons and Scandinavians. Roman Catholic groups opposed the CCF. The Ukrainians were the only predominantly Roman Catholic group to support the CCF in numbers proportionate to their share of the general population, a fact Lipset attributes to the weakened position of the Catholic Church among Ukrainians (pp. 206−8). The same trends were noted among the CCF leadership (pp. 226−28), although small ethnic group representation in the leadership of the CCF was greater than in the other political parties (p. 235). Lipset concluded that it is the upwardly mobile members of a minority who most strongly support left-wing politics. They resent social exclusion, which ignores their improved economic status.

With increasing time in Canada, the impulse to protest inequality may gain strength. Lipset noted in his data that younger non-Anglo-Saxons were more heavily represented in the CCF leadership. "The younger members of ethnic groups, who were born in Canada and speak English well, are beginning to assume their proportionate place in rural society" (p. 227). During the Depression, the CCF did rise to importance in Saskatchewan with a good amount of support from East European, non-Roman Catholic ethnic-minority groups. Milnor (1968) analysed the "ethnic revolt," and argued that while East Europeans turned to the CCF, other ethnic minorities expressed protest through support of other parties such as the Social Credit. The recent New Democratic Party (successor to the CCF) government in Manitoba was elected following a period in which the Conservative government had given little representation to non-Anglo-Saxon groups. The more recent "ethnic revolt" resulted in dramatic increases in non-Anglo-Saxon representation in the provincial Cabinet (McAllister 1971).

Post-war period. Immigration and ethnic inequality have continued in the period since the Second World War, although many post-war immigrants benefit from the general affluence. The recent response to inequality is influenced by the increased diversity both among and within groups (with many groups now having long-established second and third generational components).

In this recent period, there have been large national surveys to permit systematic study of how economic inequality is perceived in the other ethnic groups. Roseborough and Breton (1971) showed that the members of minority ethnic groups are aware of inequality, but tend to accept it as legitimate or unavoidable, perhaps expecting their own personal situation to improve. The authors compared perceptions of inequalities among British, French, and other ethnic groups. All groups see the English as having an advantage in getting the best jobs and in influencing decisions of the federal government. Of English Canadians, about one-third see themselves as having economic advantage, and one-fourth as having a political advantage. Perceptions in the "other" ethnic groups were almost identical. What is even more important is that English-Canadian and "other" ethnic group evaluations of this inequality are also similar. Of those who see the English as having an advantage in jobs, 20% of the English feel that this is fair and legitimate, and 24% of those in other ethnic groups agree with them. This shows the very great degree of legitimacy of the economic order in Canada today. Small ethnic group members may be satisfied with a lower economic position because of their immigrant status (they regard the English as having earned their position and hope eventually to earn a similar position), or because of the circumscribed nature of their comparative frame of reference (they compare themselves not with the English, but rather with their own or their parents' situation prior to immigration).

The French-Canadian view is quite different; nearly two-thirds see the English as having an economic advantage; half see them as having a political advantage. French Canadians are much more sensitive to the existence of inequality than are the "other" ethnic groups, despite the fact that their actual occupational position is roughly comparable. Moreover, only 8% see the English dominance in jobs as fair. For the French, the existing situation has a more permanent aspect. As Roseborough and Breton point out, the French are a majority group in Quebec, exercising control over local political institutions. This generates an expectation for equal status with the English.

Significant differences exist among the small ethnic groups, depending on their situation. One survey of ten ethnic groups in five cities in 1973 (O'Bryan, Reitz, and Kuplowska 1976) asked respondents their perceptions of job discrimination by Canadian employers. The groups most aware of discrimination appear to be those actually experiencing the greatest actual degree of inequality of opportunity. For example, of the ten groups, the Chinese, Italians, Greeks, and Portuguese are most often aware of discrimination (see table 4.3.4). Evidence from Goldlust and Richmond (1973) shows that these groups do experience very significant inequality of job opportunity. Thus, the perceptions of members of minority groups are not completely at odds with the facts. However, compared with other problems facing the group, job inequality is not always the major concern. The 1973 survey shows that with the exception of the Italians and Portuguese, cultural and linguistic retention is seen as a more important problem. No problem was rated as "serious" or "very serious" by a majority of the respondents in any of the ten groups.

TABLE 4.3.4
PERCENTAGE CONCERNED WITH JOB DISCRIMINATION AS "VERY SERIOUS"
OR "SOMEWHAT SERIOUS" PROBLEM FOR THEIR GROUP

Ethnic Origin	Percentage	Weighted N ($\times 1000$)[a]
Scandinavian	0.2	69
Dutch	5.1	77
German	11.1	304
Hungarian	13.3	35
Polish	13.4	91
Ukrainian	13.4	182
Portuguese	20.7	57
Greek	24.8	89
Italian	32.6	383
Chinese	38.9	58

SOURCE: O'Bryan, Reitz, and Kuplowska (1976), pp. 79–83.
NOTE: Total unweighted $N = 2433$.

None of the Canadian political parties has gained a systematic advantage among all the various ethnic minorities. Meisel's (1975, p. 13) study of voting records from the 1968 federal election showed that recent (post-war) immigrants tend to support the Liberal Party, which was in power at the time of their arrival. Earlier immigrants coming under a Conservative government had tended to support the Conservatives. This suggests a conservative tendency to favour the political *status quo* associated with immigration. Many immigrants may be thinking primarily in terms of consolidating the position established by coming to Canada. Some immigrant groups, such as Italians in Toronto, are visibly aligned with the labour-oriented, social democratic NDP party, which also receives support from academics and liberals in the Anglo-Saxon middle class. Middle-class members of minority ethnic groups are as likely to support the traditional parties of the centre.

Inequalities experienced by the rapidly growing non-white groups has produced considerable resentment. Black communities in Canadian cities are quite conscious of discrimination. But organized action has been hampered by internal divisions and a sense of powerlessness (Clairmont and Magill 1974; Davis and Krauter 1971; Head 1975; Hill 1960; Winks 1971). Head (p. 189) showed that personal experiences of discrimination among Blacks in Toronto left them "angry" and "upset," but that only a small fraction had taken any action at all in response. The diverse origins of the black population is one factor that militates against cohesive action. The Blacks cannot be considered as a single ethnic group any more than the Asians or whites. Most are West Indian immigrants, but others are African, some are American, and still others are Canadians whose ancestry traces back several generations. There are rivalries among West Indians according to their religion and place of origin. No national action groups in Canada are comparable in strength to the American National Association for the Advancement of Colored Peoples (NAACP), Congress for Racial Equality (CORE), or Southern Christian Leadership Conference (SCLC). Specific manifestations of racism therefore tend to produce at most an *ad hoc* response on the part of those immediately affected. For example, in the Toronto area, when Milrod Metal Products (an ITT subsidiary) fired thirty-two black workers over an assembly line speed-up dispute, local action was taken ("The Milrod 34: West Indians on Strike in Canada" 1977). But local action can achieve only limited results. This is not to say that the black population is disorganized; but from the point of view of concerted action against discrimination, it so far has accomplished little.

SUMMARY

Economic inequality among ethnic and racial groups in Canada has always existed. Upward mobility among members of long-established European groups is significant, and over time, ethnic communities become more heterogeneous in terms of social-class composition. But such change is slow and there is continuing immigration from increasingly diverse sources. Job discrimination affects primarily the recently arrived immigrants of South European and non-European origins.

Inequality inevitably divides groups and creates problems for societal cohesion. When ethnic groups are divided along social class lines, tensions always arise. These tensions do not necessarily lead to overt conflict. Many members of disadvantaged ethnic groups react defensively and accept inequality as legitimate or unavoidable. Willingness to accept lower wages is one reason immigrants have been an attractive source of labour for Canadian business. Other factors also militate against more overt interethnic conflict: the small size of each group, and their internal social class, generational and cultural diversity. While some members of minority ethnic groups have participated in union activity and left-wing politics, many others have adopted an apolitical or conservative stance. Modes of response to ethnic economic inequality and the relation between ethnic conflict and other forms of conflict in society require further study.

Currently, it is the non-white groups with large components of recent immigrants that experience the greatest inequality and where greatest tensions exist. Many members of these groups are conscious of discrimination, but conflicts leading to disruption or clarification of the issue so far have not been widespread. Recent labour unrest in Canada is not generally regarded as having a strong ethnic aspect, though minority ethnic groups are often overrepresented in the affected labour group. Prospects for economic unrest among the new non-white immigrant groups are difficult to project, though given the disadvantaged position of these groups, such unrest should not be unexpected.

Relationships in Socio-Cultural Institutions

The cohesion of society is also affected by relationships in socio-cultural institutions, including educational institutions, the media, religious and various other social organizations. Issues arising in socio-cultural institutions are at a general level the same as those arising in economic ones: namely, the status accorded members of each group, the perceptions each group has of the situation, the response of the group, and the ways in which these responses and possible conflicts are handled. However, at a more concrete level, the specific issues are rather different because of the nature of socio-cultural institutions. In economic institutions, individual status is defined primarily by the economic allocation and by the extent of prevailing ethnic or racial bias. In socio-cultural institutions, individual status is defined more by the degree to which the institution serves social and cultural interests, which vary between ethnic groups. Ethnic conflict in such institutions tends to focus on access to control over culture. In Canada, this conflict has been most pronounced in education and in the media, probably because of the degree to which these institutions have been subject to centralized cultural control.

Questions relating to ethnic group survival become particularly important in this context because, rightly or wrongly, socio-cultural, and not economic, institutions are seen as being the primary instrument of that survival. A key question is whether minority groups will be satisfied with a degree of cultural autonomy sufficient to ensure group survival.

INEQUALITY OF CULTURAL STATUS

Inequality of cultural status among ethnic groups in Canadian society is reflected in differential ethnic group representation, recognition, and control over culture within the major institutions of society. Culture in educational institutions and in the media is dominated by the English, and in certain areas also by the French ethnolinguistic groups. The influence of other cultural groups within these institutions is slight.

In educational institutions, for example, curriculum represents "other" ethnic groups from the point of view of the dominant groups, if it represents them at all. This fact pervades history, culture and language curricula, and textbooks at all levels of public education. In the media as well, minority groups are treated as second- or third-class components of Canadian culture. When newspapers print feature articles on particular ethnic groups, the treatment may be positive or negative, but it is usually clear that the group being featured is not the group making the presentation.

The dominant cultural groups tend to be sympathetic to the elimination of cultural and racial biases within their institutions, within the context of continued control by their own cultural group. In educational institutions, the policy is to replace texts whose content may offend a particular cultural group because of the depiction of that group.

The relative cultural statuses of various minority ethnic groups are not the same. European-origin groups and groups having a long history within Canada tend to have somewhat higher cultural status. Measures of overall ethnic status presented in chapter 4.2 reflect to some degree cultural status, though economic and other factors also influence overall ethnic status. Generally, francophone status within anglophone institutions, though small, is greater than the influence of any of the small groups. Across Canada, there may be localities in which large concentrations of minority groups exercise little influence, whereas the English and French exercise varying degrees of influence, regardless of local population balance. This is a consequence of centralized control over cultural institutions.

Alternative cultural resources and control are available to each ethnic community within its own institutions (ethnic schools, press, electronic media, and so on). For most groups, access to control over educational and media facilities now exists primarily within their own ethnic community institutions, not within common social institutions. Whether increased cultural status for the minority groups is best achieved by increasing their control within the dominant institutions or by increasing the resources of their own community institutions is an important part of the debate over cultural inequality. It corresponds to a parallel question in economic institutions, whether to seek mobility in economic institutions controlled by the dominant groups or in autonomous economic domains controlled by a minority group.

In Quebec ethnic cultural inequality raises special problems. There, the francophone group attempts to prevent increased domination by anglophones. The tendency for small-ethnic-group members to choose anglophone institutions in Quebec as a result of economic realities has increased tension with the French. Their efforts to influence this choice, whether through economic incentives or by government regulation, has clear implications for the interests of the small ethnic groups.

The issues of cultural status generally and of language choice in Quebec both give rise to interethnic conflicts. The development and implications of these two conflicts will be discussed separately here, though they are related to each other because both are related to linguistic and regional conflict in Canada.

RESPONSES: MULTICULTURALISM ISSUE

One response to cultural subordination is that of resignation and acceptance. This has been the typical response of small ethnic groups in Canada up to the recent past. Acceptance of a negative self-image often engenders attempts at cultural conformity. Emulation of characteristics and attitudes of a group one hopes or expects eventually to join is sometimes called "anticipatory socialization." But the wish or expectation is not necessarily realized, particularly in the case of racial minorities or groups otherwise encountering obstacles to assimilation. Demoralization and apathy can result from social, and self, rejection.

Origins of multiculturalism movement. The conditions under which a minority ethnic group rejects inequality, reaffirms its culture, and engages in efforts to improve its status are not well understood. In some instances, economic change or conflict is involved. Groups that accept low economic status frequently accept low cultural status as well. Groups engaging in militant attempts to combat and eliminate economic inequalities often reject negative cultural status and seek an improved ethnic self-image. Claims to equal cultural status help justify expectations of equal economic status. In other instances, expectations for higher cultural status may be a consequence of improved economic status. Those who become successful and achieve high status in the economic sphere eventually may come to expect consistent status in terms of culture.

The importance of strong religious institutions or other cultural institutions is suggested by the example of the Jewish struggle against anti-Semitism. Jews may find a source of higher self-esteem in their own religious and other traditions, and seek toleration and acceptance without assimilation.

A multiethnic society may become committed to cultural equality as a central value after a long history of ethnic conflict. In that context, minority cultural groups more often assert their right to acceptance. Each group may use the other's cultural status as a point of comparative reference, affecting expectations they have for their own status. In the United States, it is often observed that the black liberation movement gave rise to cultural self-assertion on the part of many ethnocultural groups and other status groups, such as women, the aged, and the gay community. Legitimacy accorded black claims to cultural equality has emboldened other groups to make similar claims.

In Canada conflict over the cultural status of the "other" ethnic groups during the 1960s and 1970s has been greatly affected by the French-English conflict and the legitimacy given new cultural claims of French Canadians. Across Canada, and particularly outside Quebec, increased French cultural and linguistic presence has raised the expectations of "other" ethnic groups for improved cultural status and recognition.

When tensions between French and English increased following the post-war ''Quiet Revolution'' in Quebec, the Liberal government of Lester B. Pearson established, in 1963, a Royal Commission on Bilingualism and Biculturalism. This commission led to the passage of the Official Languages Act of 1969, improving the status of French as an official language. Another outcome was to antagonize members of small ethnic groups. Ukrainian Canadians, particularly those in the western provinces where they constitute a relatively large minority, were most vocal in protest (Bociurkiw 1978). Their general objection was to the idea of group rights for the French that were not extended to other groups. They felt that if small concentrations of francophones outside Quebec have special language rights, then similar rights should be extended to similar, often larger, concentrations of Ukrainians. Certainly they objected to the title of the commission, which recognized only two ethnic cultures in Canada.

Minority group leaders began to advocate an official policy of ''multiculturalism'' rather than ''biculturalism'' (Palmer 1974). This would give equal status to anyone regardless of ethnic origin, and imply no pressure toward assimilation into either English- or French-Canadian culture. Furthermore, the group leaders wanted the government to give active support to ethnic groups wishing to develop their cultural heritage. As Jackson (1977) points out, the French-Canadian emphasis on language, raising the possibility of government-promoted bilingualism across Canada, directed the attention of other groups, such as Ukrainians, to this aspect of their own culture. Government assistance to ''non-official languages'' became an issue. The French-English duality in Canada may focus political attention on ethnic culture in general, but this does not necessarily promote cultural retention. The hypothesis that the French-English context in Montreal fosters minority ethnic cohesion was not supported in a study by Ossenberg (1964).

Attitudes among immigrants and their descendants toward multiculturalism and language retention in that context were studied by O'Bryan, Reitz, and Kuplowska (1976) in a survey of ten ethnic groups in five Canadian cities. The study showed that the label ''multiculturalism'' is not well known, but that the great majority is in favour of the basic idea (69.1%), and is also in favour of language retention as a major component and means toward cultural retention (71.1%). The importance of language retention is felt most strongly by immigrants (74.9%), and only somewhat less so in the second (66.4%) and third (59.3%) generation. Support for multiculturalism is uniformly high in all generations (69.1%, 69.4%, 64.5%). That is, the general principle of support for cultural retention is endorsed uniformly across generations.

French-English conflict affected the emergence of multiculturalism, but other conditions operate to produce variations from one ethnic group to another. Economic status and change are relevant. Ethnic groups having achieved fairly high economic status may shift attention to social and cultural status. Of these upwardly mobile groups, some place greater emphasis on cultural retention while others more often seek acceptance through assimilation. Table 4.4.1 shows that the Ukrainians are more concerned by cultural loss than the Scandinavians or the Dutch. The Ukrainian response is related to fears for the survival of Ukrainian culture in the Soviet Union. It may also be affected by the previously low economic status of Ukrainians in Canada, and persisting social descrimination. Groups currently having lower economic status—Portuguese, Greeks, Italians, and Chinese—tend to be relatively more concerned by economic problems such as job discrimination. Note that the Greeks and Chinese are concerned about cultural retention as often as are the Ukrainians. Multiculturalism finds support within ethnic groups most firmly established in the middle class, though not only within such groups.

Actions required to raise the status of non-English and non-French language and culture are a controversial issue. Opinions vary widely across ethnic groups and regions of Canada. School curriculum is one policy area. Of minority ethnic groups surveyed for the study, about half felt that the history, language, and culture of their own group should be available as subjects in public schools, at least in areas where members of a group live near one another. A much smaller group would rely on ethnic or religious schools. As many as 40% claim public funds for such education. This belief in public responsibility for ethnic education is fairly widespread. It is more prevalent among Italians, Ukrainians, and Greeks than among Portuguese, Hungarians, or Scandinavians, however. The claim on the public purse does not disappear in the native-born generations. In the second and third

TABLE 4.4.1
CONCERN WITH VARIOUS ISSUES AMONG "OTHER" ETHNIC GROUPS

	PERCENTAGE[a] CONCERNED BY		
ETHNIC ORIGIN	Job Discrimination	Loss of Tradition	Loss of Language
Scandinavian	0.2	18.6	28.6
Dutch	5.1	18.0	28.9
German	11.1	17.1	30.0
Hungarian	13.3	15.7	25.4
Polish	13.4	20.4	34.1
Ukrainian	13.4	35.4	46.1
Portuguese	20.7	19.6	18.0
Greek	24.8	35.0	40.4
Italian	32.6	21.5	30.3
Chinese	38.9	40.5	52.7

SOURCE: O'Bryan, Reitz, and Kuplowska (1976), pp. 79–83.
NOTE: a. Percentage indicating each problem "very serious" or "somewhat serious" for group.

generations, there is more of a tendency to assign responsibility to the ethnic community. But even in the third generation, one in three feels that taxpayers generally have a responsibility.

The educational system is a key area where changes are sought, but not the only one. Support for the ethnic press, multilingual radio and television, ethnic cultural centres and activities, production and distribution of books in the ancestral language, and related scholarly activities, all are advocated. In specific locations, particular issues become more prominent in response to a local situation. For example, multilingual television has been particularly lacking in some cities such as Winnipeg; so that relatively large proportions of Winnipegers wish to see such a service introduced.

Emphasis on language retention as a means of cultural retention raises more specific issues. Is language retention really crucial to cultural retention? Is long-term, non-official language retention possible in Canadian cities? Is a high degree of cultural isolation required? What are the consequences for interethnic cohesion? The non-official languages survey provided some of the answers.

The importance of language retention as an issue has been mentioned already. Respondents in the survey gave various reasons for stressing language. First, the general value of a second language; second, the practical aspect of communication; and third, its importance in maintaining traditional culture. This ranking of reasons should not be necessarily taken at face value. Many respondents may feel that it is more acceptable to justify language retention efforts in practical terms. In each group, the trend toward language loss was seen as one of the most important problems confronting the group. In most cases, it was seen as the most important problem.

How does language retention actually affect cultural retention? To find out, it is necessary to examine experiences of the second and third generations. Language retention generally occurs as a result of very early socialization. Most native-born Canadians in the non-official language groups who learn their ethnic tongue do so at home in their first five years. Among Germans, Poles, Ukrainians, and Italians, language learning had a very marked effect on the retention of ethnic identity and ethnic community ties in the native-born generation, even after taking other socialization experiences into account (Reitz 1974). That is, for these groups, language maintenance is a central element in cultural maintenance. The same may not be true in other groups where economic pressures or other external forces can be more important. But processes internal to the ethnic communities can be significant in affecting their survival, and it appears that language learning may be one very important aspect.

Current survival rates of ethnic languages across generations are very low. The survey reported a number of broad trends. Among immigrants, some non-official language use is nearly universal. Non-official languages are most frequently used at home and informally among friends, and to a significant extent also in community institutions, the media, and places of employment. Of those fluent in a non-official language, one in four uses the language at work, and three in four read the ethnic press and listen to ethnic radio broadcasts. But non-official language knowledge is lost rapidly from one generation to the next. It is retained by the second generation only to a limited degree. By the third generation, 60% have no knowledge of the language whatsoever. Over 80% rarely or never use the language. Learning one of the official languages, most often English, occurs usually within a few years of residence in Canada. For immigrants who maintain ties with their ethnic community, knowledge of English does not displace their native language, but for their children raised in Canada, it does.

In other words, the non-official languages are an important, in some cases vital, element in the lives of immigrants, but they become much less important and in fact often disappear from the lives of the subsequent generations. The appropriate response to facts of this kind is very much a topic of debate both within and between ethnic groups in Canada.

Attitudes in dominant groups. What is the response of Canadians of British and French origin to the multicultural movement? Events in the political sphere—government policies, programmes and grants—are discussed in the next chapter where the focus is on political institutions. What attitudes are popular among members of the dominant ethnic groups? The study by Berry, Kalin, and Taylor (1977) showed that the general population is as unaware of the term *multiculturalism* as are the small ethnic groups themselves. The authors found that when the question was posed to respondents, they showed ''a mildly positive attitude toward multiculturalism'' overall (p. 140). What this means is that Canadians tend to subscribe to statements like: ''there is a lot that Canadians can gain from friendly relations with immigrants'' (81% agreement, 9% disagreement), and ''it would be good to see all the ethnic groups in Canada retain their culture'' (64% agreement, 19% disagreement). Moreover, Canadians generally do not see multiculturalism as a threat to national unity. There is agreement that ''a society which has a variety of ethnic groups is more able to tackle new problems as they occur'' (52% agreement, 23% disagreement); there is disagreement that ''the unity of this country is weakened by ethnic groups sticking to their own ways'' (47% disagreement, 36% agreement).

However, while the majority view tends toward a permissive attitude to ethnic minority cultures, at the same time (and in contrast to the views of the ethnic minorities themselves), it tends *not* to uphold the principle that society should sponsor the maintenance of such cultures. Firstly, to the general statement that ''if members of ethnic groups want to keep their own culture they should keep it to themselves and not bother other people in the country,'' 49% agreed; 38% disagreed. Secondly, when persons are asked what they themselves would do to support multiculturalism, resistance is evident in that 56% would not be willing to pay taxes to support it (opposed to

29% who would). Thirdly, the majority tend to support the existing programmes that have little effect on their own lives (community cultural centres, 70%; ethnic histories, 66%; and folk festivals, 82%). But they tend to oppose programmes considered most crucial by the minority groups themselves, namely, teaching of ancestral languages in the regular schools (50% opposed, 36% in favour). The respondents also tend to oppose multilingual radio and television (46% opposed, 38% in favour), although they favour teaching non-official languages in special schools after hours or on weekends (64% in favour, 22% opposed).

In short, the majority of Canadians tend to support multiculturalism as an ideal, so long as it does not affect their own lives, the socio-cultural institutions in which they participate, or their pocketbooks. School curriculum is the arena of attitudinal conflict revealed in the interview surveys, and it is also increasingly an arena of actual social conflict in school districts across Canada.

The attitudes of French Canadians toward multiculturalism tend to be more negative than those of English Canadians, and it is clear that French Canadians feel that pressure from the ''other'' ethnic groups for more socio-cultural rights and recognition weakens their own position in Canada (Berry, Kalin, and Taylor 1977, p. 157). A summary of the French Canadian view is given by the sociologist Rocher (1976). Multiculturalism could have the effect of neutralizing the efforts of French Canadians to establish their own culture on an equal footing with English Canadian culture. This is needed to guarantee the future of bilingualism and the status of French in Canadian society. In the view of many French Canadians, English-Canadian support for multiculturalism is motivated by a desire not to upgrade minority cultures, but to downgrade French. Whether these arguments are correct has not become a topic of research. There are counter-arguments that pressures toward multiculturalism actually influence English Canadians to accept cultural diversity and therefore to be more sympathetic to French claims. Others argue that with respect to the need to decentralize control over cultural institutions all across Canada, the interests of French Canadians coincide with those of the ''other'' ethnic groups.

RESPONSES: LANGUAGE CONFLICT IN QUEBEC

Reference has already been made to the fact that members of the small ethnic groups tend to become oriented toward anglophone institutions, that this is a matter of special concern to French Canadians in Quebec, and that it has caused pressures to restrict immigration into Quebec and assert control over the linguistic decisions of immigrants in Quebec. These pressures are a source of tension not only in Quebec but across Canada where there is concern about what sacrifices are required in terms of various individual rights and economic penalties and constraints to ensure the survival of the French language and English-French accommodation.

Cappon (1978) showed that the conflict is quite clearly drawn in Montreal. French Canadians want to bolster the survival of the French language by having minority groups, such as the Italians, attend French schools. Members of minority groups want to maximize their socio-economic mobility by attending English schools.

The issue has generated conflict among French Canadians themselves. One view, formulated by the Quebec Liberal government's Commission of Inquiry on the Position of the French Language and on Language Rights in Quebec (The Gendron Commission) is presented in a volume devoted to ''the ethnic groups'' (1972). The report argues that the dangers to the French language posed by immigration had been exaggerated. Linguistic decisions of immigrants are made on economic grounds, and to ensure that French becomes the language of choice for immigrants, it must increasingly become the language of work in Quebec. Regulations restricting immigrant access to English schools are therefore seen as unnecessary.

The growing nationalist sentiment in Quebec favours a viewpoint stressing reduction in individual freedom of language of instruction for those whose mother tongue is neither English nor French. How this might be accomplished against the will of the groups affected has been an extremely controversial issue. Tests of minimal competence in English as a criterion of admission to English schools were imposed, but then abolished because they proved difficult to administer. The current law (Law 101), enacted on 26 August 1977 under the Parti Québécois government, is more clear cut. It provides access to English schools only for those whose parents had attended English elementary school in Quebec (those whose parents attended English schools outside Quebec would be allowed only if they lived in Quebec at the time the law was enacted). This law effectively ends freedom of choice of language of instruction for the other ethnic groups in Quebec. There can be no doubt of the opposition of these groups to such restriction, but the consequences of these current events cannot be assessed yet (Myhul 1978).

Supporters of multiculturalism who are sympathetic to the aspirations of Quebec nationalists and who also favour Canadian unity have advocated the decentralization of control of culture in all parts of Canada (Lupul 1978*a*). This could provide, for example, for bilingual education in French and other languages (including English) in Quebec, and for bilingual education in English and other languages (not excluding French) in other areas, depending upon local preference. Bilingualism in French and English across Canada is rejected in this approach.

SUMMARY

In socio-cultural institutions in Canada, the dominant cultures are Anglo-Saxon, and in certain contexts, French, and in this sense the status of the cultures of the ''other'' ethnic groups is rather low. This low status has been accepted, to a large degree, as legitimate by members of the various groups.

Since the 1960s, however, a multiculturalism movement has become visible. The movement seeks to promote increased status and recognition for minority ethnic cultures and support for their retention. The strength of this movement may be attributable to the improved economic status of some of the groups and their concentrations in particular communities in Canadian society, and to the improved cultural status of the French group as a result of its developing sense of identity. Both of these trends have increased expectations for acceptance and cultural tolerance. In addition, members of some groups, such as the Ukrainians and Jews, feel a special obligation to protect their cultural heritage when it is threatened elsewhere in the world. Partly because of the general significance of language as a component of culture in Canada, the small ethnic groups have stressed language retention. For these groups, language is important as a cultural symbol more than as a factor affecting access to economic or political institutions.

The multicultural movement has achieved only limited success. Various institutions, including political as well as socio-cultural institutions, have declared a policy of multiculturalism. But the dominant groups have treated the issue as essentially symbolic, and recognition of minority cultures is granted basically as a token expression of cultural tolerance. While English Canadians at least pay lip service to the abstract ideal of a multicultural society, there is strong resistance to granting minority control over cultural institutions such as schools or broadcasting facilities. Dissatisfaction with the degree of implementation of multicultural policies has not yet caused any serious interethnic tension in Canada.

The French-English conflict, which contributed to the rise of a multicultural movement, also affects the response to it. As a result of the conflict, the English group may be more inclined to grant improved symbolic status to the other groups. But not without reason, the French have seen multiculturalism as having the effect of denying them improved status. The effects of French-English relations both on ethnic group demands and on the response to such demands makes a reliable assessment of the overall impact on intergroup cohesion very difficult.

Inside Quebec, French Canadians see the small ethnic groups as aggravating the demographic balance that threatens the survival of the French language. The local authority of the French increasingly is used to encourage integration of other ethnic groups into the francophone rather than the anglophone community.

Decentralization of control over socio-cultural institutions is the general issue likely to remain significant in Canada. Decentralization satisfies local demands while creating problems of regional isolation. The political arena is crucial to the resolution of this issue and is examined in the next chapter.

Relationships in Political Institutions

National identification and the legimitacy of national political institutions are central topics of this study. Orientations of specific groups toward political institutions can be analysed in a manner parallel to the analysis of relationships in other institutions. Relevant issues include inequalities of group political status (meaning in this case inequality of access to political representation and the kinds of decisions made), the way in which political status is perceived, and the response by affected groups.

Relationships among levels of government are an important aspect of Canadian political life. Provincial governments are very powerful. Metropolitan governments have emerged in recent years as key urban areas developed rapidly. Political cohesion at provincial or local levels will be reinforced if governments attend to the distinctive economic, social, and cultural interests of their local constituencies. Some degree of decentralization is positive because it contributes to the satisfaction of local needs. Extreme decentralization may undermine national solidarity if each region becomes isolated; so that their relationship to one another becomes unsatisfactory. Depending upon political access of ethnic groups at various levels of government, the degree of decentralization needed to satisfy local ethnic group needs may affect the overall cohesion of the society.

To examine ethnic group participation in political decision making, various specific issues might be selected for close study. Those selected for inclusion here are immigration, civil and human rights, and culture. These matters have been discussed in previous chapters, providing in this chapter a basis to focus on relevant political processes. Other areas, such as economic policy or external affairs, also could be examined. Economic policies have an impact on ethnic groups because they affect the relative economic health of various regions, sectors of the economy, and occupational groups in which ethnic groups are concentrated in various ways. Foreign policy affects ethnic groups because specific groups may feel special obligations arising from their historical, cultural, and social ties to regions and countries outside Canada. Potentially, any area of policy has an ethnic aspect because of differential effects. However, little systematic research exists on the influence of ethnicity on many policy areas.

INEQUALITY OF POLITICAL ACCESS

Access to government by immigrants and their descendants differs according to the level of government. Federal politics are dominated by relations between the two major linguistic groups. This subordinates the position of ethnic groups composed of immigrants and their descendants. Any one small group, because of its size, faces serious obstacles to national political access. A group may attempt to control individual electoral constituencies; it may attempt to forge alliances with other groups to pursue common interests; or it may form pressure groups to lobby with politicians and civil servants. All of these strategies have been used by members of small ethnic groups, but with only limited success.

Lack of success by minority groups in controlling individual federal constituencies was indicated in part three. Although the small ethnic groups comprised a quarter of the population in the early 1960s, they elected only 4.4% of new members of the House of Commons, and controlled an even smaller proportion of Cabinet positions. Group members are dispersed across ridings and are a minority in most of them. The groups, of course, are split among themselves. Even if all minority ethnic groups together constitute a majority in a particular riding, the British or French groups still remain the largest single group. Candidate selection is influenced by events outside a riding, and social groups within must be well organized to prevail.

Support for the major political parties at the federal level is divided primarily along regional and linguistic lines. The Liberals, Conservatives, and New Democrats all appeal to members of the small ethnic groups to bolster their overall position. No one party has emerged as spokesman for these groups. Thus, political conflicts involving small ethnic groups tend to be fought within parties rather than as part of the struggle between them.

In the face of obstacles in the electoral process, ethnic group organizations resort to lobbying as an important strategy for gaining access to the federal government. But political influence remains problematic. Government officials are often doubtful that ethnic group leaders really represent the views of the rank-and-file. Ethnic group organizations often rely on holding conferences or sending delegations to attend conferences organized by government bureaux to make their wishes known. The political impact, predictably, is small.

In provincial and local politics, minority ethnic groups appear to be better represented. In local populations, one or the other linguistic group is dominant, and the numerical position of other groups varies. Smith (1968, p. 198) analysed ethnic origins of members of the Saskatchewan Legislative Assembly over the period 1905−1964. He found steadily increasing representation by non-Anglo-Saxons. By 1964, 30% were classified as having an ethnic origin other than Anglo-Saxon, Canadian, or American. The reason for greater representation at the provincial levels may be smaller constituency sizes, and the fact that particular groups are numerically more important in certain provinces than they are in Canada as a whole. If local governments are more responsive to ethnic group interests than the central government, intergovernmental relations may be affected. But overall impacts on national cohesion are not easily identified.

DECISION MAKING AND ITS IMPLEMENTATION

Government policies in the areas of immigration, civil and human rights, and culture directly affect the interests of the other ethnic groups and are areas of conflict. Each group has different objectives and is affected differently by specific policies. The overall impact of policy on government legitimacy and identification in all groups is therefore complex and hard to assess.

Immigration policy. Immigration policies define access to Canadian society. They control the rate and social composition of the flow of persons into the country. They affect the size and characteristics of the population and the eligibility of particular individuals for admission to Canada. What positions on immigration policy are adopted by members of various ethnic groups and what is their impact on the process of policy making?

The history of immigration policy, as discussed previously in chapter 4.2, shows that immigration has been influenced very heavily by business interests in Canada and by the need to provide a manpower supply for economic development. Immigrants have occupied various positions in the occupational hierarchy, but the largest number tend to enter in relatively low-status manual occupations. Although there are attempts to select immigrants on the basis of high labour-force demand, they inevitably create more or less intense competition with persons already working in Canada. Thus, it is predictable that immigration tends to be favoured by business executives and professionals at the top end of the occupational hierarchy, much more than by skilled and unskilled labourers (Tienhaara 1974, pp. 26–27). Generally speaking, it is the opinion of the former group that has tended to make itself felt most effectively in the political process determining immigration policy. Trend data show that during the period between 1959 and 1971, the percentage of university-educated Canadians favouring immigration declined from 57% to 39%, while the percentage of high-school-educated Canadians favouring immigration fell by a smaller amount, from 32% to 26%, and the percentage of less-well-educated Canadians favouring immigration remained stable at 21%. It was following this erosion of majority support for immigration among the university-educated segment of society that the government launched its recent critical review of immigration policy.

The earlier revision of immigration regulations in the 1960s has produced a substantially increased flow of immigrants from Asia, the West

Indies, Africa, and Central and South America. Many Canadians have been disturbed by this trend. Recent controversy suggests that many are ambivalent or opposed to immigration from sources such as the West Indies and the Indian subcontinent. A major survey conducted by the Survey Research Centre at York University shows public resistance to further immigration by non-whites (Ornstein 1978).

Ethnic-group attitudes toward immigration policy vary. Reference is often made to a French-English split, with French Canadians in Quebec opposing immigration because immigrants swell the size of the anglophone community. What about the other ethnic groups? Immigrants, and their descendants who are citizens in Canada, have interests that overlap with those of other Canadians in the same linguistic community and region. As a result, members of the small ethnic groups are only slightly more likely to favour a more open immigration policy. A Gallup poll released 2 July 1975 showed that nationally, 8% English-mother-tongue Canadians and 11% French-mother-tongue Canadians favoured increased immigration, while among those whose mother tongue was neither English nor French, the percentage was only up to 14%. On the other hand, 45% of the English and 35% of the French favoured a decrease, compared with 24% of those whose mother tongue was neither French nor English. The split between dominant and minority groups is reduced in part by the fact that the more highly educated tend to favour immigration. It may be that many in the small ethnic groups are wary of increased immigration (even from their own ancestral country of origin) because they, too, fear a flooding of the job market. (Note that in this poll the English were more opposed to immigration than the French).

Interethnic conflict over immigration policy tends to focus on rules affecting individual eligibility rather than those affecting the total flow of immigrants from various sources. The main example is the conflict over sponsorship regulations. By means of sponsorship, Canadian residents can bring relatives to Canada, even if the relatives would not qualify as independent applicants. The flow of sponsored immigrants has greatly increased over the years, and to check this flow, there have been attempts to restrict sponsorship rights. Changes in sponsorship have been resisted by groups such as the Italians (Hawkins 1972) because the individual impact is so direct and immediate. Ethnic-group resistance has been effective, and new regulations instituted in April 1978 contain no change in the priority given to the unification of families.

In 1974, the government attempted to structure the on-going debate on immigration by publishing a comprehensive green paper on immigration (Department of Manpower and Immigration 1974). This document outlined alternative policies for the future, stressing the issues of total numbers and the use of various educational and occupational selection criteria. New decisions on these matters still lie in the future.

The movement toward removing inequalities in immigration has been matched by an increasing uniformity in citizenship requirements. The Citizenship Act of 1976 does away with special categories such as ''British subjects'' and ''wives of citizens'' whose qualifications were previously guided by a modified set of rules. Now all immigrants must follow the same procedure. The residence requirement has been reduced from five to three years, and the vague and very subjectively determined qualification of having to be of ''good character'' has been removed. The requirements for acquiring Canadian citizenship are that the applicant be eighteen years of age or older; that he be lawfully admitted into Canada for permanent residence; that he be resident in Canada for three of the four years immediately preceding application; that he possess an adequate knowledge of French or English, and some knowledge of Canada, and the rights and duties of a citizen; that he be willing to take an oath or affirmation of citizenship; and that he not have a deportation order or pose any risk to the security and public order of Canada.

Although most laws in Canada treat citizens and non-citizens alike, there are some legal differences between a Canadian citizen and a person who is simply a resident of Canada. A citizen is entitled to full political participation (full franchise and the right to run for office), foreign travel and freedom of return, and full economic rights (some business and professional positions, and some forms of commercial property can be held only by Canadian citizens).

Civil and human rights policies. Civil and human rights policies directly affect the interest of every ethnic group in Canada. These policies are one means for the management of conflicts between groups in Canadian society; so that individuals are treated fairly and are not subject to systematic discrimination. Comprehensive and well-enforced guarantees of equal rights are important means by which a government may establish its legitimacy among members of minority groups.

Violations of human rights in Canada have been persistent, arising from fundamental group conflicts. There also have been episodic violations as a result of temporary circumstances. Examples of the latter type arose during each of the two world wars. When German-Canadians came under suspicion, their main response was to disguise their ethnic origin. During World War I, the largely German-Canadian town of Berlin, Ontario, changed its name to Kitchener, the name of a British general, as a display of loyalty to the Crown. However, following World War I, many Canadians supported the deportation of ''enemy aliens'' who held jobs coveted by returning Canadian soldiers (Avery 1975). Activists in the trade union movement and on the left were the most common targets.

The treatment of Japanese-Canadians during World War II was extremely harsh and patently racist. Because it was feared that they might be loyal to Japan, Japanese-Canadians were incarcerated in isolated rural communities that were virtual concentration camps (Broadfoot 1977;

Schwartz 1978). No evidence was ever produced to support this fear. A similar policy of incarceration was pursued in the United States. The Japanese community in Canada, of course, was never the same again. Prior to World War II, the Japanese had established well-organized communities, such as the one in Vancouver (Young and Reid 1938). After their release, the Japanese were initially prevented from returning to their pre-war communities. Most of them scattered across Canada and avoided the formation of highly visible Japanese communities (Quo 1971). The Canadian government recently repudiated its war-time policy toward Japanese Canadians. Although the repudiation took the form of an official apology to Japan, it was clearly directed at a Japanese-Canadian audience. However, the memory of such a traumatic experience is unlikely to be so easily erased.

To prevent not only shameful episodes such as these but also more continuous violation of individual rights in daily life, Canadian civil rights policy has evolved slowly. The first steps were taken in the 1950s by the provinces, perhaps as a consequence of greater minority group representation at that level. Individual provinces passed specific pieces of legislation in the areas of human rights, employment, incomes, and housing (see table 4.5.1; and Davis and Krauter 1971, pp. 102−113). The provincial legislation has resulted in considerable unevenness. Citizens in the various provinces do not enjoy equal treatment in such matters as merit employment and public accommodations. The equality enjoyed depends upon the attitude of the particular province, its legislature, and its ability and will to endorse the principle of equality (Means 1969).

The federal government enacted a Canadian Bill of Rights on 10 August 1960 (An Act for the Recognition and Protection of Human Rights and Fundamental Freedom). This legislation contains general provisions relevant to ethnic minorities:

1. It is hereby recognized and declared that in Canada there have existed and shall continue to exist, without discrimination by reasons of race, national origin, colour, religion, or sex, the following human rights and fundamental freedoms, namely:
   (a) The right of the individual to life, liberty, security of the person, and enjoyment of property, and the right not to be deprived thereof except by due process of law,
   (b) The right of the individual to equality before the law and the protection of the law;
   (c) Freedom of religion;
   (d) Freedom of speech;
   (e) Freedom of assembly and association; and
   (f) Freedom of the press.

The Canadian Human Rights Act of 1977 extends and specifies the proscription of discrimination. These documents are not part of the Constitution, but rather have the status of statutes. The federal legislation operates under a restricted jurisdiction: it is applied only to federal questions

TABLE 4.5.1
INITIAL YEARS FOR FOUR TYPES OF PROVINCIAL CIVIL RIGHTS LEGISLATION

Human Rights Code	Equal Pay Act	Fair Employment Practices Act	Fair Accommodation Practices Act
Saskatchewan 1947	Ontario 1951	Ontario 1951	Ontario 1954
Ontario 1961	Saskatchewan 1952	Manitoba 1953	Saskatchewan 1956
Nova Scotia 1963	British Columbia 1953	Alberta 1955	New Brunswick 1959
Alberta 1966	Manitoba 1956	Nova Scotia 1955	Nova Scotia 1959
New Brunswick 1967	Nova Scotia 1956	British Columbia 1956	Manitoba 1960
Prince Edward Island 1968	Alberta 1957	New Brunswick 1956	British Columbia 1961
British Columbia 1969	Prince Edward Island 1959	Saskatchewan 1956	Quebec 1963
	New Brunswick 1960	Yukon Territory 1963	Northwest Territories 1966
		Quebec 1964	
		Northwest Territories 1966	

SOURCE: Davis and Krauter (1971), p. 123.
NOTE: Table not updated in more recent edition of work.

and not to provincial issues where civil rights in general, and minority rights in particular, are placed in greatest jeopardy. Some argue that its effectiveness could be improved if it were applied not only to Parliament and the federal government, as at present, but also to the provinces (Davis and Krauter 1971, p. 107). Its limited scope, compounded by its vague and ambiguous language, has meant that courts made almost no use of it in reaching their judgements, even in disputes involving freedom of speech or the press (ibid, p. 109).

Enforcement is a key problem with any human rights legislation. Under present circumstances, there is a great reliance on individual civil complaints to guarantee minority rights. This is an inefficient, slow, and expensive procedure, which puts a great burden upon those least able to help themselves. Canada does not have well-financed interest groups to manage a litigant's case. A Canadian Human Rights Commission has been set up to enforce the Canadian Human Rights Act. Some, but not all, provinces have established civil rights commissions or agencies mandated to defend human rights. Such commissions do not have initiatory powers (i.e., the power to act in the absence of a formal complaint), and this may reduce their effectiveness (Means 1969, p. 411). At the same time, however, improvements in legal aid services and the establishment of official ombudsmen have served to help immigrants. But lawyers serving immigrant populations often find that much of their time is spent on questions of immigrant status itself.

An overview of Canada's civil-rights policy points in a positive direction. Odious restrictions on the participation of ethnic groups in civic life have long been removed. Much overt discrimination against minority groups has been reduced by the use of fair employment or fair accommodation practices. More important is the recognition of the importance of an increasingly active and responsible role of the State in the evolution of social life and institutions. But as minority ethnic group members know, civil rights is more than legislation: it is an attitude. Laws do not touch instances of covert discrimination. Although anti-discrimination programmes necessarily are based on legislation, discrimination is not primarily a juridical problem but rather a social, psychological, and economic one. Some would advocate intensive educational programmes to deal with the problem (Eberlee 1961, p. 4; Means 1969, p. 412), but more often the call for "affirmative action" to offset entrenched or institutionalized discrimination is heard today. The latter is sometimes described as "reverse discrimination," and the possibility of a conservative reaction arises. These are chronic issues in any multiethnic society.

Cultural policy. The federal government took the lead in establishing multicultural policies in Canada. Provincial and local governments followed later. The federal lead reflects the fact that the issue of multiculturalism and the problem of recognition for ethnic cultures other than British and French arose in the context of the linguistic conflict taking place at the federal level.

Implementation of a multiculturalism programme at the federal level has not been extensive. Some observers attribute the lack of a larger programme at least in part to apathy on the part of the ethnic minorities themselves. But another reason may be that in federal institutions the very linguistic conflict that sparked the multiculturalism issue has constituted an obstacle to more complete implementation. In recent years, the participation of some provincial governments increased more rapidly, perhaps because of greater ethnic group influence at that level.

When the multiculturalism issue first arose as a political issue, the Liberal government found it difficult to respond clearly to demands of "other" ethnic groups in the area of cultural policy. It really faced a dilemma. The powerful French Canadian group in the Liberal government has stood largely opposed to this concept of multiculturalism. As a compromise, in October 1971, the Liberals announced support in principle for the idea of multiculturalism, while initially offering only token support for ethnic group activities such as cultural centres, ethnic histories, summer camps, and so on. The government's intentions for the future, particularly with respect to language, remain ambiguous. On some occasions it has been announced that since social trends toward language loss are out of tune with popular preferences in each group, something should be done to assist non-official language retention. But on other occasions, perhaps in response to pressure from French Canadian leaders or perhaps reflecting the prevailing mood of austerity, it has been suggested that the government should shift its emphasis away from culture to combatting discrimination and racism. This would be a way of dealing with group status, but it might not fully assist small ethnic groups to withstand strong pressures toward cultural conformity.

The government's attempts to find a compromise appear to have been reasonably successful politically. Organized protests from small ethnic groups have been weak. Dissatisfactions have been expressed and may be growing, but it is significant that they are expressed most visibly at conferences organized by the government itself. In fact, it appears that many ethnic group leaders have been co-opted by participation in government planning. At the same time, there is an underlying, and perhaps growing, attitude of cynicism toward the federal government's position among minority ethnic group leaders in many parts of Canada because major demands in the areas of language education in the regular schools and multilingual broadcasting through the facilities of the CBC have not been met. Whether real dissatisfaction is widespread is difficult to judge (Bociurkiw 1978; Lupul 1978*a*).

The area of education and language is the most politically sensitive. Policies in this area can be divided into three aspects: public education for all students, options available within the public educational system of special interest to students from particular ethnic backgrounds, and special supplementary courses available outside the regular school system operated by ethnic group organizations. In each case, the relative emphasis on language as opposed to other aspects of culture is important. The current federal multicultural policy does not deal with the regular public educational systems under provincial jurisdiction (though the federal government has become involved in French-English relationships at that level). Federal policy makes small grants available to ethnic organizations that operate supplementary cultural and linguistic courses outside the regular school system. The programme is intended to support teacher training, the development and production of textbooks and other teaching aids, and actual course operation. This is a new extension of policy, evidently consistent with the Berry, Kalin, and Taylor (1977) study of majority attitudes, which showed that support for non-official language instruction is acceptable (at least across the non-francophone provinces) in special schools, but not in regular schools.

Lupul (1978b, p. 15) locates opposition to multiculturalism principally in Ontario and Quebec, and notes the reluctance of the ethnic groups themselves:

> This "church-basement" approach to the teaching of ancestral languages undoubtedly reflects both the federal government's timidity before powerful voices in Quebec and Ontario, concerned that multiculturalism not become multilingualism, and the ethnic groups' own apparent indifference to learning ancestral languages.

Lupul notes that in previous years, grant applications have been insufficient to consume even the small funds available, and that even the vocal Ukrainian group has difficulty maintaining enrolments in their schools. In any case, language instruction is a complex process and formal language instruction is notoriously ineffective when not supported by informal group involvement or external incentive.

Provincial governments in provinces with large non-English and non-French populations have adopted their ówn multicultural policies as a result of pressure from ethnic minorities. Provincial governments in Canada have jurisdiction over education. In the area of general education for all students, efforts have been made to eliminate negative ethnic and racial stereotypes from textbooks, and to add content on the role of the "other" ethnic groups in Canadian history. In Ontario, for example, there are optional guide-lines for the introduction of historical materials on ethnic groups. The Heritage Language Programme offers instruction in ancestral languages, though a surcharge for enrolment has been imposed at the discretion of local school boards. It is not known to what extent various options are actually pursued in the classrooms, nor their impact. Lupul (ibid.) notes that Alberta and Saskatchewan go further to permit all languages to be languages of instruction on a par with English and French, but that only in one city, Edmonton, are there English-Ukrainian bilingual emersion courses (Royal Commission on Bilingualism and Biculturalism 1970, pp. 102−5). Some provinces are funding third-language programmes, but no analysis of their impact is yet available. Education is not the only focus for multicultural policies. For example, provinces such as Ontario give a variety of intercultural development grants to ethnic group organizations and other community groups.

The provincial governments, of course, must attempt to respond to their own situation while maintaining an acceptable relation to other parts of Canada. In western provinces, where the other ethnic groups are demographically most significant and where the French-English conflict seems most distant, proposals for greater cultural decentralization are likely to be advanced. Though unclear in their political significance, these proposals show how the regional configuration of ethnic groups in Canada can present problems for the scope of authority of the federal government.

SUMMARY

Formal representation of small ethnic groups in the Canadian federal government and House of Commons is weak. All the major parties do attempt to appeal to these groups in their efforts to build and retain a majority, both as ethnic groups and as members of the major regional and linguistic constituencies. At the provincial and local levels, ethnic representation is relatively strong.

Of the areas of political conflict reviewed here, the most important appears to be cultural policy. This is an area where at the federal level, the British, and particularly the French, groups have strongly resisted minority group pressures for increased implementation of multiculturalism. An implication is that in an important area of policy, political institutions generate a tendency toward decentralization and a reliance on provincial and local levels of government. Whether such decentralization aids societal cohesion by deflecting pressure from the federal government, or undermines it because federal institutions are perceived as less than fully responsive is not known.

In any case, it must be re-emphasized that dissatisfaction with government cultural policy at any level does not appear to be particularly widespread or deep; it is greater in some groups than others, and greater in certain segments within groups. Whether existing policies actually reflect a good political compromise between the diverse views of British, French, and various other ethnic groups is still an open question.

In general, the greater representation for small ethnic groups at the provincial and municipal levels may have diverse effects. It may contribute to the perceived legitimacy of government generally or it may intensify regional and linguistic conflicts, and thus undermine the legitimacy and effectiveness of central governmental institutions.

National Unity and Ethnic Community Cohesion

In the preceding chapters, the characteristics of a number of ethnic groups were considered. Social processes generally thought to be relevant in various ways to the emergence or development of national cohesion were examined. In this chapter, the focus is on additional information relevant to the phenomenon of national cohesion itself. How can it be measured? What indicators are available? What do they tell us about national identification and the perceptions of the legitimacy of national institutions among immigrants and their descendants?

As stressed in our general introduction, the concept of national unity is quite complex and subject to diverse interpretations. Its two main components, national identification and acceptance of institutional legitimacy, are related, but also potentially independent of one another. An individual can identify with Canada without being loyal to a particular government in power, or he can be loyal without a strong national identification. But the seemingly most pertinent concrete indicators of societal cohesion cannot be used to distinguish neatly between the two. These indicators include attitudinal questions from sample survey interviews that tap Canadian identification. Additional information on emigration, citizenship, political participation, military service, and even the extent to which members of various groups are law-abiding seems relevant. These data have to varying degrees a bearing both on national identification and institutional legitimacy. A review of available studies on these topics will contribute to an overall view of the impact that immigration and ethnicity have on Canadian cohesion, though more precise measures would be desirable.

Evidence for ethnicity and national cohesion is most meaningful when examined in relation to ethnic community survival and the maintenance of ethnic cohesion, and not only in relation to ethnic-origin collectivities. If members of a particular ethnic-origin collectivity are largely anglicized, then to that extent, they are in reality no longer really part of a minority ethnic group in the sociological sense. In that case, evidence of strong Canadian identification and acceptance of institutional legitimacy would have an entirely different bearing on the question of interethnic cohesion than it would in the case of strong intraethnic cohesion.

CANADIAN IDENTIFICATION

A crucial component of an individual's commitment to a country is his subjective feeling about that country and his own relationship to it. This is what many mean by nationalism—the feeling of membership in, and obligation to, a nation as a significant element in an individual's self-image.

What are the national orientations of immigrants? All the available information suggests that many immigrants fairly quickly accept the idea that they are in some sense Canadian. At the same time, many experience a weakening, and some an extinction, of their identification with a national origin outside Canada. The shift in national orientation occurs more quickly in some groups, and more slowly in others (O'Bryan, Reitz, and Kuplowska 1976, p. 97*ff*; Richmond 1976, p. 47).

For our purposes, we want also to know how much the adoption of a Canadian national identity is inhibited or impeded by the maintenance of ties to a minority ethnic community. The evidence indicates that the two bases of identity are to some extent in competition (Richmond 1976, pp. 48−55). But they are not necessarily incompatible. Many persons espouse a dual identity, for example, Italian-Canadian. Moreover, many of those whose Canadian identity is strong still feel a positive attitude toward their ethnic-origin group. In one survey, fully half of the minority group members whose primary identification was "Canadian" still supported the maintenance of ethnic culture and language in Canada (O'Bryan, Reitz, and Kuplowska 1976). The authors observed that:

> To be a "Canadian" is not necessarily to reject one's ethnic ancestry and the culture it represents. Instead, one may become Canadian while continuing to support a distinctive ethnic culture and even the use of a non-official language in Canada. Enthusiasm for this culture and language may wane, but it rarely turns into rejection and hostility (pp. 97−98).

The absence of rejection of the ethnic past indicates in a particularly strong way the existence of the option of dual identity.

EMIGRATION

One of the ways disaffection with a society may be expressed is simply by leaving it. Emigration therefore reflects a lack of unity. Emigration also may contribute indirectly to cohesion by providing a safety valve for discontentment.

Kalbach (1974) has studied outmigration and shows that it has been quite significant in Canada. His analyses compare emigration to immigration. Using immigration and census statistics, Kalbach showed that Canada suffered a net population loss due to the excess of emigration over immigration during the 1890s and 1930s (see figure 4.6.1). Since World War II, however, immigration has always exceeded emigration: by a factor of 3.3 during the 1950s and 2.0 during the 1960s. There can be little quarrel with

Kalbach's argument that the holding power of Canadian society is very much a function of its economic health. His interpretation suggests that Canadian unity is based to a significant extent on economic considerations. The pertinent question is: Who is leaving? Is emigration related to ethnicity? Available data distinguish immigrants from native-born and do not distinguish one ethnic group from another. Even this information is suggestive, however. Kalbach shows that the rate of emigration among immigrants is high: 27%. One in four immigrants do not remain in Canada. They either return home or move on to other countries such as the United States. (A conclusion like this must be based on an indirect calculation, since emigrants are not counted as they leave. Immigration statistics project a foreign-born population of 4.5 million in 1971. The 1971 census enumerated only 3.3 million immigrants. Subtraction indicates that 1.2 million, or 27%, left the country.) But there are also data to suggest that Canadians in general tend to emigrate, often to the United States. A Gallup Poll released 10 June 1972 showed that among all Canadians, 19%, ''if free to do so, would like to go and settle in another country.'' The rate is highest among the young. For persons eighteen to twenty-nine years of age, 30% say they would like to leave Canada. Evidently, as Canadians grow older they become more committed to permanent residence in Canada. (Of course, if the young who want to leave actually do so, those committed to Canada are found only in the older groups!) The actual rate at which the native-born leave Canada is no doubt lower than the 30% who say they would like to leave, and to this

FIGURE 4.6.1
Net Migration, Canada, 1851–1971

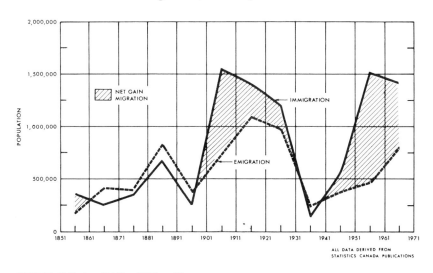

ALL DATA DERIVED FROM
STATISTICS CANADA PUBLICATIONS

SOURCE: Kalbach and McVey (1979), p. 55.

extent, Canadians generally may have a higher level of commitment to Canada than do immigrants. It may be speculated that the longer an immigrant stays in Canada, the less likely it is he will leave in the future (this is a general finding in studies of geographical mobility). Quite possibly, then, immigrants who have been in Canada for, say, ten or fifteen years may be no more likely to leave than other Canadians.

Variations in rates of emigration by ethnic origin are not known. Emigration is likely quite low for persons of East European origin because return to the homeland is politically difficult or impossible. Emigration may be quite high for members of other groups. A special study of the Toronto black population by Head (1975) showed that nearly 35% expected to return to their home country, and another 15% were uncertain whether they would remain in Canada.

CITIZENSHIP

Acquisition of Canadian citizenship by immigrants is one sign of Canadian identification and commitment to Canada. It is generally believed that immigrants to Canada are slow to acquire Canadian citizenship. The 1971 census shows that only 59.2% of the 3.3 million foreign-born persons in Canada are Canadian citizens. This overall percentage varies from 90.7% for the nearly half million persons born in East-European countries to only 46.0% for 625,000 persons from South-European countries. Of the nearly one million immigrants from the United Kingdom, 54.4% are citizens; of the 310,000 American immigrants, 53.7% are citizens. The remaining immigrants, numbering nearly one million and mostly from Western Europe, have a citizenship rate of 59.0%. The very high rate of citizenship for East Europeans undoubtedly reflects their refugee status. As British subjects, immigrants from the United Kingdom until very recently have been entitled to special privileges in Canada. For the others, the low rate of citizenship seems to raise serious questions about commitment to Canada.

A study by Neice (1978) probes this matter. Of four groups in Toronto, only 46.9% are citizens: United Kingdom, 39.8%; Italy, 39.0%; Greece, 43.3%; and Portugal and Spain, 24.0%. But of those eligible to become citizens by rules in effect at the time of the study (i.e., adults over twenty-one years of age with five years residence), figures are substantially higher: United Kingdom, 62.1%; Greece, 55.6%; Italy, 47.8%; and Portugal and Spain, 37.1%. All groups show a steady upward trend in citizenship over time, and except for persons from the United Kingdom, have a rate of over 70% for those with sixteen to twenty-five years of residence. Rates of citizenship for all persons in Canada since World War II are around 90%.

Immigrants move slowly into Canadian citizenship. They may be spurred by a national crisis such as a major war. This slow movement may mean that feelings of loyalty to Canada are there and can be mobilized, but do not lead routinely to application for citizenship in the absence of precipitating factors. Native Canadians do not pressure immigrants to become citizens. Thus, patterns of slow citizenship acquisition may reflect the absence of strong nationalistic feelings among native Canadians themselves, rather than among the immigrants.

Does a weakening of ethnic group ties lead to earlier application for citizenship? Neice's data show that Canadian citizenship status tends to be associated with use of an official language in the home (in Toronto, overwhelmingly English, of course). But an association between citizenship and language use may arise simply because the longer-term residents are both more likely to speak English and to have become citizens, not because one affects the other. There is no evidence of the relationship between citizenship and assimilation for those having been in Canada the same amount of time.

The relation of economic experiences to desire for citizenship is not a simple one. Richmond (1967) showed that among immigrants the rate of intention to become citizens is higher both for the upwardly mobile *and* the downwardly mobile. The rate is highest for those experiencing downward mobility followed by a recovery. Richmond suggests various plausible psychological explanations. But it is evident that these facts do not suggest a simple relation between economic inequality and alienation from Canada, echoing the conclusion of the earlier discussion of economic institutions.

POLITICAL PARTICIPATION

Political participation is a significant indicator of orientation toward a political system. Lack of participation may mean satisfaction with the *status quo*; it may also reflect a degree of alienation from the electoral process and from a society's central institutions. From the individual's point of view, conventional political participation such as voting is largely a symbolic rather than a rational act. By such participation, an individual signals his acceptance of political institutions. Our question here is whether small ethnic group members, particularly those retaining strong ethnic loyalties, exhibit any significant degree of political alienation by lower political participation.

Among citizens eligible to vote, at each social class level, political participation is lower for persons retaining ties to an ethnic subculture, according to data from the non-official languages survey of five Canadian cities (Reitz 1980). This is particularly true in ethnic groups most socially distant from the majority Canadian group. Thus politically, the retention of ethnic group ties does reflect a degree of political isolation.

Some interesting corroborative findings from a study of Chinese and Japanese Canadians are reported by Quo (1971). The Chinese, who retain far stronger ethnic ties than the Japanese, also tend to be more apolitical and to express cynical attitudes about Canadian government. The Japanese attitudes and behaviour parallel much more closely those of the general population (as a matter of fact, the Japanese tend to be more politically obedient and more contented). Quo concluded that socialization within an ethnic community militates against political integration. The Blacks in Nova Scotia have been isolated in ghetto-like communities, and although culturally they are conformist in many ways, they, like the Chinese, often express cynical views of politics (Henry 1973).

MILITARY SERVICE

The Canadian Armed Forces is a national organization that symbolizes in a particular way Canadian nationalism and the defence of Canadian national interests. Service in the Canadian Forces is voluntary, and therefore may reflect a kind of commitment to the Canadian national interest as defined by the government. Of course, military service is a career opportunity that may be chosen for more personal reasons. For example, black representation in the U.S. military increased greatly after World War II, primarily because of a change in the opportunities made available to Blacks. Nevertheless, few immigrants undertake military service in Canada if they maintain a commitment to a foreign nation.

Coulombe (Royal Commission on Bilingualism and Biculturalism 1969, p. 80) studied ethnic group participation in the Canadian Forces and found that of Canadian military personnel, 16% have ethnic backgrounds other than British or French. Considering that these groups comprise over 26% of the Canadian population, it is evident that there is a substantial underrepresentation of the ''other'' ethnic groups in the military. Whether this underrepresentation is restricted only to immigrants, citizens, or particular ethnic minorities, or whether the maintenance of minority group ties inhibits interest in military service in Canada are unknown.

CRIME RATES

Committing acts of violation of criminal law may be seen as antisocial behaviour that reflects low levels of social integration and commitment. Crime is one expression of social conflict. It sometimes is associated in the public mind with indigent immigrant groups who reside in ghettoes and frequently turn to crime in response to hardship and social disorganization.

Information on crime in Canada suggests that immigrants tend to be *more* law-abiding than native Canadians. Those who have studied the statistics in this field conclude that the rate of crime conviction for the foreign-born is no higher than that of the native-born, and in most cases appears to be even lower. Immigrants as a group are not causing a crime problem.

The relevant statistics are difficult to obtain. During the 1960s, it became increasingly rare to record the birth place or ethnic origin of convicted criminals. By 1970, this practice ceased entirely. A study for 1951 – 1954 showed that the rates of conviction of native-born males between fifteen and forty-nine years of age was 86.6 per 10,000, compared to 42.8 per 10,000 among foreign-born males. The rates for specific foreign-born groups range from a high of 63.1 for the American-born to a low of 16.7 for the Italian-born (Vallée and Schwartz 1961). Figures for 1961 and estimates for 1971 show that the Canadian-born males and females still have a higher probability of being convicted of an indictable offence (Giffen 1976, p. 102−5).

Rates of juvenile delinquency follow a similar pattern. In 1951, children with Canadian-born fathers had a delinquency rate of 19.1 per 10,000 males between twenty-five and sixty-four years of age, compared with 17.0 per 10,000 for those with foreign-born fathers. By 1961, the equivalent figures were 37.6 and 6.6 per 10,000 (ibid.). The conventional wisdom that children of immigrants are exposed to cultural conflicts that produce high delinquency rates is not supported by these figures.

Several reasons are offered to explain the apparently lower conviction rates among the foreign-born and their children. Our selective immigration policy may weed out those with a criminal record (tighter laws were instituted in 1906 and again in 1952). At the same time, immigration to Canada has been matched increasingly with the opening of legitimate opportunities. As was noted earlier, upward job mobility has been fairly easily available to immigrants in the recent past. Immigrants able to find a legitimate occupational niche have fewer reasons to resort to criminal means. But the social relations of immigrants also may be relevant. It takes time to assimilate the criminal norms, techniques, and associations of a new society. This may explain the higher conviction rates of males born in the United States. Tepperman (1977, pp. 192−229) notes that sponsored immigrants · are immediately embedded in a network of family and friends in Canada, and are more likely to be constrained from criminal acts by the bonds of family responsibility. They are also more likely to get financial and psychological support in times of difficulty, making crime a less probable response to hardship.

SUMMARY

The evidence may be seen as suggesting that (a) members of most of the other groups do develop Canadian identity and commitment over time; (b) the degree of their commitment to Canada is muted and restrained, though perhaps no more so than among Canadians generally; and (c) the degree of their commitment to Canada is related to a weakening of ethnic attachments and identity, but these two processes occurring together over time may not actually affect one another either positively or negatively. In other words, there is no evidence that societal cohesion is seriously undermined by the presence of a large number of persons of diverse ethnic origins or by their varying levels of attachment to an ethnic subculture. The evidence, however, is scanty and inconclusive. The situation may be different in some of the smaller and recently arrived non-white groups.

The strength of Canadian commitment depends on the aspect considered. The various minority ethnic groups tend to be law abiding. They tend to be conservative because of a desire to consolidate their positions. They are not politically disruptive. However, they may not remain committed to Canada if better economic opportunities present themselves elsewhere, something that appears to be true of anglophone Canadians generally. The problem of Canadian commitment and identity is a national problem, not an ethnic one. The persistence of ethnic communities may be to some degree a reaction to the weakness of the national community, and not a cause.

Conclusions and Implications

In the preliminary remarks of chapter 4.1, three popular alternative views of the overall impact that the "other" ethnic groups have on societal cohesion were outlined: that there is either a negative or a positive or no long-term impact because of assimilation. Related popular views of the impact on the French-English conflict were mentioned also. However, a review of the relevant theories and evidence does not lead to any simple choice among these popular conceptions. The evidence of intergroup cohesiveness is sketchy, often superficial, and permits few comparisons within and across groups.

An examination of the underlying social processes relevant to cohesion—inequality, conflict, and intergroup communication—produces some insights, but actual effects on cohesion cannot be known with any real confidence. There are many problems and hopeful signs. Conclusions therefore must be speculative. The attempt here will be to summarize briefly the overall situation, and to indicate choices confronting Canadian society that may affect national cohesion in the future.

INTERGROUP COHESION

The evidence shows that the degree of national identification and acceptance of institutional and governmental legitimacy among members of the minority ethnic groups is fairly high, or at least not significantly lower than in the dominant groups. The evidence also suggests that the growth of interethnic cohesion does not necessarily presuppose the breakdown of intraethnic cohesion. In some groups, such as the Scandinavians and North Europeans, a significant degree of assimilation occurs. In other groups, ethnic community formation is associated with some dissatisfaction with federal and provincial government policies, but there is no serious withdrawal of legitimacy. Nor does ethnic community formation appear to undermine the development of Canadian identification.

Whether overall findings apply to each individual group, or whether specific groups such as the recently arrived non-Europeans vary significantly from the overall trend in Canadian identification and acceptance of institutional legitimacy are not known. Whether the level of cohesion between francophones and anglophones is affected by the presence of these other groups has not proven to be a matter on which simple measurements are possible. With respect to the broader issue of the capacity of Canadian society to organize itself in pursuit of common goals, there is quite simply no reliable evidence on which to base any conclusion. The question of, and potential for, change is also a matter of speculation.

UNDERLYING INTERGROUP RELATIONSHIPS

Trends in basic intergroup relationships can be assessed, as they have relevance for societal cohesion, but actual consequences for cohesion have not been examined directly in many cases.

The formation of ethnic communities is associated both with interethnic conflict and social isolation of ethnic groups from one another. The extent of conflict and isolation varies from group to group. Perhaps the most serious intergroup conflicts have arisen from exceptional war-time tensions involving Japanese and German Canadians.

Often the potential for interethnic conflict is not realized. One reason is that ethnic group members are divided among themselves. They are divided by social class, region, and other social boundaries as are the dominant groups. There are also divisions that can be traced to pre-immigration experiences. Minority ethnic groups do not have a unique set of collective interests that unite them politically against other Canadians. A second reason why conflicts do not occur may be that minority group members are reluctant to assert their interests because they feel that the inequalities suffered are acceptable, or because they fear retaliation from other groups. Minority ethnic groups have tended to be poorly organized and to find it difficult to mobilize their collective resources. Some groups are able to solve their problems internally; others learn to live with their problems and accept a subordinate position in society. A third reason for the lack of interethnic conflict is that many persons who are dissatisfied with life in Canada simply leave the country to return to their country of origin or go to other countries such as the United States. This means of defusing potential conflicts is more readily available in some cases than in others.

ECONOMIC INEQUALITY

The importance of strictly economic inequality as a source of conflict has declined in the post-World War II era, at least for ethnic groups of European origin. There has been significant upward mobility for the descendants of earlier immigrants, and significantly better economic conditions for new immigrants. Reduced economic inequality has an immediate positive effect on overall societal cohesion, but it may ultimately weaken ethnic cohesion in some respects. In this sense, while interethnic cohesion does not necessarily presuppose an immediate breakdown in intraethnic cohesion, it may presuppose a long-term weakening of its social bases.

Following recent policy changes, immigration to Canada has shifted; so that non-European sources have become important. Non-whites from the West Indies and South Asia now form substantial and growing communities in Canadian cities in general, and Toronto in particular. Evidence of rather serious tensions involving these groups suggests that their experiences over the long run may not parallel those of the European-origin groups. There are some hopeful signs, notably the negative public reactions to reports of interracial violence. But Canadian experience in the area of race relations is not extensive, and existing experience does not encourage unreserved optimism.

Present legislation guarantees equal opportunity to all groups, including the new and growing racial minorities. A major choice still lying in the future is essentially whether to place priority on assisting new non-white immigrants to adapt to Canadian society in such a way that serious conflict is avoided, or to rely on present legislation to resolve the inevitable conflicts as they arise. The children of the new West Indian immigrants, for example, often encounter difficulties in school that virtually predestine them to low-paying unskilled jobs. Altering this situation to avoid future problems will require a reallocation of educational resources.

MULTICULTURALISM

Expectations have been raised in recent years for increased control or influence over socio-cultural institutions within ethnic minority groups. Rising expectations are in part a consequence of the English-French conflict, and in part a consequence of upward economic mobility and security that permit groups to give attention to non-economic concerns. Across Canada there are still only weak minority-group organization and support for the multiculturalism movement to advance the position of minority cultures, particularly in educational institutions and the media. At the same time, multiculturalism is resisted by English Canadians. French Canadians, whose own expectations are rising, even more strongly resist minority-group cultural demands. Within Quebec, there is a conflict over whether immigrant groups can choose English as the language of instruction in schools. Given the low level of contact and communication between the French Canadians and the minority ethnic groups, conflict tends to take place at the level of institutions dominated by English Canadians. In national political institutions, the power of the French is greater by far than that of the small ethnic groups. In this setting, the French often view their interests as opposed to the idea of multiculturalism, and they exert influence on English Canadians as intermediaries. The position of the French varies across regions, of course, and the multiculturalism movement may intensify regional, as well as linguistic, conflict in Canada.

Some members of the small ethnic groups see their own interests as overlapping those of the French. In this view, a reverse process is envisioned in which the multiculturalism movement increases the likelihood that various English Canadian groups will move toward accommodation with the French, thus reducing linguistic and regional conflict.

The issue of cultural status presents choices at different levels. At the most concrete level, there is the decision about the degree to which society should support minority ethnic cultures, and the form of that support, taking into account the conflicting viewpoints of British, French, and other ethnic groups. Political realities seem to dictate that the degree of commitment, in whatever form, will be rather low.

At a broader level, there is a choice of how to structure the context in which the decision about minority cultures is made. The argument of conflicting cultural interests between the French and the other groups, or between the British and the other groups seems not to have been seriously examined. Members of the other ethnic groups who argue that their cultural interests overlap with those of French Canadians and Canadians in general feel that multiculturalism proposes a new basis for Canadian cohesion. Others see such an argument as rhetoric attributable to the weakness of their position, rather than as a significant proposal for new political alignment. Serious dialogue at this level seems hampered by the social isolation of groups, and in the context of the French-English "unity crisis," particularly by the regional isolation between the French and the minority groups.

IMMIGRATION

The issue of immigration is reviewed periodically in Canada. The federal government's 1974 green paper lists alternatives for the future. From the point of view of societal cohesion, the continuing use of immigration policy as an economic tool raises clear questions. Underlying this debate are other issues: whether to reaffirm and extend the liberalization of immigration policy; whether a reaction to non-white immigration will gain attention; how to accommodate the differing perspectives on immigration held in Quebec and elsewhere.

These various choices suggest that the "other" ethnic groups could have a farther-reaching impact on social cohesion in the future than they have at present.

References and Bibliography

Allport, Gordon W.
1958 *Nature of Prejudice*. Abr. ed. Garden City, N.Y.: Doubleday & Co.
Armor, David J.
1972 "The Evidence on Busing." *Public Interest* 28 (Summer): 90–126.
Avery, Donald
1975 "Continental European Immigrant Workers in Canada 1896–1919: From 'Stalwart Peasants' to Radical Proletariat." *Canadian Review of Sociology and Anthropology* 12: 53–64.
Berry, John W.; Kalin, Rudolf; and Taylor, Donald M.
1977 *Multiculturalism and Ethnic Attitudes in Canada*. Ottawa: Supply and Services Canada.
Blishen, Bernard R.
1970 "Social Class and Opportunity in Canada." *Canadian Review of Sociology and Anthropology* 7: 110–27.
Bociurkiw, Bohdan
1978 "The Federal Policy of Multiculturalism and the Ukrainian-Canadian Community." In *Ukrainian Canadians, Multiculturalism, and Separatism: An Assessment*, edited by Manoly R. Lupul, pp. 98–128. Edmonton, Alta.: The University of Alberta Press for The Canadian Institute of Ukrainian Studies.
Borhek, J.T.
1970 "Ethnic-Group Cohesion." *American Journal of Sociology* 76: 33–46.
Broadfoot, Barry
1977 *Years of Sorrow, Years of Shame: The Japanese Canadians in World War II*. Toronto: Doubleday Publishers.
Canada, Department of Manpower and Immigration
1974 *Immigration Program*. Canadian Immigration and Population Studies. Ottawa: Information Canada.
Canada, Royal Commission Appointed to Inquire Into the Immigration of Italian Labourers to Montreal and the Alleged Fraudulent Practices of Employment Agencies
1905 *Sessional Papers*, no. 36*b*. "Report of the Commission and Evidence."
Canada, Royal Commission on Bilingualism and Biculturalism
1969 *Report*. Book 3*A*, *The Work World*, parts 1 and 2. Ottawa: Queen's Printer.
1970 *Report*. Book 4, *The Cultural Contribution of the Other Ethnic Groups*. Ottawa: Queen's Printer.

411

Cappon, Paul
1978 "Nationalism and Inter-Ethnic and Linguistic Conflict in Quebec." In *The Canadian Ethnic Mosaic: A Quest for Identity*, edited by Leo Driedger, pp. 327–39. Toronto: McClelland and Stewart.

Clairmont, Donald H., and Magill, Dennis W.
1974 *Africville: The Life and Death of a Canadian Black Community.* Toronto: McClelland and Stewart.

Clement, Wallace
1975 *The Canadian Corporate Elite: An Analysis of Economic Power.* Toronto: McClelland and Stewart.

Danziger, K.
n.d. "The Socialization of Immigrant Children." Mimeographed. Downsview, Ont.: Institute for Behavioural Research.

Darroch, Gordon
1979 "Another Look at Ethnicity, Stratification, and Social Mobility in Canada." *Canadian Journal of Sociology* 4: 1-25.

Davis, Morris, and Krauter, Joseph
1971 *The Other Canadians*. Toronto: Methuen Publications.

Deutsch, Morton, and Collins, Mary E.
1951 *Interracial Housing: A Psychological Evaluation of a Social Experiment*. Minneapolis: University of Minnesota Press.

Driedger, Leo, and Church, Glenn
1974 "Residential Segregation and Institutional Completeness: A Comparison of Ethnic Minorities." *Canadian Review of Sociology and Anthropology* 11: 30–52.

Driedger, Leo, and Peters, Jacob
1977 "Identity and Social Distance: Towards Understanding Simmel's 'The Stranger'." *Canadian Review of Sociology and Anthropology* 14: 158–73.

Eberlee, Thomas
1961 "Legal Functions Are Not Enough in Combatting Discrimination." *Human Relations* 1, no. 3.

Fine, Charles
1960 "Canadian and American Ethnic Viewpoints: A Study in Contrast." *Social Worker* 28, no. 2: 25–33.

Giffen, J.
1976 "Rates of Crime and Delinquency." In *Crime and Its Treatment in Canada*, 2d ed., edited by W.T. McGrath. Toronto: Macmillan of Canada.

Goldlust, J., and Richmond, A.
1973 "A Multi-Variate Analysis of the Economic Adaptation of Immigrants in Toronto." Mimeographed. Downsview, Ont.: Institute for Behavioural Research.

1977 "Factors Associated With Commitment To and Identification With Canada." In *Identities: The Impact of Ethnicity on Canadian Society*, edited by Wsevolod Isajiw. Toronto: Peter Martin Associates.

Gordon, Milton M.
1964 *Assimilation in American Life: The Role of Race, Religion and National Origins*. New York: Oxford University Press.

Hawkins, Freda
1972 *Canada and Immigration: Public Policy and Public Concern*. Montreal: McGill-Queen's University Press.

Head, Wilson A.
1975 *The Black Presence in the Canadian Mosaic: A Study of Perception and the Practice of Discrimination Against Blacks in Metropolitan Toronto*. Ontario Human Rights Commission. Toronto: Queen's Printer.

Henry, Frances
1973 *Forgotten Canadians: The Blacks of Nova Scotia*. Toronto: Longman Canada.
1978 "The Dynamics of Racism in Toronto." Mimeographed. Downsview, Ont.: Institute for Behavioural Research.

Hill, Jr., D.
1960 "Negroes in Toronto: A Sociological Study of a Minority Group." Ph.D. dissertation, University of Toronto.

Jackson, J.
1977 "The Functions of Language in Canada: On the Political Economy of Language." In *The Individual, Language and Society in Canada*, edited by W.H. Coons, Donald M. Taylor, and Marc-Adélard Tremblay, pp. 61–76. Ottawa: Canada Council.

Kage, J.
1962 *With Faith and Thanksgiving*. Montreal: Eagle Publishing Co.

Kalbach, Warren E.
1970 *The Impact of Immigration on Canada's Population*. Ottawa: Queen's Printer.
1974 *Effect of Immigration on Population*. Canadian Immigration and Population Studies. Ottawa: Information Canada.

Kalbach, Warren E., and McVey, Wayne W.
1979 *The Demographic Bases of Canadian Society*. Rev. ed. Toronto: McGraw-Hill Ryerson.

Kelner, Merrijoy
1970 "Ethnic Penetration Into Toronto's Elite Structure." *Canadian Review of Sociology and Anthropology* 7: 128–37.

Kerr, C.
1959 *Industrialism and Industrial Man*. Berkeley and Los Angeles: University of California Press.

Lai, Vivien
  1971 "The New Chinese Immigrants in Toronto." In *Minority Cana-*
    dians. Vol. 2, *Immigrant Groups*, edited by Jean Leonard Elliott,
    pp. 120–40. Toronto: Prentice-Hall of Canada.
Lermer, A.
  1955 "The Evolution of Canadian Policy Towards Cultural Pluralism."
    Information and Comment 16: 1–12.
Li, Peter S.
  1978 "The Stratification of Ethnic Immigrants: The Case of Toronto."
    Canadian Review of Sociology and Anthropology 15: 31–40.
Lipset, Seymour M.
  1968 *Agrarian Socialism: The Coöperative Commonwealth Federation in*
    Saskatchewan. Rev. ed. New York: Doubleday & Co.
Lupul, Manoly R.
  1978*a* "Canada's Options in a Time of Political Crisis and Their
    Implications for Multiculturalism." In *Ukrainian Canadians,*
    Multiculturalism, and Separatism: An Assessment, edited by
    Manoly R. Lupul, pp. 153–67. Edmonton, Alta.: The University
    of Alberta Press for The Canadian Institute of Ukrainian Studies.
  1978*b* "Multiculturalism and Educational Policies in Canada." *Multicul-*
    turalism 1, no. 4: 13–16.
McAllister, J.
  1971 "Ethnic Participation in Canadian Legislature: The Case of Man-
    itoba." *Canadian Ethnic Studies* 3, no. 1: 77–94.
McKenna, Marian C.
  1969 "The Melting Pot: Comparative Observations in the United States
    and Canada." *Sociology and Social Research* 53: 433–47.
McNaught, K.
  1966 "The National Outlook of English-Speaking Canadians." In
    Nationalism in Canada, edited by Peter Russell, pp. 61–71.
    Toronto: McGraw-Hill Ryerson.
Manitoba, Secretariat on Dominion-Provincial Cultural Relations
  1970 *Report of Manitoba Mosaic*. Winnipeg: Queen's Printer.
Matthews, Roy A.
  1965 "Canada, 'The International Nation'." *Queen's Quarterly* 72:
    499–523.
Means, John E.
  1969 "Human Rights and Canadian Federalism." *Phylon* 30: 398–412.
Meisel, John
  1975 *Working Papers on Canadian Politics*. 2d enl. ed. Montreal: McGill
    Queen's University Press.

Milnor, A.
1968 "The New Politics and Ethnic Revolt: 1929–38." In *Politics in Saskatchewan*, edited by Norman Ward and Duff Spafford, pp. 151–77. Toronto: Longman Canada.
"The Milrod 34: West Indians on Strike in Canada" *Race Today* (March/April): 36–40.

Myhul, Ivan M.
1978 "Ethnic Minorities and the Nationality Policy of the Parti Québécois." In *Ukrainian Canadians, Multiculturalism, and Separatism: An Assessment*, edited by Manoly R. Lupul, pp. 37–58. Edmonton, Alta.: The University of Alberta Press for The Canadian Institute of Ukrainian Studies.

Nagata, J. A.
1969 "Adaptation and Integration of Greek Working Class Immigrants in the City of Toronto, Canada: A Situational Approach." *International Migration Review* 4 (Fall): 44–70.

Neice, David C.
1978 *Ethnicity and Canadian Citizenship: A Metropolitan Study*. Ottawa: Supply and Services Canada.

O'Bryan, K.G.; Reitz, J.G.; and Kuplowska, O.M.
1976 *Non-Official Languages: A Study in Canadian Multiculturalism*. Ottawa: Supply and Services Canada.

Ossenberg, Richard J.
1964 "The Social Integration and Adjustment of Post-War Immigrants in Montreal and Toronto." *Canadian Review of Sociology and Anthropology* 1: 202–14.

Palmer, H., ed.
1974 *Immigration and the Rise of Multi Culturalism*. Toronto: Copp Clark Publishing.

Parai, Louis
1975 "Canada's Immigration Policy, 1962–74." *International Migration Review* 9: 449–77.

Pineo, Peter C.
1977 "The Social Standing of Ethnic and Racial Groupings." *Canadian Review of Sociology and Anthropology* 14: 147–57.

Pitman, W.
1977 "Now Is Not Too Late." Task Force on Human Relations. Mimeographed. Toronto: Council of Metropolitan Toronto.

Porter, John
1965 *The Vertical Mosaic: An Analysis of Social Class and Power in Canada*. Toronto: University of Toronto Press.
1972 "Dilemmas and Contradictions of a Multi-Ethnic Society." In *Proceedings and Transactions of the Royal Society of Canada*, Fourth Series, vol. 10. Ottawa: Royal Society of Canada.

Quebec, Commission of Inquiry on the Position of the French Language and on Language Rights in Quebec (Gendron Commission)
  1972 *The Position of the French Language in Quebec.* Vol. 3, *The Ethnic Groups; Other Ethnic Groups and the Enhancement and Development of French in Quebec.* Quebec: Éditeur officiel du Québec.
Quo, F.Q.
  1971 "Ethnic Origin and Political Attitudes—The Case of Orientals." *Canadian Ethnic Studies* 3, no. 2: 119–38.
Reitz, Jeffrey G.
  1974 "Language and Ethnic Community Survival." *Canadian Review of Sociology and Anthropology*, sp. no., *Aspects of Canadian Society*: 104–22.
  1977 "Analysis of Changing Group Inequalities in a Changing Occupational Structure." In *Mathematical Models of Sociology*, edited by P. Krishnan. Keele, Staffs: University of Keele.
  1980 *The Survival of Ethnic Groups.* Toronto: McGraw-Hill Ryerson.
Richmond, Anthony H.
  1967 *Post-War Immigrants in Canada.* Toronto: University of Toronto Press.
  1969 "Immigration and Pluralism in Canada." *International Migration Review* 4 (Fall): 5–24.
  1972 "Ethnic Residential Segregation in Metropolitan Toronto." Mimeographed. Downsview, Ont.: Institute for Behavioural Research.
  1976 "Language, Ethnicity, and the Problem of Identity in a Canadian Metropolis." In *Ethnicity in the Americas*, edited by Frances Henry, pp. 41–71. Chicago: Aldine Publishing Co.
Rocher, Guy
  1976 "Multiculturalism, the Doubts of a Francophone." Paper read at Second Canadian Conference on Multiculturalism, Ottawa, Ont., 13–15 February. Mimeographed.
Roseborough, Howard, and Breton, Raymond
  1971 "Perceptions of the Relative Economic and Political Advantages of Ethnic Groups in Canada." In *Canadian Society*, abr. ed., edited by Bernard R. Blishen et al. Toronto: Macmillan Co. of Canada.
Schwartz, Mildred A.
  1978 "Human Rights in War and Peace: The Case of the Japanese in Canada and the United States." Paper read at International Studies Association Annual Meeting, Washington, D.C., 23 February. Mimeographed.
Seager, Allen
  1977 "The Pass Strike of 1932." *Alberta History* 25, no. 1: 1–11.
Simpson, George Eaton, and Yinger, J. Milton
  1958 *Racial and Cultural Minorities: An Analysis of Prejudice and Discrimination.* Rev. ed. New York: Harper & Bros.

Smith, D.E.

1968 "Membership of the Saskatchewan Legislative Assembly, 1905−1966." In *Politics in Saskatchewan*, edited by Norman Ward and Duff Spafford, pp. 178−206. Toronto: Longman Canada.

Social Research Group

1965 "A Study of Interethnic Relations in Canada." Unpublished. Montreal: Social Research Group.

Spada, A.V.

1969 *The Italians in Canada*. Toronto: Italo-Canadian Ethnic and Historical Research Centre.

Tepperman, Lorne

1975 *Social Mobility in Canada*. Toronto: McGraw-Hill Ryerson.

1977 *Crime Control: The Urge Toward Authority*. Toronto: McGraw-Hill Ryerson.

Tienhaara, N.

1974 *Canadian Views on Immigration and Population: An Analysis of Post-War Gallup Polls*. Canadian Immigration and Population Studies. Ottawa: Information Canada.

Tryggvason, G.

1971 "The Effect of Intragroup Conflict in an Ethnic Community." *Canadian Ethnic Studies* 4, no. 2: 85−118.

Vallée, F., and Schwartz, Mildred A.

1971 "Report of Criminality Among the Foreign-Born in Canada." In *Canadian Society*, abr. ed., edited by Bernard R. Blishen et al., pp. 560−67. Toronto: Macmillan Co. of Canada.

Wangenheim, E.

1966 "The Ukrainians: A Case Study of the 'Third Force'." In *Nationalism in Canada*, edited by Peter Russell, pp. 72−91. Toronto: McGraw-Hill.

Winks, Robin W.

1971 *Blacks in Canada: A History*. New Haven, Mass.: Yale University Press.

Wirth, L.

1945 "The Problem of Minority Groups." In *The Science of Man in the World Crisis*, edited by Ralph Linton, pp. 347−72. New York: Columbia University Press.

Wrong, Dennis Hume

1955 *American and Canadian Viewpoints*. Washington, D.C.: American Council on Education.

Yancey, William L.; Erickson, Eugene P.; and Juliani, Richard N.

1976 "Emergent Ethnicity: A Review and Reformulation." *American Sociological Review* 41: 391−403.

Young, Charles H., and Reid, Helen R.Y.

1938 *The Japanese Canadians*. Toronto: University of Toronto Press.

Yuzyk, P.

1973 *For a Better Canada*. Toronto: Ukrainian National Association, Inc.

The Institute for Research on Public Policy
PUBLICATIONS AVAILABLE*
May, 1980

BOOKS

Leroy O. Stone &   *Canadian Population Trends and Public Policy*
Claude Marceau   *Through the 1980s*. 1977 $4.00

Raymond Breton   *The Canadian Condition: A Guide to Research in Public Policy*. 1977 (No Charge)

Raymond Breton   *Une orientation de la recherche politique dans le contexte canadien*. 1978 (No Charge)

J.W. Rowley &   *Competition Policy in Canada: Stage II, Bill C-13*.
W.T. Stanbury, eds.   1978 $12.95

C.F. Smart &   *Studies on Crisis Management*. 1978 $9.95
W.T. Stanbury, eds.

W.T. Stanbury, ed.   *Studies on Regulation in Canada*. 1978 $9.95

Michael Hudson   *Canada in the New Monetary Order—Borrow? Devalue? Restructure!* 1978 $6.95

W.A.W. Neilson &   *The Legislative Process in Canada: The Need for*
J.C. MacPherson, eds.   *Reform*. 1978 $12.95

David K. Foot, ed.   *Public Employment and Compensation in Canada: Myths and Realities*. 1978 $10.95

W.E. Cundiff &   *Issues in Canadian/U.S. Transborder Computer*
Mado Reid, eds.   *Data Flows*. 1979 $6.50

G.B. Reschenthaler &   *Perspectives on Canadian Airline Regulation*. 1979
B. Roberts, eds. $13.50

P.K. Gorecki &   *Perspectives on the Royal Commission on*
W.T. Stanbury, eds.   *Corporate Concentration*. 1979 $15.95

David K. Foot   *Public Employment in Canada: Statistical Series*. 1979 $15.00

---

* Order Address: The Institute for Research on Public Policy
P.O. Box 9300, Station "A"
TORONTO, Ontario
M5W 2C7

Meyer W. Bucovetsky, ed.   *Studies on Public Employment and Compensation in Canada*. 1979 $14.95

Richard French &   *The RCMP and the Management of National*
André Béliveau   *Security*. 1979 $6.95

Richard French &   *La GRC et la gestion de la sécurité nationale*. 1979
André Béliveau $6.95

Leroy O. Stone &   *Future Income Prospects for Canada's Senior*
Michael J. MacLean   *Citizens*. 1979 $7.95

Douglas G. Hartle   *Public Policy Decision Making and Regulation*.
                       1979 $12.95

Richard Bird (in collaboration   *The Growth of Public Employment in Canada*. 1979
with Bucovetsky & Foot) $12.95

G. Bruce Doern &   *The Public Evaluation of Government Spending*.
Allan M. Maslove, eds.   1979 $10.95

Richard Price, ed.   *The Spirit of the Alberta Indian Treaties*. 1979
                       $8.95

Peter N. Nemetz, ed.   *Energy Policy: The Global Challenge*. 1979
                       $16.95

Richard J. Schultz   *Federalism and the Regulatory Process*. 1979
                       $1.50

Richard J. Schultz   *Le fédéralisme et le processus de réglementation*.
                       1979 $1.50

Lionel D. Feldman &   *Bargaining for Cities, Municipalities and*
Katherine A. Graham   *Intergovernmental Relations: An Assessment*. 1979
                       $10.95

Elliot J. Feldman &   *The Future of North America: Canada, the United*
Neil Nevitte, eds.   *States, and Quebec Nationalism*. 1979 $7.95

Maximo Halty-Carrere   *Technological Development Strategies for*
                       Developing Countries. 1979 $12.95

G.B. Reschenthaler   *Occupational Health and Safety in Canada: The*
                       Economics and Three Case Studies. 1979 $5.00

David R. Protheroe   *Imports and Politics: Trade Decision-Making in*
                       Canada, 1968-1979. 1980 $8.95

| G. Bruce Doern | *Government Intervention in the Canadian Nuclear Industry.* 1980 $8.95 |

G. Bruce Doern &
R.W. Morrison, eds.

Canadian Nuclear Policies. 1980 $14.95

W.T. Stanbury, ed.

Government Regulation: Scope, Growth, Process. 1980 $10.95

Yoshi Tsurumi with
Rebecca R. Tsurumi

Sogoshosha: Engines of Export-Based Growth. 1980 $8.95

Allan M. Maslove &
Gene Swimmer

Wage Controls in Canada, 1975-78. A Study in Public Decision Making. 1980 $11.95

T. Gregory Kane

Consumers and the Regulators: Intervention in the Federal Regulatory Process. 1980 $10.95

Réjean Lachapelle &
Jacques Henripin

La situation démolinguistique au Canada: évolution passée et prospective. 1980 $24.95

Raymond Breton,
Jeffrey G. Reitz &
Victor F. Valentine

Cultural Boundaries and the Cohesion of Canada. 1980 $18.95

OCCASIONAL PAPERS ($3.00 per copy)

W.E. Cundiff
(No. 1)

Nodule Shock? Seabed Mining and the Future of the Canadian Nickel Industry. 1978

IRPP/Brookings
(No. 2)

Conference on Canadian-U.S. Economic Relations. 1978

Robert A. Russel
(No. 3)

The Electronic Briefcase: The Office of the Future. 1978

C.C. Gotlieb
(No. 4)

Computers in the Home: What They Can Do for Us—And to Us. 1978

Raymond Breton &
Gail Grant Akian
(No. 5)

Urban Institutions and People of Indian Ancestry. 1978

K.A. Hay
(No. 6)

Friends or Acquaintances? Canada as a Resource Supplier to the Japanese Economy. 1978

T. Atkinson
(No. 7)

Trends in Life Satisfaction. 1979

M. McLean   *The Impact of the Micro-electronics Industry on the*
(No. 8)   *Structure of the Canadian Economy.* 1979

Fred Thompson &   *The Political Economy of Interest Groups in the*
W.T. Stanbury   *Legislative Process in Canada.* 1979
(No. 9)

Gordon B. Thompson   *Memo from Mercury: Information Technology* **Is**
(No. 10)   *Different.* 1979

Pierre Sormany   *Les micro-esclaves vers une bio-industrie*
(No. 11)   *canadienne.* 1979

K. Hartley, P.N. Nemetz,   *Energy R & D Decision Making for Canada.* 1979
S. Schwartz, D. Uyeno,
I. Vertinsky & J. Young
(No. 12)

David Hoffman &   *The Dynamics of the Technological Leadership of*
Zavis P. Zeman, eds.   *the World.* 1980
(No. 13)

WORKING PAPERS (No Charge)**
W.E. Cundiff   *Issues in Canada/U.S. Transborder Computer Data*
(No. 1)   *Flows.* 1978 (Out of print; in IRPP book of same
  title.)

John Cornwall   *Industrial Investment and Canadian Economic*
(No. 2)   *Growth: Some Scenarios for the Eighties.* 1978

Russell Wilkins   *L'espérance de vie par quartier à Montréal, 1976:*
(No. 3)   *un indicateur social pour la planification.* 1979

F.J. Fletcher &   *Canadian Attitude Trends, 1960—1978.* 1979
R.J. Drummond
(No. 4)

** Order Working Papers from
  The Institute for Research on Public Policy
  P.O. Box 3670
  Halifax South
  Halifax, Nova Scotia
  B3J 3K6